In and Of the Mediterranean: Medieval and Early Modern Iberian Studies

HISPANIC ISSUES • VOLUME 41

In and Of the Mediterranean: Medieval and Early Modern Iberian Studies

Michelle M. Hamilton
and Núria Silleras-Fernández
EDITORS

Vanderbilt University Press
NASHVILLE, TENNESSEE
2015

First Edition 2015

This book is printed on acid-free paper.
Manufactured in the United States of America

The editors gratefully acknowledge assistance
from the College of Liberal Arts
and the Department of Spanish and Portuguese Studies
at the University of Minnesota;
and the Department of Spanish and Portuguese
at the University of Iowa

The complete list of volumes in the Hispanic Issues series begins on page 305

Library of Congress Cataloging-in-Publication Data

In and of the Mediterranean : medieval and early modern Iberian studies / Michelle M. Hamilton and Nuria Silleras-Fernandez, eds.
pages cm. — (Hispanic issues ; 41)
ISBN 978-0-8265-2029-6 (hardcover)
ISBN 978-0-8265-2030-2 (paperback)
ISBN 978-0-8265-2031-9 (ebook)
1. Iberian Peninsula—Relations—Mediterranean Region. 2. Mediterranean Region—Relations—Iberian Peninsula. 3. Group identity—Iberian Peninsula—History. 4. Group identity—Mediterranean Region—History. 5. Iberian Peninsula—Civilization. 6. Iberian Peninsula—Historiography. 7. Iberian Peninsula—Intellectual life. 8. Spanish literature—History and criticism. 9. Portuguese literature—History and criticism. I. Hamilton, Michelle, 1969- II. Silleras-Fernandez, Nuria.
DP86.M38I5 2014
303.48'24601822—dc23
2014013075

Contents

Iberia and the Mediterranean: An Introduction

Michelle M. Hamilton
and Núria Silleras-Fernández

In the last decade or so Mediterranean studies has gone from constituting a rather vague approach to a region imagined in geographical terms, to coalescing as a recognized field of research and teaching—a process driven in part by its inherent imperative to interrogate established categories of cultural and historical analysis. In our era of globalization, transnationalism, and oceanic and diasporic studies, the Mediterranean has come to captivate the imagination of scholars who see in it an alternative to the paradigms that have dominated scholarly discourse since the inception of the modern academy. It has provoked a reconsideration of the nation-state model and of continental and civilizational paradigms that up to now have been accepted *a priori* as the fundamental building blocks of history and culture. Even though the nation-state remains the dominant form of cultural identity and political organization, and in large part the rationale for the current organization of the nationally oriented language departments in which many of us find ourselves, a more globalizing and comparative construct, such as the Mediterranean, offers to help us understand difficult and contentious issues that sit at the foundation of our assumptions, not the least of which is the relationship between political organization and cultural and national identities. For all the lip service paid to comparative approaches and interdisciplinarity in the academy in the past few decades, national models still tend to dominate humanities disciplines—and civilizational divisions, such as "Western," "Islamic," or "African" are often taken for granted, but seldom clearly defined, let alone put to the test.

This has certainly been the case with regard to Iberian studies in the American academy. History departments inevitably place the study of the peninsula within the European concentration of the curriculum, whether the course in question is on Castile, al-Andalus, or the Almohads. This may be less true of those contemporary departments of Spanish and Portuguese that in the last decade have started to explicitly broaden the traditional category of "Spanish and Portuguese"—often imposed on them by others, but sometimes generated internally and then internalized—by reconfiguring themselves as departments or centers for Iberian and Latin American Literatures and Cultures (Resina; Menocal, "Why Iberia?" 7). Certainly this change has helped to foster an awareness of the complex nature of Iberian culture—a characteristic it shares with the Mediterranean approach. Both endeavor to loosen nationally defined fields from the geographic borders and the national shadow of hegemonic linguistic agendas and to consider them on broader, cultural terms. Such a revision is particularly apropos when one focuses on the medieval and early modern periods, when the notion of the nation-state, discretely bounded geographically, linguistically, and culturally, is clearly anachronistic. Even for a scholar such as José Antonio Maravall, who carried out a thorough study of "The Concept of Spain in the Middle Ages," Spain is primarily a geographical concept—the scene where a human group shares history, and even more importantly, historiography (17–32). But these are "imagined communities" (Anderson); for, as Patrick Geary puts it, "The real history of the nations that populated Europe in the early Middle Ages begins not in the sixth century but in the eighteenth" (15). This moving away from modern nation-state models has also given a new and deserved protagonism to languages and cultures that fell between the cracks of the national models. In the case of Iberian Studies, this broader perspective invites the inclusion of other peninsular languages and literatures, such as Catalan, Euskera, Aragonese, Galician, Portuguese, Occitan, and Latin, as well as Arabic and Hebrew, and texts and traditions, such as Aljamiado, that do not clearly fall into a single linguistic-cultural category (Dagenais 42).

As the studies in the current volume reflect, the Iberian Peninsula constituted a truly polyglossic space, in which many authors composed their works in more than one language and worked in and were influenced by several literary traditions or had the potential of doing so. In this sense, as David Wacks's points out, Iberian literatures were part of a polysystem (13). Of course, this fact is not new to scholars of Iberian history and culture, and in the studies included in *In and of the Mediterranean* the reader will find many of the primary texts in which such polyglossy can be found, including those produced at the court of Alfonso X the Learned (b. 1221, r. 1252–1284), King of Castile, León, and Galicia. The latter's cultural agenda is characterized by a preference for both Galician/Portuguese, used in the composition of the *Cantigas de Santa María*, as well as for the Castilian vernacular used in the composition of histories such as the *Primera Crónica General* and in the prose translations such as *Calila e Dimna* (1251), and is emblematic of this multilingual dynamic. The latter work, *Calila wa Dimna*, is a vernacular translation of a work with its origins in the Indic *Panchatantra*, and is but one of many translations Alfonso oversaw in his role of patron of the so-called Toledo "school of translation." Previous Iberian luminaries such as the Archbishops Raimundo of Toledo and Rodrigo Jiménez de Rada, had held similar roles as creators and patrons of the translation of literary and scientific texts translated from Arabic and Hebrew. The translations produced in Toledo and as part of the Alfonsine cultural project became foundational in the Castilian literary canon both in terms of substance and form. For example, the narrative device of the frame-tale, ubiquitous among the Hebrew and Arabic works translated into the vernacular, is adopted by subsequent medieval Castilian authors such as Don Juan Manuel in *El conde Lucanor* and Juan Ruiz in *Libro de buen amor*. The latter also reflects both formal aspects of the Arabic *maqāmāt* (Monroe 30–31, 331–32), as well as having echoes in other European literary tradition—from the Italian of Boccaccio to the English of Chaucer (Hamilton 13). The role of translation and polyglossy as part and parcel of an Iberian cultural agenda, however, extends far beyond the familiar Toledan and Alfonsine projects or the texts of the traditional Spanish canon, and are evident in the cultural realities examined in several of the essays included in the current volume, such as those of Vicente Lledó-Guillem, Gerard Weigers, Eleazar Gutwirth, and David Wacks.

Thus, the movement to broaden Iberian studies and the emergence of Mediterranean studies, although they may have developed as distinct phenomena, are obviously complementary. The aim of this volume is not to replace the notion of Iberia in Iberian Studies, but to propose an alternative and broader conceptual and comparative framework: that of the Mediterranean. The Iberian Peninsula has always been an integral part of the Mediterranean world, from the age of the Tartessos and the Phoenicians to our own era of *pateras* and the "Union for the Mediterranean," the latest iteration of the multinational political partnership created in the 1990s by the Barcelona Process.[1] Obviously, all Iberian cultural production and history can be situated by definition, "*in* the Mediterranean"—i.e., originating within the geographical region located around the Mediterranean Sea—but it is our intention in this volume of *Hispanic Issues* to consider Iberian culture "*of* the Mediterranean." In other words, to draw on the fundamental distinction articulated by Peregrine Horden and Nicholas Purcell, the purpose of the present volume is to examine what it means for medieval and early modern Iberia and its people to be considered as part of the Mediterranean ("of" rather than "in"). Each of the contributors has addressed this need and each offers a distinct perspective: to consider these cultures not as merely peninsular, but rather as corresponding to, or forming part of, cultural entities that were manifest on a regional scale, and that transcend the geographic and national boundaries normally thought to contain them. This is, of course, as true of the European context as the Mediterranean one; many Hispanists have called attention to Spain's marginalization or exclusion from the traditional master narratives of European history elaborated by northern European scholars who, consciously or not, presumed, as in the famous quip attributed to Dumas, that "Africa begins at the Pyrenees."

Spain is indeed part of Europe, but it is also part of the Mediterranean, and seeing it as such provides us with the opportunity to appreciate the peninsula's connections, not only with Africa, but also with the Middle East, as several of the articles included in this volume underscore (those of Brian Catlos, Gerard Weigers, Manuela Marín, Nico Parmley, Andrew Devereux, Luis Avilés, and Barbara Fuchs). The collection does not presume to exclude Europe and its influence from Iberian history, but it does have the effect of "provincializing" it (Chakrabarty), and, thus, constitutes in part a response to Eurocentrism (see, for example, the interventions of Catlos, Marín, Parmley, Lledó-Guillén, and Wacks).[1] As Sharon Kinoshita puts it, adopting a fresh comparative frame—"Mediterraneanizing" the object of our study—encourages us to take into account concepts such as mobility, portability of cultural artifacts, connectivity of lands and people, as well as segmentation (602). These issues are addressed in the majority of articles comprising the present volume, including those that interrogate the various forms of Iberian Imperial Mediterranean legitimacy (see Lledó-Guillem, Simone Pinet, Devereux, Ryan Giles, Avilés, Fuchs) and the mobility of people and customs (Marín, Weigers, Giles, Avilés, and Fuchs), as well as how the production and movement of cultural artifacts (manuscripts in the articles of Weigers and Parmley; printed books in that of Wacks, and both in that of Gutwirth) reveal networks of Mediterranean exchange along which Iberian thought traveled. Merely by shifting our frame of reference and deploying alternative categories of analysis, we can gain fresh insights regarding the exchange of people, texts, and other cultural artifacts.

Trade and exchange has, in fact, long constituted the subject of studies of the Mediterranean, including Fernand Braudel's *La Méditerránee et le monde Méditerranée* and S.D. Goitein's *A Mediterranean Society*. The latter, although groundbreaking, are nevertheless temporally specific studies of the Mediterranean, and scholarship has moved on to the environmentally-framed, historically-transcendent approach of Horden and Purcell's *The Corrupting Sea*. This shift, together with the tendency to move Judaic and Arabo-Islamic Studies toward the scholarly and pedagogical mainstream, has helped to provoke an interest on the part of scholars, students, and administrators in the Mediterranean as a field of inquiry and frame of comparison. Positions in history and in language and literature departments are now advertised as "Mediterranean," and a series of journals, monograph series, research institutes, and projects organized around this new field have been launched in Europe, across North America, and even in Asia.[2] At the same time, the field is still far from established or fully articulated, even by those who work in it. The daunting prospect of defying established teleologies, of mastering many languages, and of working outside of one's intellectual and disciplinary comfort zones, all present obstacles to scholars trained in nationally-oriented traditions and inculcated with disciplinary caution.

The rising popularity of Mediterranean studies in the Anglo-American and European Academy, even if it may cause some initial discomfort, is a unique opportunity for our field, which has long been pushed to the side or marginalized by the Anglophone and continental world of "theory." Mediterranean studies as conceived of by Kinoshita, Iain Chambers (who proposes the mutable Mediterranean as a space for exploring "complex, open-ended narratives"), and others recognizes the value of exchange and alternative models, including or especially those in languages other than English, and critics such as Suzanne Akbari and Karla Mallette especially underscore the encounters of Muslims and Christians as definitive of Mediterranean studies (Akbari 131). For many of us working in Spanish studies, the shift to open-ended narratives and complexity is a natural and integral aspect of not only our work, but of our field. The widening of our theoretical frame to consider Iberia as part of the shared space of the Mediterranean offers a method to examine the ways in which those living in and moving through the Iberian Peninsula—past and present—produced and responded to the richness of linguistic, cultural, and historical threads that extend far beyond the peninsula's geographical borders. In the context of the development and current state of Iberian studies, Mediterranean studies is not an unfamiliar or foreign landscape, but rather offers a new, wider forum that for many of us (including several of the contributors to this volume) will already be a familiar way of conceiving of our field and our research. The great advantage for those of us working in Iberian/Spanish studies is the dialogue that Mediterranean studies offers with our colleagues in what have been more insulated and nationally defined fields that have proven much more impervious to the currents, flows and exchange of ideas that have characterized work being done by Spanish, Catalan, Portuguese, Latin American, and American scholars (among others) who chose or choose to publish for a Spanish-speaking public.

In this sense, the work of María Rosa Menocal has been important to Iberian studies for both popularizing the history and culture of medieval Iberia and for drawing the attention of colleagues working in fields outside Iberian and even Romance studies. And while Menocal may have brought the complicated diversity and multiplicity of Iberia to the attention of a broad English-speaking public, many of us working in the field, including many of the contributors to this volume, have long appreciated the richness of Iberian medieval cultural production and modern Iberian scholarship, that since the nineteenth-century has been wrangling with these issues of multiplicity, conflict, and exchange. While an exhaustive review of such scholarship is beyond the scope of this introduction, some representative examples will help to dispel the growing myth that Spanish studies has conformed to the same insular and monolingual perspectives that have defined other European national traditions.

The early twentieth century witnessed an impressive flowering of scholarship on the Arabic and Hebrew cultural production of al-Andalus. Much of it can be found in monographs and volumes of the journal *Al Andalus*, published by the Escuela de Estudios Árabes de Madrid, which was founded in 1932 by the Spanish Arabist Emilio García Gómez (who before that held a similar post in the Centro de Estudios Históricos de Granada established in 1910) (Álvarez de Morales). *Al-Andalus* was dedicated to Andalusi Arabic (and in its first years Hebrew) literature and culture and provided a forum in which a series of Spanish (and other) Arabists—among them Ángel González Palencia, Miguel Asín Palacios, Emilio García Gómez, A. R. Nykl, E. Lévi-Provençal, Fernando de la Granja, Federico Corriente, and L. P. Harvey—and Hebraists such as José María Millás Vallicrosa and Samuel Stern published original studies, as well as editions and translations of original Andalusi texts that are to this day invaluable sources for studying the history and culture of medieval Islamic Iberia.[3] In addition, these and other scholars published important editions and studies on Andalusi works (such as García Gómez's edition and translation of Ibn Hazm's *Tawq al-Hamam*), and monographs teasing out the threads of intellectual exchange between the Andalusi world and Western Europe (such as Asín Palacios's *La Escatologia musulmana en la Divina Comedia*). *Sefarad*, a journal dedicated to the history and culture of Sephardic Jews, is yet another product of a state-sponsored institution, the Escuela de Estudios Hebraicos, which was founded by Millás Vallicrosa and the Spanish Hebraist Francisco Cantera Burgos in 1941. Like *Al-Andalus*, *Sefarad*, in addition, of course, to reflecting the political and colonial desires of the Spanish state, also, nevertheless is a testament to the Spanish academy's recognition of the diversity defining Spain's past.[4] In *Sefarad*, scholarship tracing the movement of ideas and people across the Mediterranean has been published in multiple languages for some seventy-two years, including the pioneering work of Millás Vallicrosa and Cantera Burgos. While *Sefarad* continues to be published today, *Al-Andalus* ceased to exist in 1978—to be revived two years later as *Al-Qantara*. *Al-Andalus* was created under the auspices of the Escuela de Estudios Árabes, but continued publication when the latter was subsumed into the Consejo Superior de Investigaciones Científicas (CSIC) in 1939 after the conclusion of the Spanish Civil War.[5] The CISC still functions as a research institute that houses and trains leading Spanish Arabists (such as Manuela Marín, a contributor to the current volume). Nor should the work of those scholars who investigated the rich cultural heritage of the Crown of Aragon, the Kingdom of Portugal, and the other regions and cultures of the Peninsula (such as, among others, Martín de Riquer, Lola Badia, Roque Chabás y Llorens, Carolina Michaëlis de Vasconcelos, and José Leite de Vasconcelos) be written out of any history of Iberian scholarship. The latter scholarship, in addition to *Sefarad*, *Al-Andalus*, and the CSIC offer examples of the complicated nature and history of the study and recognition of Iberia's multi-confessional, polyglossic, and diverse pasts and serve as a reminder that the history of the Spanish and Portuguese academies is not as black and white as it may seem from the outside.

The pioneering work of Américo Castro and his concept of *convivencia*—more recently rearticulated as the more nuanced concept of coexistence, or even better, Catlos's *conveniencia*, "the convenience principle" (Catlos, "Contexto social" and *The Victors* 404–8; Szpiech; Ray)—which has become so prominent in recent scholarship in English, cannot be understood nor explained without an awareness of this intellectual milieu. The latter was a thriving academic culture of scholars trained in and investigating the Arabic and Hebrew literatures and histories of Iberia, from which Castro, and his sparring partner (as discussed by Catlos in this volume) Claudio Sánchez-Albornoz, developed theories about and debated the nature of modern Spanish identity and its cultural debt to the Iberian past. Nor can the work of Menocal, to which we owe so much for her popularization and ability to finally attract the attention of an English-speaking public to what had been considered for so long, as Barbara Fuchs has shown, a place of suspiciously un-European peoples and places that were uncomfortably like the Muslim Other of the early modern and Imperial age of the eighteenth and nineteenth centuries studied by Edward Said, stand as the only voice of Iberia in the Mediterranean. In the pioneering work of other scholars working in the United States, such as James T. Monroe, Samuel G. Armistead, Francisco Márquez Villanueva, and Ángel Sáenz Badillos, we find defining voices in the twentieth-century debates concerning the role of Jews, Muslims, and Christians and their use of language, culture, and religion to articulate their identities not just as Iberians, but as members of any number of groups that transcended national or local definition, and in so doing, to truly reflect a Mediterranean sense of the world and self. While scholars in Spanish studies have long studied the literary works, the cultural debates, and the social and theoretical problems surrounding the realities and constructions of multi-faith, -linguistic and -cultural coexistence and conflict that have come to define Mediterranean studies in its current iteration, it behooves those of us currently working in Iberian studies to respond to this new interest on the part of scholars working in other fields and until recently unaware of the complexity of medieval Iberia and its role both *in* and *of* the Mediterranean and the not insignificant corpus of scholarship already generated. The studies in this volume point to this world of scholarship on the languages and cultures of Iberia (Castilian, Portuguese, Catalan, Arabic, Jewish/Hebrew) that, while perhaps not as familiar to scholars of more "European" traditions, has nevertheless formed the intellectual basis and rationale for the work of many of us currently working in medieval and, to an increasing extent, early modern Iberian literature and culture.

Needless to say, the Mediterranean is not a panacea for Eurocentrism and national and disciplinary parochialism, and it also has its critics. After all, the Mediterranean is a modern cultural construct that has to be managed with care, lest it unintentionally be reduced to a new manifestation of Orientialism—a danger that Pinet points to in her contribution to this volume (Wigen 719–720; Goddard, Llobera, and Shore; Herzfeld 45–46, 48). That said, it is no more dangerous or dubious than the other categories that we are accustomed to deploying in our scholarship, or for that matter the rarely-questioned periodization on which so much of our scholarship turns. There can be no intellectual activity, no scholarly analysis that eschews the use of categories; the imperative is to use them critically, and with a sense of self-awareness, not to reify them, and to appreciate that many different categories and perspectives may be valid and useful for examining the same phenomena. Therefore the Mediterranean should be used as a heuristic category and as an analytical tool, rather than as a taxonomical construct that aims merely to describe, classify, and systematize. In this light, we are confident that putting Iberian studies under the lamp (or the sun) of the Mediterranean will serve to further illuminate the intellectual landscape of our discipline. What Mediterranean studies offers to Iberian/Spanish studies is a theoretical space in which scholars for whom the work being done in Iberian and Spanish studies has been invisible can come to intellectually engage and exchange ideas with those of us who have been wrangling with some of the theoretical issues at the heart of Mediterranean studies for some time. Mediterranean studies offers a critical space where geneaologies and teleologies that privilege (however unconsciously) certain languages and traditions over others can meet—where past work in Castilian, Catalan, Portuguese, Andalusi Arabic, and Hebrew (among others) can come into dialogue with the scholarship and cultural production that have long dominated not only the narratives of Europe and its past, but also those recent critical studies of them. In this sense Iberian studies, like the Iberian Peninsula, is not simply prescribed and defined by the Mediterranean, but also in turn helps to anchor and define it and its critical discourses.

This Volume and Its Essays

The present volume brings together a cluster of studies that consider medieval and early modern Iberian history and cultural production from the perspective of the Mediterranean. Both the breadth of the contributions and the crosscutting approach that characterizes them reflect the natural tendency of Mediterranean studies to encourage interdisciplinary discussion and collaboration among scholars working in a range of fields. Specifically, this volume brings together a series of studies that illustrate how the various linguistic, confessional, and ethnic groups of medieval Iberia interacted with each other and conceived of themselves as belonging to communities that stretched beyond the geographical, political, and linguistic boundaries of the Peninsula itself. A collection of this sort should help us deepen our awareness of how the trade and education centers and networks, pilgrimage routes, courts, flows of ideas, and cultural mores worked to allow Iberians to consider themselves as part of larger trans-national communities and move beyond models of exceptionalism. Seen in this light, the Mediterranean becomes a Hispanic issue, and Iberia a Mediterranean one. Thus, we construe "Iberian studies" to include not only Castilian history and cultural production, but also the history and cultural production of the other regional, linguistic, and ethno-religious groups who inhabited the peninsula: Jews, Muslims, and Christians, and speakers and writers of Arabic,

Hebrew, Catalan, Portuguese, Latin, and the other languages of the peoples who lived their lives in Iberian kingdoms, as well as their legacy beyond its geographical, and often even cultural borders.

This volume is not meant to be an exhaustive survey of the potential that the Mediterranean holds for Iberian studies, but rather, as mentioned, to demonstrate through the studies featured here how Iberia is at once *in* and *of* the Mediterranean. The thirteen contributing scholars represent a range of fields, methodologies, and perspectives, reflecting the natural interdisciplinarity of Mediterranean Studies. Thus, the volume features scholars who specialize in the different Iberian literatures, historians, and scholars of religion and culture working in American, European, and Mediterranean institutions.

The first four essays address Iberia as part of the Muslim Mediterranean. Brian Catlos reminds us what is at stake in the way we frame medieval Iberian Muslim, Christian, and Jewish interactions, and points out that from a Mediterranean perspective such interactions are in fact the norm in the medieval period, contrary to the hardline positions of earlier critics, such as Castro and Sánchez-Albornoz, who debated everything but the idea that such interactions made Iberia unique. Catlos's essay is strategically placed, because in it he broaches the still fundamental question about the relevancy of the medieval past to present-day conceptions of nationhood that continue to shape our epistemological categories, including, for many of us, the institutional frameworks within which we find ourselves, as well as the type/s of knowledge we produce as a result. His dismissal of the idea of a medieval "Spain" also lays the foundation for the subsequent articles in the volume that explore various aspects of the medieval kingdoms and that for Catlos form part of a larger Mediterranean cultural ambit (and not merely provincial "Spaniards").

Gerard Wiegers looks explicitly at the mechanics of cultural transmission, focusing on how knowledge concerning the religion of Islam was translated, commented upon, and interpreted for a Christian audience by Jewish and Muslim intellectuals and, to a lesser extent, Muslim slaves and converts. Wiegers shows how the Muslim scholars of Iberia shared cultural and political beliefs with Muslims across the Mediterranean, and according to which neither translation nor transmission were neutral acts of sharing, but rather charged political acts that could be used by their political and military rivals, the Christians. While scholars such as Charles Burnett and Thomas Burman have examined the role of Jews and noticeable lack of Muslims in what scholars of Spanish Studies often teach as the great translation projects of Toledo, Weigers's study brings to the fore the important role that the medieval Mediterranean institution of slavery (an issue addressed in subsequent essays, such as those of

Luis Avilés and Barbara Fuchs) played in this important stage of Iberian cultural development.

Manuela Marín's essay brings to our attention the not insignificant political power wielded, first in Iberia, then in Morocco, by the Almoravid princess Hawwa' bint Tashufin, as well as the legacy of warrior women among Saharan Berbers and their Almohad detractors, who used their agency as a way of depicting Almoravids as culturally deficient Muslims. Few studies address the gender roles of the ruling Almoravid elite of twelfth-century Iberia, and Marín points to the inherent tension between the Arabized mores of Andalusi society and the customs of Saharan Berber women. Marín's article further underscores the cultural ties binding Andalusi and North African peoples across the Mediterranean.

Nicholas Parmley reads the canonical *Libro de Apolonio* as a counter-Crusading narrative that not only offers a model of Mediterranean sea-crossing adapted from the Arab philosophical and literary traditions of Iberia and the wider Muslim world, but that also forces its vernacular reader/s to question the larger agenda of Western Christendom vis-à-vis the Mediterranean. According to Parmley, the *Libro de Apolonio* is an example of thirteenth-century Iberian cultural production that both reflects upon the status of Mediterranean crossings for an Iberian audience and distances it from French and German narratives of the latter. Simone Pinet's contribution similarly addresses the *Libro de Apolonio* as but one of a pair of works—its imperial twin in constructing a narrative space of kingly conquest and trade being, in Pinet's opinion, the *Libro de Alexandre.* The latter begins the process of transformation by which the classical Mediterranean of Homer will be shaped in the Iberian imagination into the domesticated/colonized sea ready for the imperial desires of the Early Modern era. While for Parmley the Mediterranean as represented in the *Libro de Apolonio* offers not only the threat of misguided conquest as well as the promise of personal enlightenment, for Pinet it is a geography upon which Spanish imperial desires can be realized.

The next two essays explore specific examples of the ways in which the eastward glance of desire that both Pinet and Parmley find in the thirteenth-century narratives of the Castilian *mester de clerecía* were constructed by later Iberians in radically different literary and historical sources. Vicente Lledó-Guillem's article shows how the Aragonese nobleman and soldier Ramon Muntaner, by questioning the notion of Greek as a Mediterranean lingua franca, offers instead Catalan as the fourteenth-century alternative for a pan-Mediterranean standard language. Muntaner's linguistic position is related, as Lledó-Guillem points out, to the Catalan presence in both Greek and Byzantine territories during the thirteenth and fourteenth centuries and offers a later iteration of the imperial impulses that Pinet explores in the thirteenth-century novels of Apolonio and Alexander. However, while in Muntaner's *Chronicle* the desire for Empire may also be in part a reaction to French narratives of conquest (as both Pinet and Parmley argue was also the case for the *Libro de Apolonio* and *Alexandre*), the vernacular that Muntaner favors is that of a specific Iberian confederation, the Crown of Aragon. According to Lledó-Guillem, Muntaner's text is not only reflective of the royal position of Jaume the Conqueror, his son Jaume II, and grandson Alfons, but also reflects a nationalist ideology present in other contemporary Aragonese authors. Both Aragonese and Castilian imperial ambitions in the Mediterranean are also the focus of Andrew Devereux's study of the Catholic Monarchs' Mediterranean policy as articulated in the work of several contemporary fifteenth-century Iberian authors and statesmen, including Christopher Columbus, Pedro Navarro, and Cristóbal de Santesteban. While today we are most familiar with the legacy of Spanish imperial expansion to the Americas, Devereux's study brings to light Columbus's crusading agenda to retake the Holy Land as part of a larger political theology espoused by several voices in the royal courts of the Catholic Monarchs, who looked East and South across the Mediterranean to the spaces of former Aragonese rule (and beyond) as the theater for Spanish imperial expansion and the site of a universal Christian empire, according to which both Ottomans and North African Hafsid and Fatimid subjects would be "restored" to Christianity under the Spanish monarchs.

As do both Lledó-Guillem and Devereux, Josiah Blackmore examines the ideological import of the fifteenth-century historical chronicle, but from the Portuguese perspective, focusing on how the chronicler Fernão Lopes chooses to depict Castilian sympathizers in his *Crónica de D. João I*, a work designed to legitimate the dynastic claims of the Master of Avis over those of the Castilian monarchy. Lopes' unique historiographic narrative shuns the traditional authority of the chronicle for a style that offers a comparative perspective based on the use of several sources including, in addition to traditional *autoritates*, more popular vernacular texts such as letters, sermons and even gossip. Blackmore focuses particularly on Lopes' choice to cite the lyric *cantiga de escarnho* purportedly sung by the Castilian sympathizer Fernão Gonçalves de Sousa upon surrendering the castle of Portel. Blackmore's essay reminds us, in its study of this previously unexplored lyric insertion in Lopes' chronicle, of other Iberian texts such as the *Cantigas de Santa María* or the Alfonsine chronicles that also reflect the polyphonic culture of discourse used in narrating the Iberian past and of the polyglossy of Mediterranean Iberia.

The subsequent essays turn our attention from the legitimation of Iberian Empire and imperial culture expressed in official chronicles and court documents as addressed in the essays by Lledó-Guillem, Devereux, and Blackmore, and looks instead to how the tensions and problems of imperial Mediterranean desires (and realities) manifest in several works of Iberian imaginary fiction. The monsters and marvels that Eleazar Gutwirth has found in the Hebrew manuscripts of the Sephardim and their diaspora, particularly that of Shlomo ibn Verga's *Shevet Yehuda* and Usque's *Consolation for the Tribulation of Israel*, as well as in the margins of earlier peninsular Bibles, and that include the leviathan, behemoth, centaur, and even the Inquisition transmorphed into a monstrous beast, are prefigurations of the marvels and monsters in subsequent and better known "European" works. Gutwirth draws a line connecting Ottoman and Italian copies of these Sephardic accounts of the Expulsion to the gardens of marvels and monsters in Italian works such as *Orlando Furioso* and *Bomarzo* and from the latter to the early English print book, Peter Morwyn's *Compendious and most maruelous history of the latter times of the Iewes*. Importantly, Gutwirth relates Ibn Verga's use of the monstrous and marvelous, marked in the text in several cases by the use of the Romance instead of Hebrew, to the post-1400 Iberian interest in the monsters and the inexplicable, and as part of a rhetorical strategy designed to alert the reader that the passage or concept being discussed concerns religious polemic—whether the role of reason in questions of faith or of the Inquisition in Sephardi history. Gutwirth's essay illustrates how the Iberian conception of the marvelous and the monstrous crisscrossed the Mediterranean, and how the expulsed Iberian Jews served as cultural transmitters between Iberian, Ottoman, Italian, and English literature and popular imagination.

Wacks also explores Sephardic culture in Diaspora—including both the Sephardi manuscript and early print cultures of Italy and the Ottoman world discussed by Gutwirth—arguing that this Jewish Diasporic culture is the product of Imperial Spain and a type of "parallel shadow imperialism" that reveals how Sephardic Jews performed their Spanishness in their new diasporic homes. Wacks examines how such an interpretation explains why the Sephardi Jew Jacob Algaba chose to translate into Hebrew the Spanish book of chivalry par excellence, Montalvo's *Amadís de Gaula*, in Constantinople—the very imperial city the fictional hero conquers and incorporates into the imagined Christian Spanish empire of the text. Wacks shows how Algaba's translation de-Christianizes the text in order to make it accessible for the large reading audience it would have among Ottoman and Mizrahi Jews who constituted the public for and consumers of the sixteenth-century early print books produced in the centers of Sephardi printing such as Constantinople, Salonika and Adrianopolis. Giles, on the other hand, follows the Mediterranean crossings of the markedly unheroic Jewish *conversa* protagonist of Francisco Delicado's early sixteenth-century *La Lozana andaluza*. The eponymous protagonist goes about her business as whore and pimp while traversing the streets of Rome bearing the physical mark of a star on her forehead, variously interpreted as a syphilitic scar or as a mark of her Jewish identity. Giles offers a novel reading of Lozana's mark based on the wide but understudied Mediterranean tradition of popular magical spells and amulets, as well as Delicado's own treatise on plague and syphilis that reveals his eschatological interpretation of the disease and its relation to the fate of Rome at the hands of the invading Spanish troops of Charles V in 1527. While Lledó-Guillem points out that in the thirteenth-century Ramon Muntaner had advocated for Catalan as the *lingua franca* of the Mediterranean, Gutwirth, Giles and Wacks show in their contributions to this volume that by the sixteenth century both Castilian and, in the case of the Jews, Hebrew, came to be *de facto* Mediterranean *linguas francas* and by-products of two very different forms of cultural imperialism.

The final two essays, Luis Avilés's "Expanding the Self" and Barbara Fuchs's "Intimate Strangers," offer detailed explorations of the ways in which the Mediterranean functions in the work of Cervantes as a space for the working out of Iberian identity. In his study of the *Amante liberal* Avilés investigates the ways in which Spain's most iconic author explores the realities of Mediterranean captivity and human slavery as by-products of Iberian and Ottoman imperialism. The work's hero, Ricardo, also because of his Mediterranean experience, which entails a recognition of counter-narratives of empire and cultural exchange on the part of North African Muslims, Jewish merchants, and Turkish sailors, undergoes a personal transformation that, in Avilés's opinion, allows him to overcome his limited, parochial "Spanish" perspective and to become truly liberal, that is, capable of valuing others' opinions, particularly that of his love interest Leonisa. Fuchs explores not the hero of Cervantine drama, but the comic sideman, the *gracioso*, as the vehicle chosen by the author to explore the Mediterranean as a space of cultural engagement and hybrid cultural forms. The *graciosos* of the *Baños de Argel* and the *Gran Sultana* on the one hand give voice to anti-Semitic and anti-Muslim sentiment and, on the other, show an awareness of Jewish and Muslim cultural mores that reveal the suppressed cultural hybridity at the heart of Spanish culture itself (as explored in Fuchs's earlier studies on Maurophilia such as *Exotic Nation*). The *gracioso* of the *Sultana*, Madrigal, performs Spanishness by playing the conqueror across the Mediterranean, while Tristán of the *Los baños* is a cynical, irreverent *sacristan* with apostate tendencies. According to Fuchs, both texts invite the reader to reflect upon class and race and the contingencies and uncertainties of both. The seventeenth-century Mediterranean of Cervantes explored by both Fuchs and Avilés and defined by shifting allegiances and meaning not only marks the temporal end point of our volume, but also, nevertheless, brings us back to the beginning—recalling the constant movement of Iberian women and men across the Mediterranean from North Africa to Iberia, as well as the early imperial desires of Iberian authors and monarchs outlined in the preceding studies, and even the constant mutability that Pinet established as the defining feature of the thirteenth-century Mediterranean narratives of Apolonio and Alexander. This is in fact, as this volume shows, a hallmark of Iberia as being *of* the Mediterranean.

The essays collected in this volume thus offer an extended inquiry into the complexity of Iberia as a Mediterranean site of cultural complexity, conflict, and exchange in the Middle Ages and early modern period. The studies offered here explore the nuances and specifics of linguistic, religious, and national identities negotiated through and in the desire and realities of both diaspora and imperial expansion. It is our hope that the reader will take away from it an appreciation of the type of new scholarship the change in perspective allowed by Mediterranean Studies can have for those of us working in the history and cultural production of Iberian (and Spanish) studies.

Notes

1. The "Barcelona Process" is the name of a project embarked upon in 1995 by the European Union (and its fifteen members at the time) and fourteen Mediterranean partners with the goal of establishing a political alliance and promote cooperation. This Euro-Mediterranean partnership established the so-called "Union for the Mediterranean." See *www.eeas.europa.eu/euromed/barcelona_en.htm*.
2. Just to cite a couple of examples, the University of Minnesota, Twin Cities and the University of Colorado at Boulder both have Mediterranean Studies Groups. The Mediterranean Seminar, based at the University of California, has almost six hundred affiliates worldwide, and has been organizing and sponsoring a range of projects relating to Mediterranean studies research and pedagogy over the last decade (*www.mediterraneanseminar.org*). One of the co-directors, Brian Catlos, has contributed to the present volume. There are also a number of Mediterranean studies institutes and research projects based at universities in Europe, Asia, and the Middle East. Another indication that Mediterranean studies has in fact "arrived" is the increasing number of journals and monograph series either dedicated specifically to the Mediterranean

or publishing scholarship in this vein. These include the University of Pennsylvania Press, Brill, and Palgrave Macmillan, to name only a few.

3. Even before the establishment of the Escuela de Estudios Árabes, the Arabist Julián Ribera held a professorship of Arabic at the University of Zaragoza (Monroe, *Islam*).
4. For Franco's political desires with regard to the Arab world, see Daniela Flesler (*Return*). On the "courting" of Sephardic Jews on the part of Spanish politicians such as Ángel Pulido, who in his zeal to attract them to repatriate/resettle in Spain, helped to establish the "Instituto Arias Montano" mentioned below, see Beckwith (xliii–xlvi).
5. Once part of the CSIC, the Escuela was incorporated or subsumed under different organizational structures—first as part of the "Instituto Arias Montano," then as part of the "Instituto Miguel Asín" (Álvarez de Morales). For a thorough critical history of Spanish Arabism, see Monroe, *Islam*.

Works Cited

Akbari, Suzanne Conklin. "The Persistence of Philology: Language and Connectivity in the Mediterranean." *A Sea of Languages: Rethinking the Arabic Role in Medieval Literary History*. Ed. Suzanne Akbari and Karla Mallette. Toronto: University of Toronto Press, 2013.

Álvarez de Morales, Camilo. *Historia de la Escuela de Estudios Árabes*. CSIC: Escuela de Estudios Árabes, 2013. Web. 27 Feb. 2013.

Anderson, Benedict. *Imagined Communities: Reflections on the Origin and the Spread of Nationalism*. New York: Verso, 2006.

Armistead, Samuel G., Joseph H. Silverman, and Josep M. Sola-Solé. *Hispania Judaica: Studies on the History, Language, and Literature of the Jews in the Hispanic World*. Barcelona: Puvill, 1980.

Asín Palacios, Miguel. "Códice inexplorado del cordobés Ibn Hazm." *Al-Andalus* 2.1 (1934): 1–56.

———. *La Escatologia musulmana en la* Divina Comedia. Madrid: E. Maestre, 1919.

Badia, Lola. *Literatura catalana medieval*. Barcelona: Empúries, 1985.

Beckwith, Stacey. "Introduction." *Charting Memory: Recalling Medieval Spain*. Ed. Stacey Beckwith. New York: Taylor and Francis, 2000.

Braudel, Fernand. *La Méditerranée et le monde Méditerranéen à l'époque de Philippe II*. 2 vols. Paris: Librairie Armand Colin, 1966.

Cantera Burgos, Francisco. *La familia judeoconversa de los Cota de Toledo*. Madrid: Academia de Doctores de Madrid, 1969.

Castro, Ámerico. *España en su historia: Cristianos, moros y judíos*. 2nd ed. Barcelona: Crítica, 1983.

Catlos, Brian A. *The Muslims of Latin Christendom, ca. 1050–1615*. Cambridge: Cambridge University Press, 2014.

———. *The Victors and the Vanquished. Christians and Muslims of Catalonia and Aragon, 1050–1300.* Cambridge: Cambridge University Press, 2004.

———. "Contexto social y 'conveniencia' en la Corona de Aragón. Propuesta para un modelo de interacción entre grupos etno-religiosos minoritarios y mayoritarios." *Revista d'Història Medieval* 12 (2002): 220–35.

———. *Paradoxes of Plurality: Ethnic and Religious Diversity in the Medieval Mediterranean and Beyond* (in progress).

Chabás Llorens, Roque. *Los mozárabes valencianos.* Madrid: Boletín de la Real Academia de la Historia, 1891.

Chakrabarty, Dipesh. *Provincializing Europe: Postcolonial Thought and Historical Difference.* Princeton: Princeton University Press, 2000.

Chambers, Iain. *Mediterranean Crossings: The Politics of an Interrupted Modernity.* Durham: Duke University Press, 2008.

Corriente Córdoba, Federico. "Dos nuevos romancismos del árabe hispánico." *Al-Andalus* 43.2 (1978): 423–28.

———. *Gramática, métrica y texto del cancionero hispanoárabe de Abán Quzmán.* Madrid: Instituto Hispano-Árabe de Cultura, 1980.

Dagenais, John. "Medieval Spanish Literature in the Twenty-First Century." *The Cambridge History of Spanish Literature.* Ed. David T. Gies. Cambridge: Cambridge University Press, 2004. 39–57.

Flesler, Daniela. *The Return of Moor: Spanish Responses to Contemporary Moroccan Immigration.* Indiana: Purdue University Press, 2008.

Fuchs, Barbara. *Exotic Nation: Maurophilia and the Construction of Early Modern Spain.* Philadelphia: University of Pennsylvania Press, 2009.

García Gómez, Emilio, ed. and trans. *El collar de la paloma, tratado sobre el amor y los amantes de Ibn Hazm de Córdoba.* Madrid: Sociedad de Estudios y Publicaciones, 1952.

———. "Polémica religiosa entre Ibn Hazm e Ibn al-Nagrila." *Al-Andalus* 4.1 (1936):1–28.

Geary, Patrick J. *The Myth of Nations. The Medieval Origins of Europe.* Princeton: Princeton University Press, 2002.

Goddard, Victoria, Josep Llobera, and Chris Shore, eds. *The Anthropology of Europe: Identities and Boundaries in Conflict.* Providence: Berg Publishers, 1996.

Goitein, S.D., *A Mediterranean Society: The Jewish Communities of the Arab World as Portrayed in the Documents of the Cairo Geniza.* 6 vols. Berkeley: University of California Press, 1967–1993.

Gónzalez Palencia, Ángel. *Historia de la literatura arábigo-española*, Barcelona: Editorial Labor, 1928.

———. "Precedentes islámicos de la leyenda de Garín." *Al-Andalus* 1.2 (1933): 335–408.

Granja, Fernando. "Dos epístolas de Ahmad Ibn Burd Al-Asgar."*Al-Andalus* 22.2 (1960): 3 83–418.

———. *Maqâmas y risâlas andaluzas.* Madrid: Hiperión, 1997.

Hamilton, Michelle. *Representing Others in Medieval Iberian Literature*. New York: Palgrave Macmillan, 2007.

Harvey, L. P. "Arabic dialect of Valencia in 1595." *Al-Andalus* 36.1 (1971): 81–116.

———. *Islamic Spain, 1250–1500*. Chicago: University of Chicago Press, 1990.

Herzfeld, Michael. "Practical Mediterraneanism: Excuses for Everything, from Epistemology to Eating." *Rethinking the Mediterranean*. Ed. W. V. Harris. Oxford: Oxford University Press, 2005. 45–63.

Horden, Peregrine, and Nicholas Purcell. *The Corrupting Sea: A Study of Mediterranean History*. Oxford: Blackwell Publishers, 2000.

Kinoshita, Sharon. "Mediterranean Literature." Forum on Theories and Methodologies in Medieval Literary Studies. *PMLA* 124.2 (2009): 600–8.

Leite de Vasconcelos, José. *Romanceiro Português*. 2 vols. Coimbra: Universidad de Coimbra, 1958.

Maravall, José Antonio. *El concepto de España en la Edad Media*. Madrid: Instituto de Estudios Políticos, 1964.

Menocal, María Rosa. "Why Iberia?" *Diacritics* 36.3–4 (2006): 7–11.

———. *The Ornament of the World: How Muslims, Jews, and Christians Created a Culture of Tolerance in Medieval Spain*. New York: Little Brown, 2002.

Millás Vallicrosa, Josep María. *Poesía hebraica postbíblica*. Barcelona: José Janés, 1953.

Monroe, James T. "Arabic Literary Elements in the Structure of the Libro de Buen Amor (I)," *Al-Qantara* 32.1 (2011): 27–30.

———. "Arabic Literary Elements in the Structure of the Libro de Buen Amor (II)," *Al-Qantara* 32.2 (2011): 307–32.

———. *Islam and the Arabs in Spanish Scholarship: Sixteenth Century to the Present*. Leiden: Brill, 1970.

Márquez Villanueva, Francisco. *El concepto cultural alfonsí*. Madrid: Bellaterra, 2004.

———. *Mudejarismo: las tres culturas en la creación de la identidad española*. Sevilla: Fundación Tres Culturas del Mediterráneo, 2003.

Nykl, A.R. "Sobre el nombre y la patria del autor de la *Muwassaha*." *Al-Andalus* 2.1 (1934): 215–22.

Ray, Jonathan. "Beyond Tolerance and Persecution: Reassessing Our Approach to Medieval Convivencia." *Jewish Social Studies* 11.2 (2005): 1–18.

Resina, Joan Ramon. *Del hispanismo a los estudios ibéricos: una propuesta federativa para el ámbito cultural*. Madrid: Biblioteca Nueva, 2009.

Ribera y Tarragó, Julián. *El cancionero de Abencuzmán*. Madrid: Imprenta de Estanislao Maestre, 1914.

Riquer, Martín. *Los trovadores*. Barcelona: Planeta, 1975.

Sáenz Badillos, Ángel. *Literatura Hebrea en la España Medieval*. Madrid: UNED, 1991.

Stern, Samuel. "Les vers finaux en espagnol dans les muwassahs hispano-hébraïques. Une contribution à l'histoire du muwassah et à l'étude du vieux dialecte espagnol '*mozarabe*.' *Al-Andalus: Revista de las escuelas de estudios árabes de Madrid y Granada* 12 (1948): 299–346.

Szpiech, Ryan. "The Convivencia Wars: Decoding Historiography's Polemic with Philology." *A Sea of Languages: Rethinking the Arabic Role in Medieval Literary History*. Ed. Suzanne Akbari and Karla Mallette. Toronto: University of Toronto Press, 2013.

Wacks, David. *Framing Iberia: Maqāmāt and Frametale Narratives in Medieval Spain.* Leiden: Brill, 2007.

Wigen, Karen. "Introduction: Oceans of History." *American Historical Review* 111 (2006): 717–21.

◆ 1

Christian-Muslim-Jewish Relations, Medieval "Spain," and the Mediterranean: An Historiographical Op-Ed

Brian A. Catlos

> . . . the situation of the Jews in Spain had nothing to do with the Mediterranean but with the very innards of Spanish history.
> —Américo Castro, *The Spaniards* (8)

> . . . the uniqueness of the vital Spanish contexture is unquestionable. Spain differs from the two lineages of historical communities with which it should logically coincide. It cannot be enclosed within the functional structure of the Mediterranean peoples nor of the peoples of the so-called West . . .
> —Claudio Sánchez-Albornoz, *Spain, A Historical Enigma* (1:26)

For those who have worked on the history and culture of medieval Spain over the last half-century, and particularly on the subject of Muslim-Christian-Jewish relations, it is has been difficult to escape the influence of Américo Castro and Claudio Sánchez-Albornoz. These two towering figures defined the debate regarding the nature of Spanish history in the aftermath of the Civil War—a visceral conflict between parties that presented themselves as the embodiments of antithetical and incompatible ideologies.[1] Castro and Sánchez-Albornoz—both of whom were exiled as a consequence of the war—themselves present what appear to be antithetical and incompatible visions of the essence of Spanish history, each of which were related deeply to the encounter between Christian, Muslim, and Jewish cultures in the peninsula. Sánchez-Albornoz believed the "enigma" of Spanish history could be understood in the light of the "eternal Spaniard." For him, this unique peninsular personality, forged by the heat and hammering of a succession of foreign invasions from the Romans onwards on a core of Iberian steel, embodies a coherence and continuity of both physiology and spirit. For Castro, on the other hand, the Spanish character was a product of a succession of cultures, finally emerging in the Middle Ages: formally Christian, but embodying elements of the Islamic and Jewish cultures that it grappled with and internalized.[2]

The intellectual encounter between these two historians was hardly less jarring than the war that made each of them an exile. A tremendous intellectual explosion, it left behind a scarred scholarly landscape littered with the detritus of previous Spanish historiography, rent asunder by their fulminations—detritus that has been fashioned, in the case of Don Américo's ideas, into a nostalgic and idealized vision of intercultural *convivencia* (typically presented as an anachronistic and moralizing idealization of "tolerance"), whereas that of Don Claudio has been of particular appeal to a nationalistic (if not chauvinistic and xenophobic) Catholic and Castilian Right. What might be described as the "Castro school" has dominated the historiography outside of the peninsula. The tendency among postwar historians and particularly among British historians, but also in the United States, was to accept the essentially Castilian orientation of "Spain," as reflected in the syntheses of scholars such as Angus MacKay and Joseph O'Callaghan. From the late 1970s the monopoly of this paradigm was weakened by the work of scholars such as Thomas Bisson, Thomas F. Glick, J. N. Hillgarth, and Bernard Reilly, who produced their own syntheses, not to mention by Catalan and Valencian historians in Spain. Among non-Spanish historians, the notion of *convivencia* ("living together," a term which Castro himself adapted from Ramón Menéndez Pidal) came to be framed in terms of the "toleration" which certain Muslim and Christian regimes were held to have exhibited toward members of religious minorities.[3] This model has also fired the popular imagination, particularly in North America, as can be seen in a recent proliferation of nostalgically-flavored works aimed at a popular audience.[4] The present author, for his part, has been critical of this approach, and proposes a new paradigm, *conveniencia*, or "The Principle of Convenience."[5]

The influence of Sánchez-Albornoz is seen chiefly among nationalist historians (some with a markedly xenophobic and polemical bent), notably Eloy Benito Ruano, A. Cañizares, Serafín Fanjul, Vicente Palacio Atard, and César Vidal Manzanares, many of whom are associated with the Real Academia de la Historia of Madrid. This can be seen as one dimension of a broader historiographical/polemical trend that pits a savage and idealized "Islam" against a virtuous and civilizing "West," as in the later work of Bernard Lewis or the recent efforts of Sylvain Gouggenheim.[6]

In fact, Castro's and Sánchez-Albornoz's fundamental positions on the nature of history, and the historical role of Spain, are for the most part not altogether so different, and it is this, perhaps, that accounts for the ferocity of their opposition and those of their disciples. Each of them begins with the firm conviction that there is something called "Spain" and "Spanishness," that is not only an accidental political arrangement or the consequence of historical coincidence, but a coherent, distinct, fundamentally unified, and even unique historical entity, and that it has its origins in a remote past. Each of them reifies and essentializes Islam, Christianity, and Judaism. Theirs is history at its most Platonic and teleological—the culmination of a European nationalist historiography that stirred the likes of Edward Gibbon and was most forcefully articulated by Leopold Von Ranke.[7] It is hopelessly outdated, and it is very often—quite simply—wrong.[8] Nevertheless, their ideas, or the spirit behind their respective ideals, has had a profound effect—both illuminating and obfuscating—on subsequent historical and literary scholarship.[9] And if virtually no scholar cites them any more as historians, the sympathizers and partisans of their idealistic positions among historians today remain remarkably easy to spot. Arguments revolving around "tolerance" and "intolerance" in medieval Spain, the nature of the cultural and political encounters between Muslims, Christians, and Jews in the peninsula, and of *convivencia* and "clashes of civilization" all reflect or resonate with the binaries established by these two thinkers.[10]

The point of this essay is not to criticize or dismantle the arguments of either Castro or Sánchez-Albornoz; the debility of their legacy as historians obviates this need and, in any event, much continues to be written on the theme. Rather, it is to examine some of the general presumptions that underlie their views of history, and the history of the Iberian Peninsula, and to propose that in terms of Muslim-Christian-Jewish relations medieval "Spain"—far from being "enigmatic" or "unique"—can be fit into a Mediterranean historical framework, and this exercise can serve both to illuminate peninsular history and that of the region. In other words, this essay is a response to the idea of Spain as defined by the historians' vision—which is to say a Spain which is only ultimately realized as Christian Spain, and more specifically, that particular Christian Spain that is seen as the origin of the modern Spanish nation-state.

Was Medieval Spain Spanish?

Fundamental to the thought of both Castro and Sánchez-Albornoz is the idea that categories such as "Spain," "Islam," "Christianity," and "Judaism" represent the fundamental conceptual building blocks of history. Whereas I would not deny the usefulness and validity of such categories, or of their suitability as objects of study and historical forces, they cannot be understood as unified, coherent, immutable, and eternal forms. Each of them is contingent, temporal, multifaceted, and polyvalent. Words are just that. Their meaning and sense shifts with time, context, rhetorical style, author, and audience. History founded on etymologies is a dead end.

True, the Romans and the Visigoths may have referred to something called *Hispania*, and there was clearly a sense that in some ways inhabitants of the peninsula shared certain characteristics or affectations, but this is hardly evidence that there was some*thing* that could be identified as "Spain," or Spanish culture, at least in a concrete and exclusive sense. This is abundantly clear in the Middle Ages, when the Emperors of León invoked a clear plurality by referring to themselves as "Emperors of All of the Spains," and when Christian chroniclers could use the noun *Ispanos* to refer specifically to the Muslims of al-Andalus.[11] *Reconquista* and *jihād* notwithstanding, the Kings of Castile and León and their North African analogues competed to present themselves as the legitimate rulers over both Christians and Muslims, not as the architects of homogenous states.

Moreover, what is one to do with the medieval Spanish societies that were not part of the peninsula? Naples and Sicily were for centuries Aragonese. They were arguably no less "Spanish" in the fourteenth and fifteenth centuries than the Kingdom of Granada or the Kingdom of Valencia, and yet they evidently do not form part of either Castro's or Sánchez-Albornoz's Spanish essence. Twelfth-century Provence was in many ways closer to the Catalan counties, politically, culturally, and economically, than the counties were to contemporary Galicia. Indeed, this reflects a general problem with the Platonizing approach to the history of medieval Spain: much that we identify as "Spanish" was, in fact, characteristic of only parts of the peninsula, whereas other aspects were not limited to the peninsula.

Many of the apparently essential features of medieval "Spanish" culture and history were, in fact, highly localized. The ideology of the *Reconquista* and the reestablishment of a united *Hispania* under a supposedly restored Visigothic line was, of course, strongest in the lands of Castile and León; it reverberated also in Aragon and Portugal, but scarcely at all in the Catalan counties or Navarre. So, too, with the particular culture of *hidalguía* that developed most clearly in the Crown of Castile, or the culture and institutions of the municipal militias, which coalesced across the broad swathe of territory that comprised the frontier between al-Andalus and the Christian principalities in the twelfth and thirteenth centuries, and included specific parts of Portugal, Castile-Leon, Aragon, and Valencia.

Most obvious are the contrasts between the economic and institutional trajectories of the various kingdoms, most particularly the Crowns of Castile and Aragon—the former developing into a polity dominated by a narrow class of magnates and a strong monarchy, and the latter characterized by a weak monarchy, held in check by a parliamentary *pactisme* and contending with powerful noble and municipal estates. If it is the "plainsman" of the frontier who epitomizes the culture of medieval Castile, one could claim (with the same degree of inaccuracy and oversimplification) that it is the merchant and artisan who personified the Crown of Aragon in the Middle Ages. Both figures were "Spanish," so who would be correct?[12]

Nor does the situation of religious minorities lend itself any more easily to generalization in terms of physical presence, social roles, or cultural influence. The Crown of Aragon, particularly Aragon and Valencia, included a large proportion of Muslim subjects (constituting the numerical majority in these kingdoms to the thirteenth and fourteenth centuries, respectively). Generally, the *mudéjares* here were secure and reasonably prosperous, but had little direct political influence and a cultural influence that was apparently limited for the most part to architecture—and in this only in the Kingdom of Aragon. In Valencia, the direct influence of local subject Muslim communities survives chiefly in the quotidian, notably ceramics, cuisine, and so forth. In Portugal and Navarre the situation was similar, although the Muslim populations were both numerically and proportionately quite small. By contrast, the lands of Castile had a relatively small Muslim population, but one that left a strong cultural imprint, not the least on the Castilian language, but also on literary styles. The Arabisms that are the hallmark of the Castilian and Portuguese lexicon are far fewer in Catalan, whereas the Arabisms in Euskara are virtually all Castilian loanwords. Similarly, the development of vernacular literature in the Catalan lands not only predated that of Castile, but drew on distinct sources and influences. The Islamic architectural legacy also was dissimilar in the lands of Castile, where in the later Middle Ages the rulers and elite embraced a Maurophilia that idealized foreign rather than domestic Islamic culture, and which was reflected also in styles of tastes in fashion, and an appetite for the translation and appropriation of Islamic high culture that was all but absent elsewhere in the peninsula. The experience of Jews and the influence of Jewish culture across the peninsula was characterized by an analogous variety of experience, opportunity, and historical trajectory, although the specific cultural influence of the Jewish minorities was distinct from that of subject Muslims.

Much of this is obvious, and little is surprising. The peninsula had never been truly unified or uniform—even under the Romans and Visigoths, and certainly not in the Middle Ages. When the Islamic conquest provoked the emergence of a new order in the Christian lands, this was not predicated on a solidarity of purpose or identity, except in the most vague sense, or one limited to specific and limited rhetorical contexts. Each region, each principality, developed along a distinct if not always dissimilar trajectory, developing their own institutions, seeing the emergence of their own elites with their own agendas and their own popular traditions. In view of this, it is little surprise that neither political alliances nor economic relations corresponded to Christian and Islamic blocs. The political history of early medieval Spain is one of petty principalities and provinces, Christian and Muslim, working to resist the domination of Córdoba, whereas that of later medieval Spain is as much as contest between the Crown of Castile, the Crown of Aragon, and Portugal, as between Christian powers and Islamic powers. This is even clearer when commercial relations are considered; these were characterized by integration and interdependence of Christians, Muslims, and Jews within the Spanish kingdoms and between the *dār al-Islām* and the lands of Latin Christendom. Castile and Portugal would develop powerful and important commercial ties with Granada and the Maghrib (in part through the mediation of Genoa), and the Crown of Aragon with Granada, Tunisia, and Mamluk Egypt. The famous frontier between Christendom and Islam, often imagined as a constant in the medieval history of the peninsula, was elusive, contextual, and porous—a condition reflected in the epic literature, diplomatic relations, and archival evidence of the time.

And yet, in the imagination of Castro and Sánchez-Albornoz and their intellectual heirs, "Spain" is essentially Greater Castile-León, and that which is essentially "Spanish" is Castilian-Leonese. In other words, this represents a remarkable example of retroactive teleological thinking: it presents a facile paradigm that may seem to correspond to the Spain of the twentieth century, but is of limited use for illuminating the medieval history of the peninsula and its inhabitants. It effaces the subtlety of historical change, the richness of historical variety, and invites the misapplication of the conclusions drawn from evidence originating in one narrow area to the region as a whole. Of course, this view of Spain and Spanish history is not a twentieth-century invention; it has its roots in the myths of the Reconquest and Visigothic continuity fabricated by the twelfth-century Gallic clergymen who presented this as a justification for the political claims of their patrons—the Kings of Castile-León. But a myth, however ancient it may be, is still a myth.

Medieval Spain beyond the Peninsula

The idealized view of Spanish history is further complicated by the fact that much of "medieval Spain" was not restricted to the peninsula. Even Sánchez-Albornoz's beloved Visigothic kingdom was "Spanish" in neither language nor geography. On the one hand, the northeast of the peninsula was never effectively under its power, and on the other, its territories in Septimania (now France)—the original kernel of the kingdom—were also considerable. Much later, the Kingdom of Navarre too straddled what would be the modern border of Spain, and its offspring, the Kingdom of Aragon, would join with the Catalan counties to form a dynastic aggregate that not only claimed seigniorial authority over the Midi and Provence, but directly ruled over territories across the Mediterranean, from the Peloponnese to Ifrīqiya, and from Naples to the Balearics. Nor was Islamic Spain, al-Andalus, a strictly peninsular phenomenon. From the time of its establishment, it was inextricably linked with the Maghrib: bound by currents of immigration, networks of trade, structures of patronage, and institutions of political authority. In the Umayyad era it was the peninsular power that colonized North Africa, whereas after the dissolution of the Caliphate in the eleventh century it would be the other way around. By the same token, from the thirteenth century, as first Castile then Portugal swept over the Islamic south, they did not regard the Atlantic and Mediterranean shores as natural termini of expansion; the first tentative and failed attempts at the conquest of the Maghrib began in the 1200s, centuries before the subjugation of al-Andalus would be complete. In other words, each of the Spanish kingdoms was engaged in a process of political expansion that was framed in regional rather than peninsular terms—it was not an expansion framed by the rhetoric of the *Reconquista* and Crusade, but one to which the rhetoric of *Reconquista* and Crusade was forced to adapt. Economic expansion can be characterized in similar terms.

Obviously, neither the religious traditions nor the ethno-linguistic cultures that they are identified with are peninsular. Judaism, Christianity, and Islam were "world" religions, and Hebrew, Latin, and Arabic were "world" languages, spoken and read across the West by adherents of all three of these religions. The fact that they were also characterized by regional variations, some of which were particular to Iberia (or parts of it), is to be expected. Iberian Islam was no less "Islamic" by dint of the fact that Arabo-Islamic culture here was not identical to that of the Arabian Peninsula, Syria-Palestine, or Baghdad. Quite the contrary, the profound engagement of these "three cultures" with their wider traditions, both across the Mediterranean and into Africa and Europe, tempered local particularisms. This can be seen most dramatically in the abrupt decline of the Mozarabic liturgy (another example of a localized peninsular tradition commonly presented as quintessentially Spanish) in the late eleventh century, once Castile-León became politically engaged with northern Europe (and concretely Burgundy). Moreover, whether it took place in the framework of opposition or affinity, whether in the realm of theology, science, literature, architecture, art, or cuisine, potent processes of acculturation (and reaction) characterized the relationship between Muslims, Christians, and Jews in the peninsula from the eighth to the early seventeenth centuries. These processes, which led to the development, *inter alia*, of the picaresque in literature, *mudéjar* architecture, Golden Age Hebrew poetry, the Toledan translations, and Morisco Marianism, were not unique to "Spain," but can be observed across the Mediterranean, and even, although somewhat more faintly, in the more religiously and culturally homogenous Latin Christian hinterland of Europe.

Medieval Spain in the Mediterranean

Indeed, analogous developments took place across the Mediterranean as a consequence of the engagement and integration of Muslim, Christian, and Jewish societies. Scientific, linguistic, and literary acculturation can be observed in what is now Italy, not only in the well-known context of the Norman court of Sicily, but on the mainland also. Analogues of *mudéjar* architecture can be observed in Sicily and Byzantium and in Syria-Palestine. Formal translation initiatives were not only undertaken in Spain, but in Pisa, Byzantium, Armenia, Antioch, and Egypt, to name only a few locales.[13] In terms of linguistic integration, the influence of Arabic on Castilian pales with that on Maltese, whereas it simply displaced earlier vernaculars in Egypt and Syria-Palestine. And the adaption of cultural affectations, daily habits, and tastes in fashion between Christians, Muslims, and Jews was a fundamental characteristic of the region—if only for the simple reason that Mediterranean societies were so thoroughly heterogeneous, not only vis-à-vis the grand ecumenical divisions, but in terms of subgroups, and in terms of ethnic identities and other affiliations that cut across confessional lines. Slavery and concubinage had deep social and economic roots on both shores, and this was a powerful vector for acculturation. In both Christian and Islamic societies Jews and other confessional minorities (notably the Copts in Egypt and Muslims in Sicily, Iberia, and the Near East) were depended on to fill important economic and political niches. Christians, Muslims, and Jews preached to each other, debated with each other, and persecuted each other. And just as in medieval Spain, Muslims and Christians across the Mediterranean frequently fought against each other—often under the banner of a higher principle, but as often not—they just as easily allied with each other against their coreligionists.

In other words, seen from the Mediterranean perspective, "medieval Spain"—to the extent that *it* can be said to have existed—was not at all unique or exceptional, at least in terms of Christian-Muslim-Jewish interaction. But "what is the Mediterranean perspective"? The Mediterranean perspective recognizes certain common patterns, dynamics, and structures relating to the cultural, social, political, and economic competition, conflict, integration, and interdependence that developed among the array of ethno-religious communities that inhabited the region. To a certain extent these arose as a consequence of its specific geographic environment as described by Peregrine Horden and Nicholas Purcell—a fragmented aggregate of highly varied micro-ecologies, ill-suited to economic autarchy, but which embodied tremendous productive potential which could be realized when these regions were linked by trade.[14] Thanks to the particular disposition of the Mediterranean, which was amenable to incremental maritime navigation, or "cabotage," an intensive trade characterized the region as early as the Neolithic.[15] In the Middle Ages ethno-religious communities identifying with grand ecumenical cultures (e.g., Latin Christianity, Judaism, Islam, Byzantine Christianity) lived not only side by side, as it were, but profoundly mixed, cohabiting the same spaces as subjects of the same principalities, and frequently as members of the same collectives. These communities may have been signified or defined to a certain extent by specific religious practices and beliefs, languages, and customs, but they did not practice them exclusively or exercise a monopoly over them. The economic, social, and political interdependence of members of these groups, coupled with their common religio-cultural orientation (i.e., "Abrahamic" and Perso-Hellenic) acted as a catalyst for political and social accommodation and polyvalent currents of acculturation, and as a framework for competition and conflict. Seen thusly "medieval Spain" does not stand alone as exceptional, but perhaps provides many of the clearest examples of what were undeniably regional characteristics and trends.

Hence, by examining medieval Spain in the Mediterranean context, we can gain clearer insights into the forces at play in the peninsula, as well as abroad. "Provincializing" Spanish history in this way enriches it.[16] For example, our understanding of the anti-Jewish violence of 1391 is deepened if we view it in the context of anti-Jewish violence (and pro-Jewish policies) elsewhere in the Mediterranean. This enables us to factor out specifically local elements. Similarly, by comparing it to anti-Christian policy in the Islamic Mediterranean (or, for that matter, anti-Byzantine and "Oriental" Christian policy in the Frankish Mediterranean) we can better assess the extent to which such violence had specifically religious roots, as opposed to other causes. The tension and competition between Karaite and Rabbinical Jews in Egypt was not only echoed directly in Sepharad, but may present parallels to Roman-Mozarabic struggles in the peninsula. Looking at both the influence of the Copts in the Fatimid and Mamluk administrations and their vulnerabilities as religious minorities sheds light not only on the position of Muslims in Norman Sicily, but of the Jews in Castile and the Crown of Aragon. Similar illustrations can be drawn for matters as diverse as the study of institutional adaptation, technical and intellectual diffusion, artistic and literary developments, and the relationship between religious ideology and political policy. In the broad context of confessional relations the Iberian Peninsula in the Middle Ages represents not one, but several discrete manifestations of the trends and dynamics that were features of the Mediterranean region as a whole.

National, Continental, and Mediterranean Perspectives

This is not to say that one cannot speak of "medieval Spain" in a meaningful way—although, to be sure, "medieval Iberia" is preferable, unburdened as it is by anachronistic conceptual baggage and modern political associations. Obviously the peninsula and its people share common characteristics, habits, and experiences, if only by virtue of their proximity and their common environment. But this is not to say that these common characteristics are essential or eternal, or embody some ontological privilege. Nor is it to say that they are constant over time or consistent geographically. The Spain that attracted the earliest bands of *homo sapiens* migrants from East Africa in the Paleolithic is not the same Spain that attracts hordes of "low-cost" tourists from North Europe today. Historically, Galicia, Andalucia, and Catalonia differ by as much as they have in common.

In this sense, "Spain" is little different from "France," "Germany," "Italy," or "Europe"—national categories that are also applied anachronistically and inappropriately to the Middle Ages. It is a useful and valid category of analysis when applied critically, fully conscious of its contextual limitations, and careful not to allow its inherently anachronistic formulation to skew the historical narrative. Much of this may be obvious, but—casting an eye around the academy (which remains for the most part straitjacketed by nineteenth-century nationalist paradigms, and which is resistant to interdisciplinary and comparative revision) or around a popular media that remains enamored of essentializing models of religious and national identity, and of grand, moralizing, self-affirming narratives—it is necessary. The same intellectual spirit that imagines the "clash of civilizations" in the context of religious cultures manufactures eternal nationalisms. These are powerful, compelling models, if only because of the simplicity they embody and the certainty they convey. But not unlike Galenic medicine or Ptolemaic geography—whose principles had been proven incorrect by observation in the late Middle Ages and early modern period, but which nevertheless continued to be held to represent authoritative Truth—the time has come that that we should recognize that however canonical such concepts have become, they do not correspond to much of the evidence as we observe it, and they should be jettisoned. Better to work with no model than an incorrect model. It may be true that few Hispanists today subscribe directly to the theses proposed by Castro or Sánchez-Albornoz, and most admit that as perspectives they are obsolete, but for all that, Hispanists have been for the most part unable to escape the pull of these paradigms, to escape their vocabulary and terminology, to engage in comparative work beyond the geographic bounds of the peninsula, or to systemically question or propose alternatives to the concepts and presumptions regarding the nature of history in which they are rooted.

In sum, *contra* Castro, the comparative, the study of the Jews of Medieval Spain has *everything* to do with the Mediterranean, precisely because, *contra* Sánchez-Albornoz, in the context of Muslim-Christian-Jewish interaction Spain *can* be "situated within the functional structure of the Mediterranean." Spanish exceptionalism is, in fact, the Mediterranean norm, viewed as anomalous only when subjected to inappropriate comparisons with distinct developments taking place in the Latin Christian heartlands of northern Europe. The proof—aside from the preponderance of evidence in its favor—is that doing so enriches our understanding not only of the history of that interaction, but of that-which-we-call-Spain itself.

Notes

Thanks are due to Núria Silleras-Fernández and Michelle M. Hamilton for asking me to contribute to this volume of *Hispanic Issues*, to Carolina López-Ruiz for inviting me to the College of Arts and Sciences of The Ohio State University to present "Exceptional Iberia or Normative Mediterranean? Contexts of Ethno-religious Relations in the Middle Ages"—the talk upon which this essay is based—as well as to the faculty and graduate students present at the talk who offered comments, criticisms, and questions. Thanks are due also to Alejandro García Sanjuán (Universidad de Huelva) for pointing me toward recent works of the "Sánchez-Albornoz school." And, finally, I feel this is an appropriate occasion to signal my respect and fondness for María Rosa Menocal, Sterling Professor of Humanities at Yale University, who so recently passed away—a generous and original scholar who did so much to transform our understanding of Muslim-Christian-Jewish relations both in the Iberian Peninsula of the Middle Ages, and beyond. Except for the historiographical discussions, and the rare occasion where I refer to concrete data, I have not cited sources. In my defense I cite the fact that the general events and broad trends I discuss are regarded as established fact and should be recognized as such by scholars of medieval Iberia and the Mediterranean, and are attested to in the many general surveys that cover these regions in this period.

1. The two works that kicked off the debate were Castro's *España en su historia* (1948) and Sánchez-Albornoz's reaction, *España: un enigma histórico* (1956).
2. Much ink has been spilled recapitulating and analyzing the controversy, and grappling with the issues that lie at its heart. Early critiques include P.E. Russell, "The Nessus-Shirt of Spanish History," Thomas F. Glick and Oriol Pi-Sunyer, "Acculturation as an Explanatory Concept in Spanish History," and J.N. Hillgarth, "Spanish Historiography and Iberian Reality," each of which address the intellectual impasse that resulted from the entrenchment of such positions.
3. Some recent works that argue in terms of "toleration" or *convivencia*, or respond to these paradigms include Stéphane Boissellier, "Une tolérance chrétienne"; Giulio Cipollone, "From Intolerance to Tolerance"; Marcel Launay, "Tolérance et dialogue"; María Rosa Menocal, *The Ornament of the World*; Cary Nederman, "Introduction," and *World of Difference*; Alex Novikoff, "Between Tolerance and Intolerance"; Jonathon Ray, "Beyond Tolerance"; Maya Soifer, "Beyond Convivencia"; Abdelaziz Testas, "Models of Cultural Exclusion"; Kenneth Wolf, "*Convivencia* in Medieval Spain"; and Perez Zagorin, *How the Idea*. Both the introduction and the various chapters in Cynthia Robinson and Leyla Rouhi, *Under the Influence*, are useful. The most recent review of the terms *convivencia* and "toleration," in this context can be found in Ryan Szpiech, "The *Convivencia* Wars."
4. See, for example, María Rosa Menocal's *The Ornament of the World*, Chris Lowney's *A Vanished World*, Richard Rubenstein's *Aristotle's Children*, and David Lewis's *God's Crucible*.
5. See Brian Catlos, "Contexto social y "conveniencia," "Mudéjar Ethnogenisis," in *The Victors and the Vanquished*, pp. 390–408, and the forthcoming, *Paradoxes of Plurality*.
6. For an overview of the historiography of the reactionary Right, see García Sanjuán, "Al-Andalus."
7. For nineteenth-century historians like Leopold von Ranke, writing about Germany, and ideologues like Giuseppe Mazzini, writing about Italy (both in the 1830s)—the

fundamental reality of the nation and its role in shaping culture was evident, even in the absence of a unified state.

8. The fact that neither Castro nor Sánchez-Albornoz were Arabists or Hebraists, and each limited himself to a narrow range of data, did not restrain either of them from making broad inferences and generalizations that simply do not stand up.
9. See the works cited, in n. 3, above.
10. See nn. 4–6, above.
11. See, for example, Caffaro's description of the siege of Tortosa (1148), where he refers to the Muslim defenders sending for help "ad Ispanorum regem et ad omnes Ispanos," in reference to the Muslims of al-Andalus (see Caffaro, *De captione Almerie et Tortosue*, 34).
12. Compare to Charles Julian Bishko's seminal article, "The Castilian as Plainsman."
13. The work of Charles Burnett, among others, has laid to rest the notion that Toledo was a singular or unique center of the translation and transmission of Arabo-Islamic science and learning. See, for example, Burnett, "The Transmission of Arabic Astronomy."
14. This is a rather crude summary of Horden and Purcell's argument in *The Corrupting Sea*.
15. This is the thrust of Horden and Purcell's environmental argument, and is indeed, born out by the evidence of Neolithic societies (such as those of Menorca and Malta) that produced monumental architecture indicative of populations that were clearly more populous than could have been sustain by the rather meagre native resources of those islands.
16. I borrow the term from Chakrabarty's *Provincializing Europe*.

Works Cited

Benito Ruano, Eloy, ed. *España. Reflexiones sobre el ser de España*. Madrid: Real Academia de la Historia, 1998.

Bishko, Charles Julian. "The Castilian as Plainsman: The Medieval Ranching Frontier in La Mancha and Extremadura." *The New World Looks at Its History*. Ed. Archibald F. Lewis and Thomas F. McGann. Austin: University of Texas Press, 1963. 47–69.

Bisson, Thomas N. *The Medieval Crown of Aragon. A Short History*. Oxford: Clarendon, 1986.

Boissellier, Stéphane. "Une tolérance chrétienne dans l'historiographie portugaise de la reconquête (XIIe–XIIIe siècles)?" *La tolérance: Colloque International de Nantes, mai 1998: Quatriéme Centenaire de l'Edit de Nantes*. Ed. Guy Saupin et al. Rennes: Presses Universitaires de Rennes, 1999. 371–83.

Burnett, Charles. "The Transmission of Arabic Astronomy Via Antioch and Pisa in the Second Quarter of the Twelfth Century." *The Enterprise of Science in Islam: New*

Perspectives. Ed. J. P. Hogendijk and A. I. Sabra. Cambridge, Mass.: MIT Press, 2003. 23–51.

Caffaro. *De captione Almerie et Tortosue*. Ed. A. Ubieto Arteta. Valencia: Facsímil, 1973.

Cañizares Llovera, A. *El esplendor visigótico, momento clave en la edificación de España y para su futuro: Discurso leído el día 24 de febrero de 2008 en el acto de su recepción pública*. Madrid: Real Academia de la Historia, 2008.

Castro, Américo. *España en su historia. Cristianos, Moros y Judíos*. Buenos Aires: Losada, 1948.

———. *The Spaniards: An Introduction to their History*. Berkeley: University of California Press, 1971.

Catlos, Brian A. "Contexto social y "conveniencia" en la Corona de Aragón. Propuesta para un modelo de interacción entre grupos etno-religiosos minoritarios y mayoritarios." *Revista d'història medieval* 12 (2002): 220–35.

———. "Cristians, Musulmans i Jueus a la Corona d'Aragó medieval: un cas de "conveniència." *L'Avenç* 236 (November 2001): 8–16.

———. *Paradoxes of Plurality: Ethnic and Religious Diversity in the Medieval Mediterranean and Beyond*. Forthcoming.

———. *The Victors and the Vanquished: Christians and Muslims of Catalonia and Aragon, 1050–1300*. New York: Cambridge University Press, 2004.

Chakrabarty, Dipesh. *Provincializing Europe. Postcolonial Thought and Historical Difference*. Princeton: Princeton University Press, 2000.

Cipollone, Giulio. "From Intolerance to Tolerance: The Humanitarian Way, 1187–1216." *Tolerance and Intolerance: Social Conflict in the Age of the Crusades*. Ed. Michael Gervers and James M. Powell. Syracuse: Syracuse University Press, 2001. 28–40.

Fanjul, Serafín. *Al-Andalus contra España: la forja del mito*. Madrid: Siglo Veintiuno, 2000.

———. *La quimera de al-Andalus*. Madrid: Siglo Veintiuno, 2004.

García Sanjuán, Alejandro. "Al-Andalus en la historiografía del nacionalismo españolista (siglos XIX–XXI). Entre la reconquista y la España musulmana." *A 1300 Años de la conquista de al-Andalus (11–2011): historia, cultura y legado del Islam en la Península Ibérica*. Ed. Diego Melo Carrasco and Francisco Vidal Castro. Coquimbo-Chile: Centro Mohammad VI para el Diálogo de Civilzaciones, 2012. 65–104.

Gibbon, Edward. *The Decline and Fall of the Roman Empire*. Ed. J. B. Bury. 7 vols. London: Methuen, 1909–1914.

Glick, Thomas F. *Irrigation and Society in Medieval Valencia*. Cambridge: Harvard University Press, 1979.

———. *Islamic and Christian Spain in the Early Middle Ages*. Princeton: Princeton University Press, 1979.

Glick, Thomas F., and Oriol Pi-Sunyer. "Acculturation as an Explanatory Concept in Spanish History." *Comparative Studies in Society and History* 11 (1969): 136–54.

Gouguenheim, Sylvain. *Aristote au Mont-Saint-Michel: les racines grecques de l'Europe chrétienne*. Paris: Seuil, 2008.

Hillgarth, J.N. "Spanish Historiography and Iberian Reality." *History and Theory* 24 (1985): 23–43.

———. *The Spanish Kingdoms, 1250–1516.* 2 vols. Oxford: Clarendon, 1976.

Horden, Peregrine, and Nicholas Purcell. *The Corrupting Sea: A Study of Mediterranean History.* Malden, Mass.: Blackwell, 2000.

Launay, Marcel. "Tolérance et dialogue inter-religieux: une problématique." *La Tolérance.* Ed. Guy Saupin, et al., 351–61.

Lewis, Bernard. *What Went Wrong?: The Clash Between Islam and Modernity in the Middle East.* New York: Perennial, 2003.

Lewis, David L. *God's Crucible: Islam and the Making of Europe, 570 to 1215.* New York: W.W. Norton, 2008.

Lowney, Chris. *A Vanished World: Medieval Spain's Golden Age of Enlightenment.* New York: Free Press, 2005.

MacKay, Angus. *Spain in the Middle Ages: From Frontier to Empire, 1000–1500.* New York: St. Martin's, 1977.

Menocal, María Rosa. *The Ornament of the World: How Muslims, Jews, and Christians Created a Culture of Tolerance in Medieval Spain.* Boston: Little Brown, 2002.

Nederman, Cary J. "Introduction: Discourses and Contexts of Tolerance in Medieval Europe." *Beyond the Persecuting Society: Religious Toleration Before the Enlightenment.* Ed. John Christian Laursen and Cary J. Nederman. Philadelphia: University of Pennsylvania Press, 1998. 13–24.

———. *World of Difference: European Discourses of Tolerance, c. 1100–1500.* Philadelphia: University of Pennsylvania Press, 2000.

Novikoff, Alex A. "Between Tolerance and Intolerance in Medieval Spain: An Historiographic Enigma." *Medieval Encounters* 11 (2005): 7–36.

O'Callaghan, Joseph F. *History of Medieval Spain.* Ithaca: Cornell University Press, 1975.

Palacio Atard, Vicente. *De Hispania a España. El nombre y el concepto a través de los siglos.* Madrid: Temas De Hoy, 2005.

Ray, Jonathan. "Beyond Tolerance and Persecution: Our Approach to Medieval Convivencia." *Jewish Social Studies* 11 (2005): 1–18.

Reilly, Bernard F. *The Medieval Spains.* Cambridge: Cambridge University Press, 1993.

Robinson, Cynthia, and Leyla Rouhi, eds. *Under the Influence: Questioning the Comparative in Medieval Castile.* Leiden: Brill, 2005.

Rubenstein, Richard E. *Aristotle's Children: How Christians, Muslims, and Jews Rediscovered Ancient Wisdom and Illuminated the Dark Ages.* Orlando: Harcourt, 2003.

Russell, P.E. "The Nessus-Shirt of Spanish History." *Bulletin of Hispanic Studies* 36 (1959): 219–25.

Sánchez-Albornoz, Claudio. *Spain, A Historical Enigma.* 2 vols. Madrid: Fundación Universitaria Española, 1975. [Orig.: *España: un enigma histórico.* Buenos Aires: Editorial Sudamericana, 1956.]

Soifer, Maya. "Beyond Convivencia: Critical Reflections on the Historiography of Interfaith Relations in Christian Spain." *Journal of Medieval Iberian Studies* 1 (2009): 19–35.

Szpiech, Ryan. "The *Convivencia* Wars: Decoding Historiography's Polemic with Philology." *A Sea of Languages: Literature and Culture in the Pre-modern Mediterranean*. Ed. Susan Akbari and Karla Malette. Toronto: University of Toronto Press, 2013.

Testas, Abdelaziz. "Models of Cultural Exclusion and Civilizational Clashes: A Comparison Between Huntingdon and Siddiqui." *Islam and Christian-Muslim Relations* 14 (2003): 175–89.

Vidal Manzanares, César. *España frente al Islam. De Mahoma a Ben Laden*. Madrid: Esfera, 2004.

Von Ranke, Leopold. *History of the Latin and Teutonic Nations from 1494 to 1514*. Ed. and trans. Philip A. Ashworth. London: George Bell and Sons, 1887.

Wolf, Kenneth Baxter. "Convivencia in Medieval Spain: A Brief History of an Idea." *Religion Compass* 3 (2008): 72–85.

Zagorin, Perez. *How the Idea of Religious Toleration Came to the West*. Princeton: Princeton University Press, 2003.

◆ 2

The Role of Jews, Muslims, and Christians in Iberia in the Transmission of Knowledge about Islam to the Western World: A Comparative Perspective

Gerard Wiegers

Introduction

The Mediterranean region, and especially Christian Iberia, is well known as the region par excellence in which during the medieval and early modern period the transmission of knowledge from the Islamicate world to the "Christian" world took place.[1] Twelfth-century Toledo and Sicily, for example, attested to a concentration of translation activities. In the twelfth century Toledo was populated by Arabic-speaking Christian (Mozarab), Jewish, and Muslim minorities. From studies undertaken so far, it appears that Arabic scientific and philosophical learning in the city attracted (Christian) students from many places in Europe, focusing on the translation of works of Aristotle and Averroes from Arabic into Latin. Philosophy and science occupied a central place in the transmission of knowledge compared to Islam as a religion (Burnett 19). But it is this last aspect, knowledge about Islam as a religion (and as a culture) in the framework of networks of knowledge among and between Christians, Jews, and Muslims from the twelfth until the beginning of the seventeenth century, on which I focus in this essay.

The most important object of study of Christians interested in Islam was undoubtedly the Qur'an. As Thomas Burman has shown, medieval Christian scholars were not exclusively engaged in polemics with Islam in general and the Qur'an in particular, but also studied the text with an eye to a better understanding of how Muslims themselves understood it. Refuting the Qur'an can of course be attempted without sound knowledge of it, but, as Latin students were quick to find out, attempts to discuss the Qur'an on the basis of such efforts failed to impress a Muslim audience. Understanding and translating the Qur'an proved impossible without knowledge of Arabic and Muslim interpretations. Indeed, for Muslims themselves, the ongoing work of interpretation and commentary is an intrinsic part of their religious tradition and reading of the Qur'an. How could non-Muslim scholars of the Qur'an get acquainted with that tradition? Grammars and other linguistic tools in Latin were rare in medieval Iberia. The answer is that in many instances students of Arabic texts made use of informants and translators who were acquainted with the language. A case in point is the very influential translation of the Qur'an by Robert of Ketton (fl. 1137–1157), which was part of the famous *Corpus Cluniacense* (c. 1142). In the correspondence about the translation mention is made of the fact that one Muhammad was part of the team of translators, viz., that "Muhammad was the name of the Muslim [interpreter]."[2] We do not know anything about this man, but we may assume that he assisted Robert and the other Christian interpreters involved especially with regard to works of commentary and interpretation—*tafsir* in Arabic—the influence of which is evident in Robert's work. He may have been a *mudéjar* (i.e., a Muslim who lived as a practicing Muslim in Christian dominated territory), but in view of what we know about the existing practices, which I will discuss in more detail below, he may also have been a Muslim captive of war or a slave.

In this essay I am interested in the role which Muslim translators played in the transmission process compared to Jews and Christians. Does this role confirm the idea that Christian Iberia was marked by what has been called *convivencia*, the harmonious living together of three religious communities (Soifer)? Let me start by remarking that there are many aspects of the process of transmission that we still do not understand well. As Burman's study shows, we often do not know who the Arabic-speaking translators and informants were. In his study on extant translations of scientific works, Charles Burnett gives a list of translators' names, most of them Christians, some Jews, but no Muslims, and discusses Christian scholars who refer to *magistri* and to "a certain Arab," who had taught them Arabic, while the religious affiliation of these teachers remains unknown ("Arabic into Latin" 370). The written evidence suggests, therefore, that few of the informants were Muslims and most of them Christians and Jews. This is also the case with regard to religious texts, for example, the case of the famous translation of the Arabic text of the legend of Muhammad's ascension into heaven, translated into Romance at the court of Alfonso X by Abraham of Toledo in the thirteenth century. The latter appears to have belonged to a well-known family of learned Arabophone Jews.

In addition to studying the evidence of the names of translators and informants, another way to proceed is to focus on the "material" aspects of the manuscripts that are extant in public and private libraries both in Europe and the Middle-East. An interesting contribution in this regard is represented by Van Koningsveld's study of Andalusian Arabic manuscripts, i.e., Arabic manuscripts written in Andalusian script, copied in Christian Iberia. Arabic manuscripts (i.e., codices) copied in Christian Spain were written by and circulated predominantly among three minority groups, the Mozarabs, the *mudéjares* (and later the Moriscos), and the Jews. From the study of the contents and the data about dating, localization, and the identities of authors and copyists, the following picture emerges. Manuscripts in Muslim possession were copied in smaller towns and villages by scribes who are usually connected to Muslim religious institutions: they are imams or other servants of mosques. Usually, their contents are religious, reflecting middle and lower levels of Islamic religious learning (Van Koningsveld, "Andalusian-Arabic Manuscripts" 85–88). The Andalusian-Arabic manuscripts of the Jews living in Christian Spain, on the other hand, demonstrate quite different characteristics. They come from the urban centers, mainly in Castile, and were owned by "secular" scholars, court physicians and men of the world. Sometimes, the copyists of these manuscripts were Muslims, who were held as captives and slaves by both Christian and Jewish owners in Christian Spain, as attested to by the prayers and other remarks they made in the colophons of the manuscripts, sometimes invoking God to liberate them and bring them back to Islamic territory. The Arabic manuscripts of the Mozarab minority are mainly attested to in the twelfth and thirteenth centuries when that minority dispersed. Indeed, the evidence I have been able to find thus far seems to confirm the impression that during a large part of the Middle Ages, Jewish and Christian scholars played a markedly different role in the transmission of learning than Muslims. In fact, there are strikingly few instances of Mudejars, i.e., Muslims who lived as tolerated minorities in Christian Spain, who cooperated with Christians and/or Jews in translating Muslim lore.

On the basis of the extant evidence, we may distinguish the following four categories of Muslims and corresponding patterns of transmission:

(1) The first category consists of Muslims living in Christian Spain (Mudejars) or Muslims coming from abroad. I know at present of only one example: the *mudéjar* Içe of Segovia. Who was this figure? We know very little about Içe's

life. The first external evidence about him suggests that in the first half of the fifteenth century he was a member of the official religious and judicial Islamic hierarchy in fifteenth-century Castile, which consisted of an *alcalde mayor* (Islamic judge, or qadi) at the top level and close to the king, and local *alcaldes* in the towns and villages (Echevarría Arsuaga, "De cadí a alcalde mayor"). According to a letter written by one of these *alcaldes mayores*, Muhammad ibn Yūsuf al-Qaysī, don Isa, his *alcalde* and *alfaqui* in the city of Segovia could be consulted on matters of the divison of inheritances according to the principles of Islamic Law (Wiegers, *Islamic Literature* 147). In 1455, Içe left Segovia and travelled to the French village of Aiton (near Grenoble) in order to make a literal translation of the Qur'an into Romance. He did this at the request of the Christian theologian Juan de Segovia who wished to have a literal translation in order to convert Muslims in a peaceful way (i.e., *per viam pacis et doctrinae*) (Cabanelas Rodríguez; Wiegers, *Islamic Literature*; Roth and Glei). Juan de Segovia's correspondence shows how difficult it was to find *mudéjares* who were willing to cooperate in such an enterprise. We will return to this below.

A second example of a person who fits in this category is indirect (that is, no direct involvement in works translated into Latin or Romance is known in this case). I am referring to the interesting case of the philosopher and physician Muḥammad b. Aḥmad al-Riqūṭī al-Mursī, who taught "Muslim sciences" in Murcia using, according to the Granadan scholar Ibn al-Khaṭīb, "the languages of the peoples."[4] This was at the time of the conquest by Alfonso X in 1266, when the city accepted the terms of surrender and became a vassal city of the Castilian king. However, under mounting pressure from the Christian king to convert to Christianity, al-Riqūṭī migrated to Granada, where he was held in high esteem by the Nasrid sultan and continued his teaching activities.

(2) The second category includes Muslim slaves and captives. An early example of a "translator" in this category is a certain ᶜAbdallah al-Asīr, mentioned in an anti-Christian Arabic text written by Muḥammad al-Qaysī, a Tunisian captive, who lived in Lérida at the beginning of the fourteenth century (Van Koningsveld and Wiegers 183). From this Arabic text it appears that al-Qaysī knew texts written by the said ᶜAbdallah al-Asīr, literally "Abdallah, the captive," who had disputed with a monk (Arab. Al-rāhib) about anthropomorphisms. ᶜAbdallah, who according to al-Qaysī lived in France, is perhaps to be identified as the slave of Ramon Llull who killed himself after his master had allegedly slapped him for insulting Christian doctrine (Van Koningsveld, *Islamitische* 17; Van Koningsveld and Wiegers 183). Another example (though no translations are known) is the learned slave of Nicholas Cleynaerts, Kharūf, who was used by this Flemish Arabist in his studies of Arabic. Cleynaerts had bought his

learned slave from the Moroccan city of Fez in Granada at the beginning of the sixteenth century (Van Koningsveld "Mijn Kharuf"). Undoubtedly the most famous example in this category (though he also belongs the category of the converted Muslims) is the Granadan learned scholar and diplomat, ambassador in the service of the sultan of Fez, al-Ḥassan al-Wazzān, alias Leo Africanus (born at the end of the fifteenth century), who was captured by the Spanish while returning from Cairo to Fez in 1518 and selected to be a servant to Pope Leo X because of his intellectual capacities and cultural skills (Davis 54). Indeed, it seems that Muslims slaves and captives were often selected for their intellectual capacities to perform such tasks in the service of their new masters (Van Koningsveld, *Islamitische slaven* 26; Davis 56).

(3) The third category of translators are Muslim converts who had converted individually and of their own accord. Perhaps the companion of Egidio da Viterbo, the Italian bishop, who traveled to Spain, fits into this category. Egidio da Viterbo sought and found in 1518 a suitable translator for the translation of the Qur'an that he wished to make, one Iohannes Gabriel Terrolensis, apparently a converted *mudéjar* from Teruel who made a translation for him, which he took with him to Italy (Davis 71). Later, after having returned to Italy, Egidio found an Arabic teacher in the said Leo Africanus, who revised Gabriel's Latin translation (Burman 151; Davis 243).

Another famous example is the *mudéjar* from Xàtiva, Juan Andrés (d. after 1520), who was before converting a *faqih*, and who wrote his *Confusión o confutación de la secta Mahomética y del Alcorán* at the beginning of the sixteenth century (Wiegers, "Review Juan Andrés," "Moriscos and Arabic Studies"). This polemical work against Islam, based on his thorough acquaintance with Arabic sources, which he quotes in Arabic throughout the work, had a major influence on Orientalist studies in Europe (for example on the seventeenth-century Leiden Arabist Jacobus Golius, 1596–1667) and was eventually translated into many European languages.

(4) The fourth category consists of Muslims who had been converted under duress as a result of popular forcible baptisms and official edicts (roughly between 1499 and 1525) and were expelled from Spain in 1609. Some of these Moriscos, as they were called, cooperated either in Spain or, after their expulsion, in Morocco and elsewhere, with non-Muslim students of Arabic. A famous example is Aḥmad b. Qāsim al-Ḥajarī al-Andalusī, a colorful diplomat, scholar, and translator, who was born in about 1570 in the village of Hornachos in Extremadura (Spain) (al-Ḥajarī 1997). His Spanish Christian name was Diego Bejarano. At a time in which it was forbidden to practice Islam, he (as

well as many other new Christians of Muslim descent, the so-called Moriscos) was raised secretly as a Muslim in an Arabophone family. In about 1598 he was involved in translating the so-called Lead Books, lead plates inscribed with Arabic texts that were famous forgeries found buried in the slopes of the Sacromonte near to the city of Granada. Shortly afterwards Bejarano fled to Morocco, where he became secretary and Spanish interpreter to Sultan Mawlāy Zaydān in Marrakesh. After his secret migration from Spain he was entrusted with a mission to France in 1611 whose goal was recovering goods stolen from fellow Moriscos who had been transported from Spain to Morocco during the expulsion of the Moriscos in 1609–1610 on board French ships. He visited the Netherlands as well and returned in 1613. He left Morocco in 1634 and after performing the *ḥajj* wrote in about 1635 in Egypt a work called *Riḥlat al-shihāb ilā liqā al-aḥbāb*, i.e., "The Journey of the Meteor (his *laqab* was Shihāb al-dīn) to Meet his Beloved." In 1046/1637 he composed a summary of that (now lost) work entitled *Kitab nāṣir al-din ala 'l-qawm al-kafirīn*, viz., "The Supporter of Religion against the Infidel," focusing on his polemical encounters with Christians and Jews in the Netherlands and France. Al-Ḥajarī translated several works into Arabic, among which was a Spanish treatise on gunnery, an astronnonomical treatise, and also parts of Qāḍī Iyād's *Kitāb al-Shifā'* into Spanish. In about 1640 he lived with his family in Tunis, and it seems likely that he died there as well. The historical circumstances in which Muslims such as al-Ḥajarī worked differed considerably from the period before the forced conversions and the coming into being of Arabic studies as a field of study in the Western world. Al-Ḥajarī was an eyewitness to the birth of that field in France and the Netherlands, where he met such Arabists as Etienne Hubert, Thomas Erpenius, and Jacobus Golius. Having acquired an official diplomatic status, he oversaw the power shifts in Europe and the possibilities that alliances between Muslims states (Morocco, the Ottoman Empire) and emerging powers in the North offered.

Analysis

The evidence discussed above seems to suggest that in the transmission process of both religious and "scientific" culture from the Islamicate to the Christian worlds, Muslims themselves were far less involved than Jews and Christians and indeed seem to have mostly participated in subordinate positions. The religious and social groups mainly involved in the transmission process were Christians and Jews, not Muslim scholars. How is this to be explained?

First, as Van Koningsveld's studies indicate, and my own findings confirm, Muslim scholars were unable to compete with learned Arabic-speaking Jews in Christian Spain with regard to their learning in general and the natural sciences of the Muslim world, which attracted much more attention than Islam as a religion. Hence, Arab-speaking Jews were more suited as translators than Muslims. *mudéjares* formed the lowest level of Christian society, and were in general far less involved in higher learning than the other groups. This lack of *mudéjar* involvement in the transmission of knowledge was exacerbated by the migration of the *mudéjar* scholars, who usually quickly migrated to Islamic territory when their lands fell into Christian hands, while the less educated laborers, farmers, and artisans remained behind.

Second, we find that during a great part of the Middle Ages Muslims were reluctant to participate in Christian projects involving the study of Islam and translation of Islamic texts for fear of the potential defamation and criticism of Islamic dogma. Reservations were expressed on several occasions. Written responsa (*fatwas*) were even issued prohibiting the teaching of Islamic dogma and tradition (in particular the Qur'an) to non-Muslims. Such *fatwas* are attested in several periods, from the early medieval period until the early sixteenth century (Van Koningsveld "Mon Kharuf"). According to one *fatwa*, the dominant view among the Malikite *madhab* was to prohibit this, for Mālik (ibn Anas) had stated, "It is prohibited that a Muslim teaches the Qur'an and Arabic to an unbeliever, because they will dishonor it with it." Moreover, Christian scholars who traveled to Muslim territory in order to study Arabic texts there were not viewed in a positive light by Muslims, viz., as robbers of their literary heritage. According to Ibn Abdūn, writing at the turn of the twelfth century about and for Muslims in Seville, the latter "should not sell to the Jews or Christians books concerning sciences [because] they translate them and attribute them to their co-religionists and their bishops" (qtd. in Burnett 236). It is only in the writings of the said Içe of Segovia in the fifteenth century that we come across a different attitude. Içe contemplated that it would be a pious act to provide the unbelievers with a translation of the Qur'an in Romance. In one of his writings he speaks about "that lofty authority which commands us and tells us that any creature who knows something of the Law [i.e. Islam] ought to teach the Qur'an to all creatures in such a language that they understand it" (Wiegers, *Islamic Literature* 207ff). This suggests that he may have had missionary motives in cooperating with Juan de Segovia.

Third, the context in which we find Muslims involved often seems highly polemical, i.e., the Christian party is interested in refuting Muslim thought and practice rather than in merely the "neutral" translation of texts. This also holds true for translations of religious texts, and even for the translation of the *mi'raj* (night journey) of the Prophet Muhammad at the court of Alfonso X (Echevarría Arsuaga, "Eschatology"; Fierro).

The preceding factors should be considered in the light of the fact that the Muslim and Christian worlds were at war with each other and Muslims and Christians were political and military rivals. Hence Muslims living in the Christian Kingdoms were all drawn into the existing political and military rivalry, while Jews did not constitute a military threat. The competition and the social hierarchies that connected Muslims and Christians are expressed, for example, in an interesting way in how slavery functioned with regard to these groups. Slavery, as is well known, was an important institution in the medieval and early modern Mediterranean. It was one of the pillars, for example, of the colonial Christian Kingdom of Valencia, as Meyerson explains. It is very interesting to observe that neither Jews nor Muslims were allowed to have Christian slaves. Moreover, in the social hierarchy of Christian Spain, it was possible, and indeed a frequent phenomenon, that Jews possessed Muslim slaves. Muslims, however, never possessed Jewish slaves. According to Meyerson the reason for this was the following:

> Consequently, while some Jews owned Muslim slaves, one does not encounter the inverse. Although in subsequent centuries the Jews were displaced from royal government, their essential dependence on the crown did not change. *They never constituted a political threat—not even an imaginary one—and therefore did not warrant the kind of restraints of which Mudejares were the object.* (148; emphasis mine)

Hence, even though no written prohibition preventing Muslims from owning Jewish slaves seems to have existed in Christian Spain, the macro relations between the Muslim and Christian worlds led to an uneven distribution of power among the three religious communities and hence to a social hierarchy in which it was impossible for Muslims to possess slaves. Rather, many of the latter were slaves. According to Maya Soifer, "Increasingly, scholars are becoming convinced that a colonizing agenda informed cultural, artistic, and legal productions that until now have been understood as clear manifestations of Christian tolerance and *convivencia*" (30).

Conclusion

In the transmission of knowledge in the Mediterranean, philosophy and the sciences (including the occult sciences) elicited a much greater interest than the Islamic religion, which has been the focus of my interest here. Moreover, the present explorative study of the involvement of members of the three religious communities in the transmission of knowledge about Islam in the form of translations from Arabic into Latin and Romance seems to indicate that Muslims in Iberia were far less involved in it than Christians and Jews. The examples we have discussed above are scattered and taken from different periods, and further study may refine or challenge my findings, but the preceding survey of the sources makes it clear that there were few Muslims in Iberia taking part in it. In fact, the four categories of Muslim translators we have distinguished (*mudéjares* who were able to cooperate more or less freely; slaves, viz., captives; and Moriscos who had converted of their own accord or who had been forced to convert under duress), show that few *mudéjares* were involved. With regard to the involvement of Muslim slaves and captives, the evidence of the studies discussed above suggests that their involvement was no coincidence, but the result of selection by their masters in search of specific qualities with regard to knowledge of Arabic and Islamic dogma and tradition. This search for suited informants, teachers, and translators, we may conclude, took place in various parts of the Mediterranean. This does not mean that Muslims were entirely devoid of agency. The involvement of figures such as Içe of Segovia seems to indicate that they had. However, as I have shown, Içe remains an exception.

The evidence discussed in this essay—from the *Corpus Cluniacense* (c. 1142) to the work of a Morisco diplomat and polemicist, al-Ḥajarī (born c. 1570)—suggests that several factors may explain why the involvement of Muslims in the transmission of knowledge about Islam was rare. First of all, Muslim scholars in Christian Iberia were few, since the majority had migrated during the conquest of Muslim territory and they were unable to compete with learned Arabic-speaking Jews in Christian Spain with regard to relevant learning. Hence they played a minor role in the knowledge networks. Secondly, they were reluctant to participate for religious reasons. Two exceptions are explored in this essay: Içe of Segovia, who felt translating the Qur'an could serve missionary goals, and Juan Andrés, a Mudejar *faqih* who, after converting to Christianity, authored a polemical treatise against Islam. The latter points to the third factor explaining the lack of Muslims in the translation of Islamic texts into European vernaculars during the medieval and early modern period. As the case of Juan Andrés reveals, interest in the Muslim tradition was often marked by a highly polemical interest on the part of the dominant majority: the refutation of Islam and the conversion of Muslims. This polemical interest, I suggest, was closely connected to the political and military struggle between Muslim and Christian powers that took place in the wider Mediterranean area.

Notes

1. Also presented as a seminar paper at the Summer School of the University of California, Santa Cruz (Barcelona, July 2012). I want to thank the organizers, Dr. Brian Catlos (University of Colorado, Boulder) and Dr. Sharon Kinoshita (University of California, Santa Cruz) for inviting me as faculty, and the participants of the summer school for their very stimulating discussions. It is my pleasure to thank the editors of this volume, Michelle Hamilton and Núria Silleras-Fernández, for their valuable comments.
2. "Sarraceni Mahumet nomen erat." See Burman (46 and 221 n71) for bibliographical references.
3. Echevarría calls him Abraham ibn Wacar, physician and Arabic interpreter ("Eschatology" 150; cf. Van Koningsveld, "Andalusian-Arabic Manuscripts" 92). The Banu Waqqar were a well-known learned family from Guadalajara. Echevarría points out that that the translation (or rather paraphrasis) had a polemical function, aiming to discredit the Prophet.
4. Ar. yuqra al-umam bi-alsinatihim, quoted in Van Koningsveld, "Andalusian-Arabic Manuscripts" 81.

Works Cited

Burman, Thomas E. *Reading the Qur'ān in Latin Christendom, 1140–1560*. Philadelphia: University of Pennsylvania Press, 2007.

Burnett, Charles. "Arabic into Latin: The Reception of Arabic Philosophy into Western Europe." *Cambridge Companion to Arabic Philosophy*. Cambridge University Press, 2006: 370–404. Cambridge Companions Online. Web. 5 Sep. 2012.

———. *Arabic into Latin in the Middle Ages: The Translators and their Intellectual and Social Context*. Farnham: Ashgate, 2009.

Cabanelas Rodríguez, Dario. *Juan de Segovia y el problema islámico*. Madrid: Universidad de Madrid, 1952.

Davis, Natalie Zemon. *Trickster Travels: A Sixteenth-Century Muslim Between Worlds*. New York: Hill and Wang, 2006.

Echevarría Arsuaga, Ana. "De cadí a alcalde mayor. La élite judicial mudéjar en el siglo XV." *Al-Qantara* 24.1 (2003): 139–68 (part 1); *Al-Qantara* 24.2 (2003): 273–90 (part 2).

———. "Eschatology or Biography? Alfonso X, Muhammad's Ladder, and a Jewish Go-Between." *Under the Influence: Questioning the Comparative in Medieval Castile*. Ed. Cynthia Robinson and Leyla Rouhi. Leiden: Brill, 2005. 133–52.

Fierro, Maribel. "Alfonso X 'The Wise': the Last Almohad Caliph." *Medieval Encounters* 15 (2009): 175–98.

Hajarī, Ahmad b. Qâsim al-. *Kitāb nāsir al-dīn ʿalā l-qawm al-kāfirīn (The Supporter of Religion against the Infidels).* Fuentes Arábico-Hispanas 21. Ed. and trans. P.S. van Koningsveld, Q. Al-Samarrai, and G.A. Wiegers. Madrid: CSIC, 1997.

Koningsveld, P.S. van. "Andalusian-Arabic Manuscripts from Medieval Christian Spain: Some Supplementary Notes." *Festgabe für Hans-Rudolf Singer: zum 65. Geburtstag am 6. April 1990 überreicht von seinen Freunden und Kollegen*. Vol. 1. Ed. Martin Forstner. Frankfurt: Peter Lang, 1991. 811–823.

———. "Andalusian-Arabic Manuscripts from Christian Spain: a Comparative Intercultural Approach." *Israel Oriental Studies* 12 (1992): 75–110.

———. *Islamitische slaven en gevangenen in West-Europa tijdens de late Middeleeuwen*. Leiden: Reichs Univeriteit, 1994.

———. "'Mijn Kharûf: Over de Arabische leermeester van Nicolaas Cleynaerts." *Sharqiyyât* 9.2 (1997): 139–61.

———. "'Mon Kharûf': Quelques remarques sur le maître tunisien du premier arabisant néerlandais, Nicolas Clénard (1493–1542)." *Nouvelles approches des relations islamo-chrétiennes à l'époque de la Renaissance (Actes de la Troisième Rencontre Scientifique tenue du 14 au 16 mars 1998).* Zaghouan : CEROMDI, 2000: 123–141.

Koningsveld, P.S. van, and G.A.Wiegers, "The Polemical Works of Muhammad al-Qaysi (fl. 1309) and their Circulation in Arabic and Aljamiado among the Mudejars in the Fourteenth Century." *Al-Qantara* 15 (1994): 163–99.

Meyerson, Mark. "Slavery and the Social Order: Mudejars and Christians in the Kingdom of Valencia." *Medieval Encounters* 1.1 (1995): 144–73.

Roth, Ulli, and Reinhold Glei. "Die Spuren der lateinischen Koranübersetzung des Juan de Segovia-alte Probleme und ein neuer Fund." *Neulateinisches Jahrbuch* 11 (2009): 109–54.

Soifer, Maya. "Beyond Convivencia: Critical Reflections on the Historiography of Interfaith Relations in Christian Spain." *Journal of Medieval Iberian Studies* 1.1 (2009): 19–35.

Wiegers, Gerard. *Islamic Literature in Spanish and Aljamiado: Yça of Segovia (fl. 1450), His Antecedents and Successors*. Leiden: Brill, 1994.

———. "Moriscos and Arabic Studies in Europe." *Al-Qantara* 31.2 (2010): 587–610.

———. "Review Juan Andrés: Confusion". *Aljamía. Anuario de información bibliográfica* 16 (2004): 254–61.

3

The Princess and the Palace: On Hawwa' bint Tashufin and Other Women from the Almoravid Royal Family

Manuela Marín

Almoravids (Arab. Al-Murabitun) ruled over the Islamic West—the Maghrib and al-Andalus—during the second half of the eleventh century and the first half of the twelfth century.[1] Of Saharian Berber origins (Sanhaja), Almoravids unified the Maghrib and the Iberian Peninsula for the first time since the arrival of Islam to these regions in the eighth century and established their political capital in the south of Morocco, where they founded the city of Marrakesh.[2] Berbers have been present in al-Andalus since the Islamic conquest, but it was only with the arrival of the Almoravids that they took over political power on both sides of the Straits of Gibraltar. The Mediterranean West thus became a new political entity, in which converged Andalusi and Berber social and cultural traits. By this time, Andalusi elites had already built a high culture based upon Eastern Arab models that, as happened in other places of the Islamic world, were to some extent influenced by local and pre-Islamic characteristics. In what follows, I intend to examine how the Almoravid elites, and more precisely women pertaining to them, can be considered an exemplary case of cultural change in the political process accompanying Berbers from North Africa to the Iberian Peninsula.

In 1147, another Berber dynasty, the Almohads (Arab. Al-Muwahhidun), rivals and successors of the Almoravids, conquered Marrakesh, putting an end to Almoravid power. Almohads had been fighting the Almoravids in battlefields all over the Maghrib, accompanying their military operations with a powerful and very efficient propaganda campaign against their enemies.

Almohad allegations used to demean Almoravids were primarily of a theological character. The Almohads presented themselves as restorers of the true Islam, which they maintained had been corrupted by the Almoravids (Fierro, "La religión"; Serrano, "¿Por qué?"). In a similar vein, Almohad propaganda used other topics, focusing on what was presented as the decomposition of social and individual morality. Chief among these accusations was the alleged misdemeanor of Almoravid women who, as they said, did not cover their faces in public and combed their hair in extravagant ways to attract men's attention (Marín, "On Women").

In an often-quoted text, 'Abd al-Wahid al-Marrakushi, a pro-Almohad author writing in the first part of the thirteenth century, even claimed that the participation of Almoravid women in public affairs during the reign of the second Almoravid emir, 'Ali b. Tashufin (r. 1106–1143), had caused the decline of political and religious attitudes. According to al-Marrakushi, although the sovereign was a pious and learned man, he had no interest in public affairs; as a result, women from the leading Almoravid Berber tribes (Lamtuna and Massufa) were allowed to take on positions of power, being supported by all kinds of delinquents and people of bad reputation who were protected by these powerful women ('Abd al-Wahid al-Marrakushi 260, 273).

Attributing the decline or fall of a dynasty to the intervention of women in the political arena is a recurrent *topos* in traditional historiography, both in the Christian West and in the Islamic realm. Here, however, the charge of 'Abd al-Wahid al-Marrakushi against the Almoravids should be examined beyond its obvious propagandistic intention and biased formulation. It is indeed a fact, attested by the Arabic sources dealing with the Almoravids, that women of their ruling family and the aristocratic elites were much more visible and active than women usually are in the historical accounts of other medieval dynasties in the Islamic West. In her article on the political role of Almoravid women, 'I. Dandash has shown their implication in public affairs, opening a scholarly path that I would like to follow here, adding to her findings what I propose as a new way of interpreting the different models governing Almoravid women's behavior as reflected by Arabic sources (Dandash, "Adwar sisyasiya"). To do that, I shall begin with an analysis of the biographical data related to the Almoravid princess Hawwa' bint Tashufin. In the second part of this essay other examples of Almoravid women's behavior will be taken into account in an attempt to establish connections between the traditions of the Saharan nomad Berbers to which they belonged, and the changes experienced throughout their expansion in the Islamic West and their establishment in an urban and cultured context.

Hawwa' bint Tashufin: The Princess and the Palace

It has already been noted that the ruling Almoravid family was a "close knit aristocratic élite" which widely practiced endogamy among the descendants of Ibrahim b. Turjut, the grandfather of the first Almoravid emir, Yusuf b. Tashufin (r. 1062–1106) (Norris, *Berbers* 121; *Saharan Myth* 106).[3] The place of Hawwa' in this family group is a striking example of this practice.

The father of Hawwa', Tashufin, was a half-brother of the emir Yusuf. After losing her first husband, Yusuf's father, the widow married 'Ali, her husband's brother, giving birth to Tashufin, Hawwa's father, and another son, Sir. So, as Arab sources underscore, Yusuf and Tashufin were at the same time brothers and paternal cousins (Ibn 'Idhari, *Al-Bayan al-mughrib* 56; Dandash, "Adwar siyasiya" 55). Hawwa', Tashufin b. 'Ali's daughter, was the niece of the powerful emir of the Almoravids, doubly related to him through the patrilineal genealogy of the family.

Hawwa' was first married to her paternal cousin Sir b. 'Ali (d. 1113) who, as has been shown, was brother and cousin of Yusuf b. Tashufin. Sir was one of the most important military commanders of the Almoravid army. In August of 1091, the emir ordered him to depose the Andalusi king of Seville, al-Mu'tamid, and to proceed with the conquest of Seville and Badajoz, which he swiftly did (S. Nasr Allah 123–24). For the next twenty-three years, Sir b. 'Ali was the governor of Seville, thus becoming one of the most powerful members of the dynasty (*Kitab al-Hulal al-mawshiya* 72; Ibn 'Idhari, *al-Bayan al-mughrib* 105). The union of Sir and Hawwa' followed the pattern of intermarriage among the Almoravid ruling family and offered her a high position as the wife of the *de facto* ruler of al-Andalus and representative of the emir.

It seems, however, that Hawwa' had ideas of her own as to her duties as Sir's wife. According to the findings of I. Butshish, who quotes in this respect an unpublished text by Ibn Luyun, she refused to leave Marrakesh and follow her husband to Seville, and she only complied with her wifely obligations when ordered to by the emir Yusuf b. Tashufin (Butshish 39). If we accept Butshish's interpretation of Ibn Luyun's text, this would have been the first time that Hawwa' rebelled against the constraints to her freedom of sojourn. As we will soon see, there are other and very significant examples of how she related herself to her places of residence.

In October 1113, Hawwa' and Sir left Seville, accompanied by a great retinue and a crowd ready to enjoy the occasion. Hawwa' was taking their daughter, Fatima, to Marrakesh, where Fatima was to be married to the emir, 'Ali b. Tashufin (thus reiterating the intermarriage system of the ruling family: Fatima was the daughter of two paternal cousins of the emir). Sir had probably planned to go with his wife and daughter for the first part of their journey and take leave of them near Seville, to avoid leaving his political responsibilities for a long time. But on the first night of their trip he fell ill, and he died on the following morning (Ibn 'Idhari, *Al-Bayan al-mughrib* 56). A funeral procession was quickly organized to go back to Seville carrying the corpse. Hawwa's plans for visiting Marrakesh were, of course, abandoned and she returned to Seville to attend the funeral ceremonies.

One of the most significant episodes in Hawwa's life took place in the cementery of Seville. The text describing the event is not found in a historical chronicle, as happens with most of the other accounts related to her, but in the collection of fatwas by the famous jurist Ibn Rushd (d. 1126). What interests us now is the first part of this text, in which the figure of Hawwa' acquires a new relevance as she asserts publicly her wishes and her intentions.

According to the text reproduced by Ibn Rushd, Sir's body was removed from the palace of government in Seville, put on a stretcher, and carried to the cemetery. Hawwa' followed the funeral procession and stayed in the cemetery until the burial was finished. She was at the edge of the tomb, the ceremony having been completed, when somebody among those present told her:

> "You can now get up and go back to your residence." Hawwa' then answered: "Which residence do you mean?" "Your own place, from where you have come," replied the man. "I swear—said Hawwa'—to give in alms the third of my possessions, to fast for a year and to enfranchise my slaves if I ever go back to this residence. Where are the noblemen whom I have met in this place and to whom I have given shelter in it?" (Ibn Rushd, *Fatawa* 2.1223, n 395)

The "residence" mentioned in this exchange between Hawwa' and her anonymous interlocutor is obviously the *dar al-imara*, the palace in Seville where the Almoravid governors resided (Valor Piechotta; Tabales Rodríguez). Hawwa' would have lived there for the most part of her conjugal life, whose length is not recorded by Arabic sources. But it is clear from the words of Hawwa' that for her the palace was a place of her own, where her status as a prominent member of the sovereign family was adequately acknowledged. The loss of her husband deprived her of this unique space, where she was surrounded by patricians and noblemen; in other words, she was losing the court of attendants that, by their presence, attested to her privileged place in society. For the princess, the palace was the essential mark of her rank, and she could not think of going back to a building where she would be obliged to relinquish her former status.

Other aspects of the text quoted above deserve to be commented upon. First, the presence of Hawwa' at the burial of her husband, following the strechter carrying Sir's corpse, and standing on the edge of his tomb does not conform to the social uses prevalent among Andalusi elites. Jurists and moralists strongly disapproved the participation of women in burial ceremonies, and even their visits to the tombs of their relatives (Marín, *Mujeres en al-Ándalus* 233). Was Hawwa' following the norms of the Almoravids in this respect, as distinct from Andalusi practice? If this was the case, it would be possible to detect here another evidence of the singular place of Almoravid women in society, namely, their access to public places which was usually restricted to men.

Secondly, the text illustrates how Hawwa' used the palatial space as a place of interaction with select members of society. As the location of political and military power, embodied by the governor, the palace was the apex of the masculine hierarchy. But Hawwa' was able to encroach into this space and build up her own courtly environment, in which she mixed freely with men not belonging to her family. Although nothing is said in the text about the identities of those who frequented Hawwa' in the palace, many were probably men of letters and culture. As we will now see, the next step in Hawwa's life shows a similar but much more detailed picture of her dealings with these kinds of people.

After Sir's death and her refusal to go back to the Sevillian palace, Hawwa' returned to the capital city of the Almoravids, Marrakesh. The then-emir, 'Ali b. Yusuf, was married to her daughter Fatima; as a cousin and mother-in-law of the sovereign, Hawwa' could assert herself in Marrakesh in ways closed to her in al-Andalus. To do that, she chose a path of her own that was probably a reproduction of her role in the palace of her husband in Seville: a female member of the Almoravid family acting as a patroness of belles lettres and making her own imprint on literary circles.

The description of Hawwa's activities in this respect, recorded by the Maghribi historian Ibn 'Idhari, is worthy of attention because of its richness of information and detail (Ibn 'Idhari, *Al-Bayan al-mughrib* 57). The text, which quotes a disciple of the Andalusi philosopher and jurist Ibn Wuhayb (d. 1131), begins with a definition of Hawwa': she was a woman of letters (*adiba*) and an excellent and shrewd poetess.[4] While living in Marrakesh, the text adds, she gave orders for organising a gathering of poets and writers (*majlis*), which she personally attended, taking part in the learned discussions of the participants and showing her intelligence and cleverness.

To exemplify these qualities, Ibn Wuhayb's disciple depicts an occasion in which Hawwa' appeared at the poets' *majlis*, overcoming them with her wit. As the account of the facts goes, Hawwa' arrived at the poets' meeting place. Among them were two renowned Andalusis, Ibn al-Qasira and Ibn al-Murkhi.[5] The author explains that the latter's surname alludes to the fact that he did not have a deep knowledge of classical Arabic.[6] The group of poets had been practicing the impromptu composition of verses, but the first hemistich proposed by Ibn al-Murkhi ("I am the brother of the full moon") found no satisfactory rejoinder by any of the participants in the poetic session. When Hawwa' entered the room, she greeted her guests, and Ibn al-Murkhi improvised a poetic welcome, saying, "Let God give you life, o my moon, o my flower!" Far from feeling herself flattered by Ibn al-Murkhi's extemporization, Hawwa' tersely replied: "By God! You have compared me with what hides and what withers." Then she asked what they had been occupied with before her arrival, and after knowing about the hemistich proposed by Ibn al-Murkhi, she promptly completed the full verse. The all-male audience was, of course, duly astonished by Hawwa's witticism (Ibn 'Idhari, *Al-Bayan al-mughrib* 57).

This tale offers a new perspective on Hawwa's personality. Until now, what is preserved on her life presents her as a powerful woman, clearly conscious of her place in society. Hawwa' followed, although in her own way, the norms and rules of the Almoravid Berber elite to which she belonged, especially with regard to her status as wife and mother inside the close-knit sovereign family. But the picture of the literary salon she established in Marrakesh shows her adopting a cultural role prevalent in Arab culture and traditions. No information is offered, in the sources dealing with Hawwa', as to where and how she was educated, but her command of Classical Arabic and of the rules of Arab metrics speak to a careful and long training in both matters, part of which could have been attained, or improved, during her years of residence in Seville.

Moreover, the structure of the scene described by Ibn Wuhayb's disciple corresponds to a common pattern in Arab literature, an "anecdotal type" of man and woman in a verbal contest, won by the woman by her witty word play.[7] In her reply to Ibn al-Murkhi, Hawwa' adroitly deflects the poet's adulation, pointing out that his choice of words, comparing her with the moon and a flower, is most unfortunate, as the moon hides and flowers wither. Equally recurrent in many poetical anecdotes is the capacity of a woman to complete the first part of a verse, something that appears to have been an attribute especially connected to women, slave-girls, and singers. One of the most famous literary (and historical) examples of this kind pertains to the history of the 'Abbadid kings of Seville, and shows al-Mu'tamid falling in love with the slave al-Rumaykiya on one such occasion (Garulo, *Diwan* 13–14; Rubiera).

That Hawwa' established—probably in the royal palace in Marrakesh—a literary salon over which she presided was not an exceptional occurence in aristocratic circles, although it was more commonly restricted to male patrons.[8] The *majlis*, a characteristic feature of Arab-Islamic culture, was the favorite place for exchanging views and producing innovations in all kind of cultural and scientific subjects ("Madjlis"). Poetry was usually associated in the *majlis* with music (and more often that not with wine-drinking), giving way to the presence of slave-girls well trained in playing instruments and singing. Nothing similar, however, seems to have been going on in the *majlis* presided by Hawwa', who, by her mere presence as the patroness of the literati, was inverting the hierarchy of this kind of gatherings. She governed her guests by the strength of her social standing, but she could not have fulfilled her role without her knowledge and intelligence.[9]

A literary *majlis* like the one founded by Hawwa' was also a place of political significance. The only two members of the *majlis* identified by the author of the text were not only poets and men of letters, but also played an important role in the administrative machinery of the Almoravid empire. Both Ibn al-Qasira and Ibn al-Murkhi were of Andalusi descent, as were many other chancery secretaries or scholars attracted to Marrakesh by the power of the then masters of the Islamic West (Dandash, "Ziyarat"). The gatherings of these elite members could not have been exclusively dedicated to the discussion of poetry and related matters, and, as happened in the *salons littéraires* in *Ancien Régime* France, the *majlis* could and did become a locus of exchange of influences and information. For Hawwa', too, the *majlis* widened her area of power beyond the circle of her family and her patronage probably benefitted her as well as her protégés.

In a courtly environment the *majlis* acquired an added symbolic status, both a sign of prestige and an instrument of propaganda in favor of the ruler. In societies where poetry was considered the highest form of cultural production, poets wrote well-rewarded panegyrics for their patrons, praising their conduct and virtues. Promoting a *majlis* of her own was also, for Hawwa', a form of adopting one of the most efficient ways of self-representation available in Arab-Islamic culture. Hawwa' was certainly aware of the posibilities of having a renowned poet ready to write a piece glorifying his patron: the Andalusi poet al-Aʿmà al-Tutili (d. 1130), who lived in Seville, had done precisely that in her honor, and the poem he dedicated to her is preserved in the collection of al-Aʿmà's poetry (Al-'Amà al-Tutili 15–18).[10]

Hawwa' seems to have found in the palatial space of Marrakesh what she had longed for since leaving Seville: a prestigious place as a member of the ruling family, allowing her share in the political sphere. Her position, however, would be threatened by a second marriage, as will now be shown.

No information is found in the sources as to why Hawwa' married again, and we can only guess that this new alliance was in response to family politics. The husband belonged, as was to be expected, to the inner circle of the Almoravid kin: he was Abu l-Tahir Tamim, eldest brother of the emir, ʿAli b. Tashufin, himself, as we have seen, paternal cousin and son-in-law of Hawwa'. She was marrying, then, another cousin, and a brother of her son-in-law.

As a son of the first Almoravid emir, Yusuf b. Tashufin, Tamim was a prominent member of the administrative and military elite ruling over the Islamic West. During his father's life he had been in charge of the government of the southern regions of Morocco, including Marrakesh; in 1122 his brother ʿAli appointed him as governor of Seville.[11]

Once married to Tamim, Hawwa' again found that she would have to leave Marrakesh to stay with her husband in al-Andalus. This she refused to do, claiming that she could not live in the palace in Seville that she had sworn never to enter again. The circumstances of Hawwa's oath has been mentioned above, as recorded in the juridical consultation addressed to Ibn Rushd by Tamim himself. Going back to this text, we find there that Tamim had in fact obliged Hawwa' to go with him to Seville, but it was probably through her insistence on the question of the oath that he asked Ibn Rushd to give them his learned opinion on the matter. It is obvious that what has survived in Ibn Rushd's text is only an abstract of the original letter from Tamim, but some interesting details are preserved, such as Hawwa's claim that she was unable to comply with the terms of her oath. As recorded above, Hawwa' had pledged to "give in alms the third of my possessions, to fast for a year, and to enfranchise my slaves if I ever go back to this residence." But she maintained that by now she had already lost this third of her possessions, while keeping only her slaves; therefore she could not fulfill the economic conditions for the transgression of the oath (Ibn Rushd, *Fatawa* 2.1224).

If Hawwa' expected to be given her freedom of residence thanks to a juridical opinion, she was wrong. Ibn Rushd was a very intelligent jurist and he probably did not wish to go against the wishes of the governor of Seville. In his answer to Tamim, Ibn Rushd interpreted Hawwa's oath as a refusal to go back to the palace if this was not made under the same circumstances previously enjoyed by her, that is, as the wife of the governor. Being married again to a man who held this very charge, nothing could oblige her to comply with the terms of her oath. As Ibn Rushd put it, "oaths should be understood through the intention of who pronounces them, and not on the literal sense of the words said." This, he goes on, giving several examples, is the opinion of the Malekite school of law, although Hanafites hold a different position. This final touch was a brilliant move of Ibn Rushd, as Almoravids were staunch supporters of Malikism (Wuld al-Salim). The fatwa by Ibn Rushd is notable in more than one way. Among other things, it shows the important role of oaths in social and individual practices, and the awareness of Hawwa' of the implications of her binding promise. While she was unsuccessful in her attempt, by making it she could have won her case and stayed in Marrakesh. As things went, she went back to Seville with Abu l-Tahir Tamim.

From this period of Hawwa's life we have a last documentary trace. It belongs to the medical treatise written by Abu Marwan 'Abd al-Malik Ibn Zuhr (d. 1162, known as "Avenzoar" in Medieval Latin sources), the most famous member of an Andalusi medical dynasty, the Banu Zuhr (Azar). This book, the *Kitab al-Taysir fi l-mudawat wa-l-tadbir*, contains many references to Abu Marwan's dealings with the Almoravids, whom he served as a medical doctor, following the path of his father, who had held the same position with the Sevillian 'Abbadids (Dandash, "Ahdath murabitiya"; Expiración García).

Abu Marwan recorded, in his *Kitab al-Taysir,* his medical treatment for a number of different illnesses. In the chapter on hypochondria, he remembers one of his most difficult cases, which he took as a young man at the beginning of his training as a doctor with his father, Abu l-'Alà Zuhr (d. 1130) (Álvarez Millán). Things happened, Abu Marwan wrote, when he was called to treat the governor of Seville, Tamim (Ibn Zuhr 97; Dandash, "Adwar siyasiya" 58). After describing his symptoms, Abu Marwan gives an account of his treatment (rose water and apple juice with sandal and mastic), which made Tamim recover. But, after another visit to Tamim accompanied this time with his father, Abu l-'Alà, the governor fell ill again. Abu Marwan then suspected that the cause of Tamim's illness was "something external going inside his body," an elegant way of hinting that the governor was being poisoned. He spent several nights in the palace, taking care of his patient, until he discovered that the water Tamim drank, served to him by his servants, contained traces of ground putrefied meat. This was, according to Abu Marwan, the cause of his illness.

Having made this dreadful discovery, Abu Marwan doubted, he says, the right path to follow. He was afraid, he admits, of the consequences of his telling the truth, and among them he mentions explicitly the anger of Hawwa', Tamim's wife, and her attendants. One of Tamim's slaves and Abu Marwan's medical colleagues advised him to keep quiet on the whole matter. According to his version of the facts, Abu Marwan refused to contribute to the deception, and Tamim finally recovered, but not before he was isolated by his brother, the emir 'Ali b. Tashufin, from his own family and attendants. The relationship between Abu Marwan Ibn Zuhr and the Almoravids was not easy. As he says at the end of this text, he saw Tamim again in Marrakesh, where he, Abu Marwan, was in jail by order ot the emir 'Ali b. Tashufin.[12] Tamim was again in good health, Abu Marwan notes, but without mentioning Hawwa' and her alleged role in the failed poisoning of her husband.

It is not surprising that, on the basis of Abu Marwan's text, Dandash attributes the intent of poisoning Tamim to Hawwa', who, as we have seen, did not want to accompany him to Seville ("Adwar siyasiya" 58). But Abu Marwan also hints, in his record of the facts, to another reason: desire for Tamim's inheritance. Abu Marwan does not point to anyone in particular, although Hawwa' could have been, of course, one of the interested parties in the affair.

If Abu Marwan Ibn Zuhr's account is to be considered truthful (and it is not possible to check his information against any other source), Hawwa's actions reveal the lengths she would go to in order not to reside again in the palace in Seville and to avoid losing her position in the palace in Marrakesh. The scarcity of the data found in Arabic sources prevents us from fully understanding her motives and the decisions she took. It remains a mystery why she married Tamim, for instance; nor can we know what real weight she had in the inner struggles of the royal Almoravid family. But it seems quite evident that Hawwa' found in it a place of her own, through whatever means possible.

It is not known, either, when she died.[13] Tamim only spent a year and four months as governor in Seville and was then transferred to the same post in Granada. In 1126 the Almoravid emir removed him from office at the request of Ibn Rushd, who had traveled to Marrakesh after the king of Aragón, Alfons I, suddenly attacked, seriouly threatening the Andalusi lands under Almoravid control, and Tamim had failed to answer to it adequately (*Kitab al-Hulal* 98; Serrano, "Dos fetuas"). If Hawwa' was still alive, she could have found, in Ibn Rushd's intervention to dismiss her husband from office, a kind of retaliation to the fatwa he had delivered some time before taking her husband's side.

A last note on Hawwa' pertains to the way she is named in the sources, where her personal name is usually preceded by the term *ḥurra* ("free woman"). This was a title used for women of noble descent first introduced by Almoravids (Marín, *Mujeres* 44). In the case of Hawwa', this was a particularly apt designation, or so it seems to us, for a woman who so strongly asserted her freedom of behavior and residence—although not always successfully and sometimes through, to say the least, unconventional means.

Hawwa' bint Tashufin and Other Almoravid Women: Patterns of Behavior

The attention paid to Hawwa' up to this point should not obscure the fact that other Almoravid women shared with her a singular position in the history of their dynasty. Paramount among them is Zaynab al-Nafzawiya, wife to Yusuf b. Tashufin, the first Almoravid emir. Zaynab's figure deserves to be studied in full, a task which is beyond the scope of this essay.[14] But it is important to mention, very succinctly, that she played a crucial role in the accession to power of her husband, to whom she offered her substantial wealth to sustain his career, and whose advice Yusuf always followed—to his own and his dynasty's advantage.

A powerful woman figure, then, was instrumental in the opening years of the Almoravid dynasty, sharing with her husband the administration of public affairs. In this she was undoubtedly exceptional, as was the fact that she was not a member of the close-knit family unit that so closely governed the marriage alliances of the ruling elite.

Hawwa' belonged to the next generation of Almoravid rulers, led by her cousin and later son-in-law, 'Ali b. Yusuf b. Tashufin. As we have seen above, Hawwa' was a cultured woman, well trained in the Arab literary heritage, and whose poetical abilities were praised by authors who mentioned her in their chronicles. In these same texts, 'Ali b. Yusuf represents a masculine version of the process by which the Almoravid elite, without losing its Berber cultural origins, adopted gradually the most prestigious signs of Arabization, as was shown in the case of Hawwa'.

Arabization (adopting Arabic as a language as well as Arab cultural mores and social traditions) and Islamization are, of course, two different processes, which may happen simultaneously or not. While the Almoravids, Sanhaja Berbers, were well Islamized and contributed to the spread of Islam in the Western Sahara, their Arabization was slower and did not erase certain peculiarities of their social habits (Dandash, *Dawr al-murabitin*).[15] Of the first emir, Yusuf b. Tashufin, one of his biographers said that he could not speak Arabic, although he understood the language quite well (Ibn Khallikan 7.114). In traditional Western historiography, in fact, Almoravids are frequently presented as ignorant nomads who overran the "brilliant" Andalusi culture and could not understand the subtleties of Arabic poetry.[16] But, as has been stated earlier, the second generation of the Almoravid sovereign family had fully adopted classical Arab culture. Hawwa' was not the only female member of the family to distinguish herself in this respect.

Tamima bint Yusuf b. Tashufin, a sister of the second emir, 'Ali, and therefore a cousin of Hawwa', was the subject of a short biography by the Andalusi writer Ibn al-Abbar (Ibn al-Abbar nº 2875; Codera 118).[17] In this text she is described as a lady of great beauty and sharp intelligence, who lived in Fez, the northern capital of Morocco. She was renowned for her good manners (*adab*) and her nobility. To illustrate this flattering picture, Ibn al-Abbar reproduces one of these "anecdotal situations" so common in Arab literature and which heavily influenced the emerging Romance texts: one day, Tamima requested the presence of one of her secretaries, whose accounts she wished to check. When she met the man and looked at him, something in his countenance made Tamima understand that he was in love with her; beckoning him to come over, she recited two verses identifying herself with the sun, whose residence is the sky and to whom he could not ascend, nor the sun could descend to him.[18]

Of another woman from the ruling Almoravid elite it was said that, among other virtues, she knew by heart a great amount of poetry. This was Zaynab bint Ibrahim b. Tifilwit, of whom Ibn al-Abbar said also that she was an excellent and pious woman, much given to the practice of charity and the giving of alms (Ibn al-Abbar n 2876; Ibn 'Abd al-Malik al-Marrakushi VIII–2, n 289).[19] Zaynab (or Maryam, as she is called in a poem by Ibn Khafaja) was the daughter of one of the most important military commanders of the Almoravids—and cousin of 'Ali b. Tashufin, who was appointed governor of Zaragoza in 1115 and surrounded himself there with a literary court that featured renowned poets like Ibn Khafaja and philosophers like Ibn Bajja (Avempace) (Dandash, "Adwar siyasiya" 58; Ibn 'Abd al-Malik al-Marrakushi VIII–2, nº 289, n1125; Bosch 190–91; Viguera, *Aragón musulmán* 227).[20] Another daughter of Ibn Tifilwit, Hawwa', is summarily described by Ibn al-Abbar as being adorned with the same virtues of her sister Zaynab/Maryam (Ibn al-Abbar no. 2877).[21]

We may conclude that the process of Arabization of the Almoravid governing elite involved men and women, and that the latter adopted patterns of behavior common among female members of other dynasties in the Arab-Islamic world, like the Abbasids or the Fatimids. The fact that prominent poets of their times, such as al-A'mà al-Tutili or Ibn Khafaja, addressed poems to women of the Almoravid family bears witness to the political relevance of these women, who wielded authority and influence in the inner circle of the palace. It was there that their role acquired its significance, and in this sense, their pattern of behavior distinguished them from the singular life-story of Zaynab al-Nafzawiya, the wife of Yusuf b. Tashufin. In several ways, Hawwa' bint Tashufin, Tamima bint Yusuf, and the daughters of Ibn Tifiwilt, Zaynab and Hawwa', exemplify the striking social and cultural changes accompanying the political and military progress of the Almoravids from the Sahara to the Iberian Peninsula.

We do not know to what extent this Arabization of the elite Almoravid women affected other women of lesser rank. It could have been that, outside the walls of palaces, Berber women kept their old Saharan traditions, although urban surroundings and new conditions of life might have affected them and their families; but this is not the kind of information that would be included in the sources at our disposal. There is, however, a remarkable case that confirms that one of the roles traditionally ascribed to women in some Berber regions—that of warriors—did survive.[22]

The leading character in the story is Fannu, daughter of 'Umar b. Yintan, a vizier of 'Ali b. Tashufin, and the scene, the royal Almoravid palace in Marrakesh, under siege by the Almohads in 1147, during the last days of the Almoravid Empire in the Maghrib.[23] The narrator is al-Baydhaq, a strong supporter of the Almohads, who describes Fannu's role in the sieges:

> Marrakech was conquered by the sword. The battle in the palace lasted until midday, and it was impossible to go into it until Fannu bint 'Umar b. Yintan died. On this day, she fought against the Almohads dressed like a man. The Almohads were astonished by how she fought and the strength of her courage, awarded to her by God. She was a virgin. After she died, the palace was invaded. The Almohads only discover that she was a woman after her death. (Al-Baydhaq 64; Lévi-Provençal 170–171)[24]

A few other examples of Almoravid women taking part in military actions have been extracted from contemporary accounts, but only the terse text by al-Baydhaq renders, in a poignant way, the tragic tale of a heroine who fights like a man and better than other men until she dies defending the last stronghold of her army (Butshish 50).[25] The added touch to her individuality, the fact that she was a virgin, confers to Fannu a special status: as such, she is a desexualized woman, who dressed and behaved like a man. Thus her actions transcended gender boundaries and could be registered without reservations by a pro-Almohad author like al-Baydhaq.

Nothing more has been preserved in Arabic sources about Fannu, and so we do not know why she was singled out as a female warrior in the last days of the Almoravid empire. Was she an exceptional case, as the text of al-Baydhaq implicitly suggests? This she certainly was in her own family. Two of her sisters, Tamaghunt and Maymuna, and a brother, 'Umar, were made prisoners by the victorious Almohads and their lives were spared only because when he visited Marrakesh during the reign of the Almoravid 'Ali b. Tashufin, their father had played a key role in commuting the Almohad *mahdi* Ibn Tumart's death sentence (Al-Baydhaq 27–28; Lévi-Provençal 27–29).[26] It would therefore seem that among her female siblings, Fannu was the only one to assume the warrior role that Almoravid society allowed, however partially, to women.

Yet she did not do this in an open battle, as was the custom for her Berber predecessors, but defending the urban and closed space of the royal palace. The powerful image of the Almoravid princesses in the palace, which I have tried to recover in the first part of this essay, acquires here a new meaning. The last recorded feat of an Almoravid woman underscores both the changes experienced by the Sanhaja Berbers through out their imperial expansion and the survival of age-old traditions. Patterns of womanly behavior appear thus as adapting to circumstances and proving that Almoravid elite women could and did choose among them according to their own decisions.

Notes

1. Research for this essay has been done in the framework of the research project *La arquitectura en Andalucía desde una perspectiva de género: estudio de casos, prácticas y realidades construidas* (Proyecto de Excelencia, Consejería de Economía e Innovación de la Junta de Andalucía, HUM5709), directed by Prof. María Elena Díez Jorge (University of Granada, Spain).
2. See Bosch Vilá, *Los almorávides*; Nasr Allah, *Dawlat al-murabitin*; Viguera, "Los almorávides," with an excellent bibliographical essay; Hajji "La salida;" Messier *Almoravids,* and Fierro, "Los almorávides y los almohades."
3. See also Huici Miranda; Lagardère 167.
4. Ibn Wuhayb, born in Seville, died in Marrakesh. He was a vizier and judge for the emir 'Ali b. Tashufin. See Fierro, "La religión" 438, 440, 447, 459, and 471; Molina, "Instituciones administrativas" 151; and Serrano and Forcada, "Ibn Wuhayb, Malik."
5. Ibn al-Qasira (d. 1114) had been a member of the court of the Sevillian king al-Mu'tamid. After some time, he became the head of the chancery for Yusuf b. Tashufin, and later on, for 'Ali b. Yusuf, whose letter of appointement as heir of the Almoravid Empire he supposedly wrote. See Álvarez de Morales, "Ibn al-Qasira;" Molina, "Instituciones administrativas" 150 and 160–161; and García Sanjuán, "Ibn al-Qasira."
6. The Arabic root R.Kh.A has, among other meanings, that of "loosen, relax, lower."

But this interpretation of Ibn al-Murkhi's surname could be a rhetorical way of enhancing the following account.

7. More on this topic in Fedwa Malti-Douglas, *Woman's Body* 33–34.
8. See Deverdun, *Marrakech* 1.91–98, on the location and archaeological remains of 'Ali b. Yusuf's palace in Marrakech. The palace was distroyed by the Almohads to make place for the building of the Kutubiya mosque.
9. Compare Hawwa's activity in this respect to that of the Umayyad Andalusi princess Wallada (eleventh century), who distinguished herself as a poetess and held a literary salon in Cordoba. See Garulo, "La biografía," 105.
10. On al-A'mà, see W. Saleh Alkhalifa "Al-A'mà al-Tutili." Saleh Alkhalifa mentions that al-A'mà wrote several panegyrics for the emir 'Ali b. Tashufin, and another "for a woman called Hawwa', probably a member of the Banu Tashufin dynasty." The editor of *al-Bayan al-Mughrib*, Professor Ihsan 'Abbas, had already identified this woman with Hawwa' bint Tashufin in 1967; see Ibn 'Idhari, *Al-Bayan* 57n 2.
11. On Tamim's long career and different appointments in the Maghreb and al-Andalus, see 'Alawi, "Tamim b. Yusuf b. Tashufin." As governor of Seville, Tamim succeeded another of his brothers, Ibrahim b. Yusuf b. Tashufin (Kuhne 437).
12. On the circumstances and dates of Abu Marwan's imprisonment, see Kuhne, "Aportaciones."
13. Dandash, "Adwar siyasiya" 58, suggests that Hawwa' could have died before Tamim returned to Morocco in 1126.
14. See an account drawn from Arabic sources in Dandash, "Adwar siyasiya," and H. T. Norris, *The Berbers*, 132, with a translation of the text on Zaynab in Ibn 'Idhari, *Al-Bayan al-mughrib*.
15. Such as the veiling of men but not of women, or the traces of matrilineal lineages in men's names; Norris, *Saharan Myth* 39.
16. A significant example of this attitude, in García Gómez, "Un eclipse de la poesía en Sevilla," where Yusuf b. Tashufin is described as a "coarse Berber," and the author laments the eclipse of poetry in Seville, due to the ignorance of the Almoravids rulers of the city.
17. See also Gannun 1.82; Norris, *The Berbers* 137; and *Saharan Myth* 109.
18. The self-identification of Tamima with the sun is underlined by the fact that the word "sun" (*shams*) in Arabic is a feminine.
19. According to Ibn al-Abbar and Ibn 'Abd al-Malik al-Marrakushi, Zaynab had been the wife of Abu l-Tahir Tamim who, as shown above, later married Hawwa' b. Tashufin.
20. On the relationship of Ibn Khafaja with Almoravid princes and governors, see Schippers, "Prosopography of the Almoravid Addressees of Ibn Khafaja's Poems."
21. In Ibn al-Abbar the edited text reads Hayya (no 2877). Ibn 'Abd al-Malik al-Marrakushi (VIII–2, nº 288) confuses this Hawwa' with Hawwa' bint Tashufin. See Ávila, "Las mujeres sabias en al-Andalus," 45 and 106.
22. See in this respect Lourie 196–197. (My thanks to Maribel Fierro, to whom I owe this

reference). On examining an impressive array of sources the problematic information about the presence of (black) women in the Almoravid army which besieged Valencia in 1094, Lourie concludes that "Almoravids came from a society that did not regard the idea of women warriors as contradictory in terms of gender" (197).

23. Sources differ in calling him 'Umar b. Yintan or Yintan b. 'Umar; Molina 151.
24. The text of al-Baydhaq is summarized in Ibn 'Idhari, *Al-Bayan al-mughrib* 28. See Norris, *The Berbers* 146 and Butshish 48, 50.
25. On twentieth-century examples see Pennell.
26. Molina 151 and Lagardère, *Les almoravides, Le djihad* 303, suggest that Tamaghunt and Maymuna could be the same woman. Bargach (60–62) wrongly asserts that Tamaghunt (called by him Tamakkaunat) was a daughter of Hawwa 'bint Tashufin and Sir b. Abi Bakr, but offers what seems to be a popular account of her destiny and that of other Almoravid women prisoners of the Almohads.

Works Cited

'Abd al-Wahid al-Marrakushi. *Al-Mu'jib fi talkhis akhbar al-Maghrib*. Ed. Muhammad Sa'id al- 'Aryan and Muhammad al-'Arabi al-'Alami. Casablanca, 1950.

Abu l-'Alà' Zuhr. *Kitab al-mujarrabat*. Ed. C. Álvarez Millán. Madrid: CSIC, 1994.

Abu Marwan Ibn Zuhr. *Kitab al-aghdiya*. Ed. E. Garcia, Madrid: CSIC, 1992.

Al-A'mà al-Tutili. *Diwan*. Ed. I. 'Abbas. Beirut, 1963.

'Alawi, Hasan Hafizi. "Tamim b. Yusuf b. Tashufin." *Ma'lamat al-Maghrib al-Aqsà*. Vol. 8. Salé: al-Jam'iya al-Maghribiya li-l-Ta'lif wa-l-Tarjama wa-l-Nashr, 1985. 2567–68.

Álvarez de Morales, Camilo. "Ibn al-Qasira: un diplomático andalusí en la corte de los almorávides." *Cuadernos de Historia del Islam* 8 (1976–77): 85–94.

Ávila, María Luisa. "Las mujeres sabias en al-Andalus." *La mujer en al-Andalus: reflejos históricos de su actividad y categorías sociales*. Ed. María J. Viguera. Madrid-Sevilla: Editoriales Andaluzas Reunidas, 1989. 139–84.

Azar, Henry. *The Sage of Seville: Ibn Zuhr, His Time, and His Medical Legacy*. Cairo: American University Cairo Press, 2008.

Bargach, Mohamed. *La femme sans voile dans l'histoire du Maroc*. Casablanca: Editions Maghrébines, 2000.

Al-Baydhaq. *Akhbar al-Mahdi b. Tumart wa-bidayat dawlat al-muwahhidin*. Ed. 'Abd al-Wahhab b. Mansur. Rabat: al-Matba'a al-Malakiya, 2004.

Borrego Soto, Miguel Ángel. "Ibn al-Murji, Abu Bakr (el abuelo)." *Biblioteca de al-Andalus. De Ibn al-Labbana a Ibn al-Ruyuli*. nº 876. Ed. Jorge Lirola Delgado. Almería: Fundación Ibn Tufayl, 2006.

———. "La alquería de Jarana y los Banu l-Marji." *Al-Andalus-Magreb* 12 (2005): 19–38.

Bosch Vilá, Jacinto. *Los almorávides*. Tetuán: Editora Marroquí, 1956. 2nd ed. Intro. E. Molina López. Granada: Universidad de Granada, 1990.

Butshish, Ibrahim al-Qadiri. *Al-Maghrib wa-l-Andalus fi 'asr al-murabitin. Al-Mujtama', al-dhihniyat, al-awliya'*. Beirut: Dar al-Tali'a, 1993.

Codera, Francisco. "Familia real de los Benitexufin." *Estudios críticos de historia árabe española (segunda serie)*. Madrid: Imprenta Ibérica, 1917. 75–165.

Dandash, 'Ismat. "Adwar siyasiya li-l-nisa' fi dawlat al-murabitin," *Buhuth al-Multaqà al-Isbani al-Maghribi al-Thani li-l-'Ulum al-Ta'rikhiya. Al-Ta'rikh, al-'Ilm wa-l-Mujtama'*. Madrid: AECI, 1992. 49–65.

———. "Ahdath murabitiya min Kitab al-Taysir li-Ibn Zuhr." *Adwa' jadida 'alà l-murabitin*. Beirut: Dar al-Gharb al-Islami, 1991. 119–39.

———. *Dawr al-murabitin fi nashr al-Islam fi gharb Ifriqiya 430–515 h/1038–1121m*. Beirut: Dar al-Gharb al-Islami, 1988.

———. "Ziyarat al-andalusiyin li-balat al-murabitin bi-Marrakush." *Adwa' jadida 'alà l-murabitin*. Beirut: Dar al-Gharb al-Islami, 1991. 101–116.

Deverdun, Gaston. *Marrakech, des origines à 1912*. Rabat: Editions Techniques Nord-Africaines, 1959.

Fierro, Maribel. "Los almorávides y los almohades." *De árabes a moriscos (711–1616): una parte de la historia de España*. Córdoba (in press).

———. "La religión." *El retroceso territorial de al-Andalus. Almorávides y almohades. Siglos XI al XIII. Historia de España Menéndez Pidal*. VIII–II. Madrid: Espasa Calpe, 1997. 437–57.

Gannun, 'Abd Allah. *Al-Nubugh al-maghribi fi l-adab al-'arabi*. Beirut: Dar al-Kitab al-Lubnani, 1975.

García, Expiración. Introductory Essay. *Kitab al-aghdhiya*. By Abu Marwan Ibn Zuhr. Ed. Expiración García. Madrid: CSIC, 1992.

García Gómez, Emilio. "Un eclipse de la poesía en Sevilla. La época almorávide." *Al-Andalus* 10 (1945): 285–343.

García Sanjuán, Alejandro. "Ibn al-Qasira." *Biblioteca de al-Andalus. De Ibn al-Labbana a Ibn al-Ruyuli*. nº 954. Ed. Jorge Lirola Delgado. Almería: Fundación Ibn Tufayl, 2006.

Garulo, Teresa. "La biografía de Wallada, toda problemas." *Anaquel de Estudios Árabes* 20 (2009): 97–116.

———. *Diwan de las poetisas de al-Andalus*. Madrid: Hiperion, 1986.

Hajji, Mohamed. "La salida de los almorávides del desierto. Fundación de la confederación sinhayí y el surgimiento del movimiento almorávide." *Mauritania y España, una historia común. Los almorávides, unificadores del Magreb y al-Andalus (s. XI–XII)*. Granada: El Legado Andalusí, 2003. 17–34.

Huici Miranda, Ambrosio. "La salida de los almorávides del desierto y el reinado de Yusuf b. Tasfin." *Hespéris*, 1959. 155–82.

Ibn al-Abbar. *Al-Takmila li-Kitab al-Sila*. Ed. Maximiliano Alarcón. *Miscelánea de estudios y textos árabes*. Madrid: Centro de Estudios Históricos, 1915.

Ibn 'Abd al-Malik al-Marrakushi. *Al-Dhayl wa-l-takmila*. VIII–2. Ed. Muhammad Bensharifa. Rabat: Akadimiyat al-Mamlaka al-Maghribiya, 1984.

Ibn ʻIdhari. *Kitab al-Bayan al-mughrib fi akhbar al-Andalus wa-l-Maghrib. Al-Juz' al-rabi'. Qit'a min ta'rikh al-murabitin*. Ed. Ihsan 'Abbas. Beirut: Dar al-Thaqafa, 1967.

———. *Al-Bayan al-mughrib fi akhbar al-Andalus wa-l-Maghrib. Qism al-muwahhidin*. Ed. Muhammad Ibrahim al-Kattani et alii. Beirut: Dar al-Gharb al-Islami, 1985.

Ibn Khallikan. *Wafayat al-a'yan*. Ed. Ihsan 'Abbas. Beirut: Dar al-Thaqafa, 1971.

Ibn Rushd. *Fatawa*, Ed. al-Mukhtar b. al-Tahir al-Talili. Beirut: Dar al-Gharb al-Islami, 1987.

Ibn Zuhr. *Kiyab al-Taysir*. Ed. Mishil al-Khuri. Damascus: Dar al-Fikr, 1983.

Kitab al-Hulal al-mawshiya fi dhikr al-akhbar al-marrakushiya. Ed. Suhayl Zakkar and 'Abd al-Qadir Zamama. Casablanca: Dar al-Rashad al-Haditha, 1979.

Kuhne, Rosa. "Aportaciones para esclarecer alguno de los puntos oscuros en la biografía de Avenzoar." *Actas del XII Congreso de la U.E.A.I. (Málaga, 1984)*. Madrid, 1986: 431–46.

Lagardère, Vincent. *Les Almoravides jusqu' au règne de Yusuf b. Tasfin (1039–1106)*. Paris: L'Harmattan, 1989.

———. *Les almoravides. Le djihad andalou (1106–1143)*. Paris: L'Harmattan, 1998.

Lévi-Provençal, E. *Documents inédits d'histoire almohade*. Paris: Paul Geuthner, 1928.

Lourie, Elena. "Black Women Warriors in the Muslim Army Besieging Valencia and the Cid's Victory: A Problem of Interpretation." *Traditio: Studies in Ancient and Medieval History, Thought, and Religion* 55 (2000): 181–209.

"Madjlis." *Encyclopaedia of Islam: New Edition*.Vol. V. Leiden: E.J. Brill, 1986. 1031–33.

Malti-Douglas, Fedwa. *Woman's Body, Woman's Word: Gender and Discourse in Arabo-Islamic Writing*. Princeton: Princeton University Press, 1991.

Marín, Manuela. *Mujeres en al-Ándalus*. Madrid: CSIC, 2000.

———. "On Women and Camels: Some Comments on a *Hadith*." *O ye Gentlemen: Arabic Studies on Science and Literary Culture in Honor of Remke Kruk*, Leiden: Brill, 2007. 485–93.

Messier, Ronald A. *The Almoravids and the Meanings of Jihad*. Santa Barbara: Praeger, 2010.

Molina, Luis. "Instituciones administrativas: visires y secretarios." *El retroceso territorial de al-Andalus. Almorávides y almohades. Siglos XI al XIII. Historia de España Menéndez Pidal*, VIII–II. Madrid: Espasa Calpe, 1997. 149–167.

Nasr Allah, Sa'dun 'Abbas. *Dawlat al-murabitin fi l-Maghrib wa-l-Andalus*. Beirut: Dar al-Nahda al-'Arabiya, 1985.

Norris, H.T. *The Berbers in Arabic Literature*. London: Longman, 1982.

———. *Saharan Myth and Saga*. Oxford: Oxford University Press, 1972.

Pennell, C.R. "Women and Resistance to Colonialism in Morocco: the Rif, 1916–1926." *Journal of African History* 28 (1987): 107–18.

Rubiera, María Jesús. "Algunos problemas cronológicos en la biografía de al-Muʻtamid de Sevilla: la conquista de Silves y el matrimonio con Rumaykiyya." *Actas de las Jornadas de Cultura Árabe e Islámica (1978)*. Madrid: IHAC, 1981. 231–36.

Saleh Alkhalifa,W. "Al-A'mà al-Tutili." *Enciclopedia de al-Andalus. Diccionario de autores y obras andalusíes*, vol. I, Granada: El Legado Andalusí, 2002. 20.

Schippers, Arie. "Prosopography of the Almoravid Addressees of Ibn Khafaja's Poems." *Medieval Prosopography* 23 (2002): 185–201.

Serrano, Delfina. "Dos fetuas sobre la expulsión de los mozárabes al Magreb en 1126." *Anaquel de Estudios Árabes* 2 (1991): 163–82.

———. "¿Por qué llamaron los almohades antropomorfistas a los almorávides?" Ed. P. Cressier, M. Fierro, and L. Molina. *Los almohades: problemas y perspectivas* 2. Madrid: CSIC, 2005. 815–52.

Serrano, Delfina. and Miquel Forcada. "Ibn Wuhayb, Malik." *Biblioteca de al-Andalus*, vol. 5. Ed. J. Lirola Delgado. Almería: Fundación Ibn Tufayl, 2007. 603–8.

Tabales Rodríguez, Miguel Ángel. "La transformación palatina del alcázar de Sevilla, 914–1366." *Anales de Arqueología Cordobesa* 12 (2001): 195–213.

Valor Piechotta, Magdalena. *La arquitectura militar y palatina en la Sevilla musulmana*. Sevilla: Diputación Provincial, 1991.

Viguera, María Jesús. *Aragón musulmán. La presencia del Islam en el valle del Ebro*. Zaragoza: Mira Editores, 1988.

———. "Los almorávides." *El retroceso territorial de al-Andalus. Almorávides y almohades. Siglos XI al XIII. Historia de España Menéndez Pidal*, vol. VIII–II. Madrid: Espasa Calpe, 1997. 41–64.

Wuld al-Salim, Hama-hu. "Al-Usul al-fikriya li-dawlat al-murabitin." *Al-Islam wa-l-Thaqafa al-'arabiya fi l-Sahra' al-Kubra*. Beirut: Dar al-Kutub al-'Ilmiya, 2010. 14–49.

4

Medieval Mediterranean Travel as an Intellectual Journey: Seafaring and the Pursuit of Knowledge in the *Libro de Apolonio*

Nicholas M. Parmley

> Humans live their lives and build their institutions on dry land. Nevertheless, they seek to grasp the movement of their existence above all through a metaphorics of the perilous sea voyage.
> —Hans Blumenberg, *Shipwreck with Spectator*

The *Libro de Apolonio* has a rich and complicated history, both pagan and Christian, that stretches from the second century to the thirteenth century A.D. and from Asia Minor to the Kingdom of Aragon in the northeast of the Iberian Peninsula.[1] The thirteenth-century Castilian version of the story of Apolonio of present concern is in fact a poetic rendering of a much earlier Latin work known as the *Historia Apollonii Regis Tyri*.[2] The great majority of scholarship on the *Libro*—when not concerned with the *mester de clerecía* genre—has tended to focus on religious typology and the Christianization of a pagan text (Weiss, Rico, Pickford, Brownlee, Kelley, Surtz). The efforts of scholars such as Manuel Alvar and Patricia Grieve have largely been focused on the eponymous protagonist, Apolonio, as scholar king and Christian pilgrim. And Alan Deyermond has emphasized the text's relationship to European ecclesiastical tradition and folklore ("Motivos folklóricos"). Studies by Harriet Goldberg and, more recently, Matt Desing have begun to emphasize less researched characters such as Apolonio's daughter Tarsiana, who is a talented minstrel and clever riddler, and Apolonio's wife Luciana, who becomes both priestess and abbess ("Luciana's Story"). Surprisingly, though, for a tale of travel that is literally centered geographically and narratively on the Mediterranean Sea, very little has been written about this maritime space or travel through it. Many scholars, including Deyermond and Brownlee, simply mention the sea in passing or disregard it as nothing more than the medium by which the poet moves the plot or by which the protagonist lives a life of Christian pilgrimage.

Such readings of the sea in the *Libro*, in the context of the Christian *peregrinatio vitae*, while insightful, remain beholden to a decidedly European Christian ecclesiastical perspective, and are thus conspicuously underscored by the narrative of twelfth-thirteenth-century crusading chronicles, which depict the eastern Mediterranean—the geographic backdrop of the *Libro*—as a space of religiously inspired imperial conquest and colonization. But such approaches neglect the reality of thirteenth-century Iberia's participation in a much broader and more intellectually nuanced and shared cultural Mediterranean space. It is precisely during this time of crusade and conquest that the author of the *Libro* offers not simply a Christian, but a decidedly Mediterranean perspective of travel: seafaring is no longer relevant only to commerce or the religio-political violence of the crusading cause, but a (necessary) medium for access to knowledge and tradition, wherever and with whomever such knowledge might be found (Muslim, Christian, or Jew). That is, the impetus to travel at the heart of the *Libro* reveals Christian Iberia's intimate relationship with a broader medieval Mediterranean tradition of travel, according to which the (sea) voyage is intimately connected to the pursuit of knowledge and understanding. Simply stated, the *Libro de Apolonio* is a book indicative of its location in both time and space: as a medieval Mediterranean tale of dubious Greek origin and composed in Castilian, it draws upon both Muslim and Jewish views of the voyage as an intellectual journey. As such, the narrative of Apolonio's travels is necessarily set on the eastern Mediterranean Sea, the space in which these traditions coalesce and collide.

Moreover, in the poem's description of the intellectual journey and the complexity of the sea space as both poison and cure, there is perhaps a thinly veiled critique of the failed ethics of crusading. The images on the pages of the *Libro de Apolonio* reveal a fascination with the East and a yearning for distant lands and unknown places. Looking east for the thirteenth-century Iberian Christian invoked a sense of itinerant pilgrimage and a nearly inevitable confrontation with the anxiety of the Crusades. During the Crusades, wave after wave of crusading armies would march across the continent or traverse the turbulent waves of the great sea toward the eastern shore. But the conflicting ambition of leaders and the jealousies of regional factions over several centuries revealed the impossibility of such a task.[3] The discord and failure to cooperate and the inability or lack of impetus to effectively and consistently invest

Western resources in the East turned what was at first rapid progress into precipitous decline and failure.[4] It is in the midst of this historical milieu that the *Libro* presents its literary map of the region. The eastern Mediterranean as a violent space of the crusade and its corresponding religio-political violence and conquest is repurposed in the *Libro de Apolonio*. In view of the failed efforts of the Crusades, to which even Christian pilgrimage was intimately related, an analysis of the sea voyage and its corresponding motivations to travel in the *Libro* reimagines the sea and that same Mediterranean space as an intellectual path—a space where the failed ethics of crusade are replaced with the ethos of the intellectual (*ṭalab al-ʿilm*) and religious (*ḥajj*) journey.

As such, in this essay I would like to move away from an exclusively Christian reading of the *Libro de Apolonio*. To do so, I will discuss the maritime voyages of Apolonio within the framework of Muslim and Jewish traditions of travel and learning, as distilled from Greek (Neo-platonic) notions about the pursuit of knowledge. In particular, I am interested in how the Arabo-Islamic concept of the *riḥla* might help to explain the motivation behind Apolonio's travels, which I contend reflects what Houari Touati has called the "intellectual journey," in reference to a similar motif in Mediterranean Muslim tradition from the eighth-thirteenth centuries. Moreover, I aim to demonstrate how the image of the sea, particularly in storm, is the manifestation of that same intellectual space, where the sea strips the traveler (philosopher) of both physical vestments and intellectual vanities in order that he may first gain awareness of his ignorance, and only then pursue the true path to knowledge and wisdom. I contend that the traveler and his movements in and throughout the maritime space as intellectual journey can be understood in the context of medieval Arab and Jewish philosophical notions of perplexity and incoherence, terms distilled by medieval Iberian readers from Aristotle and Plato's understanding of the Greek *aporia* (ἀπορεία); it is both a state of confusion and wandering, and a necessary path to understanding. With this, I will demonstrate two interrelated points. First, that Apolonio's motivation to travel and the various episodes that narrate the sea he sails reveal a text that participates in—was a product of—a more broadly conceived and shared multicultural medieval Mediterranean space. And second, that Apolonio's intellectual journey, as a movement from perplexity to understanding, is made possible only by way of the voyage: by sailing on stormy seas, and learning from experience both the blessings and travails of travel. Without this experiential knowledge, Apolonio lacks the practical intelligence and wisdom to adequately interpret his surroundings, for his inability to interpret well is inextricably linked to his inexperience as a traveler. Put positively, travel leads to wisdom and correct interpretation.

Before we directly address the text of the *Libro de Apolonio*, however, and in particular Apolonio's motivations to travel, it is imperative that we contextualize our analysis within the framework of medieval Mediterranean notions and traditions of travel.

Traditions of Travel

In *Travel in the Middle Ages*, Jean Verdon contends that "[f]or a land civilization like that of the Middle Ages, the sea could only provoke fear, anxiety, and repulsion" (55). The sheer number of people that took to the sea, however, seems to problematize this view. S.D. Goitein writes in *A Mediterranean Society* that despite nature's caprice and the perfidy with which it could render any journey a hazardous undertaking, "Mediterranean man in the Middle Ages was an impassioned and persevering traveler" (1.273). That is, despite even natural deterministic elements that disrupted the environment, there was constant movement that connected the region(s) of the Mediterranean and the peoples that inhabited them. In his study on the documents of the Cairo Geniza, Goitein reminds us of a vibrant maritime community in which both the lack of comfort and the danger involved in seafaring were in the end insufficient to discourage travel (273).

Even for the people of pre-Islamic Arabia, travel was a way of life. As a consequence, the concept of travel was an important component of *jāhilīyah*, or pre-Islamic poetry, and an integral part of the *qaṣīda*, the predominant form of the Arabic poem. According to ninth-century anthologist Ibn Qutayba, the *qaṣīda* or ode had a strict thematic order: it began with an erotic prelude (*nasib*), followed by a woeful yet skillfully composed tale of travels (*riḥla*), and concluded with a panegyric (*madīḥ*) (Ibn Qutaybah). The poetic form of the *qaṣīda*, and in particular the importance of the *riḥla*, would continue to dominate Islamic poetry and eventually make its way into al-Andalus (Netton). However, as Islam spread rapidly westward, the importance of the voyage became not just a poetic conceit, but also a matter of practical religious and intellectual concern. Consequently, Islamic tradition conceived of a philosophical journey distinct from the *riḥla* of Arab poetry: *al-riḥla fi ṭalab al-ʿilm* (travel in search of knowledge), what I will refer to as the intellectual journey.

By the eighth century Islam was forced to deal with the problem of disappearing sources of knowledge and shifting authoritative centers into the Mediterranean (Touati 25–28). The Prophet and his companions were dead and those who had gleaned knowledge from them were also passing; thus, the difficulty of safe-guarding the transmission of knowledge and *al-ḥadīth* from their sources grew more difficult ("Hadith"). And it is specifically in this period that Islam is becoming a Mediterranean presence. As Muslims had once moved from Mecca to Medina, they were now moving into and across the Mediterranean space. Jews too experienced anxiety over shifting sources of Talmudic and Halakhic knowledge, and a concern over *qabbalah*, as both oral tradition and received doctrine. In fact, like the Jewish *qabbalah*, the Muslim *ʿilm*, as knowledge related to Islamic tradition, conceived of genealogical knowledge which called for all *ḥadīth* to be authenticated by an unbroken chain of transmission (*isnād*). And as authoritative centers were moving westward (i.e., to Damascus, and as far as Córdoba), the gathering of this information required travel—eastward. This is carefully and copiously documented in a genre of Islamic literature called *tabaqāt* (generations) or *ʿilm al-rijāl* (knowledge of the transmitters of *ḥadīth*). Intended to evaluate the narrators of *ḥadīth*, it is at times necessary for the author to recount their travels in order to verify the authenticity of the *isnad*.[5] But knowledge was not confined to the authority of tradition; for the intellectually curious medieval Mediterranean man, knowledge came in many forms, and could be found in many places. One *ḥadīth* in particular cites the Prophet as encouraging his followers to "seek knowledge, even if it be in China" (Netton).

An example of this can be found in the travels of medieval Muslim scholar and jurist Ibn Battuta, who set out from Morocco on an intellectual journey across Ifrīqiya, the Arabian Peninsula, and China. His initial motivation to travel was the Islamic pilgrimage to Mecca known as the *ḥajj*, itself emblematic of a multivalent use and understanding of travel. Though primarily a religious pilgrimage, the *ḥajj* was also—or could be—"a study tour . . . of the heartland, and opportunity to acquire books and diplomas, deepen one's knowledge of theology and law, and commune with refined and civilized men" (Dunn 30). Both part of and apart from the Crusades, medieval Christians also carried out pilgrimages to holy sites throughout the Mediterranean. And though for some the philosophical journey can be found among their many motivations to travel, depictions of medieval Christian itinerant intellectuals are limited, or rather undermined, by chronicles of the Crusades and violent accounts of colonization and empire. Of course, Muslims were not alone in their understanding of travel as the pursuit of knowledge. Benjamin of Tudela was a twelfth-century Jewish geographer, ethnologist, and historian who traveled from northern Iberia to Europe, Asia, and Africa in search of authenticated knowledge.[7] As Touati contends, it is thus that the paradigm of hearing and voyage became important to the acquisition of knowledge; the Arabic *ʿiyān* 'observation' resembled the *autopsia* 'to see with one's own eyes' of the ancient Greeks, such that a sense of witness was both seeing and hearing (9). The Geniza letters of both Muslims and Jews echo this idea, revealing a frequent maxim of medieval seafarers that "a man who is present sees what he who is absent cannot see" (Goitein 274). This emphasis on the importance of experiential knowledge is also central to medieval philosophical texts, such as Muḥammad Ibn Ṭufayl's allegorical novel *Ḥayy ibn Yaqẓan*, where inquiry and investigation are essential components of the intellectual journey, a notion widespread in Andalusi philosophical works.[8]

The Iberian Jewish philosopher Moses Maimonides, heavily influenced by Ibn Rushd and Aristotelian thought, wrote *The Guide for the Perplexed* (*Dalālat al-Ḥā'irīn*), as a guide to the reconciliation of religious duty and reasoned philosophical study, and a caution against interpretive dangers which lead men into perplexity (71–72). Ibn Rushd, an Arabic source for, and strong influence on, Maimonides' Aristotelian commentaries, published his philosophical work, *The Incoherence of the Incoherence* (*Tahāfut al-Tahāfut*) as a defense of his Aristotelian views in contrast to the problems of Islamic Neo-platonic thought claimed by al-Ghazali in *The Incoherence of the Philosophers* (*Tahāfut al-Falāsifah*) (Van Den Bergh xii). Another Andalusi polymath and contemporary of both Ibn Rushd and Maimonides, Ibn Ṭufayl was also heavily influenced by a marked Aristotelian rationalism. He wrote his short philosophical novel, *Ḥayy ibn Yaqẓan* (*Life, Son of Awake*), as a philosophical thought experiment of the intellect and self-discovery, in which he creates a fictional character in order to explore one's ethical formation as a movement from ignorance to knowledge, where "what a man achieves for himself is more satisfying than what he inherits from convention" (Colville xv). This is precisely what the *Libro* contends of Apolonio, first suggested by the image of court library as representative of an incomplete access to knowledge, and developed throughout the text as Apolonio gains greater wisdom through the experience of travel. Just as for Ibn Ṭufayl, Ibn Rushd, and Maimonides, the intellectual pursuit cannot be separated from a sense of spiritual awakening, for the author of the *Libro*, Apolonio moves toward holy knowledge (to use Desing's terminology) not by abandoning reason, but by embracing it. For Ibn Ṭufayl, societal convention, whether religious or secular—perhaps such as that codified in the texts of Apolonio's library—were not enough. And for Maimonides, the pursuit of philosophy was "the highest degree of Divine worship, surpassing even the study of the Law and the practice of its precepts" (34). One who is in a state of perplexity has yet to reconcile the two.

Notions of intellectually driven wanderlust can also be found in the fictionalized narratives of the *maqāmāt*, such as Judah al-Ḥarizi's *Sefer Takhemoni*, in which the protagonist narrates his travels throughout the Islamic world (including the Mediterranean), as well as in translated narratives such as *Kalīla wa Dimna*. Whether out of concern for teleological and genealogical authority, the pursuit of philosophical truth, or the individual search for meaning, in no uncertain terms, knowledge and wisdom were products of the voyage—they necessitated travel.

One might ask what benefit it is for us to read the work of a thirteenth-century Christian cleric in the context of the Arabic and Hebrew intellectual journey. Heir to the cultural advances of al-Andalus (Muslim Spain), thirteenth-century Iberia was inhabited by large populations of Arabic and Hebrew speakers. Nearly all the Iberian kings of the period—Pere IV of Aragon, Sancho IV of Castile, and Alfonso X—employed Muslim and Jews in their courts. And some scholars believe Pere I of Aragon even spoke Arabic (Menéndez Pidal). Arabic and Hebrew speakers were hired as prized composers and musicians of learned Andalusi song and verse, translators, physicians, and bureaucrats. Many participated in the ambitious intellectual projects of Christian universities and translation schools, such as Alfonso X's scriptorium, known as the Toledan School of Translators. Here, texts of intellectual voyage such as *Calila wa Dimna* were translated into Latin and Romance for the consumption of a broader Christian readership. Together, these interactions and relationships created a shared space of cultural and intellectual contact and exchange. It was a space, I argue, in which a thirteenth-century author writing in the northeast of the Iberian Peninsula would have been familiar with the knowledge and wisdom recorded in Semitic and Greek, at least in translation. And perhaps his own adaptation of the tale of Apolonio's travels was inspired by a shared notion of the intellectual voyage.

Motivations to Travel

As a space of representational meaning, the textual space of departure connects the initial stages and motivations of Apolonio's adventures to the broader Mediterranean tradition of the *al-riḥla fī ṭalab al-ʿilm*, the intellectual journey discussed above. King Apolonio's movement from land to sea, from the relative safety of the shore into the treacherous space of maritime travel, is motivated by a matrix of intellectual anxieties, fears, and curiosities. But, to arrive at a clear understanding of Apolonio's travels, the reader must navigate the varying perspectives of narrators and protagonists who relate the king's departure, as well as the king's inconsistent and, at times, inaccurate understanding of events. Apolonio's inability to correctly read the circumstances of his journey problematizes our understanding of the intellectual identity of the *Libro*'s central protagonist and namesake, and perhaps speaks to a more nuanced complexity of the identity of the text that tells his tale. Apolonio's motivation when he first ventures from his native Tyre seems obvious: he is on a quest for the hand of King Antioco's daughter. Yet the king's departure does not appear to be motivated simply by amorous sentiment or matrimonial pretension; rather this opening scene suggests Apolonio's travels are a matter of intellectual significance. That is, in order to win the fair maiden, Apolonio, like all her suitors, is required to solve a riddle that encodes the King of Antioch's incestuous relationship with his daughter. The penalty for failure is harsh, however. A wrong answer will cost him his head: "la cabeça o la soluçión" (21d) (your head or the solution). None had yet successfully solved the riddle and consequently many were decapitated as a result. The danger does not seem to deter the king, however; rather, the poet suggests Apolonio is adequately prepared for the task. "Como era Apolonio d*e* letras p*ro*fundado, / por soluer argume*n*tos era bien dotrinado; / entendió la fallença y el suçio pecado / como si lo ouiese por su ojo pr*o*uado" (22a-d) (Given Apolonio's profound knowledge of letters / and his ample training in the art of solving riddles / he understood the king's failure and his appalling sin / as if he had seen it with his own eyes). This is the first reference in the text to Apolonio's intellect. Here it appears that he is a learned man, knowledgeable and well read. The poet suggests the king's book collection includes philosophical texts and treatises on rhetoric, which allowed him to solve riddles (*soluer argumentos*). Was he reading commentaries on Aristotle and Plato and/or the original works of Averroes, Maimonides, and Ibn Ṭufayl, representative of the diverse intellectual culture reflected in his tale? This question, as relevant for Apolonio as it is for the author, will be discussed below. For now, we turn to the king's demonstration of his intellectual prowess in the scholarly play of riddling. Was it this intellectual challenge that enticed him to travel?

Riddling was a common form of play in medieval literature (Deyermond, Clark, Goldberg). As Harriet Goldberg points out, often riddling can be intrinsically unfair: "The poser wields absolute power" (59). Alan Deyermond stresses the importance of the riddle in setting the narrative in motion, but it is specifically Antioco's misuse of riddling that puts Apolonio in motion and sets the stage for his sally out to sea. Moreover, the poet suggests that Apolonio decides to unveil the hidden truth to King Antioco and his court, not out of moral necessity or to rebuke Antioco's unethical conduct, but in order to demonstrate his intelligence so that he may not be considered stupid. "Mas, por tal q*ue* no fuese por bauieca tenido, / dio a la pregu*n*ta buen responso conplido" (23c-d) (Yet, so that he might not be taken for a simpleton / he answered the question with a correct response).

The riddle, then, becomes a device by which the reader is made privy not only to Apolonio's intellectual prowess, but also his intellectual anxieties. Throughout the episode the poet emphasizes how important knowledge and learning are to the king; he desires that others recognize these qualities in him. Yet it seems that in the midst of attempting to demonstrate his intellectual competence and rhetorical dexterity (solving the riddle), he reveals precisely the opposite: a lack of wisdom and situational awareness.

Patricia Grieve, in her study of Apolonio as a Christian king, contends that Apolonio falls into Antioco's trap not because he is ignorant, but because his intellect is misdirected: "When he attempted to solve King Antioco's riddle, Apolonio turned to his secular books and did not turn to God at all" (162). Grieve bases her conclusions on the fact that upon Apolonio's return to Tyre after the riddling debacle, he cloisters himself in his private chambers seeking the right answer among his books and manuscripts. "Encerr[ó]se Apolonio en sus cámaras p*ri*uadas, / do tenié sus escritos y sus estorias notadas. / Rezó *sus* argume*n*tos, las fazanyas passadas, / caldeas y latin*e*s, tres o quatro vegadas" (31a-d) (Apolonio cloistered himself in his private chambers / wherein he stored both writings and historical commentaries. / He consulted their arguments, the events of history, / (in) Caldean and Latin, three or four times). Here the poet describes nothing less than the contents of a medieval royal library. As Manuel Alvar remarks, "vemos que hay libros (en latín y en hebreo), comentarios, tratados de retórica—en el amplísimo sentido medieval—, historias. Es decir, una colección que conformaba el saber de un hombre laico del siglo XIII" (52) (we see that there are books [in Latin and Hebrew], commentaries, rhetorical treatises—in the broadest medieval sense—histories. That is, a collection which comprised the knowledge of a thirteenth-century layman).[9] In particular, we read that Apolonio consults his annotated and commented (*notadas*) volumes, and, suggesting a sense of mastery, he then recites (*rezó*) their arguments, presumably from memory. He then consults exemplary and notable narratives of past events (*fazanyas passadas*), whether in the Semitic or Latin tradition. And he does this repeatedly in his attempts to understand the enigma of Antioco's riddle. Grieve suggests that this moment of intellectual curiosity and confusion reveals Apolonio's secular bookish acumen at the expense of his theological training and that even when surrounded by shelves of knowledge, Apolonio remains confused (162). Both Grieve and Alvar suggest that these works in Latin and Chaldean exclude Scripture. However, Latin was the language of the Church and its writings, not to mention the Vulgate; and Hebrew and Aramaic—possible referents for *caldeo*—were the original languages of the *Tanakh* (Hebrew Bible). Consequently, it is not only possible but probable that Apolonio's library contained Scripture, or at a minimum Christian theological texts in Latin. This does not, however, contradict Grieve's observation of Apolonio's inability to skillfully interpret texts or our assertion of his need to travel in pursuit of practical wisdom. He was confident, if not arrogant, in his intellect and learning, and now fails to comprehend the cause of his misfortune: "En cabo, otra cosa no*n* pudo entende*r*" (32a). In the end, the king who is supposedly *de letras profundado* and *bien dotrinado*, simply does not understand.

The fact that the author of the *Libro* begins the text with a riddle, I argue, serves to contextualize the event and text in the rhetorical vestments of the intellectual journey (discussed above), central in Iberian philosophical tradition, itself based on a larger Mediterranean tradition stretching back to Aristotle. Central to this journey, as we shall see, is the idea that the knowledge one seeks is found in the very path one travels. That is, knowledge is to be found not in places (i.e., ports as the beginning and end of maritime travel), but in and through the space of the intellectual journey: here, the sea and seafaring. But the sea Apolonio travels is the Mediterranean of the past: it is the Mediterranean of Homer and of Aristotle, of Greek and Eastern philosophy, dotted by ancient place-names—Tyre and Antioch, Tarsus and Mytilenem (Lesbos)—relevant to thirteenth-century Iberia as a space of a shared historical memory. As such, Apolonio's journey is the legacy of a larger Mediterranean tradition of travel but articulated on the Peninsula through the Andalusi and Judeo-Iberian tradition of travel and learning. And these are distilled from Greek (Neo-platonic) notions about the pursuit of knowledge; in particular, the Arabo-Islamic concept of *al-riḥla fī ṭalab al-ʿilm*.

When Apolonio sets sail toward Antioch, he does so to solve riddles, and to begin to work his way out of confusion. Though Apolonio clearly fails at this endeavor, such engagement is a crucial step in the process of his self-awareness. For many of the foremost Iberian intellectuals of the Middle Ages (whether Christian, Muslim, or Jew), the philosophical quest was not on an inevitable collision course with religion; rather, the enlightened individual was required to reconcile the paths of reason and revelation, to find the space where Scripture and philosophy converge. As such, medieval Iberian philosophy—in which the *Libro de Apolonio* participates—asserted that the truest intellectual quest was not an abandonment of secular knowledge for holy knowledge, but an understanding that the two are inseparable.

Medieval Iberian philosophers conceived of this intellectual space as a state of confusion akin to the Greek *aporia*. Aristotle defines this as a philosophical puzzle, while Plato views it as a cognate for mental confusion, where the mental state of perplexity is necessary for man to begin the path to knowledge, for it "divests the interlocutor of the presence of knowledge in a particular area and [brings] him to a recognition of his ignorance" (Politis 88). However, it would have been best known to contemporary Iberians, and perhaps the author of the *Libro*, through the philosophical notions found in Maimonides' *The Guide for the Perplexed* and Ibn Rushd's *Incoherence of the Incoherence*. It is precisely these authors (Christian, Muslim, and Jew) and their ideas that would have been circulating in thirteenth-century Iberian and informed the culture environment in which the author of the *Libro* composed his verse—and perhaps shed some light on the texts found in Apolonio's library, *caldeas y latines*.

Returning to the text of the *Libro*, and the king's failed attempt at solving Antioco's riddle, Matt Desing sees in this scene Apolonio's negative association with texts, which he is unable to use skillfully, "Despite the aid of his texts, . . . he is unable to put positive action behind his correct answer to Antocio's riddle" (9). Desing's use of the term "action" is instructive; though Apolonio's intellectual understanding of the riddle is technically correct, Apolonio lacks the practical wisdom to adequately interpret the situation and act accordingly. His failure to put knowledge into action can be taken quite literally. As I mentioned previously, Apolonio's inability to interpret well is linked to his inexperience as a traveler. Put positively, action (travel) leads to knowledge and understanding—and correct interpretation.

While hiding from his own people, Apolonio realizes that even his native Tyre cannot provide him the intellectual comfort and refuge he has long enjoyed. Tyre as a synecdoche for a house of learning and the knowledge stored in books is now rejected by the king. The methods of learning fostered and promoted in this space have failed him. And his decision to abscond entirely from his native land may be seen as a rejection of the learning that heretofore had fashioned his understanding of self. In deciding to leave, the king weighs his options, pondering whether to literally get lost (*perderse*) or take this opportunity to seek adventure and change his luck: "mas q*ue*ría yr p*er*dersse ó la uent*u*ra mudra . . . metióse en auent*u*ras por las ondas del mar" (34b, d) (but he wanted to lose himself or seek adventure . . . he undertook adventures amidst the waves of the sea). By wanting to lose himself, Apolonio reveals his desire for self-imposed exile; shame and fear have forced him to flee his homeland. On the other hand, travel, and particularly seafaring, could provide him an opportunity for adventure and the possibility of redemption. Inaction has failed him; perhaps action can save him.

The space of departure, as prologue to Apolonio's seafaring adventures, is perhaps best contextualized in terms of his relationship with the citizens of his native Tyre. The expressed criticism of Apolonio by his own people is that he lacked intelligence and skill, and was diminished in some capacity as a ruler *because* he had not traveled. By way of open criticism, they invite Apolonio to the voyage for the purpose of gaining that which he lacked: practical knowledge and wisdom. "Biuía en reyno viçioso y onrrado, / non sabía d*e* cuyta, biuiya bien folgado, / teníame por torpe y por menoscabado / porq*ue* por muchas tierras no*n* auía andado" (125a-d) (I lived in a kingdom of honor and plenty, / I knew not trouble, lived in great peace, / they took me for simple and diminished / because I had not yet journeyed to many lands). As such, Apolonio's fear of being thought of as simple or stupid (*bauieca*) in the courts of Antioch comes into sharper focus now not only as a prideful act of intellectual vanity but perhaps as a response to his countrymen's implied desire for him to travel in the pursuit of knowledge.

Apolonio may have found subsequent justifications for his travels in love, fear, and humiliation, but it becomes readily apparent through his sorrow on the shores of shipwreck that the king ventured out onto the seas in order to do the very thing his subjects asked him to do: visit *muchas tierras*, and in doing so, gain the knowledge, wisdom, and experience they thought he lacked. This criticism of Apolonio reveals a specific cultural understanding of the concept, and benefits, of travel. And in this manner, the text suggests a causal connection between the voyage and understanding. We are before a familiar trope: the intellectual journey, in which the desire for knowledge motivates men to travel to distant lands, different peoples, and distinct cultures. The text suggests that one's homeland becomes an insufficient source of knowledge, and wisdom is attainable only by crossing the seas. But what does the Mediterranean space of this intellectual journey look like? And what wisdom is Apolonio to gain from it?

The Space of the Sea

Indicative of Maimonidean intellectual concerns over correct interpretation, the initial riddle scene suggested Apolonio lacked the practical intelligence and experiential knowledge to adequately interpret his surroundings; he was in a state of perplexity. And it is for this reason that Apolonio was motivated to travel. But as he moves from the safety of the shore into the perilous depths of the sea, I argue that Apolonio enters a larger *space* of complexity. In the Neoplatonic sense of engaging ambiguity in the material realm, the sea is presented as a space of confusion and contradiction, marked by joy and suffering, life and death. The windswept waves hold within their grasp both the terror and promise of the examined life, where travel on the tempestuous sea first divests the traveler (Apolonio) of all intellectual pretenses in order that through a process of self-discovery he might find the knowledge and understanding he seeks.[10] Thus, the various episodes which narrate the adventures and misadventures of Apolonio's maritime exploits reveal the sea to be a space of perplexity as well as a path to understanding. And it is a necessary path, for Apolonio's intellectual journey from ignorance to understanding is made possible only by way of the voyage. And as we have suggested, with the knowledge one gains from the voyage, Apolonio stands not only to overcome his intellectual anxieties and thus gain greater understanding, but to reclaim his honor, reunite with his family, and return triumphant to his native Tyre. Let us now turn to the space of Apolonio's travels and his intellectual journey. Though there are numerous episodes that take place at sea, I will narrow our focus to two voyages in particular that shed light on the nature and complexities of this space.

The first voyage concerns Apolonio's flight from Tarsus to Pentápolin, taken in response to a violent decree sent by King Antioco.[11] The trip to Pentápolin begins with straight and steady winds and the sailors who steer the ship are "bue*n*os marineros q*ue* sabién ‹bien› la marina" (103c) (good sailors who know the ways of the sea). For these initial moments of the journey all is calm and seemingly under the control, but the seasoned sailors, the texts tells us, "conosçen los vientos q*ue* se camian aýna" (103d) (they know well these winds are prone to sudden change).

The scene that follows provides the first of many descriptions of what we may call the sea turn. That is, from calm seas to violent gales—"Avién vientos derechos, façiénles bien correr" (106b) (With steady winds, they traveled swiftly)—the reader and rider experience abrupt and menacing fluctuations in the ocean's temperament: mimicking, and influenced by, the similarly capricious nature of the wind, the sea "cámiase p*ri*uado" (107b) (quickly changed). Importantly, the sea not only changes quickly, it angers easily: "ensányase rafez" (107b) (easily angered). In a moment's notice, the wrath of the sea is provoked and steady winds become violent tempests presaging nothing but the sailor's destruction and death in the darkness of the sea's depths. With the wind's swift transformation, the sea is troubled and tossed into a fury; the sea has turned. "Boluiéro*n*se los vientos, el mar fue conturbado; / nadauan las arenas, [a]l çiello leuantando; / non auié hí marin*ero* q*ue* non fuese cont*ur*bado" (108b-d) (The winds were turned, / the sea was confounded; / sand was stirred, / lifted to the heavens; / not a sailor was left untroubled).[12] The violent tempest stirs and lifts the sands of the sea floor, whipping them around the ship, mucking the waters (109a). The powerful torrent of rain and wind reaches into the depths and thus the storm completely surrounds them from all directions, not only from all sides, but from above and below. The storm is sudden, it rises, and men are confounded.

This description of the maritime space is similar to scenes found in contemporary eleventh-thirteenth-century Iberian works, such as Alfonso X's *Cantigas de Santa María* (*CSM*) and the verse of the Jewish poet scholar Judah Ha-Levi. In *CSM* 33 we read, "Hûa nv'ya per mar" (15) (A ship journeyed by sea), when suddenly, "tormenta levanter / se foi" (17) (a storm arose). In *CSM* 112, the battered ship is surrounded by a turbulent and murky sea, "d'agua volta con arena" (32) (water stirred with sand). And in *CSM* 267, the physical and psychological state of a storm-battered sailor emulates the sea: "coitado" (63) (distressed) and "atormentado" (73) (storm-battered). In Ha-Levi's poem *Halev beyam* (Heart at Sea), we read that both man and ship are helpless before the might of the sea in tempest. Stout men, like strong cedar, are overwhelmed, and the tricks of the trade prove useless in the hands of even the most experienced sailor: "The mast's might is useless, / the veteran's wiles as well" (Cole 165–67).

Similarly, and perhaps expectedly, the mariners on Apolonio's ship are frightened and distressed by their sudden change of fortune and the imminent prospect of wreck. In the confusion of tempestuous swells and violent winds, the sea asserts its influence on the sailors not only in physical terms, but psychologically as well. The ship and men not only flounder on, and in, the sea, but they are emotionally anguished and troubled (*conturbados*). It is compelling that prior to this moment in the text, the term *conturbado* is used only to describe the volatile temperament of the sea. And as it is here ascribed to the sailors, the reader thus perceives that the sea has overwhelmed them. And as a consequence the sailors have lost all control, of both self and sails.

> los q*ue* era maestros non podién goue*r*nar;
> alçáuanse las naues, q*ue*ríense trastornar
> tanto q*ue* ellos mismos non se sabién conseiar.
>
> Cuytóles la tempesta y el mal temporal:
> perdiero*n* el conseio y el gouierno capdal;
> los árboles de medio todos fueron a mal. (109b-d)

(Those who were masters were unable to govern; / the ships lifted trying to break / such that even they were unable to steer. / The storm and wicked winds troubled them: / they lost the rudder and their way; / the center masts all came crashing down.)

Then, as somewhat of a recapitulation of the event, we read:

Quando en la mar entramos, fazié tiempo pagado;
luego q*ue* fuemos d*e*ntro, el mar fue conturbado.
Qua*n*to nu*n*ca traýa allá lo he dexado;
tal pobre qual tú veyes, abez só escapado. (129a-d)

(When we first set out upon the sea, all was well; / then once we were within it, the sea was disturbed. / What I brought with me, there I have left it; / as deprived as you see me now, barely have I escaped.)

For Monedero, the concept of losing *conseio* 'counsel/way' and *gouierno* 'physical or mental control' signifies a loss of direction and steering: "perdieron el rumbo" (Monedero 130) (They lost their way). And as the ship still rises and falls with the menacing waves, the poet describes the sea as not only threatening the sailors, but wanting or trying (*quererse*) to capsize the ship. Unable to withstand the violence of the thrashing winds and waves, the center-mast fails, crashing into the deck. Indeed, not long after, the ship is torn to pieces and none survive but the king. And through the ambivalent use of pagan and Christian imagery, it is Apolonio's good fortune that God desired to save him from the sea. The sole survivor of this terrible tempest, the king clutches to a small piece of wood; alone he washes up on the shores of Pentápolin.

Following this violent landfall, and as a survivor of shipwreck, Apolonio narrates for the reader his own account of the voyage through a sorrow-filled inner monologue. His perspective reiterates familiar images of disaster, but adds to them a fairly straight forward critique of the maritime space: "Nunq‹*u*›*a* deuía om*ne* en las mares fiar, / traen lealtat poca, saben mal solazar" (120ab) (Never should man put his trust in the seas, / they have little loyalty and knowingly deceive). That is, one should never trust the sea(s), for it is disloyal and plays a sinister game of deception. Is this a philosophical game, a riddle, *aporia*?

The second voyage of our investigation concerns the king's journey from Pentápolin to Tarsus upon the death of his rival King Antioco. With wife and unborn child in tow, Apolonio and his men steer their vessel out into favorable winds and manageable waves that lay flat and calm over the deep. Yet this serene setting proves to be nothing more than the "buena cara" (good side) of the deceitful sea, here presented as a pair of siblings, joy and suffering: "q*ue* del gozo, cuyta es su ermana" (265d) (trouble is the sister of joy). The reader now awaits the appearance of joy's malevolent counterpart. Indeed, not long after, Fortune is ambushed, the poet tells us, as the sea's wrath is unleashed on the unsuspecting travelers: "tóuoles la vent*ur*a hu*n*a mala çellada" (266a,c) (upon them Fortune played a wicked trick). And in the midst of crashing waves and violent winds—perhaps as a consequence of it—Apolonio's wife Luciana begins to suffer the pangs of labor. Another duplicitous scene unfolds. Though Apolonio expresses great joy at the birth of his daughter, he is forced to endure the pain of the perceived death of his wife. Due to labor complications, Luciana is believed dead, and in order to protect those on board from her decaying body, she is tossed into the sea. There is no shipwreck, but the reader is not denied a tragedy. The description of this voyage powerfully depicts the personal experience of disaster at sea; in the midst of the sea's wrath we are privy not only to calamity, but the human response to misfortune. This is what makes the *Libro* fundamentally different from contemporary Crusade chronicles. As Goitein demonstrates in *A Mediterranean Society*, this maritime space was not used solely as a path of destruction for crusading armies or political tyrants. In his discussion of the written record of families, traditions, and institutions, the Mediterranean space is revealed as a multicultural community and a vibrant marketplace inhabited by real people, who lived, loved, and died around and in the Mediterranean Sea. As such, Apolonio's second voyage provides the reader with a more intimate portrayal of the individual lives that enter and cross the maritime space.[13]

Moreover, in comparison to the Muslim and Jewish intellectual travelers and traditions mentioned throughout this essay, depictions of medieval Christian itinerant intellectuals are limited, or rather undermined by chronicles of the Crusades and their violent accounts of colonization and empire. We see this in the anonymous *Gesta francorum*, Albert of Aachen's *Historia Hierosolymitana* or the *Liber* of Raymond of Aguilers in which we encounter countless stories of plunder and pillage. Even the staunchest apologists of the Crusades, such as Guibert of Nogent, who in his *Gesta Dei per Francos* depicts crusaders as divinely inspired idealists eschewing material wealth and embracing only pure spiritual transformation, is in the end forced to describe how sanctioned political land-grabbing and violent informal acquisitions in the form of plunder and looting not only decimated the landscape on the path of "pilgrimage" but transformed the Crusades (however idealist or purely intentioned) into a zealous religio-political and economic movement of avarice, and a violent conflict of civilizations and ideologies (Riley-Smith).

In contrast, Apolonio's imagined voyage depicts not a space of violence, but the intellectual path. And though this intellectual process is intimately connected to the notion of pilgrimage—he is repeatedly referred to, or refers to himself, as *peregrino, romero,* or *palmero*—Apolonio's path of pilgrimage is presented as an alternative to the narrative of crusade. For example, none of the ports or hinterlands that Apolonio visits is a destination on the march of war, as Jerusalem so clearly is in the crusader narrative. In fact, there is no specific geographic destination for Apolonio's travels; rather, in the *Libro*, the journey is the destination. And whereas the chronicles of Crusade generally depict what we might call a movement of collective pilgrimage (e.g., *Gesta dei per Francos*), the travels of Apolonio are clearly depicted as an individual pilgrimage and personal philosophical journey, taken so that he might become a better and more suitable ruler and king. Moreover, the crusader narrative from the very beginning is concerned with confronting the other (e.g., *Gesta francorum Jerusalem Expugnantium*), while Apolonio's journey is about confronting the intellect; it is a nonviolent conquest of the philosophical self. But, in the broader Mediterranean context we have thus far been describing, this inward pilgrimage requires that Apolonio travel beyond the intellectual boundaries of his homeland, into the space of the sea, particularly because doing so is dangerous and unpredictable.

What are we to make of these maritime journeys? In the various scenes that narrate the maritime adventures and misadventures of Apolonio, the sea is depicted as troubled and violent (*conturbado*) and frequented by perilous storms (*mal temporal*), revealing the capriciousness and unpredictability of the sea (*cámiase priuado*). More importantly, however, the episodes that narrate the mariners' interaction and response to the unpredictable nature of this maritime space further define the sea space as one of perplexity and incoherence, of violence and vulnerability. The space of the sea, then, serves as a constant reminder that Apolonio is not in control. It has brought him to a space of confusion, but perhaps also self-awareness. Much more than simply a medium by which the poet moves the plot, as some scholars have suggested, the maritime space, and its storms in particular, serves as an important component of the pursuit of knowledge.[14] The perilous storms and treacherous winds of the sea are, and create, an intellectual space in which the wandering and probing philosopher king (Apolonio) travels toward self-knowledge and ultimately understanding.

After Apolonio finishes his woeful tale of loss and suffering on the shores of Pentápolin, a Tarsian fisherman describes this space more clearly—as means and end.

> El estado deste mundo siempre así andido,
> cada día sse camia, nu*n*ca q*ue*do estido;
> en toll*er* y en dar es todo su sentido,
> vestir al despoiado y despoiar al vestido.
>
> Los que las auent*ur*as quisieron ensayar,
> a las vezes p*er*der, a las vezes ganar,
> por muchas d*e* man*er*as ouieron d*e* pasar;
> queq*ui*er q*ue* les abenga anlo d*e* endurar. (134a-135d)
>
> (This has always been the way of the world, / every day it changes, never staying the same; / all it knows is give and take, / clothing the dispossessed and dispossessing the clothed. / And to those who wish to try their luck, / sometimes you lose, sometime you win, / and such will happen in many a way; / but whatever happens, you must endure.)

Like the sea upon which Apolonio has just traveled, the fisherman describes the unpredictability of this world. It gives and takes away, and it has always been that way. But if one wants to know fortune (*auenturas*), he must first experience misfortune (*majaduras*); if one desires wisdom, he must first set out to sea. "Nunq‹*u*›*a* sabrién los om*n*es qué era*n* auent*ur*as / si no [prouassen] p*ér*didas ho muchas majaduras; / quando an pasado por muelles y por duras, / después sse torna*n* maestros y cren las escripturas" (136a-d) (Men will never know what adventure is / if they do not experience both loss and misfortune; / but when they have seen both joy and sorrow, then they become masters and believe the scriptures). Monedero suggests that "por muelles y por duras" can be read as analogous to the phrase *por duras y maduras* (137) (through thick and thin). Importantly however, to describe that which is beneficial, the fisherman uses the nautical term *muelle*: pier, jetty, or quay. It is inviting to conclude that for a man to gain wisdom, he must not only experience the safety of the harbor, but venture out into the sea and suffer the inevitable travails of maritime travel. Here sea travel is necessary for the acquisition of an experiential knowledge that not only serves as a *regimen principium,* but ultimately as a path to theological wisdom: "*después* sse torna*n* maestros y cren las escripturas" (136d, emphasis mine) (*then* they become masters and believe the scriptures).

Grieve writes concerning this passage, "Mastery, then, becoming 'maes-tros,' comes not from the accumulation of learning from books, but from life experience and an awareness of the deeper meaning of the Scriptures" (152).[15] However, as explored above, it is only in the midst of the voyage that one experiences the great joys and intense sorrows of life; and only *after* gaining the knowledge that comes from traveling (experiential inquiry) does one gain understanding, and thus believe (*cren*) the Scriptures. Consequently, what is of primary import is not Apolonio's lack of scriptural knowledge (though certainly a relevant concern), but his inexperience as a traveler. This has fascinating consequences. The sea not only becomes a synecdoche for the path to wisdom, and perhaps salvation, but echoing Desing, travel (seafaring) becomes a metaphor for interpretation; the sea is a cipher—of riddles, texts, and even Scripture. Apolonio, then, does not err in the initial riddle scene simply because he favors secular knowledge over scriptural wisdom, as Grieve suggests. Rather, Apolonio was unable to successfully navigate the treachery of the riddle because he had yet to navigate the treachery of sea, and thus lacked the necessary interpretive acumen one gains therein. In the end it was a riddle only his travels could solve.

Indicative of Ibn Ṭufayl, Ibn Rushd and Maimonides' notion of renouncing the vanities of this world, in the midst of Apolonio's adventures and misadventures, all intellectual pretenses are stripped away—like the clothes of a castaway on the shores of shipwreck.[16] Stormy seas and ruin reveal his weakness and ignorance, and ultimately take his identity. After washing up onto the shores of Pentápolin, Apolonio has lost everything at sea: "p*er*dió qua*n*to traýa" (156c) (he lost all he had). Responding to those who inquire even of his name, he can only respond that this too is lost: "el nombr*e* que hauía, p*er*dílo en la mar" (172c) (the name he had, he lost at sea). Not all is lost, however. Apolonio remembers where he is from, and instructs his inquirers to ask for him there: "el mío linage, en Tiro te lo sabrién contar" (172c) (of my lineage, in Tyre they will know what to tell you). Later, when he is described in a letter, it is remarked that only his body was salvaged from the wreck: "con el cuerpo solo estorçió de la mar" (223d) (with his body alone he escaped from the sea). And when he returns to Pentápolin after his brief exiles, the people hardly recognize him: "abés te con*n*oscemos" (333b) (we barely recognize you). Coupled with the lack of physical and mental control emblematized throughout the scenes of seafaring, again, the space of the sea serves to remind the reader of Apolonio's lack of control—that he is in a state of confusion and incoherence, but also self-awareness. It is precisely when Apolonio is in the process of being stripped of his physical comforts and intellectual vanities that the reader begins to witness the progress of the intellectual journey. And though Apolonio weeps and laments this state, it becomes a necessary place from which to begin the pursuit of knowledge. For Apolonio and the people of Tyre, though tragic and painful, this is perhaps the desire and purpose of the invitation to the voyage.

In the end, the lessons of the tempestuous sea, the words of a wise fisherman, and the advice of his loving people appear to have led him out of the darkness of ignorance and into the light of self-knowledge in the pursuit of wisdom. Standing on the shores of his native Tyre, reunited with his wife and child, Apolonio has returned from his intellectual journey: "El curso deste mu*n*do . . . lo as p*ro*uado" (339a) (The way of this world . . . you have experienced). And to the very people who thought him lacking and ignorant, and who encouraged him to set sail onto the perilous space of the sea, Apolonio is now able to proclaim: "buena fue la tempesta, d*e* Dios fue p*ro*metida, / por onde nós ouiemos a fer esta venida!" (547c, d) (blessed was the storm, by God it was promised, / for through it we may celebrate this arrival). It is only after such a realization that the king's words ring truest: "sano es Apolonyo" (546b) (restored is Apolonio).

Conclusions

The *Libro de Apolonio* reveals that Iberian Christian scholars and intellectuals conceived of an alternative model of Mediterranean travel based on Iberian philosophical notions of the voyage as an intellectual journey. And the tale of King Apolonio forms only part of a larger web of representation. Together with the anonymous *Libro de Alexandre* and the Alfonsine compiled *Calila e Dimna*, Ibn Ṭufayl's *Ḥayy ibn Yaqẓan*, and the philosophical works of Ibn Rushd and Maimonides, the *Libro de Apolonio* becomes part of a medieval Iberian and broader Mediterranean intellectual tradition (that includes the likes of Ibn Battuta and Ibn Tudela, not to mention earlier models found in Herodotus and Saint Augustine). Consequently, medieval Iberian Christians were also "firmly tied to a world in which intellectuality and adventure were closely linked," as Touati contends of medieval Muslim and Jewish men of letters (42). In fact, the idea that "one cannot truly inhabit knowledge without shipping off on a trip" seems to be a collective principle, upheld and defended in the geographically broader and culturally more diverse Mediterranean of the thirteenth century, of which Iberia not only formed the westernmost boundary, but played a central role (2). As such, the idea of the eastern Mediterranean as a space of religio-political violence and conquest is repurposed. In view of the failed efforts and ethics of Crusading, an analysis of the sea voyage and its corresponding motivations to travel in the *Libro de Apolonio* reimagines the sea and that same Mediterranean space as the representative and necessary path of the intellectual journey. No longer defined solely by the efforts of violent imperialism, the sea becomes a space where one seeks knowledge. This is not a rewriting of history, e.g., Christian failures as victories; rather, the text provides a literary framework and filter through which the confusion of imagery and symbols can be both read and understood. As with a legend on a map the reader is equipped to more skillfully interpret the space before him. In the waning years of repeated calls to crusade, the *Libro de Apolonio* offers an alternative: an invitation to the voyage and an intellectual journey. Thus, the sea is, or can be, a space of learning, perhaps shared learning, where travel leads not to conflict, but to knowledge, wisdom, and perhaps salvation.

Notes

1. The *Libro*'s primary sources are the *Historia Apollonii Regis Tyri*, the *Gesta Apollonii Regis Tyri metrica*, the *Phanteon* of Godofredo de Viterbo, the *Gesta Romanorum*, and the *Carmina Burana*. See Monedero 15–25 and Corbella 17–26.
2. G.A.A. Kortekaas contends that the earliest extant Latin manuscripts of the Apolonio tradition are translations of a lost Greek Christianized version, which in turn is a later recension of an "original" pagan Greek text. Hard evidence for this supposed pagan Greek original, however, is scanty at best.
3. Peter Thorau writes of the Frankish crusading contingent that they were "politically irresponsible" and were thus "torn apart by internecine struggle," exhausting themselves in the pursuit of policies which revealed "a serious lack of consistent thought" (150).
4. Admittedly, this is a topic of some debate. For two distinct views on the subject, see Jonathan Riley-Smith, *The Crusades: A History*, and H.E. Mayer, *The Crusades*.
5. See, for example, *The Great History* by Muhammad al-Bukhari and *al-Jarḥ wa al-Ta'dīl* by Ibn Abī Hātim.
6. On the economic factor among European crusaders, see Lopez and Raymond, *Medieval Trade in the Mediterranean World*, "Growth of Merchant Class," doc. 31.
7. This interest in historiography, geography, and ethnology shows how both Jews and Muslims were modeling themselves on Herodotus and, in general, Greek and Latin sources of Antiquity. In the *Kitāb al-Fihrist* (*The Book of the Index*), Ibn al-Nadīm suggests that the works of Plutarch, Plato, and Plotinus, as well as Homer and Herodotus, among others, were well known and even quoted in Arabic writings of the tenth century. See El Daly, *Egyptology* (26, 62); Pines, "An Arabic version of the *Testamonium Flavianum* and its Implications"; and Dodge, *The Fihrist of al-Nadim*.

8. Medieval Iberian intellectuals' familiarity with Ancient Greek philosophy is undisputed. Beginning with the Graeco-Arabic translation movement in eighth-tenth-century Baghdad known as the *Bayt Ul-Hikma* (House of Wisdom), and continued with vernacular translations of Greek and Arabic knowledge in the thirteenth-century courts of Alfonso X, medieval Mediterranean scholars and theologians had unprecedented access to the wisdom of Greek Antiquity. Steven Wasserstrom, in *Between Muslim and Jew*, reminds us that "S.D. Goitein characterized the relationship of Jews with Muslims in the first centuries of Islam as one of 'creative symbiosis'" (3). See Gutas, *Greek Thought, Arabic Culture* and Lyons, *The House of Wisdom: How the Arabs Transformed Western Civilization*.
9. Though my conclusions ultimately lie with Grieve and Alvar, it is unclear why the terms *caldeas* and *latines* should necessarily exclude Scripture. Moreover, *caldeo* is not a fixed linguistic referent in medieval Iberian literature; in works such as the *Caballero de Zifar* it is used to refer to Arabic (Walker 31–32). That there might also be Arabic philosophical or religious texts in Apolonio's library only serves to underscore Iberia's active participation in a much broader intellectual Mediterranean space.
10. The reader will remember Aristotle's contention that "[t]hose who search without first engaging with *aporiai* are like people who don't know where they need to be going; moreover, they do not even know whether or not they have found what they are searching for. For the end [of a search] is not clear to such a person, but it is clear to the person who has first considered the *aporiai*" (Politis 90). Concerning the "unexamined life," see Plato's *Apology*, 38a.
11. "Del rey Antioco eres desafiado, / nin en çiudat ni en burgo no*n* *ser*ás albergado: / quie*n* matarte pudiere *ser*á bien soldado. / Si estorçer pudieres, *ser*ás bien auenturado" (70a-d) (King Antioco has declared you his enemy, / neither city nor village will your refuge be: / a man of fortune you are if you can be saved, / for he who kills you will be well paid). It is worth noting that King Apolonio's journey to Tarso from Tyre was not a particularly safe or pleasant one. We are not given great detail, but after arriving at port, the poet tells us: "Quando llegó, como llazdrado era, / fizo echar las áncoras luego p*or* la ribera. / Vio logar adabte, sabrosa [co]stanera / por folgar del lazerio y de la mala carrera" (63a-d) (Being in such a poor state, upon his arrival, / he called for the anchors to be released along the coast. / He then saw a suitable place and a welcoming shore / upon which to heal from his suffering and the trying journey). No further information is given regarding what in particular made this a *mala carrera*, a difficult journey.
12. Given the description of the disturbed sand (*nadauan las arenas*) presumably from the sea floor combining with the wind and waves and being lifted to the heavens, it appears the ship is still within sight of land when said danger appears. We are told also that the ship had only sailed about two hours from land when the winds suddenly changed. Can such trouble and danger befall a ship that remains so close to the shore? In *A Mediterranean Society*, S.D. Goitein remarks that when a ship had

"passed out of sight," that is, it was referred to as the "crossing" or *ta'diya*. The term is used to describe the event when a ship crossed from coastal waters out into the high seas and out of sight (Goitein 319). Interestingly, Goitein notes that such phrases are reported with a sense of relief, not concern. Thus it seems that coastal waters could be just as dangerous as the open seas.

13. A further example of perilous seas and the sailors' inability to deal with it is found in Apolonio's journey from Tarsus to Tyre (455a–456b).
14. Simone Pinet writes that the shipwreck event in the Byzantine romance (e.g., *Libro de Apolonio*), "is quite literally a pretext, the goal being the deliverance of the protagonists to this or that shore" (389). It is not the main event of later texts, she contends.
15. Monedero suggests the word *escripturas*, "puede valer tanto para la Biblia, atendiendo a 137a,b, en que parece aludir a Dios, como para los libros de aventuras, en donde son las hadas benéficas las que protegen, 137c,d" (137).
16. Hans Blumenberg writes that "Shipwreck, as seen by a survivor, is the figure of an initial philosophical experience" (106). In one sense, it is a type of conversion. As an example he cites Vitruvius, who reports that the Socratic philosopher Aristippus, after being shipwrecked on the island of Rhodes, went from being a lover of money and pleasure to a believer in the idea that "one ought to provide one's children with only such possessions as could be saved from a shipwreck (*quae e naufragio una possent enatare*)" (106). See *Ad adolescents*, 4. He mentions also Basil the Great, Bishop of Cappadocia in the fourth century, who reduced what one could salvage from shipwreck to virtue: "Homer calls on us in the same way: You must be concerned with virtue, which even swims out with the shipwrecked man, and lends him an appearance that commands respect, even if he comes onto the shore naked." (106). See also *Patrologia Graeca*, 31.572. In her study of shipwreck and perspective, Simone Pinet adds to this the concepts of self-awareness. For the subject who looks [back] upon shipwreck from the safety of the shore, "Philosophy is not a taking of a position, but an awareness of where one stands or gazes from" (393).

Works Cited

Alfonso X, King of Castile and León. *Lapidario: según el manuscrito escurialense H.I.15.* Ed. Sagario Rodríguez M. Montalvo. Madrid: Gredos, 1981.

Alvar, Manuel. "Apolonio, clérigo entendido." *Symposium in honorem prof. M. de Riquer.* Barcelona: Universitat de Barcelona, 1984.

Brownlee, Marina Scordilis. "Writing and Scripture in the *Libro de Apolonio*: The Conflation of Hagiography and Romance." *Hispanic Review* 51.2 (1983): 159–74.

Blumenberg, Hans. *Shipwreck with Spectator.* Trans. Steven Rendall. Cambridge: MIT Press, 1997.

Clark, Doris. "Tarsiana's Riddles in the *Libro de Apolonio*." *Medieval Hispanic Studies Presented to Rita Hamilton*. Ed. A.D. Deyermond. London: Tamesis, 1975. 31–43.

Cole, Peter. *The Dream of the Poem: Hebrew Poetry from Muslim and Christian Spain 950–1492*. Princeton: Princeton University Press, 2007.

Colville, Jim. *Two Andalusian Philosophers*. London: Kegan Paul International, 1999.

Desing, Matthew. "De pan y de tresoro: Sacrament in the *Libro de Apolonio*." *La Corónica* 40.2 (Spring 2012): 93–120.

———. "Luciana's Story: Text, Travel, and Interpretation in the *Libro de Apolonio*." *Hispanic Review* 79.1 (2011): 1–15.

Deyermond, Alan. "Emoción y ética en el *Libro de Apolonio*." *Vox Romanica: Annales Helvetici Explorandis Linguis Romanicis Destinati* 48 (1989): 153–64.

———. "Motivos folklóricos y técnica estructural en el Libro de Apolonio." *Filología* XIII (1968–69): 121–49.

Dunn, Ross E. *The Adventures of Ibn Battuta*. Berkeley: University of California Press, 2005.

El Daly, Okasha. *Egyptology: The Missing Millennium: Ancient Egypt in Medieval Arabic Writings*. London: UCL Press, 2005.

Encyclopaedia Judaica. Ed. Michael Berenbaum and Fred Skolnik. 2nd ed. Vol. 11. Detroit: Macmillan Reference USA, 2007. Web. 4 March 2013.

Encyclopedia of Religion. Ed. Lindsay Jones. 2nd ed. Vol. 11. Detroit: Macmillan Reference USA, 2005. Web. 4 March 2013.

Goitein, S.D. *A Mediterranean Society: the Jewish Communities of the Arab World as Portrayed in the Documents of the Cairo Geniza*. Vol. 1. Berkeley: University of California Press, 1967.

Goldberg, Harriet. "Women Riddlers in Hispanic Folklore and Literature." *Hispanic Review* 59.1(1991): 57–75.

Grieve, Patricia E. "Building Christian Narrative: The Rhetoric of Knowledge, Revelation, and Interpretation in *Libro de Apolonio*." *The Book and the Magic of Reading in the Middle Ages*. Ed. Albrecht Classen. New York: Garland Publishing, 1998. 149–69.

Gutas, Dimitri. *Greek Thought, Arabic Culture: The Graeco-Arabic Translation Movement in Baghdad and Early 'Abbasid Society (2nd-4th/8th-10th centuries)*. New York: Routledge, 1998.

"Hadith." *Encyclopaedia of Islam*, 2nd ed. Brill Online, 2013. Web. 4 March 2013.

Ibn Qutaybah. *Kitāb al-shi'r wa al-shu'arā'*. Ed. M.J. de Goeje. Lieden, 1904.

Ibn Rushd. *Averroes' Tahāfut al-Tahāfut: The Incoherence of the Incoherence*. Trans. Simon van den Bergh. London: Luzac, 1954.

Kelley, Mary Jay. "Mixed Messages in the *Libro de Apolonio*." *Journal of Interdisciplinary Literary Studies* 2 (1990): 1–11.

Kortekaas, G.A.A. *Commentary on the Historia Apollonii Regis Tyri*. Lieden: Koninklijke Brill, 2007.

Libro de Apolonio. Ed. Carmen Monedero. Madrid: Clásicos Castalia, 1987.

Libro de Apolonio. Ed. Dolores Corbella. Madrid: Cátedra, 1992.

Lopez, Robert S., and Irving Raymond. *Mediterranean Trade in the Mediterranean World*. 3rd ed. New York: Columbia University Press, 2001.

Lyons, Jonathan. *The House of Wisdom: How the Arabs Transformed Western Civilization*. New York: Bloomsbury Press, 2009.

Maimonides, Moses. *The Guide for the Perplexed*. Trans. M. Friedlander. New York: Cosimo, 2007.

Manuel, Juan. *El Conde Lucanor*. Ed. Sánchez Cantón. Madrid: Editorial Saturnino Calleja, 1920.

Mayer, H.E. *The Crusades*. Trans. John Gillingham. Oxford: Oxford University Press, 1988.

Menéndez Pidal, Ramón. *Poesía juglaresca y juglares: Aspectos de la historia literaria y cultural de España*. Madrid: Espasa-Calpe, 1962.

Netton, I.R. "Riḥla." *Encyclopaedia of Islam*. 2nd ed. Brill Online, 2012. Web. 5 March 2013.

Pickford, T.E. "Apollonius of Tyre as Greek Myth and Christian Mystery." *Neophilogus* 59 (1975): 599–609.

Pinet, Simone. "Where One Stands: Shipwreck, Perspective, and Chivalric Fiction." *eHumanista* 16 (2010): 381–94.

Politis, Vasilis. "*Aporia* and Searching in the Early Plato." *Remembering Socrates*. Ed. Lindsay Judson and Vassilis Karasmanis. Oxford: Clarendon Press, 2006.

Rico, Francisco. "La clerecía del mester." *Hispanic Review* 53.1 (Winter 1985): 1–23.

Riley-Smith, Jonathan. *The Crusades: A History*. 2nd Ed. New Haven: Yale University Press, 2005.

———. "The Motives of the Earliest Crusaders and the Settlement of Latin Palestine." *The English Historical Review* 98:389 (October 1983), 721–36.

Surtz, Ronald E. "El héroe intelectual en el mester de clerecía." *La Torre: Revista de la Universidad de Puerto Rico* 1.2 (April-June 1987): 265–74.

Thorau, Peter. *The Lion of Egypt: Sultan Baybars I and the Near East in the Thirteenth Century*. Trans. P.M. Holt. London: Longman, 1992.

Touati, Houari. *Islam and Travel in the Middle Ages*. Chicago: The University of Chicago Press, 2010.

Verdon, Jean. *Travel in the Middle Ages*. Notre Dame: University of Notre Dame Press, 2003.

Walker, Roger M. *Tradition and Technique in* El Libro Del Cavallero Zifar. London: Tamesis, 1974.

Wasserstrom, Steven. *Between Muslim and Jew: The Problem of Symbiosis Under Early Islam*. Princeton: Princeton University Press, 1995.

Weiss, Julian. *The* Mester de Clerecía*: Intellectuals and Ideologies in Thirteenth-Century Castile*. Woodbridge, UK: Tamesis, 2006.

◆ 5

Between the Seas: Apolonio and Alexander

Simone Pinet

> And just as sailors are guided in the darkness of the night by the magnetic needle which shares the qualities of both the stones and the stars, and shows them where to go, in bad, as well as in fine weather; so those whose duty it is to advise the king should always be guided by justice.
>
> —Alfonso X

At Sea

It must come as no small surprise to anthropologists or historians that literary scholars have only recently decided to embrace the Mediterranean as an analytical category. Not only has the term been debated and criticized for decades in those fields, it actually seems to have run its productive course and even has been declared dead after fading out into fuzzy definitions.[1] My own wariness with such a category within literary studies stems from divergent, not often explicitly so, and even contradictory conceptualizations of what is meant by "Mediterranean" in any given reflection in the vastly termed "literary" fields: a geography (with varying zones which at times include mainlands and hinterlands, at others just the coasts or the waters themselves), a cultural unity, a "zone of exchange," a babel of commercial tongues. It is the lens of trade as hallmark of these Mediterranean studies that I have been most exposed to as a Hispanomedievalist, as colleagues from different disciplines approach the term metaphorically and metageographically as a locus for the exchange and production of identities, the sharing and hybridization of forms and subjects, the interconnectivity of ideas.[2] These are recognizable keywords, and the utility these scholars argue they pose is desirable even if many of such topics have been addressed before under other headings: the possibility of interdisciplinarity; the breaking out of national boundaries; the freeing of cultures and peoples to move beyond frontiers seen as imposed on them by scholarship or by misguided nationalisms; or, as is sometimes personalized, the liberation from the influence of the short-sightedness of a few repressed and culturally racist conservatives.

I am disinclined to make uncritical use of a category that presents itself so frequently as (morally) superior when its main conceptual structure, that of economics, remains for the most part undefined and/or unquestioned in its pertinence or suitability for the literary fields. The argument that this is a lesser evil than other approaches does not make me an enthusiast either. The celebratory tone in which terms such as "exchange," "circulation," "production," "connectivity" move about without others, such as "exploitation," "subjection," "hegemony," and "politics" continues to trouble me as the analytical category of the Mediterranean in literature reaches field status on campuses, in a new Orientalism of sorts. For some, there seems to be a need for the classification of studies either on the side of the trade and ethics approach, or on the politics and microhistory one, and while I am unsure this is a real dichotomy we must face—and there is enough rigorous work being produced eschewing this straw man's choice—the fact that there is so much arm-twisting and shaming involved in choosing the first approach is reason enough to spell out how one understands and uses these terms in a particular study.

I should clarify, therefore, that I will use "Mediterranean" here for what I sense has become the dominant view, its "commonplace," that is, as a catchword for the trade model that is used for the interdisciplinary analysis in this (new) field, especially when dealing with the early modern period.[3] In this essay, "Mediterranean" will be the trope that signifies the economic, the exchange, the business of movement and trade. This presupposes a semantic shift from the geographic to a network of ideas centered on economics. Such an emptying out of the geographic element in the understanding of the Mediterranean does not go against the way in which the texts I study here think of the sea. The sea—unspecified and unlabeled—for the poets of the thirteenth century whom I will be reading here only vaguely retains a geographic notion, mostly linked to the East. The Greek regional sea, with its classical and biblical connotations—one not experienced but merely known as a reference—inhabits the maritime imaginary of these texts. This goes along, in a way, with the most currently held position on the Mediterranean as a field of study, for as Horden and Purcell remark in a recent article, "the definition of the Mediterranean as a region was not . . . a by-product or concomitant of ancient imperialism . . . Nor did it appear in medieval or early modern European thought" but was, indeed, conceived of as maritime for the longest of times and invented as a region only in the nineteenth-century, associating itself, for better or worse, with other imperialisms (728). As placeholder, Mediterranean will be set against a notion of a (smaller) archipelagic sea (from *arche-pelagos*, the Aegean), from where medieval notions, tropes, and metaphors about the sea come to structure Iberian texts and their maritime imaginary.

As counterbalance to this Mediterranean background, I want to posit an imaginary inherited from the classical world. The Hellenic world could be said to have had two spatial imaginaries, that of agriculture, and that of the sea, a mirroring evidenced by lexical parallels, such as plow and ship. These parallels receive interesting elaborations in the notion of government, originally a nautical term for the control of a ship, as seen in Pindar, which was imported onto land as part of the technical vocabulary of the *polis* (Marcotte 38).[4] This coincidence of vocabulary, this sharing of meaning is what I want to use as a framework to argue for competing and supplementary perspectives on the sea, where this political or cultural emphasis, which we might call "Greek," underlies any conception of the sea in the medieval mind. As a poetics of the sea, the articulation between instruments of politics and seafaring techniques as articulating a particular vision of culture is in tension or as palimpsest with the economic, "Mediterranean" perspective. I will explore these two "seas" as overlapping perceptions on how a focus on the sea as stage, trope, or metaphor, plays out in two canonical romances of thirteenth-century Spain.

The *Libro de Alexandre* and the *Libro de Apolonio* are roughly contemporary, the *Alexandre* being slightly earlier, composed in the first third of the thirteenth century in the Northern Christian kingdoms of Iberia, most probably in the Rioja region and related perhaps to the short-lived *studium generale* of Palencia and the circuit of courts and monasteries in the area. Both of these works are part of a genre, mode of composition, or group of works known as *mester de clerecía*, works of clerisy self-proclaimed as learned literature, emphasizing syllabic count, pronunciation, Latinate syntax, and especially linked to a general project of translation that is part of an enterprise both pedagogical and political as clerics circulate and gain visibility both in the monastery and the court.[5]

The protagonists of these two works are kings: Apolonio is a king belonging entirely to the world of literature; Alexander is a king of history, whose fame extends to myth, and whose myth was widely recorded in the verbal and visual arts of the Middle Ages. I want to emphasize them both as bookish figures translated as models of sovereignty for thirteenth-century Iberia, especially because in the medieval mind both kings were considered historical figures, their biographies compiled side by side in chronicles and historical accounts. This association reinforced a new model of royalty emphasizing *curialitas*—courtly behavior or politeness, and *sapientia*—learnedness, next to courage and liberality, put in place in the second half of the twelfth-century, as Adeline Rucquoi details.[6] Through romance, conceived as strategy (following Barbara Fuchs's definition), these two texts stage different views of kingship on the sea and its borders. Thus, we might anticipate the strategy of these works, the *Libro de Alexandre* and the *Libro de Apolonio*, as being that of romancing the seas, positioning themselves as strategies or itineraries—*derroteros*, in Spanish—in the narration of kingship.[7]

Coastlines

The biography of one of the Desert Fathers, Columban, written in the sixth century, illustrates the relation of similitude that enabled the relocation of the forest imaginary to the sea, as he tells us that the wandering monks "*desertum in pelago intransmeabili invenire obtantes*" (hoped to find the desert in the unsurmountable sea). Such a space had been greatly anticipated by the same traditions informing the forest of the romance.[8] Fear of the sea—drowning, shipwreck, but also storms, sea monsters, getting lost—was not only a reminder to use common sense, but a serious philosophical question.[9] One can even hypothesize that sea travel was only possible among the islands of the Cyclades in the Aegean because, at all times, at least one of them was in sight. In this sense, the sailor was never really engulfed—*empelagado*, or *engolfé*, as Spanish and French put it. In fact, throughout the sixteenth century ocean travel was still a feat, one that was only attempted when a profitable result was guaranteed to come of it (Braudel 46–47).

Travel, displacement, and movement across the seas certainly tie the Greek perspective to the Mediterranean one, across a continuum with only slight changes of emphasis. As Remo Bodei writes, sea travel in search of adventure, for example, might seem a modern invention, when it is not a cliché, but not even incessant travel is exclusive to modernity, as stories such as the Wandering Jew or the Flying Dutchman will remind any self-congratulating frequent-flyer (26). It is perhaps only the normalization of travel, its stabilization or lack of mystery, propelled by the absence of a destination, that we may leave for modernists to claim as their own. To travel by sea in the Middle Ages, whether to evangelize, to found a monastic enclave, to find riches or holiness, to fight or wage war, or to return home, is travel with a clear destination or goal, overcoming with this determination the real and philosophical dangers it might entail, and thus marking the sea as a privileged site for adventure. Thus travel by sea is quite common in medieval literature of all latitudes, in hagiography, as in the *Book of Margery Kempe*, the story of Constanza in Gower's *Confessio amantis*, in the miracles of *Nuestra Señora* or those of Santiago; in the poetry of *cantigas* and *romancero*; in epic and poetic fiction. Sea travel is a *navigatio vitae*, as Curtius traces through the Argonaut tale in the European Middle Ages.[10]

That the story of King Apolonio is placed ambiguously, floating about the waters, is not merely a generic condition—with purported echoes of Byzantine romance—that would restrict an interpretation of the element of water to a fictional convention.[11] Antiquity, the "historical" frame for this *Libro*, condemned sea travel based on the idea that the ocean is a given, natural frontier, a preexisting limit to human activity, thus a natural limit, but it also formulated the ocean as a juridical limit, since the sea is related to what has no law (Blumenberg 8). In this opposition to land, the sea emerges as the space for criticism of whatever is on land, that is, the sea is the reflection, the opposite of the continent. The sea boundary obviously frames prohibition and at the same time is an invitation for transgression, a breaking of a law signifying not properly a sin, but a will to excess, a lack of moderation or inappropriateness. This active trespassing of a frontier, the willful crossing of the shoreline illustrates a sort of "original sin," in Hans Blumenberg's words: "The idea that here, on the boundary between land and sea, what may not have been the *fall* but was certainly a mis*step* into the inappropriate and the immoderate was first taken, has the vividness that sustains lasting *topoi*" (9; emphasis in the original). Sea travel was thus characterized as a form of madness, foolishness, a recipe for failure, or, at best, an ordeal to be survived, undesirable, not something anyone would go through willingly or subject him- or herself to purposefully—except if lured by the promise of quick profit, of luxury to be had, of "the 'culture-critical' connection between two elements characterized by liquidity: water and money" (9).

It is, first of all, such limiting and, secondly, the excess or lack of moderation that breaking the limit implies in terms of risk or ordeal, that links sea travel in the books of *Apolonio* and *Alexandre* over and above any generic relations one might assume. How the limit is marked and how their travel is framed, however, and how the spaces that come to inhabit that limit are elaborated in the two poems, propose two models of kingship, an imperialist one and a commercial one, figured through two poetics of the sea with overlaps but with distinct positions that are not always compatible. While there is in both poems a persistence of the economic as frame or trope, both texts also link the economic to virtue and virtuosity in divergent directions. Finally, both are bound to the East, to an Oriental Mediterranean that is as geographic as it is textual and bookish, mirroring other texts in circulation at the time, such as the *Fazienda de Ultramar* or the *Semejança del mundo*.

Mixed Metaphors

For Horace, there are forbidden journeys by sea, a prohibition marked by the sea's throwing itself against the ship, protecting an original division that the journey attempts to erase. It is also Horace who introduces the idea of the "ship of state" in political rhetoric, with the ensuing Quintilian interpretation of the "tempest" as civil war. Horace will compare the transgression of the limit of the ocean with that of Prometheus, who stole fire; and with that of Daedalus, who violated the forbidden space of air (Blumenberg 11–12). Land is the only element appropriate to humanity. Thus, within this elemental framework, stepping out of the boundaries of humanity is what explicitly structures the Alexander legend, and implicitly characterizes Apolonio from the beginning of his story. Extreme danger, risk, and the promise of profit of some kind link both stories on the socioeconomic side of the trope. To propose that Alexander and Apolonio constitute models for princes as they control the ships of state is implicit in this blending of metaphors, but one should mention that the clerics who propose such an association would also consider their own role in that metaphor as that of pilot: Cicero, Aristotle, and Seneca proposed metaphors of state and philosophy related to navigation, so that philosophy as a pilot or helmsman for the navigation of life would be in tune with both Alexander's and Apolonio's clerical education, and with the model for royalty, advanced by Rodrigo Jiménez de Rada, which associated the role of king with that of master through the virtue of *sapientia*.[12]

Apolonio, as we know, is characterized early on as having been trained in letters—the text says he is *de letras profondado*, "steeped in books," for he has been trained in solving riddles, *por solver argumentos era bien doctrinado* (st. 22)—allowing him to solve the enigma of Antioco's incest. This early characterization prepares the contrast between his clerical knowledge and his lack of worldly experience as he is confounded by Antioco's refusal to accept his answer. Thus is set up the opposition that has characterized interpretations of this romance, between knowledge understood as theoretical, bookish knowledge and the experience understood as life adventures. The failure of this clerical knowledge, and the shame the protagonist feels, prompt Apolonio to set sail, taking up adventures at sea (st. 34). Uría underlines that the shame at the failure of clerical knowledge to bring about the marriage is something not present in the Latin source but added by the Castilian poet, an addition that Uría reads as the initial mark of conversion from pagan to Christian king that will be further elaborated from the shipwreck to the final verses of the story, in a process of conversion that structures the Iberian version of the story ("El *Libro de Apolonio,* contrapunto").[13] While the marks of hagiography are clear in the narration of Apolonio's life, it seems to me the poet would not want to characterize clerisy as failure. The failure—and ensuing humiliation, as I read it—is one of insufficiency, a clerical knowledge that must be supplemented with the experience of a life led virtuously, a virtue cast in economic terms.[14]

The first stanza announces a story of the good king Apolonio *and his courtesy*. This binary presentation highlights the role of courtesy, as *curialitas*, as a supplement to Apolonio's kingship that will be detailed in the story itself. Immediately in stanza 2, the logic of loss and recovery that structures the poem is introduced after using a general metaphor of "storm," *temporal*, to signify all of his troubles. The poet introduces the episode of Antioco, linking Apolonio to the plot in stanza 18:

El rey Apolonio, que en Tiro regnaua,
oyó daquesta duenya qu'en grant preçio andaua;
queria casar con ella, que mucho la amaua,
la hora del pedir veyer non la cuydaua.

(King Apollonius, who reigned in Tiro, / heard of this lady who was much coveted; / he wanted to marry her, for he much wanted her, / he couldn't wait to ask for her in marriage.)

The framing of Apolonio's initial embarkment is thus *cupiditas*, doubly understood as lust and as greed: it is implied he covets or wants (*amaua*) Antioco's daughter because of the triangular desire that has increased her value (*preçio*). Apolonio's setting sail for Antioch's court is here not narrated, for he is next seen solving the riddle hiding Antioco's incest. In stanza 23, *before* giving an answer to the king, the poet tells us that Apolonio understands the sin that the riddle hides and thus repents from having gone to Antioch, understanding that he has fallen into a trap. Even then, so as not to be taken for a fool, he provides the truthful answer, making Antioco's secret public. Antioco does not receive the answer well and demands, on threat of death, for Apolonio to find a different response to the riddle. Apolonio returns to Tiro and retires to his chambers to find a way out, detailing once again his clerical background in stanza 23, but he finds no alternative answer in his books that can get him out of the trap. The stanzas that follow are particularly interesting:

> En cabo, otra cosa non pudo entender
> que al rey Antioco pudiese responder;
> cerró sus argumentos, dexóse de leyer,
> *en laçerio sin fruto non quiso contender.*
> *Pero mucho tenìa que era mal fallido,*
> *en non ganar la duenya t ssallir tan escarnido;/*
> quanto más comidia qué l'auìa conteçido,
> tanto más se tenìa por peyor confondido.
> *Dixo que non podìa la vergüença durar,*
> *mas querìa yr perdersse o la uentura mudar;*
> de pan t de tresoro mandó mucho cargar,
> metiòse en auenturas por las ondas del mar. (st. 32–34; emphasis mine)

> (In the end, he could not find anything / to respond to king Antioco; / he closed his books, stopped reading, / *in suffering without fruit he did not want to insist. // However he felt he had been wronged, / not winning the lady t being so scorned* / the more he thought about what had happened to him, / the more he took himself to be destroyed. // *He said he could not withstand the shame, / but would rather get lost or change his fortune;* / much bread t treasure he ordered be loaded, / he went for adventures in the sea waves.)

Apolonio does not search for a second, *true*, new answer—for he knows the answer he gave Antioco was the right one—but for a way out of Antioco's trap. In this reading the only answer that clerical knowledge can provide is truth; no alternative for that is possible, and therefore his search in books proves fruitless. Apolonio himself deems such a search without results impractical, which one must read in terms of politics. The conclusion that the hard work of a bookish search is not worth it because no results will come of it, it will not solve the situation, anticipates the reflection in the next stanza on profit. For as the poet remarks with a *pero*, and this is crucial, Apolonio has not remained the same as he was when he left for Antioch: his setting sail to get himself a coveted wife as profit has left him wifeless and scorned. His journey not only did not bring in the reward he sought, but has discredited him. It is this loss that provokes shame and triggers his departure from his kingdom, which he feels he has failed, linking thus the risk and profit model to his sovereignty. This much is confirmed later on by the people of Tiro, who retell the events to the traitor Taliarco, sent by Antioco to kill Apolonio. Apolonio's failed journey and the ensuing shame and discredit frame a new kind of sea travel, taken up in secret, in which abandonment of the kingdom is both a self-exile (or a paradoxical search for homelessness) and an abandonment of power, a journey without a clear goal and thus much more dangerous.[15]

The story shifts back to Antioco, where the theme of *cupiditas* will be reasserted: Antioco's lust for his daughter will correspond to the greed he incites in men to kill or apprehend Apolonio, echoing Apolonio's own initial ambition. The duplicated vocabulary that is used here to express these nuances of *cupiditas* is telling of how much it structures the romance's moral dimension: *cobdiçia* and *adulterio*, literally, but also in general *pecado* and *error*, emphasizing their power to (re)produce more sin, to turn and transform men. Apolonio's journey, from here on, will sway between both poles of *cupiditas,* and his—and his family's—broaching of these situations are the core of the simultaneously moral and economic lessons in the romance. Using Uría's conversion model as a first level, we can supplement the moral dimension with an economic one, where to the structure of *largesse* or generosity that characterizes sovereignty in other texts one can oppose a model of charity, subtly criticizing the excesses of liberalness and framing the economic within morality.[16]

Alexander's clerical education is not just assumed, as is Apolonio's, but in fact detailed in the first well-known stanzas of the *Libro de Alexandre*, as Aristotle's tutoring of the conqueror was one of the best-loved episodes of Alexander's biography. Ronald Surtz, in an article on Apolonio and Alexander as intellectual heroes, details how Alexander is presented in the *Libro de Alexandre* as warrior and equally as cleric, a trait copiously exemplified through the many erudite digressions in the poem. Set against the Cluniac and Cistercian spiritual reforms and their anti-intellectual programs, Surtz reads the characterization of both kings as a questioning and further legitimizing of clerical knowledge framed within a Christian perspective, one particularly linked to staying within the limits of one's role in the world: "The message of the *Libro de Alexandre* turns out to be the same as that of the *Libro de Apolonio*. The sage in his poem, the king in his governing, the warrior in his battles, he who exercises his task appropriately, will receive the prize or punishment he deserves" (273). I have mentioned above how the focus on the sea allows us to see how these limits are first set, then breached and broken. While Apolonio himself will *oppose* clerical knowledge to traveling, linking the sea to *cupiditas* and ultimately to economics, Alexander's clerical knowledge will be positively and intimately tied to his successful traveling across the seas to reach the lands he must conquer. In stanzas 115–119 Apolonio, as the sole survivor of the shipwreck that pushes him onto the Pentápolin coast, reflects on what it is that has forced him onto sea: it is sin, specifically his own greed, seeking marriage, and then others' greed seeking the reward offered by Antioco; Antioco's sin itself seeking its revenge against the truth offered by Apolonio's knowlege, that have repeatedly conspired with the sea, resulting only in loss for Apolonio.[17] The king himself, telling his tale to the fisherman, explains that what initially moved him out of Tiro was his own sense of worthlessness at not having traveled: "teníame por torpe t por menoscabado / porque por muchas tierras non auía andado" (they took me for a fool and for a good-for-nothing / because I had not traveled through many lands).[18] Similarly, it will be Alexander's excessive curiosity that will move him to break the limits of human appropriateness and seek to discover Nature's secrets, in a spectacular fall from grace that condemns not knowledge, and particularly not clerical knowledge, but the excess of one's own capabilities, ciphered in the *Libro de Alexandre* by placing the limit not at the meeting of sea and land, but between the human and Nature. From the beginning, in fact, clerical knowledge, for Alexander, is not marked as insufficient, as it is for Apolonio, but as inadequate for his problems: "Grado a ti, maestro, assaz sé sapïençia; / non temo de riqueza aver nunca fallençia. / ¡Mas vivré con rencura, morré con repentençia, / si de premia de Dario non saco yo a Greçia!" (st. 46) (I thank you, master, I have great knowledge / I fear not of ever lacking any riches. / But I will live with rancor, die with sorrow, / if from subjection from Dario I don't relieve Greece!). Alexander's knowledge and wealth are sufficient and great, but do not help him with his political troubles, framed as were Apolonio's in terms of shame and dishonor (st. 47). Thus, in many stanzas, Alexander prepares himself to move politically. Once outfitted with advice and proper attire, he will first survey the lands and mountain passes, seeking adventure and later announcing his destiny with the provocation of Darius; knighted and then crowned, he will challenge and subject the Armenians, Athenians, and Thebans. In stanza 245, after pacifying the lands, he will set sail as a natural extension of his power, picking up the thread of the initial provocation of Darius's request for tribute payments. The preparations and the narration of this change of scenery do not betray any ambivalence toward the sea, there is no warning or premonition that clouds the expedition, no moral digression on the part of the poet that tells the reader that this is a limit that must not be broken, no caution on water as an element foreign to humanity, or beyond power. Here, the desire to extend power across the seas is not coded negatively, but transitions calmly onto the waters and into the ship. Moreover, clerical knowledge will be instrumental for the articulation of a military strategy for the many conquests that follow, as in the multiple *mappamundi* that inhabit Alexander's strategic rooms, whether as he plans his extraordinary travels or as he recedes into his own habitations, or as rhetorical capability of transforming his resources into powerful weapons that will enable movement, displacements across land and sea.[19]

Embarkments

Alexander's travels by sea are described twice, in very different terms. In stanzas 250–254, Alexander embarks in the direction of Asia.

Alexander's impatience for setting sail contrasts with the grief—and fear of death—sailors and sailors' wives display by dragging their feet, delaying departure, and general bawling. Alexander admonishes them saying that love of land makes cowards of many, and invokes a series of heroes whose defiance of the ocean's limit brought them greatness: Alcides (or Hercules) in Spain, Bacus in India, Jason's victory and prize in the search for the Golden Fleece, thus linking clerisy itself to the violation of limits.[20] Alexander does not look back once, suggesting both courage and disaffection for his land, or extreme ambition. As they take distance from home, the tears subside and Asia appears on the horizon, implying that the sailors do not lose sight of land. Alexander shoots an arrow to the coast, inaugurating the new limit set from the sea, the penetration of another land, its domination, all of which frames the introduction of the *mappamundi* digression that follows. Sailing the sea to Asia has proven to be swift, safe, eventless. Most importantly, Alexander is not condemned by this horizontal displacement. Narration does not even hint at a threat from the sea, it does not spend time on it; as the gaze from those left behind is muddled by the tears, the narrator seems to turn his head, blink, and see Asia on the other side. They set up camp on shore and begin the campaigns on land, forgetting the waters behind them.

Apolonio's first encounter with the sea is less glorious. At the beginning of the poem, he does not emphasize the risk of setting sail, he seems almost unaware of possible danger at this early stage in the poem, which supports his bookish knowledge and further highlights his lack of experience. It is those on shore, similar to Alexander's story, who bemoan his departure, and the poet who cautions against the sea's movable condition:

El mar, que nunqua touo leyaltat ni belmez,
cámiase priuado et ensányase rafez;
suele dar mala çaga más negra que la pez. . . . (st. 107)

(The sea, which never had any loyalty or offered protection, / changes secretly and becomes enraged easily; / it can make one's fate blacker than tar. . . .)

The moral connotations linked to the liquidity of the medium, that is, mutability and trickery, are mirrored positively in King Apolonio himself, whose loyalty and charity, fidelity and honesty will characterize him throughout. Without any complications other than sadness and tiredness from the trip, Apolonio and his crew arrive in Tarso. The tempest that will threaten him there will be one of economics: greedy men search for him seeking to win Antioco's reward, meanwhile the city of Tarso, encumbered by hardship and high prices, may not be able to guarantee his safety. Apolonio here exercises another type of knowledge, his economic skills as merchant, and is able to guarantee a safe, if temporary, home for himself in Tarso by selling his cargo of food for a fair price to the town, then using the profit to build the walls around the city.

Both kings thus approach the sea without fear, with no sense of the danger with which it threatens them. They both seem blind to the general knowledge of the sea's treachery, of which their crews and, in Apolonio's case, the poet himself, seem keenly aware. It is this blindness, and our foreknowledge of the betrayals that both kings will be subjected to—Apolonio by Antioco at the beginning of the poem, Alexander by his own man at the end of his story—that is bound up with the kings' first navigation.

Intrusions

Holding on to a piece of wood, Apolonio will be thrown by the sea to its limit, *a término*, that is, to shore, losing men and riches, arriving in Pentápolin. Upon regaining consciousness the king will now lament that destiny has thrown him onto the ocean, which has sided with Antioco against him:

Nunqua deuía omne en las mares fiar,
traen lealtat poca, saben mal solazar;
saben, al reçebir, buena cara mostrar,
dan con omne ayna dentro en la logar. (st. 120)

(Never should man trust the seas, / they bring little loyalty, know not how to comfort; / They know to show a good face when welcoming you, / Only to trick you, once inside.)

It is with this shipwreck scene that the danger of sea travel is confirmed in the text for the protagonist and that an elaboration of the limit between land and sea as *shore*, as a place for the negotiation of those limits, of risk and profit, of loss and recovery, begins to be articulated in the *Apolonio*. While the negotiations that allowed him to remain in Tarso could have been taken for a stroke of luck, a sudden and interested trade of sorts, the encounter with the fisherman is one in which Apolonio has nothing to trade but his own story, itself a commonplace exchange. To the king's request for counsel, the fisherman offers stories of experience, tales of change of fortune and, at the end, is able to produce from less than nothing a gift for Apolonio.[21] The shipwreck, then, is framed at this other end not with a negotiation based on liberalness or generosity, as was the case with Tarso, but with one based on charity.

Courtesy will bring him back to his status as king, through sport and song and cunning, marrying Luciana to the delight of Architrastes, her father, who has seen in Apolonio an equal. It will be strolling on the beach that another shore character, a sailor passing time on an anchored ship, will beckon Apolonio to sail again, this time to reclaim both his own throne and that of Antioch, now that the incestuous couple has been struck by lightning as punishment for their sins. While the sea is agreeable and calm for most of the trip, they are about to cross it when fortune strikes again and Luciana, giving birth to Tarsiana, is struck with a deathlike condition that makes everyone believe she is dead. Carefully placed in a richly decorated coffin on the waves, the body and treasure arrive to the port-city of Efeso. Found by a doctor who happens to live by the sea, they discover she is still alive and bring her back to health. Restored to life, but lost to her family, she must remain there in a monastery built on the shore next to Efeso. Tarsiana, Apolonio's and Luciana's daughter, thirteen years later, betrayed by her tutors and sold as a slave, finds a home at a bordello in the port city of Mitalena, on the island of Lesbos. While the numerous transactions involving women's bodies cannot be detailed here, I want to recall not only the emphasis on market, trade, ports, and shores that structures the stories of both Luciana and Tarsiana, but also the emphasis on language (as prayer or as storytelling and singing) that allows them to participate in this world of exchange, using language as a form of conversion: the poet remarks that all of the men who visit Tarsiana in the bordello are, as is Antinágora, *converted* by her words (st. 419).

Meantime, Apolonio will repeatedly lecture on fortune as logic of loss and recovery, set sail for Egypt and return ten years later to discover the betrayal of the tutors. Disconsolate, he sets sail for home, Tiro, but fortune intervenes, and the sea takes away his power to govern the ship and God himself throws the pilgrims, *romeros*, to the shores of Mitalena. The episode of negotiation of identity between Apolonio and Tarsiana will take place entirely on the shore, on board the ship anchored at the port of the city. In stanza 547, the sea as God's instrument will be credited with the recovery of his daughter. Now that the sea as instrument of God has been introduced, an angel will instruct Apolonio to go to Efeso and find Luciana. By now, he has established that his life matters must be negotiated in the space between land and sea and in stanza 613 Apolonio enters Tiro, accumulating recoveries, reputation, and profit in his itinerary home.

Julian Weiss has paid close attention to such mercantile characterization of Apolonio. He begins by explaining *cortesía* as a concept that should be extended to include spaces and relations outside the court, and mentions the world of commerce, but resists the temptation to appeal to a rise of the middle class to justify confusion between courtesy and exchange. In my view, it is precisely in that confusion that the text gains actuality, making relevant the story of Apolonio in the context of thirteenth-century Castile, marking not only a distance from the Latin model, but an alternative to the model of sovereignty in the *Libro de Alexandre*. According to Weiss, "*cortesía* functions as an ideological mechanism to remove individual identity from the realm of history and changing social relations: it negotiates the unstable process of acquiring, circulating and potentially losing material wealth, and confronts challenges posed by new forms of economic production" (504). Thus, *cortesía* would be the stable ground against which a commerce characterized by instability would be staged. I read in this text, however, that travel as form of knowledge, travel by sea, and even commerce itself are what characterize Apolonio not only as courtly king but *also* as successful and ethical merchant, capable of dispensing justice by distributing wealth and goods appropriately.

In order to support a tension or an opposition between courtesy and commerce, Weiss refers to Elánico's refusal to be paid a reward from Apolonio's treasure to compensate his honesty: "amiztat vender non es costumbre nuestra / Quien bondat da por preçio malamiente se denuesta" (st. 76) (it is not our custom to sell friendship / he who is kind for money offends himself). Weiss presses the point by saying that what has been traded in the name of friendship is not commerce, but a just price, "once again, though this time in relation to a specifically Christian identity, the poem denies that a contractual social relationship can be established on monetary terms" (508). However, what has actually happened is that Apolonio has traded in ethics—just price—which seem to overshadow the economic transaction that has occurred. By matching Antioco's bet on the greediness of men with generosity and gratefulness, Apolonio manages to transform the client bond between the men into one of friendship. It is in this two-fold level where Apolonio, melding courtesy and merchantry, is king.

Weiss's analysis begins to suggest such a reading of the *Libro de Apolonio*:

> a commercial transaction is not openly repudiated, but silently assimilated into the hero's courtliness. The point is reinforced by having the commercial transaction immediately commuted into an act of courtly *magnanimitas*. This transformation of commerce into courtliness is effected by having the money reinvested in the construction of the town walls . . . he transforms a commercial exchange into an act of *cortesía*, and in the process creates a space where *cortesía* (acts of the court) can take place. (509)

But just one step further, and where Weiss stops, is the idea that this characterizes Apolonio with an identity that lies *beyond* that of cleric, king, or merchant, in a rhetorical combination that is capable of transforming the product of one of these identities into another by virtue of words. That is, it is within language where courtesy, sovereignty and commerce coexist and may be traded for each other. When Tarsiana, in Weiss's words, "translates economic exchange into a moral and spiritual practice," and "[h]er customers end up buying not her body but her life story, and with it their own moral redemption," it is precisely *in* language, as *translation*, where economics and spirituality trade in each other, overlap or merge in order to produce a new object of exchange: again, language, a story, produced within *curialitas* (510). Thus, it is through language and virtue that Apolonio is able to curb the danger of greed, codified as the danger of sea travel, in order to make it work for him, to render it profitable. The violation of the sea is mollified through careful administration of morality and ethics, nevertheless obtaining the *preçio* for which the king has put himself at risk.

The best-known maritime episode in the *Libro de Alexandre*, because it so appropriately illustrates how again and again the hero defies Nature, is Alexander's descent into the sea by having a sort of submarine built for him to go to the bottom of the ocean.[22] A few stanzas before, however, this journey—different from any other—is framed explicitly as the breaking of a boundary. Alexander's council mean to restrain their leader's urge to go further, calling it specifically greed, *cupiditas*, by addressing the king in this way: "La tu fiera cobdiçia non te dexa folgar; / señor eres del mundo: non te puedes fartar. / ¡Nin podemos saber nin podemos asmar / qué cosa es aquesta que quieres ensayar!" (st. 2274) (Your fierce greed does not let you rest; / you are lord of the world: but you are not satisfied. / We cannot know and we cannot judge / what it is that you wish to attempt). The council warn that no reward can ever be great enough to make such risk-taking worthwhile: "Non es honra nin preçio pora omne honrado / meterse a ventura en lugar desguisado" (2270ab) (There is no honor or worth for honorable men / in venturing into uncharted places).[23] In stanza 2289, as Alexander harangues his men to follow him further, he argues that of the seven worlds God made, only parts of a single one have been dominated. He refers here to the Earth as sphere as being conquered only in its landmass, most obviously by Alexander himself, suggesting that of the Earth itself both the seas and the skies remain to be explored. Alexander claims that God has sent him and his men to those parts precisely to discover the secrets of these realms, claiming that the risk entailed must be assumed in order to gain anything, to profit, following Aristotle's advice.[24]

Alexander's men respond to his rhetoric, and they promise to follow him everywhere and set sail to a calm sea, with good winds, with no destiny or defined goal: "ivan e non sabién escontra quál lugar" (2297d) (they went without knowing where they were going). They swiftly sail into open seas, where they wander aimlessly, and where the poet remarks once again the unheard-of willful navigation without having land in sight, through uncharted waters (2299cd). The mutability of winds changes the waves, and the sea becomes enraged, while the king's weapons—remarks the poet—cannot tame them. The danger increases as they go further into the sea, the storms multiply; but Alexander does not falter in his determination, to the admiration of his men. To this horizontal challenge of uncharted open sea, the poet now adds—if incredulously—the story of Alexander's submarine exploration:

> Dizen que por saber qué fazen los pescados,
> cómo viven los chicos entre los más granados,
> fizo arca de vidrio con muzos bien çerrados;
> metiose él de dentro con dos de sus crïados. . . .
> Mandó que lo dexassen quize días durar;
> las naves, con tod'esto, pensassen de andar:
> assaz podrié en esto saber e mesurar
> e meter en escripto los secretos del mar. (2306, 2309)

> (They say that to know what fish do, / how the little ones live among the grander ones, / he made a glass ark with all openings closed; / he went in it with two of his servants. // . . . He ordered to be left there fifteen days; / after which the ships could prepare to leave: / with this he could know and measure / and write down the secrets of the sea.)

Even though he finds more trouble than Ulysses himself, with tempests and high winds scaring the sailors at high sea, where they know not how to pilot the ships, Alexander reaches the site to have himself lowered in his glass chamber into the waters, where the inhabitants fear and tremble in his presence, kneel their fins and pledge their scaly allegiance to the Conqueror.[25] If Alexander's submersion exemplifies the excess in the hero that will be translated as *superbia*, this excess seems to be one that is considered in its verticality: the prohibition to enter the water seems to be codified negatively only in *submersion*. If greed was assimilated to the horizontal dare of sailing into open seas, it is not greed but vainglory, arrogance, and pride that codify this vertical crossing of limits. Alexander comes back successful from his challenge of the surface of the seas, he survives storms and enraged seas and fierce winds; but his challenge of the depths of the sea with the explicit intent of discovering its secrets and putting them to writing is what triggers the digression, framed in terms of *superbia,* that will end with his betrayal and murder. Natura, who suffers the affront of the crossing of (human) boundaries that Alexander undertakes, recruits the devil with God's approval, and they send Antípater, to punish Alexander's sin of pride in stanzas 2324–2457 (which include the interpolated description of the kingdom of Hell).

The contrast in moral lessons—and the ensuing nuance as models for sovereignty—between the stories of Alexander and Apolonio, emblematized in the sins of *superbia* and *cupiditas*, are interesting in themselves but especially in their parallel use of an economic language and prowess that allows both kings to get what they want: superhuman knowledge, *secretos*, in the case of Alexander; profit, *ganançia*—in the logic of loss and recovery—in Apolonio's. The characterization of maritime space as one of risk, danger and profit is similar, but the sins that threaten such endeavors are distributed differently: while for Alexander the horizontal, the surface economics of the sea is always profitable and it is only his intent to access depth that proves deadly, for Apolonio movement across water is always structured upon the careful negotiation at the start of every journey, his arrival and departure at every port, that marks his fortune and salvation.

Spacing Limits

Several conclusions can be drawn from this difference in the presentation of the limits between sea and land, that is, Alexander's characterization of that limit as a coastline, and only as inviolable limit in depth, and Apolonio's elaboration of the limit as a space, as shore, where morality and economics are negotiated. First, a coastline reminds one of an aerial view of a bi-dimensional cartographic representation, supported by the many interventions of the cartographic in the romance that supports a surface, cultural view of the world, one particularly linked to power. This cartographic representation in turn works as imperial model and as a reminder for the limit of the worldly as it points to the timelessness and spacelessness of salvation, with which warning the poem ends.

Apolonio's shoreline is a perspective from the land, a horizontal look from the ship or from the port town looking in to the market, a point of view that is underlined through the statues of Apolonio built in that precise space, mediating land and sea. As Apolonio sets sail for Egypt, leaving his daughter with Dionisia and Estrángilo, unable to overcome the death of his wife, the Latin source marks this new identity—a new voyage, not as father or husband, nor as emperor of Antioch, for these identities have been taken from him or relinquished out of grief, but as merchant, *sed funga potius opera mercatus*, the Latin source remarks. The Spanish version characterizes this as a pilgrimage, but Tarsiana herself, Apolonio's daughter, will waver between the merchant and *romero*, making them alternatives to each other, similar and thus exchangeable: "Dios te salve, romero o merchante" (st. 489b) (God save you, be you pilgrim or merchant). Alexander talks of his own craft in weapons and strategy in the beginning of the poem (st. 69) as his merchantry, his trade, *merchantería*, bringing the parallels between kings closer.[26]

The *Libro de Alexandre* and the *Libro de Apolonio*, as has been pointed out many times before, propose models for kingship that should not be seen as contradictory but as evolving visions, modeled on the past, forged for the future, sustained by a moral framework. Alexander's is a continental, military project, while Apolonio's is a portuary, mercantile model. Alexander conquers and colonizes, Apolonio negotiates; Alexander's success is predicated upon his ambition and cautioned in its extreme version of pride; Apolonio's deferred deliverance is built on containment and careful calculation of profit. These two models, built upon the sea, articulate different models of land: while Alexander merely sets camp on a coastline that he has set off as a starting limit for his military exploits through the arrow that marks Asia as his for the taking, Apolonio moves within a wider space than that of the ebbing waves. His is a shore, a port city; his fellow characters are kings as well, but also fishermen and merchants.

These two texts experiment with two possible models with underlying tones of imperialism and mercantilism that play out as alternatives only as long as the limits of (Christian) ethics are kept in check. A few decades later, Alfonso X will himself bring together the sea and the space of royalty, mixing once again the metaphors of sovereignty or governance and of sea travel, when quoting the ancient sages in the second *Partida* as saying that "the court of the king is like that sea," for as the sea, the court gives place to any and all, and delivers judgment, counsel, and liberalness, and is subject to calmness and tempest (*Partida II*, tit. 9, law 28).

At the end of the Middle Ages, historically, blending imperialism and mercantilism, as Bodei writes, the ocean's movements became normalized, depriving the sea of its specificity. Instability not only did not any longer provoke fear or respect but, as it became normal or habitual, mutability itself came to be seen as something more durable and substantial. Whether we take the journey to be one of empire or of economics, when variations—rebellion, treason, and civil war as well as inflation, interests, or speculation—are seen as normal, they are in turn interiorized. Seen as the condition within, they do not provoke fear, they are not seen as abstractions but as substantial; they are not perceived as temporal but as the most permanent of conditions. This naturalization of space traceable through romance elaborations, first that of the forest, then that of the sea, as Ferdinand Braudel said, made of the literary Mediterranean facing the early modern world barely a puddle in the map of possible opportunities.

Notes

1. See for instance J. R. Llobera's article and ensuing debate, summarized in the introduction to the collective volume *The Anthropology of Europe*: "The Mediterranean was invented in 1959, and had already outrun its usefulness in the 1980's." This assertion is referred to by historian Michael Herzfeld in his contribution to *Rethinking the Mediterranean*. See his objections to the revival of the concept, as well as some constructive criticism in "Practical Mediterraneism."
2. Wigen's introductory piece to the *American Historical Review's* issue on maritime studies is concise and to the point, summarizing the potential that scholars seek in Mediterranean (and Atlantic, and Pacific) studies as new area/regional studies within global historiography, and pointing out problems. Harris's compilation of conflicting assessments and instrumentalizations of "Mediterranean" (*Rethinking the*

Mediterranean) as an answer to Horden and Purcell's *The Corrupting Sea* illustrates the unresolved fuzziness of the terms, and offers healthy debate: Oxford University Press even markets the collection as subjecting the "currently popular topic of Mediterranean studies to a fresh critical gaze."

3. Horden and Purcell's definition of what they present as a specific methodology for their project as an "ecologically driven interdependence that weaves the fabric of the region" is not useful for the study of literary texts here: the environment described in these poems is one imagined and produced not from experience but from reference, it is an almost mythical past and place of books, including those of history. On the other hand, in the same article, even when Horden and Purcell distinguish their notion of the Mediterranean from that of the ancient world, they collapse the analyses by saying, for instance, that "Plato was too sanguine in thinking that at ten miles inland, even in mountainous Crete, his ideal city would escape the `corruption engendered by the complex ecology of the sea," when only a few paragraphs before, Plato's reasons for this distancing of cities is quoted as one fleeing "mercantile vice." Thus, the argument for Mediterranean as mercantilism in a strict sense, and in a general sense, economics, emphasizing production, distribution, exchange, etc. is naturalized as the *ecology* of the region, avoiding the details of any specific social and political economic model.
4. See Péro, *Les Images maritimes de Pindare*, for general references on these tropes.
5. For a list of parallels between the *Apolonio* and the *Alexandre*, see Uría's article comparing both poems ("El *Libro de Apolonio*, contrapunto"). Uría analyzes the opposing exemplary trajectories of the characters; in a way my study follows the same intuition that the protagonists of these stories offer complementary visions of sovereignty. Surtz also looks at parallels between the protagonists of these stories, however his analysis, based on the (failed) intellectual heroism of the kings, stems from his reading of pride as the main trait of both characters. All quotes from the *Libro de Alexandre* (*Alexandre*) are from Casas Rigall's edition; all quotes from the *Libro de Apolonio (Apolonio)* from Corbella's. Both of these editions have introductions detailing problems of authorship, transmission and history of the criticism, but see Uría's *Panorama* for a general and comprehensive contextualization of *mester de clerecía*. All translations are my own. I have not translated names of characters or place-names.
6. Rucquoi analyzes this model traced through Jiménez de Rada's and Lucas de Tuy's characterization of Alfonso VIII's kingship as model for thirteenth-century royalty. The *Historia Apollonii Regis Tiri*, or *HART*, the Latin source for the Spanish, and other vernacular versions of the story of Apolonio, was copied alongside chronicles, often along with Alexander's, strengthening the ties between both romances and between them and figures of royalty.
7. The most interesting article to elaborate on fiction as part of the textual network composing and responding to royal figures is Arizaleta, "El *Libro de Alexandre:* el clérigo."

8. See Navarro González, *El mar en la literatura medieval castellana*, for a catalogue of scenes with seascapes in different genres up to the fifteenth century.
9. For an analysis of the fear of drowning and shipwreck, from Greece and Rome to romanticism, see Blumenberg, *Shipwreck with Spectator.*
10. Biaginni, "*Todos somos romeos,*" argues for pilgrimage as an allegorical dimension of all works of *mester de clerecía*, fundamentally through Berceo's *Milagros* but looking to it also as poetics in the *Alexandre* and the *Apolonio.*
11. This is a reference to *Apolonio*'s filiation to Greek or Byzantine romance; see Brownlee.
12. I here follow Rucquoi's analysis of images of sovereignty in the thirteenth century (222); her study can be complemented by Arizaleta's work on clerics at court (see, among other other articles by her, *Les Clercs au palais*).
13. Surtz's remarks on Apolonio's reliance on knowledge that comes from books, and not from God, as in the Latin source, reinforces this conversion model ("El héroe intelectual," 265).
14. Shortly after Apolonio sets sail, a storm shipwrecks the fleet and Apolonio is the only survivor. While Uría reads this as the event itself marking conversion (leaving the humiliation as a preparation for this event), Surtz reads in the shipwreck a punishment for the protagonists' desire to seek adventure in the sea. As an expected trope in sea travel, the shipwreck serves to characterize the sea as unstable, as a space inappropriate for humanity, as a space for trial from which one may emerge successful or fail and die forever lost. The symbolic dimensions of the sea, widely elaborated in medieval literatures, were of course always present.
15. As a model for sovereignty, Apolonio seems to lack that bond between *sapientia* and *fortitudo*, for to his bookish, clerical knowledge there is no chivalric, battling self to correspond to it, as there is in Alexander and both historical and fictional kings of the twelfth and thirteenth centuries (see Aurell, especially 67–70). If this model, which Aurell relates to the matter of Rome is absent here, it is because, I argue, *fortitudo* is presented in another guise, substituted by another form of subjection of both medium and the other: economic prowess.
16. Shell studies this as a chronological shift taking place in the twelfth and thirteenth centuries, where the model of *largesse* as the highest virtue in kings, using as examples Charlemagne and Alexander, undergoes a revision, shifting to a model of *charity*. *Largesse* or liberalness will be increasingly linked to *cupiditas* in relation to the reciprocity it demands. Shell calls the change from an economy of desire to one of grace, where it is God who will be responsible for corresponding the gift, a *conversion*, and it is this layer of meaning that I suggest here is added to—not substituting—to Christian morality as a model for sovereignty (35 and ss.)
17. Fui buscar contienda, casamiento famado / gané enamiztad, salí dende aontado, / et torné sin la duenya, de muerte enamiztado. // Con toda essa pérdida, si en paz me xouiés' . . . Mouióme el pecado, fízom' ende sallir, / por fer de mí escarnio, su maleza complir; / dióme en el mar salto, por más de desmentir, / ovo muchas

ayudas por a mí destrouir. // Fizo su atenençia con las ondas del mar, / viniéronle los vientos todos a ayudar. . . . (I went to seek a challenge, a famous marriage, / I won enemies, left dishonored, / and returned without the lady, on threat of death. // With all this loss, if I had stayed . . . Sin [the greed of others] displaced me, forced me to leave, / to scorn me, to fulfill its evil; / it ambushed me at sea, to further discredit me, / it was aided by many in my destruction. // It [sin, greed] conspired with the waves of the sea, / all the winds came to help. . . .).

18. Surtz reads this same stanza as a condemnation of clerical knowledge, where I see no signs of a condemnation of erudition but simply a statement of curiosity.
19. See for instance my "Será todo en cabo a un lugar," which I have now considerably expanded, to appear in a forthcoming book.
20. Arizaleta ("El *Libro de Alexandre*: el clérigo," 90), following González Jiménez (87–88), suggests a parallel between this harangue of Alexander for the Asian expedition and Fernando III's harangue in Muñó, recorded in the *Chronica regum castellae*, inciting the war against Muslims.
21. The fisherman's sharing of his poor dress is, as has been noted many times, one more link to hagiography, both to the episode in the life of Martin de Tours, and to other works of *mester de clerecía* (*Vida de Santo Domingo*) in which the same scene is mentioned. Note that it is an episode of charity that is being presented here.
22. The poet remarks that all of the men who visit Tarsiana in the bordello are, as is Antinágora, *converted* by her words (st. 419).
23. See Cacho Blecua's remarks on knowledge with regards to Nature in *Alexandre*.
24. Neither Cañas nor Casas Rigall provide insight into *desguisado*, so I extrapolate from the meaning of *guisa*: manner, care, will, form; and *aguisar*: to make, to prepare, to set up.
25. As Casas Rigall notes in his edition, the "seven worlds," probably a reference to Isidore's *Etymologies* but likely to have been brought into the body of the text from a marginal note, as happens elsewhere in the *Libro de Alexandre*, does not appear in Gautier (note to 2289, p. 639).
26. I have detailed specific instances of economic language in the *Libro de Alexandre*, if with other intentions, in my "Towards a Political Economy in the *Libro de Alexandre*."

Works Cited

Arizaleta, Amaia. *Les clercs au palais: chancellerie et écriture du pouvoir royal (Castille, 1157–1230)*. Paris: SEMH, 2010. Web. 5 Sept. 2012.

———. "El *Libro de Alexandre*: el clérigo al servicio del rey." *Troianalexandrina* 8 (2008): 73–114. Brepols Periodica and Miscellanea Online. Web. 5 Sept. 2012.

Aurell, Martin. "Le *Libro de Alexandre* dans son contexte: clergé, royauté et chevalerie lettrée au XIIe siècle." *Troianalexandrina* 8 (2008): 59–71. Brepols Periodica and Miscellanea Online. Web. 5 Sept. 2012.

Biaginni, Oliver. "*Todos somos romeos que camino passamos*": *homo viator* dans le *mester de clerecía*." *Cahiers d'études hispaniques médiévales* 30 (2007): 25–54.

Blumenberg, Hans. *Shipwreck with Spectator*. Cambridge, Mass.: MIT Press, 1997.

Braudel, Ferdinand. *El mediterráneo y el mundo mediterráneo en la época de Felipe II*. Mexico: Fondo de Cultura Económica, 1953.

Bodei, Remo. "*Navigatio vitae*." *La letteratura del mare: atti del Convegno di Napoli, 13–16 settembre 2004*. Rome: Salerno, 2006. 21–36.

Brownlee, Marina. "Writing and Scripture in the *Libro de Apolonio*: The Conflation of Hagiography and Romance." *Hispanic Review* 51 (1999): 159–74.

Cacho Blecua, Juan Manuel. "El saber y el dominio de la Naturaleza en el *Libro de Alexandre*." *Actas del III Congreso de la Asociación Hispánica de Literatura Medieval*. Ed. M. I. Toro Pascua. Salamanca: Universidad de Salamanca, 1994. 197–207.

Curtius, E. R. *Literatura europea y Edad Media latina*. 2 vols. Mexico: Fondo de Cultura Económica, 1955.

Goddard, V. A., J. R. Llobera, and C. Shore. *The Anthropology of Europe: Identities and Boundaries in Conflict*. Providence, R.I.: Berg, 1996.

González Jiménez, Manuel. *Fernando III el Santo*. Sevilla: Fundación José Manuel Lara, 2006.

Harris, William V. *Rethinking the Mediterranean*. Oxford: Oxford University Press, 2005.

Herzfeld, Michael. "Practical Mediterraneanism: Excuses for Everything, from Epistemology to Eating." *Rethinking the Mediterranean*. Ed. W. V. Harris. Oxford: Oxford University Press, 2005. 25–63.

Horden, Peregrine, and Nicholas Purcell. "The Mediterranean and the New Thalassology." *The American Historical Review* 111.3 (2006): 722–40.

Las Siete Partidas: Medieval Government: The World of Kings and Warriors (Partida II). Trans. Samuel Parsons Scott. Ed. Robert I. Burns, S.J. Vol. 2. Philadelphia: University of Pennsylvania Press, 2000.

Libro de Alexandre. Ed. Juan Casas Rigall. Madrid: Castalia, 2007.

Libro de Alexandre. Ed. Jesús Cañas. Madrid: Cátedra, 2003.

Libro de Apolonio. Ed. Dolores Corbella. Madrid: Cátedra, 1992.

Marcotte, Didier. "Peripli nell'antichità: la sintasi greca del mare." *La letteratura del mare: atti del Convegno di Napoli, 13–16 settembre 2004*. Rome: Salerno, 2006. 37–50.

Navarro González, Alberto. *El mar en la literatura medieval castellana*. La Laguna: Universidad de la Laguna, 1962.

Péro, J. *Les images maritimes de Pindare*. Paris: Klincksieck, 1974.

Pinet, Simone. "Será todo en cabo a un lugar: Cartografías del *Libro de Alexandre*." *Actes del X Congrés internacional de l'Associació hispànica de literatura medieval*. Eds. Rafael Alemany, Josep Lluís Martos, and Josep Miguel Manzanaro. Valencia: Institut Universitari de Filologia Valenciana, 2005. 1321–34.

———. "Towards a Political Economy of the *Libro de Alexandre*." *Theories of Medieval Iberia. Diacritics* 36.3 (Fall 2006): 44–63.

Rucquoi, Adeline. "La royauté sous Alphonse VIII de Castille." *Cahiers de linguistique hispanique médiévale* 23 (2000): 215–41.

Shell, Marc. *Money, Language, Thought: Literary and Philosophical Economies From the Medieval to the Modern Era.* Berkeley: University of California Press, 1982.

Surtz, Ronald. "El héroe intelectual en el mester de clerecía." *La Torre* 1 (1987): 265–74.

Uría Maqua, Isabel. "El *Libro de Apolonio*, contrapunto del *Libro de Alexandre*." *Voz románica* 56 (1977): 193–211.

———. *Panorama crítico del mester de clerecía*. Madrid: Castalia, 2000.

Weiss, Julian. *The* Mester de clerecía: *Intellectuals and Ideologies in Thirteenth-Century Castile*. Woodbridge: Tamesis, 2006.

Wigen, Kären. "Introduction." *The American Historical Review* 111.3 (2006): 712–21.

◆ 6

The Catalan Standard Language in the Mediterranean: Greece versus Sardinia in Muntaner's *Crònica*

Vicente Lledó-Guillem

The *Crònica* by Ramon Muntaner (c. 1270–1336) is considered one of the best examples of linguistic patriotism in the Middle Ages, particularly with regard to Catalan language and identity.[1] The author narrates the history of the Crown of Aragon from the birth of Jaume I (1207) to the coronation of Alfons the Benign (1328). Jaume Aurell explains that the *Crònica* can be divided in two parts: the first one covers the thirteenth century by focusing on the reigns of Jaume I (r. 1213–1276), Pete the Great (r. 1276–1285), and Alfons the Liberal (r. 1285–1291). In the second part Muntaner "shifts to a passionate autobiographical account of the heroic deeds of the Catalan Company" in the eastern Mediterranean "where he serves as a knight and ruler" (*Authoring the Past* 72). Pierre Vilar indicates that the Catalan linguistic situation was a unique and, at the same time, very clear example in the pre-modern period of language as the clearest symbol of a political identity that could even be called a nation-state (448). However, certain language attitudes that appear in the Catalan text have not been analyzed yet. In this study I will focus on the importance of the language ideology of the *Crònica* in a Mediterranean context. I will demonstrate that, from a linguistic point of view, there is an ideological polyphony in the text: on the one hand, we find a clear support of the ideology of the standard language, which naturalizes the idea that the more unified and homogeneous a language is, the more perfect it is. According to Susan Gal, the concept of the standard language is still the dominant linguistic ideology in Europe (14). This support of the standard language ideology appears when Catalan is compared to some of the Romance and Germanic languages, and, especially, when the text describes the Greek language. The *Crònica* stresses the importance of linguistic homogeneity or uniformity, and, at the same time, blurs the difference between written and oral language. This aspect leads to a redefinition of the *diglossia* in the Greek-speaking world, as well as a questioning of the Greek language as a suitable Mediterranean *lingua franca*. On the other hand, the *Crònica* opposes the ideology of the standard language. The clearest example takes place when the Catalan text narrates the preparations for the conquest of Sardinia. The author of the *Crònica* explains that he wrote a lyric composition to give advice concerning how to invade Sardinia. Muntaner indicates that he sent a minstrel, En Comí, to sing the composition in front of King Jaume II (r. 1291–1327) and his son Prince Alfons in Barcelona. The text of the *Sermó*, which appears in chapter 272 of the *Crònica*, puts into question both the association between language and identity, and the linguistic division of the Romance World that had reached its zenith during the thirteenth century. The *Sermó* denies the linear continuity of the *langue d'oc* and shows that the Catalans can adopt the language of the enemy and give it a new beginning as a symbol of a Catalan identity. Therefore, the Catalan text is heteroglossic or polyphonic as far as the relationship between language and identity is concerned.[2] The linguistic patriotism of the text is not as homogeneous as one may think.

Language Uniformity and the Standard Language

In chapter XXIX the *Crònica* makes a linguistic description of the Mediterranean World:

> E negú no es pens que en Catalunya sia poca província, ans vull que sàpia tothom que en Catalunya ha comunament pus ric poble que negú poble que jo sàpia ne haja vist de neguna província, si bé les gents del món la major part los fan pobres . . . D'altra part, vos diré cosa de què us meravellarets, emperò, si bé ho encercats, així ho trobarets: que d'un llenguatge solament, de negunes gents no són tantes com catalans. Que, si volets dir castellans, la dreta Castella poc dura e poc és, que en Castella ha moltes províncies qui cascun parla son llenguatge, qui són així departits com catalans d'aragoneses. E, si ben catalans e aragoneses són d'un senyor,

la llengua no és una, ans és molt departida. E així mateix trobarets en França e en Anglaterra e en Alemanya e per tota Itàlia e per tota Romania: que els grecs qui són de l'emperador de Costantinoble són així mateix moltes províncies, així com de la Morea e del realme de l'Arta e de la Blaquia e del realme de Salònic e del realme de Macedònia e del realme del Natolí e d'altres províncies moltes, en les quals ha aital departiment de los llenguatges com ha de catalans a aragoneses. (68)

(And let no one imagine that Catalonia is a small province; rather do I wish everyone to know that Catalonia has, in general, a richer population than I know of or have seen in any other province, though most people in the world imagine it to be poor . . . Besides, you will wonder at a thing I will tell you, though, if you examine it well, you will find it is so, namely, that of people of the same language there are none so numerous as the Catalans. If you speak of Castilians, the true Castile is of small extent and importance; for Castile has many provinces, each with its own language, as different from each other as Catalan from Aragonese. For though Catalans and Aragonese are under one lord, their languages are very different. And so likewise will you find it in France and in England and in Germany and in all Romania, as the Greeks, who are subjects of the Emperor of Constantinople form many provinces, such as the Morea and the Kingdoms of Arta and of Vlachia, and in the Kingdom of Salonika, and in Macedonia, and in Anatolia and many other provinces, amongst which there is as much difference in the language as there is between Catalan and Aragonese.) (61)[3]

According to the text, the criterion to establish the size and authenticity of a community is the existence of a common and unified language. Consequently, having a common king or emperor is not a decisive factor to consider that a community really exists, since there has to be a common and unified language. In fact, from a linguistic point of view, the Catalan text is questioning the uniqueness of established kingdoms such as Castile and France. Moreover, the *Crònica* denies the linguistic identity of the Germans, and with it of the Holy Roman Empire, as well as the Byzantines, because their respective languages are not uniform or homogeneous enough. Ideologically speaking, a common language represents a common identity, although the common language needs to have a certain degree of uniformity (Milroy 576) or homogeneity (Watts 596). Consequently, there is an identification between language and standard language as a genuine basis of an identity. The Catalan text supports this ideology by applying it to the linguistic context of the Crown of Aragon: the identity that the *Crònica* supports is the Catalan identity as opposed to the Aragonese.

They have the same king but there is a linguistic difference that separates them. Ferran Soldevila stresses the importance of this differentiation in his edition of the *Crònica* when he indicates that in this passage "there is a clear distinction between Catalan and Aragonese as separate languages" (68). Moreover, the linguistic differentiation that the text describes in the Crown of Aragon does not correspond to a political division of the Crown, since the Kingdom of Valencia is included as a linguistic part of the Catalan identity, as I will explain later when analyzing chapter XVIII of the *Crònica*.[4]

The ideology of the standard language had been spreading in Western Europe for a couple of centuries, but it was only in the thirteenth century when the political, social, and economic conditions made possible, first, the appearance of the concept and, later, its naturalization as an ideology.[5] Roger Wright has indicated that

> the wide monolingual Romance continuum that had existed well into the twelfth-century Renaissance was in its last stages . . . but the poison of nationalism was invading perceptions of language, as different sociopolitical units wanted to focus their own individual status more distinctively, and at that time a separate orthography of their own, even for pan-Romance lexical items, seemed an essential part of their national and social identity. ("Linguistic Standardization" 269)

The linguistic fragmentation in Europe, particularly in the Romance World, was the result of metalinguistic factors and not the product of a natural linguistic evolution. Only those linguistic varieties selected, codified and elaborated to become standard languages that represented a political power became languages from an ideological point of view. This naturalization of the existence of an independent language required a lot of energy and resources including literary and administrative influence (Penny 51–52). One of the Romance languages that achieved the status of the standard language of an independent monarchy was Catalan. During the Albigensian Crusade (1209–1229), Pere II of Aragon (r. 1196–1213) was defeated and killed by the French at the Battle of Muret (1213). After this event, the Catalan-Aragonese chances of expansion in the south of France were almost completely eliminated. Jaume I of Aragon chose the Iberian Peninsula and the Mediterranean as potential areas of military conquest and political influence. One of the consequences of this political change was the beginning of the standardization of the Catalan language as one of the official languages of his kingdom. First, there was a selection of a linguistic variety that would become the basis of the standard language: the political and economic supremacy of the city of Barcelona and the good relationship between the monarchy and the Catalan oligarchy made the linguistic variety of Barcelona the best candidate (Nadal and Prats 362). In fact, Catalan was the language of the merchants and the nobility that supported the Aragonese monarchy in its Mediterranean expansion (Lledó-Guillem 156–57).[6] Second, in 1276 Jaume I of Aragon supported the process of codification of the Catalan language by requesting that all the administrative documents in Catalan from the different Catalan-speaking areas of the Crown were written in a homogeneous Catalan language.[7] Finally, the process of elaboration by which a language acquires the necessary registers for those areas of knowledge that had been monopolized by other more prestigious languages was carried out by means of the writing of Catalan historiography, legal documents such as *El Llibre del Consulat de Mar*, and a large corpus of administrative documents that can be found in the Archives of the Crown of Aragon.[8] The process of standardization of the Catalan language is particularly interesting ideologically because, from a political point of view, the *langue d'oc*, which was and still is very similar to Catalan, was one of the languages of the Kingdom of France. It was very important to stress that Catalan was different from the *langue d'oc* so that Catalan could become the main language of the monarchy, and the *langue d'oc* could be iconized as one of the different languages of France that prevented the existence of a pure French identity based on a single and uniform language. The first part of the fragment quoted above: "If you examine it well, you will find it is so, namely, that of people of the same language there are none so numerous as the Catalans," conveys the idea that among all the languages that have initiated the process of standardization and uniformity, the only one that can be considered a model of complete standardization and uniformity is Catalan. Consequently, Catalans are the best example of a group in which there is a perfect correspondence between language and identity.

Nevertheless, the *Crònica* had to face the problem of the linguistic varieties of the Catalan language. It is difficult to assess the degree of linguistic variation in the Catalan-speaking area in the first half of the fourteenth century. From a sociolinguistic point of view, we must bear in mind that "language is variable at all times" (Milroy 582) and that standardization is an imposition of uniformity upon language, which is by nature variable (Milroy 576). The Catalan chronicle establishes a synthesis between uniformity and variability by describing what nowadays is called dialectal leveling in chapter XVIII:

> E axí mateix venc ab madona la reina altre honrat fadrí qui era de comte fill, e era parent de madona la reina, qui havia nom En Corral Llança, e una sua germana, nina e fadrina, e nodrí ab madona la dita reina. E aquest En Corral Llança eixí

dels bells hòmens del món e el mills parlant e pus savi; sí que en aquell temps se deïa que el pus bell catalanesc era, del món, d'ell e d'En Roger de Llòria. E no era meravella, que ells, així con davant vos he dit, vengren molt fadrins en Catalunya e nodriren-se tota hora ab lo senyor infant; e així apreseren del catalanesc de cascun lloc de Catalunya e del regne de València tot ço qui bon ne bell era, e així cascun d'ells fo lo pus perfet català que anc fos e ab pus bell catalanesc. (51)

(And, likewise, there came with my Lady the Queen another high-born boy, who was the son of a count and related to my Lady the Queen, and who was called En Conrado Lansa, and a little sister of his, quite young, who had been brought up with my Lady the Queen. And this En Conrado Lansa came to be one the handsomest men in the world and one of the wisest and one of the best speakers. Indeed, at that time, it was said that the most beautiful Catalan was that spoken by him and by the said En Roger de Luria. And it is no wonder for, as I have told you already, they came very young to Catalonia and, in every place in Catalonia and in the Kingdom of Valencia they acquired what was best and most beautiful in the language. And so they became perfect Catalans and spoke the most beautiful Catalan.) (39–40)

This is another example of the close relationship between language and identity that the *Crònica* supports. Both En Roger de Luria and En Conrado Lansa have acquired "the most beautiful Catalan" and, as a result, they have attained a perfect Catalan identity. In this passage the Catalan text establishes a balance between the process of selection of a variety as the basis of the standard language and the process of acceptance. According to the text, the perfect Catalan is the result of a dialectal leveling in which the best and "most beautiful" features of the different varieties are selected to create a perfect and beautiful Catalan language. This dialectal leveling is described as a natural and personal experience and it helps the process of erasure of the linguistic hierarchy that the selection of a variety and the creation of the standard language imply. The best example of the standard language in which the *Crònica* is written, based above all on the variety of the merchants and oligarchy of Barcelona, is depicted as the result of the leveling of different varieties. Consequently, the hierarchical process of standardization is erased.[9] The *Crònica* is part of the planning of the status of the Catalan language as a unified language that needs to be accepted in all the Catalan-speaking areas. Because of the political division between the Principality of Catalonia and the Kingdom of Valencia since Jaume I The Conqueror, the process of selection of the variety of Barcelona as the dominant one in the creation of the standard language has to be erased.

The Description of the Greek Language According to Western Premodern Standards: Searching for a Mediterranean Lingua Franca

Once it has established that the Catalan language represents the ideal standard language in Western Europe because of its uniformity, the *Crònica* compares Catalan with the Greek language. This is, in fact, a description of the extent to which the Greek-speaking area in the Eastern Mediterranean follows the linguistic rules of the West, here accepted as natural and appropriate, and therefore, constitutive of a linguistic ideology.[10] However, the Greek-speaking territories had not naturalized these Western linguistic ideas, since their political and social context was different. In the area of the Eastern Mediterranean where Greek was spoken there was a diglossic situation according to which the different varieties of Greek coexisted and were used for different purposes following quite a strict functional differentiation.[11] R. H. Robins quotes a fragment of a letter from Michael Acominatus (1140–1220), Archbishop of Athens:

> Truth to tell, I have become barbarized dwelling so long in Athens, and what is worse, I am forgotten as if I were dead, and I am forgetful myself. I went down to the deepest extremity, whose imprisoning bars are eternal . . . Why should we suffer those who are beyond the scope of all learning and among whom there is a barbaric mob, alienated from all philosophy, and where former speakers of Attic Greek are now barbarized in their speech? In the past three years one has scarcely understood their dialect, except for names which survive uncorrupted, like *Peiraeus*, *Hymettus*, the *Aeropagus* . . . (10)

This is an important testimony of the linguistic ideology in the Greek-speaking world at the end of the twelfth and beginnings of the thirteenth century. Before the year 1204, when the Western crusaders invaded Constantinople, there was a quite stable linguistic situation that consisted of two varieties of the Greek language with different functions: on the one hand, "the language of classical Greek and its derivative *koiné* (*diálektos*) [common or standard dialect], well represented in the Greek New Testament." On the other hand, "the more colloquial Greek *Umgangssprache*, the first language of most Greek speakers and the only language of the less educated" (Robins 12). It is possible to refer to a classicizing variety H, or High variety, which would be used by the Church, the Court of the Emperor, education, high culture, and the administration of the state during the Byzantine Empire. This variety H had a high level of standardization, although there were some differences between the Classical

Attic style, the *koiné*, and, as Horrocks indicates, some other "practical styles" (229). The variety L, or Low variety, which represented the varieties of the spoken languages, had a very low degree of standardization and was not supposed to be used for literary or administrative functions. Robins believes that at the end of the ninth century Classical Greek was becoming a second language that needed to be taught and studied (11). Blumenthal and Kahane state that "after the archaizing renaissance of the tenth and eleventh centuries, the split between the written and the spoken languages became a mark of Greek culture" (189).

However, the diglossia of the Greek language was influenced by the western presence, to such an extent that, particularly in the territories dominated by the Latins, after 1204, the strict functional distinction between the High and the Low variety suffered important changes. One of the best examples of this attack on the stability of the diglossic functional distribution of the Greek language appears in the *Chronicle of Morea* (1300).[12] Robert Browning indicates that it is difficult to know exactly what the original language of this poetic chronicle was because there are several translations in French, Italian, and Aragonese. It has been said that the original version was in French and it was translated into Greek soon after. "At any rate the Greek version, whether original or translated, is the work of a man who had little or no contact with Byzantine tradition or with the literary tongue. He was probably a second or third generation French settler, Hellenised in language . . . This is a document of almost pure spoken Greek" (73). Horrocks has pointed out that the literary use of the Romance languages in the fourteenth and fifteenth centuries had an influence on the use of vernacular Greek in fictional literature, especially in romances that were either translated from Romance languages into Greek or were originals in written vernacular Greek (216–17). Western linguistic ideology put in jeopardy the stability of the Greek diglossia, and, consequently, questioned the universal value of this linguistic system. The West had already had an influence before the Catalan *Crònica* had been written. In other words, the Franks had disrupted the functional difference between the High and the Low varieties of the Greek language. A historical narrative had been written in the Low variety of the Greek language due to the influence of the Western part of the Mediterranean.

Nevertheless, the Catalan text questions the validity of the Greek diglossia in a different way. The *Crònica* stresses the lack of uniformity of the Greek language by describing how the different areas where Greek is spoken show different varieties of the language. Having analyzed the diglossic linguistic situation of the Greek language it is not difficult to notice that the Catalan text does not make a differentiation between written and oral language. Because the ideal of the standard language consists on having a perfect harmony and uniformity between the oral and written registers, the Greek diglossia is not a valid linguistic situation. In fact, the *Crònica* does not even refer to the written standard that the Byzantine Empire used until the fifteenth century, which was based on the High variety of Greek. This lack of reference to Classical Greek, either Attic Greek or the Greek *Koiné*, brings up the contrast between the linguistic ideology of the West and the East of the Mediterranean. The equivalent of Classical Greek in the West was Latin. Latin was still a very important language in Western Europe, since it was the language of the Church, the language of the universities, and the international language or *lingua franca* of the West. However, since the rise of several European monarchies with a high degree of centralization in the thirteenth century, the vernacular languages started a process of standardization that carried with it a high degree of elaboration to oppose the linguistic monopoly of Latin in certain areas of knowledge. After this process of standardization a diglossia in Western Europe similar to the one in the Eastern Mediterranean with the Greek language was almost impossible. Muntaner's text makes this very clear and, at the same time, naturalizes the inferiority of the Greek language in relation to Catalan. As far as Catalan was concerned, it was possible to describe ideologically a language that showed a perfect harmony and correspondence between the oral and written registers, but the Greek language could not show this, since the High register was not used in ordinary speech, and the Low register had rarely been used in writing except after the Western influence, with the *Chronicle of Morea* being the best example. The Catalan reference to the Greek language implies ignoring the written register. The Greek standard that appears in the context of the diglossia is very different from the Western ideal standard that entails much more proximity between the oral and the written registers. After proving that Catalan is superior to the rest of the languages in Western Europe that have gone through the process of homogenization, the *Crònica* compares Catalan and Greek. The *Crònica* tries to prove that Catalan is superior to Greek as a standard language. This comparison is not simply between two languages, but between two ways of understanding the concept of language and identity: the Western way based on the ideal of a uniform standard language versus the Eastern way based on diglossia.

In the *Crònica* this opposition between the Western standard language, whose best example in the West is Catalan, and the Greek diglossia is placed in another semiological system. The result is another opposition that has important political and economical resonances: Catalan is the ideal *lingua franca* of the Mediterranean, whereas Greek is not. This conclusion is the result of fractal recursivity, which, according to Judith T. Irvine and Susan Gal, "involves the projection of an opposition, salient at some level of relationship, onto some other level" (38). The linguistic analysis that the *Crònica* has carried out by comparing the languages of the Mediterranean has important ideological connotations. The most important one is that Catalan, as the ideal standard language is the best and natural candidate to become the *lingua franca* of the Mediterranean. Greek was a strong rival since "during the period of western rule after 1204 . . . and even in the Ottoman period, Greek retained something of its status as a diplomatic language in the eastern Mediterranean, and the style employed for such purposes by foreigners and Greeks operating outside the sphere of the Constantinople establishment was rather closer to that of the educated speech of the relevant periods" (Horrocks 222). Certainly, this interest in proving the superiority of the Catalan language over Greek is related to the Catalan presence in the Aegean and in the Byzantine territories.[13]

The *Langue d'Oc* as a New Language for the Crown of Aragon: A New Voice in the *Crònica*.

Chapter CCLXXI explains how the King of the Crown of Aragon Jaume II summoned the Catalan Courts in Girona in 1322 demanding support to send his son, Prince Alfons, to Sardinia. Once the military campaign had been approved, Muntaner, as a character in the *Crònica*, explains that he himself sent a *Sermó* to both Jaume II of Aragon and the Prince to give them advice before the military confrontation in the Mediterranean. The author of the *Sermó* sent a minstrel, En Comín, to sing the *Sermó* to them in Barcelona. I will demonstrate that this poetic composition in chapter CCLXXII of the Catalan Chronicle proves that any language can be used to support the Aragonese expansion.

The *Sermó* has 240 lines in the Catalan text. The English translation has 233 lines and has been divided into twelve stanzas. I reproduce here the most important fragments for my study:

> En nom d'aicell ver Déus, qui fé el ceel e el tro,
> en son de Gui Nantull farai un bell sermó
> a honor e a laus del casal d'Aragon.
> E per tal que així sia, la salutacion
> diga xascús, si el plats, que la Verge nos dón
> seny e-s enteniment, que en façam nostre pro
> per est món e per l'altre, e que a salvació

véngon trastuit li comte, vescomte e baró,
cavaller e burgès, mariner e peó,
qui en est bon passatge de Sardenya a bandó
metran, si e sa terra e sa provesió,
e segran l'alt enfant N'Anfós, que és ganfanó,
e de trastota Espanya creiximent e cresó.
De llevant a ponent, mitjorn, septentrió,
tremblarà tota gent qui en subjecció
de sos paires valents, rei Jacme, ja no só.
E vull sàpia xascús que aquest és lo lleó
que Sibil·la nos dits que, ab senyal de bastó,
abatria l'ergull de manta alta maisó;
que ges er non dirai, que bé m'entendon pro. (446–50, 1–20)

(In the name of that true God who made Heaven and the thunder,
In the meter of Guy de Nanteuil I shall make a fine sermon
To the honor and praise of the House of Aragon.
And in order that suitable be the salutation
Let every one of you say, if you please: the Virgin grant us
Sense and understanding to work for our good,
In this world and the next, and that to salvation
May come every count, viscount and baron
Who in this fine expedition of Sardinia, without reserve
Engages himself and his land and his property;
And follows the noble Infante En Alfonso, who is its gonfalonier,
And gives all Spain increase and glory.
From East to West and South to North
Will tremble all those who under the sceptre
Of his valiant father, King En Jaime, are not yet.
And I wish you all to know that this is the lion
Of whom the Sibyl tells us, he with the device of the pales,
Will cast down the pride of many a noble manor.
Who they are I will not tell now; you well understand me.) (I, 1–19)[14]

The long poem starts with an invitation to pay homage to the House of Aragon. At the end, as Ferran Soldevila explains, we find the war cry that Catalan and Aragonese soldiers would normally use: "*Aragó e Sant Jordi*," although the two parts do not appear together (Soldevila 457):

e que el nom d'Aragon ne sia exalçats,
e que pisàs ne altres no el pusquen falsetats
bastir ne ordonar; e sant Jordi, al lats
de l'alt senyor infant, li sia acompanyats. (456–57, 237–40)

(And that the name of Aragon be exalted,
And that neither Pisans nor others may treachery
Carry out or ordain, and that Saint George going by the side
Of the noble Lord Infante, be his companion.) (XII, 230–33)

The *Sermó* is, therefore, a discourse used to enhance the House of Aragon and to encourage the King and his son in the conquest of Sardinia and Corsica, although the text focuses especially on the occupation of the former. Before the introduction of the text of the *Sermó*, the Catalan Chronicle has described how after the support provided by the Catalans and the King of Mallorca (the later being Juame II's vassal at the Courts of Girona), Jaume II of Aragon received the help of the Kingdoms of Aragon and Valencia. Consequently, the *Sermó* is described as the project of the whole Crown of Aragon.[15]

The content of the *Sermó* consists of military advice as well as an emphasis on the unity of the Aragonese army against the Pisans. The *Sermó* also contains important religious references with examples such as:

xascús s'hi lleu en peus, e trastui que diats
de paternostres tres per santa Trinitats
e a honor de sa Mare qui fo ses tots pecats.
Que eu prec lo seu car fill que ens sia atorgats
e que el nom d'Aragon ne sia exalçats. (456, 233–37)

(Let all stand up and all say
Of Paternosters three for the Holy Trinity,
In honor of His Mother who was without sin,
That she entreat her dear Son, that it be granted to us
And that the name of Aragon be exalted.) (XII, 226–30)

However, from an ideological and linguistic point of view, the most important aspect of the poem is the language used to pay homage to the House of Aragon and its expansionist policy. The main question we must ask is: in what language is the poem written? First of all, it is definitely not the Catalan language that has been used in the text in prose of the *Crònica*. In other words, a *Sermó* that constitutes an homage and enhancement of the House of Aragon does not use the standard language in which three of the four Catalan Chronicles had already been written: the *Llibre dels Fets* by Jaume I the Conqueror, the *Llibre del rei en Pere d'Aragó e del seus antecessors passats* by Bernat Desclot, and most of the *Crònica* by Ramon Muntaner.[16] Certainly this could be attributed to the fact that until the fifteenth century there was a literary diglossia in the Catalan-speaking area. Catalan was used for prose, whereas the *langue d'oc* was used for poetry.[17] This is a phenomenon that we already find in Ramon Llull (1232–1315), who has been traditionally considered the father of Catalan prose. It would seem that we already have an explanation of why the *Sermó* is not written in the same language as the one used in the Catalan Chronicles. Nadal and Prats refer to the *Sermó* as "poema provençalitzant" (409), whereas Martí de Riquer calls some Provençal elements of the *Sermó* "solucions provençals." The Catalan scholar even points out one example of hypercorrection typical of a Catalan trying to write in the *langue d'oc*: for the word "all" the text of the *Sermó* uses "*trastruits*" instead of the standard "*trastotz*" (Riquer 463). Even if we consider that the *Sermó* is a Provençal poem, it is important to bear in mind that the minstrel En Comín is told to sing the poem by using the melody of Gui Nanteuil, which had been used to sing a French epic poem in *langue d'oïl* that describes the deeds of the hero Gui de Nanteuil (Soldevila 450). This means that the *Sermó* is going to be sung in front of Jaume II of Aragon and his son Alfons in a language that is different from the Catalan used in the *Crònica* and that is very close to Provençal. Moreover, the melody is foreign too.

The second question that needs to be asked is: does this *Sermó* represent a real support of the imperial policy of the Crown of Aragon, despite its linguistic features? The answer is yes, but the linguistic connotations of the poem constitute an opposition to the ideology of the standard language that the text had supported in chapter XXIX, and a different way of praising the Aragonese imperial expansion. On the one hand, the *Sermó* stresses the lack of continuity of both the *langue d'oc* and the *langue d'oïl*. Since 1213 these two languages had represented the Crown of France, and this phenomenon speeded up the standardization of the Catalan language starting with the *Cancelleria Reial* created by Jaume I the Conqueror.[18] Consequently, including a poem in *langue d'oc* with a melody used to recite an epic poem in *langue d'oïl* had important linguistic implications. A language that belongs from an administrative point of view to the Crown of France, the *langue d'oc*, is used along with the most important standard language, also from an administrative point of view, of the Crown of

Aragon: *catalanesc* or Catalan. Moreover, this poem in *langue d'oc* is one of the strongest complements to the House of Aragon, since there are constant references to Aragonese symbols such as the cry of war and, according to Lady Goodenough, even the "coat of arms of Catalonia" in the following fragment: "And I wish you all to know that this is the lion / Of whom the Sibyl tells us, he with the device of the pales" (545). The continuity of the *langue d'oc* has been questioned, since this language has a new beginning in the *Sermó*. This new beginning implies that the language is at the service of the Aragonese monarchy and, as a result, it has been created again or recreated. The *langue d'oc* could be considered a language of the Crown of Aragon, at least during the reign of Pere II of Aragon.[19] However, after the Albigensian Crusade and the Battle of Muret (1213), the *langue d'oc* was not a symbol of the Aragonese monarchy any more, although it was used for lyric poetry. This is why a process of standardization of a new language, Catalan, had started. However, when the new Catalan language that had been elaborated to be used in historiography, legal documents, and for administrative purposes appears in Muntaner's *Crònica* along with the *Sermó* in *langue d'oc*, there is a clear opposition to the ideology of the standard language. The *Sermó* proves that Catalan, the main standard language of the Crown, does not need to be the only legitimate language to support the Catalan Aragonese expansion in the Mediterranean. Other languages can represent the Catalan identity. In this particular case, a language that was used to support the French invasion of Catalonia in 1285 is used by Muntaner, who has described these events in his *Crònica*, to support the Aragonese conquest of Sardinia. Furthermore, the *Sermó* in *langue d'oc* is sent directly to the King of the Crown of Aragon.

Therefore, the inclusion of the *Sermó* has two consequences: First, languages can be instruments of any identity because they can be transformed and remade by every person and every social group. Second, when a language is created again it has a new beginning and, consequently, the continuity of the language and the constant identity that it is supposed to represent are denied. Standardization does not limit the heteroglossic character of languages. When the Catalan text uses the *langue d'oc* to support the Aragonese political and military expansion in the Mediterranean, the Chronicle is creating a new language, since it is placing the *langue d'oc* in another context and is expanding and showing the multiple possibilities of the *langue d'oc* and every single language. Tony Crowley has explained the heteroglot nature of language when referring to the Irish language and English:

> Heaney describes how Irish writers have taken the language imposed upon their forebears and created it anew. Joyce of course is identified as the most striking forger of all . . . What occurs instead is a revelation of the heteroglot nature (though they are not necessarily best represented in this light) of all languages and consequently all forms of identity. Rather than a secure form of purity, what Heaney ends with is the hailing of the creativity and novelty of a new form of language, inherited from the past but made new in the present. It is a language which scorns the policing of linguistic and cultural borders and even questions their very necessity. In the context of the divisions and static positions taken by all sides at various points in the historic conflict, and the importance of all sorts of physical and mental borders, the diversity, plurality and openness of this account of heteroglossia can be read as a radical vision. It can also be read as an indirect comment on the significance of an understanding of language in history. (198-99)

Hence language cannot be the marker of the beginning and continuity of an identity because it can be "created anew." The Catalan *Crònica* creates a new *langue d'oc* by means of the *Sermó*, since this *langue d'oc* becomes a different language associated to the Crown of Aragon. It has been transformed. This transformation is stressed by the use of a melody that corresponds to an epic poem written in *langue d'oïl*. Yet, at the same time, this transformation of the *langue d'oc* into a new language puts into question the stability and continuity of all the standard languages that had been selected, codified and elaborated in thirteenth century Europe to represent the identity of certain European monarchies. When the Catalan text questions the continuity of the *langue d'oc* by creating it "anew," it opposes the ideology of the standard language in general because it is also denying the stability and continuity of the Catalan language. Catalan can also be "created anew" and lose its continuity as a symbol of the Catalan identity in order to represent another one.[20] If we read the passage of chapter XXIX in which Catalan appears as the perfect ideal of the standard language because of its uniformity and index of the Catalan identity, we realize that there is a clear contradiction in the text that I would prefer to call polyphony or heteroglossia by choosing Bakhtin's terminology quoted above. The text of the *Sermó* proves that a language cannot be a permanent index of an identity. Therefore, the superiority of the Catalan language based on its uniformity and power to represent the Catalan identity is questioned. The text contradicts itself and shows its polyphony.

This study has proven that it is important to analyze how language relates to the socio-historical context in the premodern period.[21] By focusing on the linguistic ideology of the *Crònica* of Ramon Muntaner in a Mediterranean context I have been able to show the potential similarities with the contemporary world and, at the same time, the possibility of questioning certain ideas about language and identity that have been accepted as natural. Muntaner's *Crònica* and its polyphony are an invitation to analyze the relativity of certain language attitudes and to deepen our study of medieval Catalan literature from a language in history point of view. Furthermore, the linguistic ideological study of this text shows that it is not easy, let alone convenient, to separate the study of language, literature, and history in our field, particularly in the premodern period. The different voices that appear in Muntaner's *Crònica* are better understood by placing the work in a Mediterranean context. The linguistic and ideological comparison between the different political entities in the West and the Greek-speaking area in the eastern Mediterranean have made us realize that there were different ways of thinking about language in the premodern period. The Sardinian context has also contributed to reinforce this conclusion. A Mediterranean perspective helps us question certain ideas about language that seemed permanent and universally valid, such as the standard language, the intimate connection between language and identity, and the supposedly natural linguistic frontiers. Had we not adopted a Mediterranean point of view the results would have been much more difficult to obtain. This study should serve as an example of the need to establish similar connections and comparisons in the premodern Mediterranean, so that we can expand our understanding of the period.

Notes

1. The earliest manuscript of the *Crònica* is at the *Biblioteca Nacional de Madrid*, Manuscript 1803, on paper, year 1342. In the *Biblioteca de Catalunya* we find the second earliest version: Manuscript 4, on paper, year 1353 (Soldevila 19).
2. In other words, there are some ideological tensions inside the *Crònica* that correspond to what Mikhail Bakhtin described as "the acute and intense interaction of another's world" in the same work (536).
3. In this essay I will use Lady Goodenough's translation of Ramon Muntaner's *Crònica*. Surprisingly, the translation of this passage has not included the reference to the linguistic situation in Italy that appears in the Catalan original.
4. Wright indicates that Aragonese "was not the main official chancery language of the state of Aragón; that was the function of Catalan (or Latin)," and this is why Aragonese did not have a centralized or standardized norm (271).
5. I use linguistic ideology as "a set of cultural notions in the anthropological sense:

a frame, not always conscious or within awareness, through which we understand linguistic practices" (Gal 15).

6. Jaume Aurell explains that the four Catalan chronicles by Jaume I the Conqueror (1213–1276), Bernat Desclot, Ramon Muntaner, and Pere IV of Aragon (r. 1336–1387) were written in Catalan to provide "important support and narrative justification for Barcelona's policy" ("Medieval Historiography and Mediation" 98). Pierre Vilar indicates that Barcelona shows a great economic, political and diplomatic strength compared to the rest of the regions of the Crown of Aragon (434).
7. With Peter the Ceremonious (1336–1387) the Royal Chancery was reformed and it became an important cultural center (Martí i Castell 324; Nadal, Prats 431).
8. As far as the description of the process of standardization is concerned, I use the explanation provided by José del Valle and Luis Gabriel Stheeman (26). David Rojinsky explains that relatives of Alfonso X the Wise (1252–1284), such as his father in law James I of Aragon (1213–1276) and Frederick II (1194–1250) of Sicily, implemented the status of the vernacular languages of their kingdoms at the expense of Latin. Rojinsky indicates that none of the Castilian King's relatives "oversaw a promotion of the vernacular textuality on the same scale as Alfonso X," especially his cousin Louis IX (1226–1270), since French did not become the official language of government until 1539 (87).
9. I follow the definition of "erasure" provided by Judith T. Irvine and Susan Gal: "*Erasure* is the process in which ideology, in simplifying the sociolinguistic field, renders some persons or activities (or sociolinguistic phenomena) invisible. Facts that are inconsistent with the ideological scheme either go unnoticed or get explained away" (38–39).
10. It is important to bear in mind that the term "Romania" in the fragment does not refer to the area where Latin languages were spoken but to the Byzantine Empire.
11. I use Ferguson's definition of "diglossia:" "DIGLOSSIA is a relatively stable language situation in which, in addition to the primary dialects of the language (which may include a standard or regional standards), there is a very divergent, highly codified (often grammatically more complex) superposed variety, the vehicle of a large and respected body of written literature, either of an earlier period or in another speech community, which is learned largely by formal education and is used for most written and formal spoken purposes but is not used by any sector of the community for ordinary conversation" (336).
12. The term "Morea" refers to the Peloponnesian Peninsula in Greece. This area was occupied by the Franks after the fourth Crusade (1204). For more information see Lock.
13. Between 1311 and 1388 the Duchies of Athens and Neopatria were dominated by the Catalans. For this crucial period in Catalan history see Peter Lock, Lluís Nicolau D'Olwer, Kenneth M. Setton, and Antoni Rubió i Lluch.
14. In the translation, I use the Roman numerals to indicate the stanza according to the division established by Lady Goodenough. The Arabic numerals indicate the lines.

In the Catalan original I have indicated the page number of the edition followed by the number of the lines. The reader will notice that the number of lines of the English translation does not correspond exactly to the number of lines of the Catalan text.

15. As Soldevila indicates, the *Sermó* has been studied by Milà i Fontanals (243–75), Riquer, and Perugi (Soldevila 450).
16. The fourth Catalan Chronicle is *Crònica dels reys d'Aragó e comtes de Barcelona* (c. 1366), also known as *Crònica de Pere III el Cerimoniós*, written under the supervision of the King Pere IV of Aragon (1336–1387). There are four versions of this chronicle: three long versions in Latin, Catalan, and Aragonese, and a short version in Catalan (Riquer 480). See Catherine E. Léglu for the language use in literature in the Catalan, French, and Provençal areas.
17. In this context, I use the term diglossia with a different meaning, which would imply a functional distinction in the use of two languages, instead of two varieties of the same language. This meaning corresponds to the concept of diglossia that Joshua Fishman established: the use of two linguistic varieties of any kind with different functions (129).
18. Lledó-Guillem has studied this linguistic political association of both the *langue d'oc* and the *langue d'oïl* with the Crown of France in the Chronicle by Bernat Desclot and in the poetic debate in *langue d'oc* between the French and the Catalans during the French invasion of Catalonia in 1285.
19. The Catalan-Aragonese presence and influence on the Provençal-speaking area in the south of France was particularly important during the reign of Peter II. However, after the defeat of Muret (1213) against the French army under Simon de Montfort, and especially after the Treaty of Corbeil (1258) the Crown of Aragon lost a great amount of political influence in the area. This had important consequences regarding the linguistic map of the area. Politically it was important for the Crown of Aragon to stress that Catalan was different from the *langue d'oc*. A process of standardization and differentiation started. Had the political situation been different, the distinction between the two languages would have been much more difficult to naturalize and there could have been a common language across the Pyrenees. For more information see Lledó-Guillem. Also Wright, "Linguistic Standardization," and Penny, "Linguistic (Dis)continuity."
20. The study of the *Sermó* in the *Crònica* would invite us to adopt a post-philological approach, which, according to Michelle Warren, would entail the narration of the history of the language without taking for granted the coherence of the linguistic systems and by paying attention to hybrid processes rather than normative ones (36).
21. Roger Wright has indicated how important it is to study the texts of the past, but also the socio-historical context of the human beings who wrote them. He has also provided a name for this methodology: Sociophilology ("La fragmentación románica," 534).

Works Cited

Aurell, Jaume. *Authoring the Past. History, Autobiography, and Politics in Medieval Catalonia*. Chicago: University of Chicago Press, 2012.

———. "Medieval Historiography and Mediation: Bernat Desclot's Representations of History." *Representing History, 1000–1300: Art, Music, History*. Ed. Robert Maxwell. Princeton: Princeton University Press, 2010. 91–108.

Bakhtin, Mikhail. "From *Discourse in the Novel*." *The Critical Tradition: Classic Texts and Contemporary Trends*. 2nd ed. Ed. David H. Richter. Boston: Bedford, 1998. 530–39.

Blumenthal, Henry, and Renée Kahane. "Decline and Survival of Western Prestige Languages." *Language* 55.1 (1979): 183–98.

Browning, Robert. *Medieval and Modern Greek*. 2nd ed. Cambridge: Cambridge University Press, 1983.

Crowley, Tony. *Language in History. Theories and Texts*. New York: Routledge, 1996.

del Valle, José, and Luis Gabriel-Stheeman. "Nacionalismo, hispanismo y cultura monoglósica." *La batalla del idioma. La intelectualidad hispánica ante la lengua*. Ed. José del Valle and Luis Gabriel-Stheeman. Madrid: Iberoamericana, 2004. 15–33.

D'Olwer, Lluís Nicolau. *L' expansió de Catalunya en la Mediterrània Oriental*. 3rd. ed. Barcelona: Proa, 1974.

Ferguson, Ch. "Diglossia." *Word* 15 (1959): 325–40.

Fishman, Joshua A. *Sociología del lenguaje*. Trans. Ramón Sarmiento y Juan Carlos Moreno. Madrid: Cátedra, 1979.

Horrocks, Geoffrey. *Greek: A History of the Language and its Speakers*. 2nd ed. Oxford: Wiley-Blackwell, 2010.

Gal, Susan. "Migration, Minorities, and Multilingualism: Language Ideologies in Europe." *Language Ideologies, Policies, and Practices: Language and the Future of Europe*. Ed. Clare Mar-Molinero and Patrick Stevenson. New York: Palgrave MacMillan, 2006. 13–27.

Irvine, Judith T., and Susan Gal. "Language Ideology and Linguistic Differentiation." *Regimes of Language: Ideologies, Polities, and Identities*. Ed. Paul V. Kroskrity. Santa Fe: School of American Research Press, 2000. 35–83.

Léglu, Catherine E. *Multilingualism and Mother Tongue in French, Occitan, and Catalan Narratives*. University Park: Pennsylvania State University Press, 2010.

Lledó-Guillem, Vicente. "Bernat Desclot's Response to Bernat d'Auriac's *sirventés*: The Battle of Castellammare and the Rise of Catalan as a Royal Language." *La Corónica* 39.2 (2011): 145–62.

Lock, Peter. *The Franks in the Aegean 1204-1500*. New York: Longman, 1995.

Martí i Castell, Joan. *Llengua catalana*. Barcelona: Edhasa, 1986.

Milà i Fontanals, Manuel. *Obras completas*. Vol. 3. Ed. Martín de Riquer. Barcelona: CSI, [1959]–1966.

Milroy, James. "Sociolinguistics and Ideologies in Language History." *The Handbook of*

Historical Sociolinguistics. Ed. Juan Manuel Hernández Campoy and Juan Camilo Conde-Silvestre. Oxford: Wiley-Blackwell, 2012. 571–84.

Muntaner, Ramon. *Les quatre grans Cròniques. III. Crònica de Ramon Muntaner*. Ed. Ferran Soldevila. Revisió filològica de Jordi Bruguera. Revisió històrica de M. Teresa Ferrer i Mallol. Barcelona: Institut d'Estudis Catalans, 2011.

———. *Chronicle*. Trans. Lady Goodenough. Cambridge, Ont.: In parentheses, 2000. Web. 2 July 2012.

Nadal, Josep M., and Modest Prats. *Història de la llengua catalana. Vol. 1: Dels orígens al segle XV*. Barcelona: Edicions 62, 1982.

Penny, Ralph. "Linguistic (Dis)continuity in the Iberian Peninsula." *Essays in Hispanic Linguistics Dedicated to Paul M. Lloyd*. Ed. Robert J. Blake, Diana L. Ranson, Roger Wright. Newark, Del.: Juan de la Cuesta, 1999. 43–55.

Perugi, Maurizio. *Il 'sermó' di Ramon Muntaner. La versificazione romanza dalle origini*. Firenze: Olschki, 1975.

Riquer, Martí de. *Història de la literatura catalana*. Vol. 1. Barcelona: Ariel, 1964.

Robins, R. H. *The Byzantine Grammarians: Their Place in History*. New York: Mouton de Gruyter, 1993.

Rubió i Lluch, Antoni. *Los catalanes en Grecia; últimos años de su dominación, cuadros históricos*. Madrid: Voluntad, 1927.

———. *Catalunya a Grècia: estudis històrics i literaris*. Barcelona: L' Avenç, 1906.

Setton, Kenneth M. *Catalan Domination of Athens 1311–1388*. Cambridge, Mass.: Mediaeval Academy of America, 1948.

Vilar, Pierre. *La Catalogne dans l'Espagne moderne. Recherches sur les fondements économiques des structures nationales*. Vol. I. Paris: SEVPEN, 1962.

Warren, Michelle R. "Post-Philology." *Postcolonial Moves: Medieval Through Modern*. Ed. Patricia Clare Ingham and Michelle R. Warren. New York: Palgrave Macmillan, 2003. 19–45.

Watts, Richard J. "Language Myths." *The Handbook of Historical Sociolinguistics*. Ed. Juan Manuel Hernández Campoy and Juan Camilo Conde-Silvestre. Oxford: Wiley-Blackwell, 2012. 585–606.

Wright, Roger. "La fragmentación románica." *Romanística sin complejos. Homenaje a Carmen Pensado*. Ed. Fernando Sánchez Miret. Bern: Peter Lang, 2009. 527–43.

———. "Linguistic Standardization in the Middle Ages in the Iberian Peninsula: Advantages and Disadvantages." *De mot en mot: Aspects of Medieval Linguistic. Essays in Honour of William Rothwell*. Cardiff: University of Wales Press, 1997. 261–75.

◆ 7

Empire in the Old World: Ferdinand the Catholic and His Aspiration to Universal Empire, 1479–1516

Andrew W. Devereux

It is well known that Christopher Columbus sought to reach India by way of the Atlantic, and that he viewed his voyages as potentially instrumental in Spain attaining a position of economic and political primacy among the polities of Europe.[1] While attempting to discover a westerly route to the riches of Asia, the Genoese navigator's four Atlantic crossings instead led to the foundation of Castilian settlements in the Caribbean, settlements that grew into colonies that are commonly viewed as the genesis of the early modern Spanish Empire. This was an empire that was primarily Atlantic in its orientation, and one that was principally a Castilian endeavor.

Columbus's objectives, however, also contained a Mediterranean angle. His crusading agenda and interest in effecting a Christian recovery of the Holy Land is an aspect of the explorer's thought that has garnered increasing scholarly attention in recent years.[2] In late 1500 Christopher Columbus presented to Ferdinand and Isabella of Spain a memorandum advocating the conquest of Jerusalem. Rather than offering a strategy, the document presented interpretations of Scripture as evidence that the Spanish Crown was destined to recover the Holy Land for Christendom.[3] In short, Columbus saw the Atlantic as a route to India and argued, in turn, that the riches of India could finance a Spanish-led recovery of Jerusalem.

A few short years following Columbus's memorandum, the Spanish naval commander Count Pedro Navarro composed his *Memorial* to Ferdinand of Aragon (r. 1479–1516), exhorting the king to subjugate the Ottoman Empire and to conquer Jerusalem.[4] The contrast with Columbus's memorandum is striking: Navarro's text is detailed, practical, and concrete. Not only does it offer a precise strategy for an attack on Ottoman Greece and Turkey, it elaborates a coherent vision of a Spanish Mediterranean Empire while presenting a "political theology" of Spanish kingship and its proper relationship to other Mediterranean powers.

While scholars have pored over Columbus's writings, translating and publishing many of them in the process, Navarro's *Memorial* remains unpublished and little known to modern historians. I use this comparison here because it is emblematic of the discrepancy between modern scholarship on early modern Spain's imperial ventures in the Atlantic and Mediterranean basins. The sixteenth-century development of a vast territorial empire in the Americas, compared to the more modest array of Spanish imperial possessions in the Mediterranean, has determined that, until quite recently, scholars have devoted relatively little attention to early modern Spain's Old World empire.

Navarro, however, was no outlier. On the contrary, he was one of many figures close to the royal courts of Ferdinand and Isabella who viewed the Mediterranean as the principal theatre of Hispanic imperial expansion. These "Spaniards," Aragonese, Navarrese, as well as Castilians, held a well-developed set of ideologies concerning the inner sea that informed Spanish policies there and Spain's relations with other powers that vied for Mediterranean hegemony. During the decades of Ferdinand's reign, the Aragonese king attempted to forge a Mediterranean empire, bringing Spain into contact, and at times conflict, with all the major powers of the Mediterranean basin via a protracted process of expansionary ventures in Italy and North Africa. Many Spaniards close to the Crown viewed these acquisitions in the central Mediterranean as a prelude to a grander string of conquests that would bring the eastern Mediterranean, from Alexandria to Constantinople, under Aragonese dominion.

The application of national categories, such as "Spanish," to the phenomenon of early sixteenth-century Mediterranean expansion is problematic due to the political complexities of the Iberian Peninsula at the time. For much of the period that Ferdinand outlived Isabella (1504–1516), there was no standing provision for the union of the Crowns of Aragon and Castile. Consequently, Ferdinand's Mediterranean aspirations were understood as an Aragonese venture, with any lands he conquered from Algiers (modern Algeria) toward the east accruing to the Crown of Aragon, and therefore inheritable by any Aragonese successor that Ferdinand might produce. That said, the process of expansion that Ferdinand directed was not conducted solely by subjects of the Crown of Aragon. The Aragonese monarch, chronically short on funds, applied whatever resources he could muster toward the realization of his ambitions. To this end, he employed veterans of the Granada War, such as the Castilian captain Gonzalo Fernández de Córdoba, and he relied on the naval skill of the Navarrese commander Pedro Navarro. In his African policy, Ferdinand worked closely with the Castilian Cardinal Francisco Jiménez de Cisneros, while in Italy he generally appointed Catalans to administrative offices, as he did Hugo de Moncada to the position of Viceroy of Sicily (1509) and Ramón de Cardona as Viceroy of Naples (1509). In this regard, Ferdinand's Mediterranean project was in fact a "Spanish" endeavor, in so far as it involved subjects from every kingdom that ultimately comprised the early modern Spanish monarchy. Ferdinand did, on occasion, articulate his Mediterranean objectives as being Aragonese, at least in dynastic terms. More often than not, however, he employed confessional categories to express his political agenda, frequently representing his actions as being undertaken in defense of the "Christian republic," or simply of Christendom.

Underlying Ferdinand's, and others', aspiration to Mediterranean *imperium* was a coherent vision of the possibilities represented by the inner sea. These figures held economic, strategic, and ideological interests in establishing Spanish hegemony across the *mare nostrum*. The ideological component of this conception of empire was indebted to the religious history of the sea basin, and to medieval political thought on Christian universalism. Spanish interests were predicated on an understanding of the Mediterranean as the center of the world and the locus in which the Spanish hoped to establish a universal Christian empire, a form of political organization deeply indebted to medieval political theory as elaborated by writers such as Dante in his tract *On Monarchy*. The basic tenets of this imperial ideology included the attainment of a "universal" peace among the princes of Christendom, the ending of the Great Schism between the Roman and Greek churches, and the recovery of all the lands that had constituted early Christendom. Embedded within that aspiration, obviously, was a Christian conquest of the Holy Land. Ferdinand and many at his court depicted his political and religious objectives as integral to the attainment of such a universal Christian empire. The Aragonese king was but one of numerous rulers who expressed his aspirations in such terms. The French kings Charles VIII (r. 1483–1498) and Louis XII (r. 1498–1515) represented their invasions of Italy as a prelude to the forging of a universal empire, and Ottoman sultans, in particular Mehmet II (r. 1444–1446; 1451–1481) and Selim I (r. 1512–1520), articulated their expansionist policies in similar terms, albeit through an appeal to Islamic universalist ideology. Indeed, the Mediterranean in the wake of the Ottoman conquest of Constantinople was a region dominated by appeals to universalist ideologies, both Christian and Islamic.

Hindsight, of course, tells us that Ferdinand's plans for Mediterranean *imperium* were not attained in their entirety. At his death in 1516, the Kingdom of Naples, Malta, and numerous African presidios had been brought under Aragonese control. Greece and Turkey, however, remained under Ottoman rule, and the Holy Land was still ruled from Mamluk Cairo. A shift in perspective, however, yields a different view. Seen from the Ottoman capital at Constantinople, Aragon's gains in Italy and North Africa must have appeared quite threatening indeed. Moreover, viewing Ferdinand's plans to extend Aragonese dominion to the eastern reaches of the Mediterranean merely as a failed policy obscures certain salient points contained within the contemporary documents. The study of Ferdinand's aspiration to Mediterranean *imperium* is instructive, for it illuminates important strains in Hispanic political thought on universal empire just at the moment that "Spain" (united under Habsburg rule from 1516) stood poised to create a truly global empire, albeit in a setting far removed from the shores of the inner sea. Drawing on juridical tracts, memorials, and diplomatic and personal correspondence, this essay elucidates the full extent of Ferdinand the Catholic's imperial aspirations in the Mediterranean basin, while illuminating the ideologies of empire that informed this Mediterranean project.[5]

The Medieval Catalan Legacy

It is not surprising that Ferdinand should have viewed the Mediterranean as his primary sphere of interest. Although a member of the Castilian Trastámara dynasty, he inherited the political priorities of the medieval count-kings of the Crown of Aragon and, as such, he held longstanding dynastic interests in Sicily and Sardinia. Moreover, he aspired to recover lost territories that he felt rightly constituted his Aragonese patrimony. Chief among these was the Kingdom of Naples, but he also sought to recoup the Duchies of Athens and Neopatria, brought into the orbit of the Crown of Aragon through the conquests of the Catalan Company in the early fourteenth century. In addition to these medieval dominions in the central and eastern Mediterranean, the Crown of Aragon had established consuls to support Catalan merchants in a series of North African ports stretching as far east as Alexandria (Hillgarth 19).[6] Thus, there existed a fourteenth-century precedent of Aragonese interests, both dynastic and commercial, across nearly the entire breadth of the Mediterranean. These Catalo-Aragonese traditions, in effect, served as a blueprint that guided Ferdinand's political project in the Mediterranean throughout his thirty-seven-year reign.

From the moment he succeeded his father, Joan II (r. 1458–1479), as King of Aragon, Ferdinand sought to recover territories that had formerly been subject to Aragon. In particular, the Kingdom of Naples, at that time ruled by a cadet branch of the Aragonese dynasty, attracted his attention. The central Mediterranean axis of Sicily-Naples was the strategic cornerstone upon which Ferdinand hoped to erect his empire. From the first years of his rule as King of Aragon, Ferdinand took an active interest in Neapolitan affairs and exerted increasing influence in the kingdom of the Italian *mezzogiorno* ruled by his cousin, King Ferrante I (r. 1458–1494). During the first decade of his reign, however, he applied only "soft power" in pursuing his aims.[7] When Charles VIII of France invaded Italy in 1494, pressing his Valois dynastic claim to the Italian realm, Ferdinand saw an opportunity to press his own counter-claim and to return Naples to the direct rule of the Crown of Aragon.

Acting in concert, Ferdinand and Isabella dispatched an army to Naples, led by a veteran of the Granada War, Gonzalo Fernández de Córdoba. The Castilian military leader's exploits on the battlefields of Italy would earn him the sobriquet of *Gran Capitán*. The struggle for Naples, however, was not waged with the sword alone. Ferdinand and Isabella asserted a dynastic claim to the realm that derived from the thirteenth-century marriage between Pere III of Aragon (r. 1276–1285) and Constance of Hohenstaufen. Constance's grandfather, Frederick II of Hohenstaufen, had been Holy Roman Emperor (r. 1220–1250) and King of the Two Sicilies (r. 1198–1250) (meaning the island of Sicily and its mainland counterpart, commonly known as the Kingdom of Naples). In November 1503 a Castilian courtier named Cristóbal de Santesteban drew up a juridical study of Ferdinand and Isabella's rights to Naples. Likely commissioned by the monarchs, the text presents the Trastámara dynastic claim, while also illustrating the strategic and symbolic importance the Italian lands held in Spanish designs on Mediterranean *imperium*.[8] Today Santesteban and his text are little known to scholars working on the Spain of the Catholic Monarchs, but it is evident that he was a figure of some importance at the courts of Ferdinand and Isabella and later Charles V.[9]

In his elucidation of his patrons' dynastic claim, Santesteban argued that they were the rightful heirs to the thirteenth-century Hohenstaufen rulers of the Two Sicilies, and that the papal donation of the kingdom to Charles of Anjou in 1265 had been illegal. At the same time, however, he presented a discourse of legitimation through the argument that Ferdinand and Isabella's actions, in Italy and elsewhere, contributed to the defense of Christendom, and that the Spanish monarchs adhered to the ideals and standards of imperial leadership and crusading kingship.[10] Santesteban represented his royal patrons as crusaders who, in spite of ruling over the nation furthest from the Turkish threat, had nevertheless done more than any other monarchs, "se haya mouido por seruicio de dios y por remedio del pueblo xpiano que en tanto peligro estaua" (*Tratado de la succession* ch. 11) (for the benefit and succor of the Christian people, who were in such grave danger).[11]

What is more, Santesteban employed geographical arguments to portray Ferdinand and Isabella as monarchs in the process of establishing a universal empire that would soon encompass the known world. Medieval European geographers held that there were three parts of the Earth—Asia, Africa, and Europe—that, like the Holy Trinity, were indivisible.[12] This Trinitarian view found support in the biblical account of the post-diluvian division of the Earth among Noah's three sons, thus affirming the conception of the three continents as related pieces of a whole. Dante, in *On Monarchy*, used the historical example of the Roman Empire's dominions to argue that true empire consisted of the establishment of *imperium* in Asia, Africa, and Europe (Alighieri 50–53). Moreover, these three parts of the world had all been Christianized during the early history of the Church. The advent and expansion of Islam, however, had brought Muslim rule to both Asia and Africa. In the context of the ascendant Ottoman Empire, sixteenth-century Europeans viewed the "recovery" of those formerly Christian lands not only as a *desideratum*, but as a duty incumbent on the exemplary Christian prince. Such a ruler would thus create a Christian "union" of the constituent pieces of the known globe (Bunes Ibarra 117).[13]

Santesteban drew on these geographical, political, and religious ideas when he argued that Ferdinand and Isabella were the only princes who ruled lands in all three parts of the Earth: within Europe they ruled Spain, Calabria, Apulia, and Mallorca; in Africa they possessed Sicily, Sardinia, Corsica, and Melilla (only the last of which is actually on the African continent); and in Asia they held "the Indies and Terra Firma" (*Tratado*, Ch. 11). This last term was a reference to the South American continent, the north coast of which Christopher Columbus had reconnoitered during his third voyage. In 1503, when Santesteban was writing, Europeans disagreed over whether Columbus had discovered a new continent or merely a hitherto unknown part of Southeast Asia. In locating the Caribbean islands in Asia, Santesteban portrayed Ferdinand and Isabella as ruling in all three parts of the globe and as on the cusp of establishing a universal empire.

If Santesteban's tripartite division of the Earth had a center, it was the island of Sicily, a position normally reserved for Jerusalem (Philipps 34 n33).[14] Within his genealogical exposition of the Spanish monarchs' rights to the southern Italian lands, Santesteban included a panegyric to the island kingdom. He described Sicily as the crossroads of the world. Its superiority to other lands, asserted Santesteban, derived in part from its location between Asia, Africa, and Europe. From this, Santesteban concluded that "nadie llamasse sennor del mundo ni lo penso ser si a ella le faltasse" (*Tratado de la Succession* ch. 6) ([N]o one might call himself lord of the world, nor even think of doing so, without first controlling Sicily). In asserting Ferdinand and Isabella's claim to Sicily, Santesteban indicated that, in their control of this crossroads of the world, they were engaged in the task of forging unity out of plurality.[15]

In depicting Sicily as the crossroads of the world, Santesteban did not neglect Jerusalem. On the contrary, his *Tratado* represented Sicily, Naples, and Jerusalem as kingdoms rightfully belonging to a single ruler. Santesteban's position on this matter is consistent with his emphasis on the Hohenstaufen lineage, as from the time of Frederick II the three polities were linked. Although the Mamluks had captured Acre, the last remnant of the Kingdom of Jerusalem, in 1291, popes continued to invest the Kings of Naples with the title to the defunct crusader kingdom. Santesteban, therefore, argued for Ferdinand and Isabella's rights, not just to Naples and Sicily, but also to the defunct crusader Kingdom of Jerusalem. In his portrayal of Ferdinand and Isabella as rightful rulers of the Holy Land, Santesteban cast his patrons as crusading monarchs and as leaders of the princes of Christendom. Such a representation reinforced his argument that the Spanish monarchs stood poised to establish a universal Christian empire centered in the Mediterranean.

Within a month of the publication of Satesteban's *Tratado*, Spanish forces won a decisive victory over their French opponents at the Battle of Garigliano (December 29, 1503), bringing all of Naples under effective Spanish control. Less than one year later, another dramatic shift occurred. On November 26, 1504, Isabella of Castile died, leaving her daughter Juana as Queen of Castile (r. 1504–1555), to rule jointly with her husband Philip of Austria (r. 1504–1506). After having ruled as Isabella's king-consort for thirty years, Ferdinand of Aragon was relegated to the status of administrator, or governor, of the Castilian realms. It was under these circumstances that the king embarked on his most ambitious attempts to forge a Mediterranean empire. Although he exerted authority in Castile through his daughter Joanna, Ferdinand's patrimony was restricted to the lands comprising the Crown of Aragon. For most of the period from 1504 to 1516, the ultimate union of the crowns of Aragon and Castile was by no means assured (Aram 109–110).[16] Indeed, in 1506 Ferdinand married Germana de Foix, and for the remainder of his life he tried desperately to produce a male heir who would inherit the Crown of Aragon. As Ferdinand conquered and annexed territories, these lands as well as the king's projected conquests were understood to pertain to an independent Crown of Aragon, to be inherited by an Aragonese heir, should Ferdinand be able to produce one.

Through his conquest of Naples, Ferdinand brought a political unity to the Naples-Sicily axis (commonly known as the Kingdom of the Two Sicilies) that it had more often than not lacked ever since the Sicilian Vespers (1282). From 1504 until his death in 1516 Ferdinand employed his Italian possessions as a forward base from which to launch a series of conquests along the North African coast and into the eastern Mediterranean. The Italian viceroyalties of Naples and Sicily furnished soldiers, galleys, munitions, and victuals, and were used as staging points for attacks against North Africa and into the Aegean Sea (CODOIN 24:93–103).[17] In this way, beyond their geographic centrality, the axis of the Two Sicilies operated as the cornerstone upon which Ferdinand sought to erect a grander imperial edifice. The Aragonese monarch hoped to use his control of those central Mediterranean lands and coastlines as a base from which to establish his dominion over the coast of the Maghrib as well as points further east.

Spanish interest in North Africa, of course, preceded Isabella's death. As early as 1495, Ferdinand and Isabella obtained from Pope Alexander VI (1493–1503) a bull investing them as "Monarchs of Africa." In the *bula ineffabilis* (issued February 13, 1495), Alexander invested the Spanish monarchs with the rights to the conquest of the whole of Mediterranean North Africa.[18] Two years later the city of Melilla was conquered under private enterprise, and subsequently placed under the dominion of the Crown. Following Isabella's death and the consolidation of Aragonese control over Naples, Ferdinand made the conquest of the North African littoral one of the priorities of his foreign policy. Between 1505 and 1510, the Aragonese king ordered assaults that brought a string of North African strongpoints, including Mazalquivir, Orán, Bougie, Algiers, and Tripoli, under Spanish control, thus establishing Spanish hegemony in the waters of the western Mediterranean. Ferdinand did not envision these presidios as ends in themselves. Rather, the king and his royal councilors conceived of these enclaves of Spanish sovereignty on the edge of the African continent as stepping-stones from which to launch a grand crusade into the eastern Mediterranean. The projected conquests included Egypt, Ottoman-ruled

Greece and Turkey, Palestine, and lands extending eastward into a vaguely defined "Asia."

Pedro Navarro's 1506 *Memorial*, cited at the opening of this essay, expressed a clear vision of the agenda the naval commander hoped Ferdinand would pursue. Navarro's *Memorial* urged Ferdinand to initiate an attack on Ottoman-ruled Greece and Turkey. In a two-page prologue to his *Memorial*, Navarro argued that Ferdinand was the ruler best-suited to recover these formerly Christian lands that now lay under Muslim rule.[19]

Following the subjugation of the Ottoman Empire, Navarro suggested that Ferdinand use Anatolia as a launching point for a crusade toward the south, restoring the Holy Land to Christian rule. At various points throughout his *Memorial*, Navarro stated that the overarching objective of a Spanish crusade against the Ottomans ought to be: "Cumplidamente deue restituir la sangre de nuestro Saluador X.o Jhu [Christo Jesús]: al suo p*ropio* vaso" (fol. 1v) (the restitution of the blood of our Savior Christ Jesus to its proper chalice) and "restaurar el sangre de Xo [Christo]" (fol. 1v) (to restore the blood of Christ). Navarro argued that Ferdinand possessed assets that made him especially fit to effect a Christian recovery of Jerusalem. Comparing Ferdinand's resources favorably with those of the Roman Empire of Antiquity, Navarro suggested that the Christian recovery of the Holy Land was a feat that lay within Ferdinand's grasp: "Sollo Spagna Secilia: Puglia son los harneros del mundo a toda natura de victuaglias. Con sollo la Sicilia los Romanos del universo tomaron la Impresa: quanto más: y Spagna y Puglia: non al universo amas a solo restaurar el sangre de Xo [Christo]" (fol. 1v) (Only Spain, Sicily, and Apulia are the breadbaskets of the world, plentiful in all manner of victuals. With only Sicily, the Romans undertook the conquest of the universe. How much more you will achieve, as you also control Spain and Apulia. [For your task is] not to conquer the universe, but simply to restore the blood of Christ).

Navarro's exhortation to action, however, was not merely a military project. The *Memorial* is a deeply religious and political text, and one of the principle objectives that he lists is the restoration of the Orthodox Church to Rome, or the ending of the Christian schism: "Restitutio dela sancta eglesia oriental a la sancta fe cathólica" (fol. 1r) (the restitution of the holy Eastern Church to the holy Catholic faith). In his advocacy of Catholic universalism, Navarro resorts to the traditional conception of the Church in corporeal terms: he writes that Greek kings and emperors had become alienated from the Holy Mother Church of Rome, and for this reason were "membros apartados del cuerpo místico de X.o [Christo] nuestro Redemptor" (fol. 2r) (members that had become separated from the mystical body of Christ our Redeemer). This separation was the source of the corruption of the mystical body of Christendom. However, continues Navarro, in recovering Greece, Turkey, and Jerusalem, all would be unified, and in union there would be no corruption (fol. 2r).

The upshot of this course of action, argued the military commander, would be that Ferdinand would prove instrumental in bringing about a unified politico-religious world order, that there would be one shepherd and one flock. Navarro asserted that the kings and emperors of Greece were no more, and in recovering their lands all would be unified. Navarro reserved an exalted position for King Ferdinand, writing that there would be "unus deus unus princeps: sera por V*uestra* R*eal* alteza la perpetua unyon en el seruitio del omnipotente dios: y en la Gloria de V*uestra* R*eal* M*agestad*" (fol. 2r) ([O]ne God and one Prince, and that Your Royal Highness [Ferdinand] will achieve a perpetual union in the service of almighty God and to the glory of Your Royal Majesty). Navarro's argument, then, crafts for the Aragonese king a strongly spiritual role.

It is impossible to determine to what degree Navarro's *Memorial* reflected royal thought or ideology, but a few clues indicate that it did not stray far from Ferdinand's own aspirations. Navarro's *Memorial* differed in degree, but not in substance, from the writings of numerous other figures at Ferdinand's court, including Cristóbal de Santesteban, who also espoused a vision of Spanish universal empire centered in the Mediterranean. Indeed, Navarro's *Memorial* would appear to have met with approval, as he continued to occupy important positions in Ferdinand's service for six years following his composition of the text, leading Spanish military engagements in North Africa and Italy until his capture by the French at the Battle of Ravenna in 1512.

Ferdinand did not immediately pursue the course of action Navarro advocated, remaining focused instead on the conquest of the North African coastline. It is clear, however, that the Aragonese king viewed the acquisition of strategic points along the northern and southern shores of the Mediterranean as reinforcing one another, and as leading ultimately to the establishment of Aragonese sovereignty in the Levant. In 1509 Ferdinand met with his council of state and laid out a plan to restore the Duchies of Athens and Neopatria to the Crown of Aragon. In his address, he referred to the fourteenth-century Catalan Company's conquest of parts of Greece, and argued that if they could accomplish this with the limited resources of the Crown of Aragon, then surely, with the resources of Castile at his disposal, he would be able to take back those lands that comprised the defunct duchies and now lay under Ottoman rule (Doussinague 237–38, 487).

Surviving documentation does not attest to a precise timeline that Ferdinand developed for the projected assault on the Ottoman Empire, but within a year of the meeting with his council of state he would appear to have been thinking along those lines. The Italian humanist Peter Martyr, nearly constantly at Ferdinand's court during these years, recorded his impressions of Ferdinand's political designs in personal letters that he sent to friends. In January 1510, in a letter to Iñigo López de Mendoza, Martyr wrote that internal discord between the two claimants to the Ottoman imperial throne rendered it an extremely opportune moment to attack the Turkish empire, and that an alliance of Christian princes could easily topple the Ottomans.[20] In the same letter, Martyr sent news of Pedro Navarro's capture of the North African city of Bougie, interpreting the victory as a decisive moment in Spanish expansion into the Mediterranean: "¡Oh hazaña digna de encomio! De ahora en adelante nada habrá ya difícil para los españoles, nada emprenderán en vano. Sembraron el pánico en toda África." (Martyr 313) (This deed is worthy of great praise! From now on, nothing will be difficult for the Spanish, they will undertake nothing in vain. They have sown panic throughout Africa). Martyr's letter leaves little doubt that those at the royal court understood Spanish actions in Africa as intimately linked to Ferdinand's ambitions further east.

Ferdinand, and those in his inner circle, portrayed the projected conquest of Ottoman Greece and Turkey as well as the *empresa de África* as being geared toward a Christian recovery of the Holy Land. In an address to the *Cortes* of Aragon convened at the town of Monzón in April 1510, Ferdinand asked for funds to be used in a series of African conquests that would culminate in his recovery of Jerusalem. The king emphasized his right to conduct this conquest, due precisely to his possession of the Crown of Jerusalem through his acquisition of the Kingdom of Naples.[21] On July 25, 1510, Pedro Navarro attacked Tripoli (modern Libya), and quickly seized control of the city. Ferdinand's response to the news illuminates the way the African presidios fit into the king's grander Mediterranean designs: within hours of receiving word that Tripoli was now in Spanish hands, Ferdinand conveyed the news by letter to Cardinal Cisneros, writing that God had opened the path (*camino*) for the successful completion of the "holy enterprise," a crusading term that referred to the conquest of Jerusalem (*CODOIN* doc. #19, 25:464–7).[22] Ferdinand's use of the term *camino* in conjunction with the capture of Tripoli shows how he and others in his circle thought about the conquest of the string of North African presidios. The *camino* along the rim of Africa led to the eastern Mediterranean, toward Egypt and the Holy Land.

Already by late February of 1510, Ferdinand had begun to calculate a grand scheme of conquests covering the entirety of the eastern Mediterranean and stretching beyond to encompass a vaguely defined set of lands of "the East." He instructed his ambassador in Rome, Jerónimo de Vich, to procure from Pope Julius II (1503–1513) a bull affirming Ferdinand's rights in this regard. In a telling statement, Ferdinand wrote:

> Y la dicha bulla que sobrello se ha de despachar querríamos que fuesse general desdel confín del reyno de Tremecén que está hazia la parte de leuante, o començando desdel reyno de Bugía y Alger inclusiue todo lo que está desde allí hazia la parte de leuante. Por ventura podrían allá poner duda, diziendo que en esta generalidad se entendería todo lo de Grecia y Asia y a esto respondemos que no sería inconueniente que si Dios nuestro señor nos diesse gracia que ganassemos algo dello la silla apostólica nos lo concediesse desde agora ahunque no era menester expressarlo sino poner lo en general como hauemos dicho. (Ferdinand to Jerónimo de Vich, February 28, 1510, in Terrateig 95–96)
>
> (And in the said bull that you are to procure, I desire that it grant in general terms the lands from the eastern border of the Kingdom of Tremecen, or beginning from the Kingdoms of Bougie and Algiers inclusive, all the lands from there toward the East. Perhaps some might raise concerns, saying that in such generality this grant could be understood to include all of Greece and Asia, and to this I would respond that, should God favor us with a conquest of these territories, it would not be unsuitable that the apostolic See should grant us these lands, although it is not necessary to express it in these terms, but rather state your case according to the generalities that I have outlined here.)

Ferdinand emphasized that, although he desired the recognition of this right from the papacy, it was a mere formality. Citing the Italian jurist Bartolus of Saxoferrato in crafting his argument, Ferdinand claimed that his status as King of Jerusalem entitled him to conduct conquests not only in the Holy Land proper, but more generally throughout Greece and Turkey and in any other lands ruled by the Turks (Ferdinand to Jerónimo de Vich, February 28, 1510, in Terrateig 95–96).[23] Indeed, Ferdinand expanded his argument further, stating that as King of Jerusalem, he was aggrieved, not only by the infidels occupying the Holy Land, but by all infidels everywhere. This, he argued, rendered any military action he took against non-Christians a just war (Ferdinand to Jerónimo de Vich, February 28, 1510, in Terrateig 95–96).[24]

The string of eastern conquests that Ferdinand envisioned was understood to pertain to the Crown of Aragon. The king instructed Vich that the bull he was to procure should ensure the succession to an Aragonese heir, in perpetuity, of any lands Ferdinand might conquer in the Levant.[25] Indeed, Ferdinand was fixated on establishing a vast empire, centered in the Mediterranean, that he might bequeath to a hoped-for heir. His union with Germana de Foix had produced a son who lived only a few hours, and during the last years of his life, as Ferdinand entered his sixties, he resorted to a variety of measures to try to produce another son who could succeed him.[26] In 1513 Peter Martyr, in a letter to his close friend Iñigo López de Mendoza, wrote that the king had taken to eating bulls' testicles in his food in an attempt to arouse his sexual appetite so that he might produce an heir for his paternal realms (Martyr 137–38). Soon afterward, Martyr wrote another letter, in which he asserted that two appetites were killing Ferdinand: his love of the hunt, and his sexual appetite for the queen. Martyr complained that Ferdinand took Germana with him everywhere he went, presumably because he did not want to miss an opportunity to produce an heir (Martyr doc. #542).

There is no surviving documentary evidence of whether Jerónimo de Vich pressed Pope Julius II for the bull that Ferdinand desired. If the ambassador did undertake such negotiations, the result was not what the Aragonese monarch hoped for. The demands of Ferdinand's letter, however, are stunning for their audacity. In seeking the right to the conquest of all lands ruled by the Ottomans, and the perpetual succession of conquered lands to his Aragonese offspring, Ferdinand was attempting to counter the emerging Castilian overseas empire in the Americas and the Portuguese presence in the Red Sea and Indian Ocean. From August 25, 1499, on, following the return of Vasco da Gama, King Emmanuel of Portugal (r. 1495–1521) claimed the right to the conquest of a vast swath of southern lands as yet relatively unknown to Europeans. To this end, the Portuguese king styled himself "Senhor da conquista e da navegação e comércio de Etiópia, Arábia, Pérsia e da Índia" (Thomaz 37) (Lord of Conquest, Navigation and the Commerce of Ethiopia, Arabia, Persia, and India").[27] Ferdinand's solicitation of a papal bull granting him the right to the conquest of any lands ruled by the Turks is thus another volley in the contest between the Iberian kingdoms that had persisted since Portugal and Castile had clashed over rights to the Canary Islands in the early fifteenth century. What Ferdinand instructed his ambassador Vich to negotiate for him was no less than a bull of donation along the lines of the *Inter caetera* bull (4 May 1493) that had confirmed Castilian claims in the Americas following Columbus's first voyage. This gives a sense of the extent of Ferdinand's ambitions in the eastern Mediterranean and beyond.

Ferdinand justified his Mediterranean ambitions by citing his status as titular King of Jerusalem, and emphasizing Bartolus's legal argument regarding the rights of conquest said title gave a prince within lands ruled by the Ottomans or other non-Christians. Leaving no stone unturned, the Aragonese king tasked the Castilian jurist and law professor, Juan López de Palacios Rubios (c. 1447–1524), to develop an argument supporting Ferdinand's aspirations to Mediterranean empire. Sometime between 1512 and 1516, López de Palacios Rubios, author of the infamous *Requerimiento* that conquistadors read to indigenous inhabitants of the Americas when they claimed lands for Castile, composed *De insulis*, a tract offering a legal argument for Spanish claims to the Americas. Within the text, López de Palacios Rubios digressed from the New World to address Spanish ambitions in the Mediterranean. The jurist pointed out that Africa was formerly Christian, and that it had produced no less a luminary than Saint Augustine of Hippo. Asserting that the seventh-century Muslim conquest of Africa had been unjust, López de Palacios Rubios argued that sixteenth-century Christian warfare in Africa was therefore a defensive action, thus meeting the criteria of a just war. The jurist further bolstered Ferdinand's claims to the neighboring continent by arguing that Visigothic Hispania had encompassed not only Iberia, but also North Africa: "África, que antaño, en tiempos de San Agustín, Obispo de Hipona, estuvo bajo el dominio de los Reyes Cristianos de España . . . Más tarde fué esa tierra ocupada, como lo está actualmente, por los infieles y debe ser subyugada por uno de estirpe regia" (López de Palacios Rubios 64–65) (Africa, in the time of Saint Augustine, bishop of Hippo, was under the dominion of the Christian Kings of Spain . . . Later this land was occupied, as it currently is, by the infidels and it ought to be subjugated by one who comes from a royal line). The jurist applied a similar line of argumentation justifying a Spanish conquest of the Holy Land. The Muslim occupation of Jerusalem was "tyrannical," asserted López de Palacios Rubios, and Ferdinand, as titular King of Jerusalem, held the rights to the legitimate recovery of the Holy Land: "Yo sé cómo el ánimo de Vuestra Serenidad está inclinado con todo empeño a esta empresa y cómo se dispone a emplear el resto de su vida en tan santa expedición, según lo he oído muchas veces de sus propios labios" (López de Palacios Rubios 62) (I know how Your Highness's spirit is inclined with all determination toward this enterprise and how you intend to expend the remainder of your days on this holy expedition, as I have heard this profession many times from your own lips).[28] López de Palacios Rubios linked Spanish interests in Africa and in the Holy Land, through legal argumentation and through military strategy. In doing so, the jurist revealed that early sixteenth-century Spaniards viewed crusading ventures in Africa and the Levant as inextricably linked and geared toward the conquest of the Holy Land and the destruction of Islam (López de Palacios Rubios 61–69). These objectives, as we have seen, served as consistent components of Ferdinand's political and religious agenda, particularly during the twelve years of his rule following Isabella's death. López de Palacios Rubios's text thus presented a legal argument justifying Ferdinand's Mediterranean imperial project.

Conclusion

Ferdinand of Aragon did not attain the Mediterranean empire to which he aspired. He died on January 23, 1516, even as he continued to plan further assaults in the Mediterranean. His successor, Carlos I of Spain (r. 1516–1556; also ruled as Holy Roman Emperor Charles V), faced a tumultuous accession in his Spanish realms. The revolt of the *Comuneros* in Castile and the *Germanías* in Valencia and Mallorca are but the most spectacular of the examples of initial resistance to his rule. Meanwhile, at the far end of the Mediterranean, the Ottoman Sultan Selim I (r. 1512–1520) embarked on his own series of conquests (1516–1517), bringing Syria, Palestine, Egypt, and the Arabian Hijaz under Ottoman rule.

The establishment of Ottoman hegemony across the Levant, and Suleiman I's (r. 1520–1566) subsequent foundation of the Ottoman Regencies in the Maghrib at Tripoli, Tunis, and Algiers during the 1520s, fundamentally altered the balance of power in the Mediterranean basin. In spite of this shift in the geo-political landscape, though, the Spanish Crown did not turn its back on the Mediterranean. The inner sea remained a sphere of major importance throughout the sixteenth century. Charles V's conquest of Tunis (1535) was but one attempt to redress the Ottoman advances of the previous two decades that stood in the way of Spain's imperial ambitions in the Mediterranean.

While Ferdinand's hopes of an Aragonese Empire did not come to fruition, the political thought on universal empire that underlay his political and religious objectives remained a vital component of Spanish imperial ideology well into the early modern period. Thomaso Campanella (1568–1639), an Italian subject of the Spanish Crown, wrote *The Monarchy of Spain* in 1600, a text that offered a spiritual vision of what the Spanish Empire should be, a vision that accorded in most of its particulars with the plans developed in many of the documents examined in this essay. By the time of Campanella, however, the tide had turned, and those aspirations to universal empire seemed to have greater promise of realization in the New World than in the Old.

Notes

1. Columbus wrote of his interest in reaching Arabia Felix, Mecca, and the spice markets of Calicut. See: Christopher Columbus, *The Four Voyages* (275). During his fourth voyage (1502–1504) he believed that he was a mere ten days' sail from the mouth of the Ganges (288). See also Nicolás Wey-Gómez, *The Tropics of Empire*.
2. Alain Milhou, *Colón y su mentalidad mesiánica en el ambiente franciscanista español*; Pauline Moffit Watts, "Prophecy and Discovery: On the Spiritual Origins of Christopher Columbus's 'Enterprise of the Indies'"; and, most recently, Carol Delaney, *Columbus and the Quest for Jerusalem*.
3. The 1500 memorandum was compiled into the text known as the *Libro de las Profecías*. The best modern edition of the *Libro* is that of Rusconi (67–77). In further examples of Columbus's professed crusading ambitions, in 1501, in a letter to Queen Isabella of Castile, Columbus discussed the possibility of a Spanish-led crusade to the Holy Land. See Cristóbal Colón, *Textos y documentos completos*, 278. In 1502 Columbus wrote to Pope Alexander VI urging the launching of a crusade, and offering to lead the venture in person. On this correspondence, see Varela 312.
4. Pedro Navarro, *Memorial para la Magestad en orden a la conquista de Jerusalén*. Biblioteca Nacional, Madrid, Mss./19699, caja 60. The *Memorial* was composed at some point during 1506.
5. Along these lines, albeit primarily in the context of the Atlantic World, see Anthony Pagden, *Lords of All The World* and *Spanish Imperialism and the Political Imagination*.
6. The conquest of Mallorca (1229) facilitated Catalan trade with North Africa; by 1253, the Crown had established a Catalan consulate in Tunis; by 1259, one in Bougie as well. These commercial aspirations extended into the eastern Mediterranean. In 1262, Jaume I of Aragon entered into relations with Egypt, through the mediation of Manfred, King of Sicily and Naples. As a result of these negotiations, in 1264 a consul from Barcelona was established in Alexandria (Hillgarth 21).
7. Ferdinand pursued marriage alliances with the Neapolitan royal family in an attempt to increase his influence in the *Reame*. In perhaps a more telling example, he insisted to the Neapolitan king, Ferrante I, on the establishment of the Castilian military orders of Santiago and Calatrava in Naples. As these were under the direct authority of the Crown of Castile, this action represents a growing Spanish influence in the Italian kingdom. See *Documentos sobre relaciones internacionales de los Reyes Católicos* 304; Ferdinand to King Ferrante of Naples, asking him to establish the orders of Santiago and Calatrava in kingdom of Naples, and to make them subservient to the masters of the orders in Castile. Ferdinand wrote that, as Ferrante was of the same *casa*, that his realm should more closely resemble those of Ferdinand and Isabella. He encouraged Ferrante to give rents or lands that were part of Ferrante's royal patrimony to set up the military orders in Naples, as Ferrante faced nearly constant war with Muslims: "Porque de contino teneys guerra con moros" (Because you are engaged in constant war with the Moors).

8. Cristóbal de Santesteban (c. 1440–1520), *Tratado de la succesión.*
9. The most complete information pertaining to the life of Cristóbal de Santesteban is to be found in the following source: Valentín Carderera y Solano, *Iconografía española.* Entry LVII in this work is devoted to D. Cristóbal de Santesteban y Doña Isabel de Rivadeneyra. Carderera y Solano describes Cristóbal as the son of Don Francisco de Santesteban and Doña María de Tobar. "Don Cristóbal nació por los años 1440 y debió servir á los Reyes Católicos, y más tarde al Emperador Carlos V, en calidad de caballerizo suyo. Fué regidor de Valladolid y comendador de Biedma en la órden de Santiago. Formando parte de aquella generación de ilustres varones, á quienes parecía indigna de su alto linaje la ignorancia de las letras y aun indispensable su cultivo, dejó escrito un tratado sobre la sucesión de los reinos de Jerusalén, Nápoles, Sicilia y las provincias de Pullia y Calabria, que se imprimió en Zaragoza el año 1503." (Don Cristóbal was born in the 1440s and must have served the Catholic Monarchs and later Emperor Charles V as a groom. He was an alderman of Valladolid and held the commandership of Biedma in the Order of Santiago. As part of that generation of illustrious barons who placed such emphasis on the cultivation of letters, he composed a tract on the dynastic succession of the kingdoms of Jerusalem, Naples, Sicily, and the provinces of Apuglia and Calabria, which was printed in Zaragoza in 1503). No documentation survives to attest to the reception Santesteban's *Tratado* garnered at Isabella and Ferdinand's court, but it is likely it met with royal approval. Santesteban went on to hold the post of *regidor* (alderman) in the city of Valladolid and he held the commandership of Biedma in the military order of Santiago. It is possible that one or both of these positions were granted in recompense for the service he had rendered the Crown with the composition of his *Tratado.*
10. For a fuller elaboration of the linkage between these understandings of imperial leadership and service to Christendom, see Muldoon 45. Muldoon argues that in the later Middle Ages (post-Carolingian and Ottonian empires), "the emperor did not possess universal jurisdiction, but he did possess a status superior to that of any other ruler, a status that included some kind of general responsibility for Christendom." Along similar lines, see the following works: Weiler, "The *Negotium Terrae Sanctae* in the Political Discourse of Latin Christendom, 1215–1311" and Jones, *Eclipse of Empire.*
11. "Cosa es cierto de loar que syendo España la nación de toda la xpiandad q mas lexos y mas segura este del Turco: y teniendo sus altezas las guerras que han tenido: y hauiendo fecho la conquista del reyno de Granada: y escomençado a conquistar el de Fez/ se haya mouido por seruicio de Dios y por remedio del pueblo xpiano que en tanto peligro estaua a enbiar tantos cauallos y otras muchas gentes: y tan gran numero de fustas como en esta armada enbiaron: y gran honrra ha sydo para ellos y para sus reynos lo que alla ha fecho" (Santesteban, *Tratado de la succesión,* ch. 11) (Truly, it is a fact worthy of praise that Spain, being the Christian nation most removed and protected from the Turk; and that their highnesses have been

so occupied in war, and having conquered the Kingdom of Granada and begun the conquest of that of Fez; that, in service of God and for the benefit and succor of the Christian people who were in such danger, they sent so many knights as they have done with this armada. And what the armada has done there has proved a great honor to them [the monarchs] and to their kingdoms).

12. On this Trinitarian geographical conception of the world, see Lewis and Wigen 25–26, Relaño 11 and García de Valdeavellano 423. García de Valdeavellano asserts that medieval Europeans conceived of the world, in all its plurality and diversity, as a whole (un Todo), directed by God; medieval thought consisted of the subordination of the plurality to the unity (of God) (*ordinatio ad unum*).
13. Miguel Ángel de Bunes Ibarra writes that the Earth was understood as a *corpus mysticum*, with two of the three parts (Asia and Africa) now under the rule of infidels, and that it was the responsibility of Christians to restore those parts, once more bringing unity to the Earth and to God's divine plan (117).
14. Phillips writes that Jerusalem was understood to lie at the point of intersection of the three continents (Asia, Africa, and Europe).
15. While Jerusalem was more often than Sicily placed at the geographic center of the world, the link between rule in Italy and lordship of the world was not unique to Santesteban. In German lands, too, rulers viewed control of Italy as a fundamental piece in political aspirations to empire. In the context of Iberian traditions, there also existed a precedent connecting Sicily to ambitions of empire, albeit of a more eschatological nature. On these themes, see (Edelmayer 551–59). Edelmayer examines the Holy Roman Emperor Maximilian I's published pamphlets that argued that to rule the world it was necessary to rule Italy (556). Maximilian's publication of these pamphlets illustrates that in the German lands too there was an association between control of Italy and the aspirations to universal monarchy. On Iberian understandings of the island of Sicily as a foundational piece in the construction of a universal empire, specifically Arnau de Villanova's eschatological vision of Aragonese history, see Fernández-Armesto: "In 1292, Arnau began a series of writings which reflect these influences. His *De Tempore Adventus Antichristi* of 1297—intended as the first part of a trilogy on the Antichrist—was the first of his visionary works to prophecy an eschatological role for the Arago-Catalan count-kings. In the *De Mysterio Cymbalorum*, written not later than 1301, this was refined into a programme: renovation of the church, conquest of Jerusalem, extirpation of Islam, unification with Byzantium, creation of a universal Christian empire with its capital in Sicily" (67).
16. For a succinct and clear presentation of the "accident" of the union of Aragon and Castile that took place with Ferdinand's death in 1516, see Aram (109–10).
17. This excerpt is from a letter from Hugo de Moncada, viceroy of Sicily, to Ferdinand (Palermo, June 15, 1511). Moncada describes having provided Diego de Vera everything he demanded for the conquest of Tripoli. Moncada goes on to discuss the Viceroy of Naples providing provisions to Pedro Navarro, which demonstrates

the ways these Italian possessions were truly the frontline, and fundamental, for the conquest of various points along the African coast. See also the letter from Moncada to Ferdinand (Palermo, October 23, 1511) (*CODOIN* 24:112–122), in which Moncada discusses the *empresa de África* and the difficulty of populating Tripoli with Christians: "Con deseo espero la respuesta de V.A., Señor, sobre reducir á Tripol á fortalezas; porque pensar de poblarle de cristianos es excusado" (117–18) (I eagerly await a reply from Your Highness, concerning the proposal to transform Tripoli into a military fortress; because the idea of populating Tripoli with Christians is not feasible). Moncada writes that he has received letters from the Master of Rhodes, including one for Ferdinand that he is enclosing, a fact that illustrates that Sicily and Naples operated as a clearing house for news from the eastern Mediterranean: Moncada, in fact, uses the term *las nuevas que escribe de Levante* to describe the Master's letter to Ferdinand (121).

18. Bula de Alejandro VI concediendo a los Reyes Católicos la investidura de los Reinos de Africa (February 13, 1495; Simancas. Patronato Real, Leg. 60, fol. 195), printed in Doussinague, *La política internacional*, Appendix # 4: "os damos la investidura de la misma África y de todos los reinos, tierras y dominios de ella y a vosotros y a vuestros herederos y sucesores dichos con la autoridad de Vicario del mismo Señor Jesucristo de que gozamos en la tierra, para que vosotros, vuestros herederos y sucesores dichos si como esperamos las conquistáis, las poseáis perpetuamente" (524) (we grant you the investiture of Africa itself and all the kingdoms, lands, and dominions she contains . . . so that you, your heirs and successors should possess them in perpetuity if, as we hope, you conquer them . . . there you shall exalt the name of our Savior, Jesus Christ) and, "allí [a África] llevaréis y esparciréis el nombre de nuestro Salvador Jesucristo" (523) (There [to Africa] you shall carry and spread the name of our Savior Jesus Christ).
19. Navarro addresses Ferdinand's aptitude for these deeds: "Como a persona a quien más conviene" (*Memorial para la Magestad en orden a la conquista de Jerusalén* fol. 1r) (as the person best-suited to the task).
20. "Acerca de Asia y de sus proximidades, sábete que Selimsac, segundogénito del Gran Turco—que tiene el mando del Asia Menor—para sustituir a su padre, anda a la gresca con sus hermanos y está planeando la usurpación del imperio o asesinando o derrocando a su hermano mayor, aun durante la vida de su progenitor, quien, decrépito, se consume en el lecho y apenas si contiene la vida con los dientes. Estas discordias serían motivo para la fácil caída del imperio turco, si contra él se aliaran los Príncipes cristianos" (Martyr 311) (Concerning Asia and its environs, you should know that Selimsac, the second son of the Ottoman Sultan—who controls Asia Minor—intends to go with his brothers to Greece in order to plan a coup. Either through assassinating or toppling his older brother, he intends to take control of the empire, even as their father still lives, although he is decrepit, bedridden, and barely alive. This internal discord would allow the Turkish Empire to be conquered easily, if the princes of Christendom would form an alliance).

21. Pedro Abarca wrote that at the Cortes of Monzón: "Hizo la propuesta, representando la gloria provechosa de la conquista de los Reynos de Tunez, y Buxia, que tan adelantada estaba, y prometia feliz sucesso à las esperanças de otra mayor de la África, hasta llegar dentro del Asia à la Casa Santa por tan immensos espacios, que se le debían como à Rey de Aragon por los derechos, y vinculos de Napoles, y Ierusalén" (Abarca fol. 386r) (He made the proposal, referring to the auspicious glory of the conquest of the Kingdoms of Tunis and of Bougie, which was already so far advanced, and promised the success of yet another conquest even greater than that of Africa, penetrating Asia as far as Jerusalem, which belonged to him by right, as King of Aragon, due to the links between Naples and Jerusalem).
22. Ferdinand to Cisneros concerning the capture of Tripoli (August 13, 1510): "De lo cual nos le habemos dado y damos infinitas gracias, y estamos muy alegres, porque su divina clemencia nos muestra y abre cada día más el camino para que le sirvamos en aquella santa empresa" (467) (We have given, and do give, infinite thanks for this victory, and we are delighted, because with each passing day divine clemency reveals and opens the path in order that we might serve Him in this holy enterprise).
23. "Quanto más que como sabeys la conquista de Hierusalén pertenece a nos y tenemos el título de aquel reyno y de derecho, como dize Bartholo, aquel a quien pertenece la conquista de Hierusalén lícitamente puede tomar las tierras que poseen los turcos, ahunque ellos no tengan a Hierusalén, porque, según él dize, sin ganar de las dichas tierras Hierusalén no se puede conquistar, ni después de conquistado, conseruar, y a quien se concede vna cosa se concedan todas aquéllas sin las quales aquéllas no se puede fazer" (Archivo Histórico Nacional, Estado. Legajo 8605, Ferdinand to Jerónimo de Vich, February 28, 1510, in Terrateig 95–96) (As you know, the right to the conquest of Jerusalem belongs to us and we rightfully possess the title to that kingdom. As Bartolus writes, he who holds the rights to the conquest of Jerusalem may licitly take the lands ruled by the Turks, even if they do not possess Jerusalem, because, as he says, Jerusalem cannot be conquered or held without first conquering the lands ruled by the Turks. When one is granted a particular right, one is also granted the rights to everything necessary in order to fulfill that right).
24. "Demás desto ya sabeys que la Iglesia tiene indito bello y declarada guerra contra los infieles que tienen ocupada a Hierusalém y por consiguiente contra todos los otros infieles, pues son enemigos de nuestra santa fé cathólica y no reconocen a Su Santidad, y siendo ésto assí como es sigue se que todo lo que se tomare de los infieles por quienquiera que lo tome será suyo, como cosa adquirida y tomada en justa y lícita guerra; ca la regla general es que lo que se toma en justa guerra es de quien lo toma, y pues esto se toma en guerra mouida por la yglesia lo que en ella se tomare será de quien primero lo ocupare" (Legajo 8605, Ferdinand to Jerónimo de Vich, February 28, 1510, in Terrateig 95–96) (Moreover, as you know, the Church has a standing and declared war against the infidels who occupy Jerusalem and, as follows, against all other infidels, as they are enemies of our Holy Catholic faith and do not recognize His Holiness. This being the case, it follows that whatever one might

seize from the infidels will belong to him who seizes it, as with things taken in the course of just and licit war. For the general rule is that that taken in just war is the rightful property of him who takes it, and in the case of war instigated by the Church, territory taken shall belong to him who first occupies it).

25. "Querríamos que desde luego procurassedes de ganar de nuestro muy Santo Padre vna bulla en que generalmente declarasse la dicha guerra contra los infieles y diesse a nos para nos y para nuestros sucessores reyes de Aragón todo lo que con ayuda de Dios nuestro señor conquistássemos de las tierras de los infieles" (Ferdinand to Jerónimo de Vich, February 28, 1510 in Terrateig 95–96) (We would like you to do all you can to procure from the Holy Father a bull in which he declares in general terms a war against the infidels and grants to us, for us and for our successors the Kings of Aragon, all the lands we might, with the help of God, conquer from the infidels).
26. On May 3, 1509, Germana de Foix gave birth to a son, Juan de Aragón, but the boy died within the day.
27. Thomaz sees King Emmanuel's claimed title to the conquest of eastern lands as developing naturally out of the Treaty of Tordesillas (1494).
28. In regards to the Holy Land, Palacios Rubios wrote that it had been violently and unjustly occupied: "Fué ocupada violentamente por los infieles que ahora la señorean como tiranos" (It was violently and unjustly occupied by the Infidels who now control it like tyrants).

Works Cited

Abarca, Pedro. *Anales, Rey Don Fernando el Católico-Los reyes de Aragón en anales históricos, distribvidos en dos partes: al rey n. señor en sv consejo de Aragón: por el padre Pedro Abarca de la Compañia de Iesús, Mestro del Gremio de la Universidad de Salamanca, y sv Cathedrático Jvbilado De Prima de Theologia: y Prefecto de los Estudios de sv Colegio Real.* Madrid: En la Imprenta imperial, 1682–84.

Alighieri, Dante. *On Monarchy*. Ed. and trans. Prue Shaw. Cambridge: Cambridge University Press, 1996.

Aram, Bethany. *Juana the Mad: Sovereignty and Dynasty in Renaissance Europe*. Baltimore: The Johns Hopkins University Press, 2005.

Bunes Ibarra, Miguel Ángel. "El marco ideológico de la expansión española por el norte de África." *Revista Aldaba* 26 (September 1995): 113–34.

Carderera y Solano, Valentín. *Iconografía española: Colección de retratos, estatuas,mausoleos y demás monumentos inéditos de reyes, reinas, grandes capitanes, escritores, etc. desde el S. XI hasta el XVII.* 2 vols. Madrid: Ramón Campuzano, 1855–1864.

CODOIN (Colección de Documentos Inéditos), vols. 24–25. Madrid: Imprenta de la Viuda de Calero, 1854, facsimile edition: Nendeln, Liechtenstein, 1966.

Columbus, Christopher. *The Book of Prophecies Edited by Christopher Columbus*. Ed. Roberto Rusconi; Trans. Blair Sullivan. Berkeley: University of California Press, 1997.

———. *The Four Voyages*. Ed. and trans. J.M. Cohen. New York: Penguin, 1969.

———. *Textos y documentos completos: relaciones de viajes, cartas y memoriales*. Ed. Consuelo Varela. Madrid: Alianza, 1982.

Delaney, Carol. *Columbus and the Quest for Jerusalem*. New York: Simon and Schuster, 2011.

Documentos sobre relaciones internacionales de los Reyes Católicos. Ed. Antonio de la Torre. vol. 1. Barcelona, 1949.

Doussinague, José María. *La política internacional de Fernando el Católico*. Madrid: Espasa-Calpe, S.A., 1944.

Edelmayer, Friedrich. "Italia y el Sacro Imperio en la época de Maximiliano I," *El reino de Nápoles y la monarquía de España: Entre agregación y conquista (1485–1535)*. Ed. Giuseppe Galasso and Carlos José Hernando Sánchez. Rome: Real Academia de España en Roma, 2004. 551–59.

Fernández-Armesto, Felipe. *Barcelona: A Thousand Years of the City's Past*. New York: Oxford University Press, 1992.

García de Valdeavellano, Luis. *Curso de Historia de las instituciones españolas: De los orígenes al final de la Edad Media*. Madrid: Alianza Editorial, 1998.

Hillgarth, J.N. *The Problem of a Catalan Mediterranean Empire 1229–1327*. The English Historical Review, Supplement 8. London: Longman, 1975.

Jones, Chris. *Eclipse of Empire? Perceptions of the Western Empire and its Rulers in Late Medieval France*. Turnhout: Brepols, 2007.

Lewis, Martin W., and Kären E. Wigen. *The Myth of Continents: A Critique of Metageography*. Berkeley and Los Angeles: University of California Press, 1997.

López de Palacios Rubios, Juan. *De las islas del mar océano*; Fray Matías de Paz, *Del dominio de los Reyes de España sobre los indios*. Ed. and trans. Agustín Millares Carlo. México: Fondo de Cultura Económica, 1954.

Martyr d'Anghiera, Pietro. *Epistolario de Pedro Mártir de Anglería*. Trans. J. López de Toro. *Documentos inéditos para la historia de España*, vols. 9–12. Madrid: Imprenta Góngora, 1953–1957.

Milhou, Alain. *Colón y su mentalidad mesiánica en el ambiente franciscanista español*. Valladolid: Cuadernos Colombinos, 1983.

Muldoon, James. *Empire and Order: The Concept of Empire, 800–1800*. New York: St. Martin's Press, 1999.

Navarro, Pedro. *Memorial para la Magestad en orden a la Conquista de Jerusalen*. Mss. 19699, caja 60 (Pedro Navarro, *Memorial*). Madrid: Biblioteca Nacional de España, 1506.

Pagden, Anthony. *Lords of All The World: Ideologies of Empire in Spain, Britain, and France c.1500-c. 1800*. New Haven: Yale University Press, 1995.

———. *Spanish Imperialism and the Political Imagination: Studies in European and*

Spanish-American Social and Political Theory 1513–1830. New Haven: Yale University Press, 1990.

Phillips, Seymour. "Outer World of the European Middle Ages." *Implicit Understandings: Observing, Reporting, and Reflecting on the Encounters Between Europeans and Other Peoples in the Early Modern Era*. Ed. Stuart Schwartz. New York: Cambridge University Press, 1994.

Relaño, Francesc. *The Shaping of Africa: Cosmographic Discourse and Cartographic Science in Late Medieval and Early Modern Europe*. Aldershot: Ashgate, 2002.

Santesteban, Cristóbal de. *Tratado de la successión de los reynos de Jerusalén y de Nápoles y de Cecilia y de las provincias de Pulla y Calabria*. Zaragoza: Jorge Coci, 1503. Madrid: Biblioteca Nacional de España: Post-incunables R/29905(2).

Terrateig, Baron, ed. *Política en Italia del Rey Católico (1507–1516). Correspondencia inedita con el embajador Vich*. 2 vols. Madrid: Consejo Superior de Investigaciones Científicas, 1963.

Thomaz, Luís Filipe F.R. "L'idée impériale manuéline." *La Découverte, le Portugal et l'Europe*. Actes du Colloque, Paris (26–28 mai 1988). Paris: Fondation Calouste Gulbenkian, 1990. 35–103.

Varela, Consuelo. "Aproximación a los escritos de Cristóbal Colón." *Jornadas de estudios, Canarias-América* 3–4 (1984): 69–90.

Watts, Pauline Moffitt. "Prophecy and Discovery: On the Spiritual Origins of Christopher Columbus's 'Enterprise of the Indies.'" *American Historical Review* 90 (1985) 73–102.

Weiler, Björn. "The *Negotium Terrae Sanctae* in the Political Discourse of Latin Christendom, 1215–1311." *The International History Review* 25.1 (2003): 1–36.

Wey Gómez, Nicolás. *The Tropics of Empire: Why Columbus Sailed South to the Indies*. Cambridge, MA: MIT Press, 2008.

8

Singing the Scene of History in Fernão Lopes

Josiah Blackmore

When the Portuguese king Fernando I died in late 1383, there ensued a series of events over the next two years that marked, in A.R. Disney's phrasing, "the greatest dynastic crisis in Portugal since the kingdom had come into being" (117). The heir to the throne, Fernando's daughter Beatriz, was only eleven years old but had already been implicated in an arranged marriage that would favor Juan I of Castile's interests on the Portuguese crown. Queen Leonor Teles, Fernando's widow, was to act as regent until Beatriz's majority. Following Fernando's death, a struggle for power intensified between Juan of Castile and Portuguese loyalists, headed by João, Master of Avis, illegitimate son of Pedro I and Inês de Castro. In one of the more dramatic moments of this Portuguese civil strife, João murdered the Galician lover of Leonor (João Fernandes Andeiro). In 1385, he led a battle at Aljubarrota in which Castilian forces were decisively defeated, and soon after the twenty-six-year-old was acclaimed king as João I (r. 1385–1433) of the newly established House of Avis.[1]

These pivotal years between 1383 and 1385, and the first two decades of João I's reign to 1411, are the subject of the *Crónica de D. João I* (hereafter *CDJI*) by Fernão Lopes (c.1380–c.1460), Portugal's first official chronicler and one of medieval Europe's preeminent historical writers. Lopes began to hold archival responsibilities at court beginning in 1418 with his appointment as Keeper of the Royal Archive. In 1434 he was made *cronista-mor* (chronicler-royal) by Duarte I, João's successor, who charged Lopes to "poer em caronyca as estorias dos Reys que antygamente em portugal forom" (render into chronicle the histories of the previous kings of Portugal).[2] This history of kings, in Amado's analysis, was "an important instrument for political affirmation and cultural consolidation" ("Belief in History" 18). The extant chronicles that can definitively be attributed to Lopes are the *Crónica de D. Pedro I*, the *Crónica de D. Fernando*, and the *CDJI*.

The *CDJI*, in two parts, was thus the final component of a wide-ranging historical project.[3] Yet unlike the histories recounted in the earlier chronicles, Lopes's task in the *CDJI* was not only to present the *res gestae* of João's rise to power and subsequent reign but also to "demonstrate the legitimacy of a royal election that was not determined by bloodline but by the will of the people" (Amado, "Crónica de D. João I"). In addition to Lopes's exposition of João's pursuit of power and the political and national issues at stake as part of the historiographic demonstration of legitimacy, there is also in the *CDJI* a de facto legitimating function of historiographic narrative itself. Gabrielle M. Spiegel, in a study of thirteenth-century French prose historiography, notes that "chroniclers created a novel vernacular historiographic discourse, one that attempted to ground historical truth in a new system of authentication based on prose as a language of 'truth'" (*Romancing the Past* 2). Nonetheless, Lopes did not aprioristically assume an authority as chronicler—rather, he sought to establish narrative legitimacy through a careful disquisition on objectivity and historical method in the Prologue to the First Part.[4] The consultation of many sources underlies Lopes's method, and in the *CDJI* the objective is to present only the "simprez verdade" (simple truth) by critically comparing sources or competing versions of the same event. Yet this "objectivity" is necessarily linked to the political rhetoric of the chronicle, since its purpose is to consolidate João's monarchic authority and impugn other writers who would challenge it.[5] "It would be a mistake to believe that the façade of objectivity erected by vernacular chroniclers represented a genuine impartiality before the 'facts' of history," Spiegel writes; "[i]f anything, the assumption of 'neutrality' was a more powerful tool of partisanship" (*Romancing* 220). Such an understanding of the putative neutrality implied by the "simple truth" points to the ideological dimension of historiographic discourse. In marshalling information to his chronistic purposes, Lopes presents an array of letters, sermons, notarial documents, and rumors of the "comuũ poboo" (common people) in addition to more traditional *auctoritates*. These documents and reports are distinct from Lopes's own discursive creations, such as dialogues or speeches, since their origins are external to the chronicler's narrative. As a result, the authority of Lopes's text derives from a combination of external sources (written and oral) and the chronicler's own narrative shapings of voices of the past. Within this discursive multiplicity of the *CDJI*, we also find two citations of lyric poetry: one on Juan I's siege of Lisbon, and one on the surrender of the castle of Portel, a town near Évora. In this essay I consider how the lyric insertions foreground the process by which an event is narrativized or made into a historical story, and how it addresses the referentiality of language. My specific focus is on the second of the lyric moments, the one which recounts the surrender of Portel.

Yet before proceeding to the *CDJI* itself, the discursive multiplicity I mentioned above merits comment, as this is what allows for a study of Lopes through the perspective of Mediterranean studies, and this perspective enriches our understanding of the historical and literary environments that gave rise to Lopes's work. While one of the strains of historiographic writing in medieval Portugal was a tradition of annals, derived from the twelfth-century *Annales portucalenses veteres*, written in Latin and of ecclesiastical origin, another was a tradition of vernacular writing that was, in part, a legacy of the Castilian historiographic school of Alfonso X, el Sabio (1221–84). Alfonso's grandson Dinis reigned in Portugal from 1279 to 1325, and followed his grandfather's interest in cultivating a fecund literary culture. Dinis himself was a prolific *trovador*, and had an interest in historical writing. The Portuguese monarch commissioned a translation into Portuguese of part of the historical writing of the tenth-century Cordovan writer Ahmad al-Rāzī; this translation, done by Gil Peres with the assistance of Master Mohammad, is known as the *Crónica do Mouro Rasis*. Portions of this chronicle were incorporated into the *Crónica Geral de Espanha de 1344* (compiled by Dinis's illegitimate son Pedro, Count of Barcelos), which also included parts of Alfonso X's *Primera Crónica General*. Consequently, a Mediterranean context of historiographic writing partially shaped Lopes's intellectual environment, evident in the *Crónica do Mouro Rasis* and in the traditions of Arabic writing that were part of Alfonso's histories and that made their way into Portugal in the *Crónica Geral de 1344*. As Francisco Márquez Villanueva points out, a plurality of historical sources and narrative genres constituted Arabic historiographic discourse (141–59), so the Mediterranean as a category of analysis in Lopes connects the Portuguese chronicler to this vibrant historiographic tradition.

And now to Lopes's *CDJI*. The lyric insertion occurs in an episode that spans chapters 157 and 158. The year is 1384, and Nuno Álvares Pereira, the hero-general of the battle of Aljubarrota a year later which seals João's destiny as the new monarch, is traveling the Portuguese countryside to confront Castilian sympathizers and to muster support for João.[6] Pereira arrives in Portel, whose mayor is a "great Portuguese nobleman" by the name of Fernão Gonçalves de Sousa, married to Teresa, the former nursemaid of Queen Beatriz of Castile. According to Lopes, it was at his wife's urging that Sousa "tomou . . . voz comtra Portugall e se tornou Castellãao" (*CDJI* 294) (took sides against Portugal and turned Castilian). Pereira and his men manage to infiltrate the city and capture it for João's cause. Lopes begins chapter 158 by observing that "Fernam Gomçallvez . . . era o mais saboroso homem que em Portugall avia, e mui sollto em suas pallavras" (296) (Fernão Gonçalves was the most entertaining man in Portugal, and very free with his words). And, Lopes goes on to note, even though the mayor found himself in an unpleasant situation, "nom leixou dhusar daquello que per natureza tinha" (296) (he did not refrain from using that which nature had given him). At the end of the episode, after a meeting with Pereira in which the mayor is told he must side with João or leave, a resigned Fernão Gonçalves de Sousa surrenders the castle and departs, but not before calling for the trumpets to be played and then addressing his wife in the following manner: "Amdaae per aqui, boa dona, e hiremos balhando, vos e eu, a ssoom destas trombas; vos por maa puta velha, e eu por villaão fodudo no cuu ca assi quisestes vos. Ou cantemos desta guisa, que será melhor" (298) (Come this way, my good woman, and let us leave dancing, you and I, to the sound of these horns; you as a filthy old whore, and I as a common wretch buggered in the ass, since that's what you wanted. Or let's sing in this manner, which is better):

> Pois Marina baillou,
> tome o que ganou;
> melhor era Portell e Villa Ruiva,
> que nom Çafra e Segura,
> tome o que ganou,
> dona puta velha. (298)
>
> (So Marina danced,
> take what she earned;
> better would be Portel and Vila Ruiva
> than Zafra and Segura,
> take what she earned,
> old madame whore.)[7]

Lopes then explains that the mayor lost Portel and Vila Ruiva in Portugal but was given Zafra and Segura in Castile, and that he referred to his wife in this fashion because it was well-known that she had persuaded him to switch allegiance to Castile. As the mayor left Portel, Lopes notes that "estes sabores e outros hia dizemdo" (298) (he was reciting this and other entertaining things). At this point the episode ends.

Sousa's poem, with its ribald, debasing allusions to the mayor and his wife and their overtly entertaining nature, is a *cantiga de mal dizer* in the tradition of the Galician-Portuguese lyric school which originated in the late twelfth century. This is noteworthy, since scholars generally consider this poetic practice to have ended in the mid fourteenth century (c.1340) according to the dating of the last known poems composed, purportedly after which several decades of poetic inactivity ensued (Jensen, *Earliest Portuguese Lyrics* 18). Lopes's inclusion of Sousa's *cantiga* seems to show that Galician-Portuguese lyric culture was still alive in the late fourteenth century, four decades later (recall that this episode is taking place in 1384) than the accepted terminus ad quem of the Galician-Portuguese school.

This lyric insertion, much like the song included in chapter 115 on the siege of Lisbon, which is sung by unnamed women, constitutes one of what can be termed the many historical "voices" Lopes incorporates into his text.[8] Spiegel defines historiographic "voices" as sources of authority drawn on by chroniclers who seek to construct a "witness discourse" around (contemporary) events (*Romancing* 219). The *CDJI*, however, is not a witness discourse in that its events are not contemporary, although Lopes does take recourse to many sorts of documents. This multitude of documents are "voices" in Spiegel's definition, but the lyric insertions are not insofar as Lopes does not include them as sources of historical information per se to lend authority to his text. Yet we can still consider the lyrics as voices if we expand Spiegel's definition to include the historically-attested ways in which members of a culture spoke in codifiable forms of discourse, such as poetry or proverbs.[9] Lopes's inclusion of these forms of speaking does not mean that he was necessarily "less choosey about the rank of his informants" because he used popular sources (Russell 70), but rather because those popular forms of speaking or singing, in addition to written documents, are part of a polyphonic culture of discourse in narrating the past.

Let us now turn to the details of Sousa's *cantiga* and to the staging or performance of a historical scene that it represents. In the flow of the narrative, the *cantiga* transforms into a symbolic idiom certain facts already presented in the preceding prose. Specifically, it poetically restages an episode of political defeat and surrender. Lopes prepares for Sousa's improvisation of the *cantiga* by claiming that he was "o mais saboroso homem que em Portugall avia" (the most entertaining man in Portugal). The superlative qualifier suggests that it was the mayor's talent for inventive and witty speech that earned him a place in history. *Saboroso* (or the substantive *sabor*) appears frequently in the Galician-Portuguese lyric corpus to refer to an entertaining or ludic poetic capacity, as it also does in the fourteenth-century genealogical *Livro de linhagens* by Pedro of Barcelos, in which the aristocratic family trees often identify individuals with monikers or descriptive expressions.[10] For example, in the Gaia family ancestry, we find references to a "Johan'Eanes da Gaia, que foi cavaleiro de boa palavra e muito saboroso" (190) (João Eanes da Gaia, who was a knight faithful to his word and very entertaining), to his grandson "Joham da Gaia, que foi mui boo trobador e mui saboroso" (190) (João da Gaia, who was an excellent *trobador*, and very entertaining), and to a "Martim Martĩiz . . . que foi mui boo cavaleiro e mui saboroso" (190) (Martim Martins . . . who was a good knight, and very entertaining). João da Gaia's entry, in which the qualities of being a poet (*trobador*) and being *saboroso* are specified as separate characteristics, suggests that one does not necessarily imply the other. *Saboroso* indicates a use of language meant to achieve a certain effect (pleasure or laughter).

In the case of Fernão Gonçalves de Sousa, this use of language is a playful engagement with the ambiguity and polysemy of words.[11] Early in chapter 158, Lopes establishes this by describing a scene in which the mayor, on witnessing a sudden, drunken attack on the castle at Portel by some of Pereira's men and some of the locals: "disse comtra os seus em sabor: Vistes numca mais estranha cousa que esta, que Portell combate Portell?" (*CDJI* 296) (he wittily said to his men, Have you ever seen a stranger thing than this, where Portel fights Portel?). Lopes explains that the abundance of wine in Portel was the reason for the attack, so here the mayor displays a penchant for double meanings. In the poem, the mayor exploits the circumstance of political defeat by restating it in the idiom of the *cantigas de mal dizer*. Generally speaking, his *cantiga* participates in that subgroup of Galician-Portuguese joke poems on political themes, such as those on the traitorous *alcaides* of Sancho II (1223–48), or the political *sirventeses* of Alfonso X.[12] The Sousa family, in fact, was one of the most powerful of the Portuguese aristocracy (Jensen, *Medieval Galician-Portuguese Poetry* lxxvii), so the mayor's abasing self-portrait, as well as the use of *puta* to refer to his wife, effects an inversion of status and social standing in the metamorphosis of historical into poetic personae; the deliberate use of *cantar* (to sing) in the penultimate line of the first stanza signals a shift from historiographic to poetic discursive register, and to the improvised performance as an entertainment for an observing public. Sousa's quality of being "o mais saboroso homem que em Portugall avia" implicitly invests this inversion and the performance of the *cantiga* with a humorous quality, one that depends on an interplay of several factors.[13] The first is the demotion from *fidalgo* ("huũ gram fidallgo portuguees" (294) (a great Portuguese nobleman) to *vilão*. This demotion, in the first instance, indicates Sousa's adoption of a social rank more fitting with that of a *jogral*, one of the ranks of performers of Galician-Portuguese *cantigas* who usually came from lower social classes (Jensen, *Earliest* 26; Menéndez Pidal 17). To proclaim this jocular demotion Sousa commands that horns be played. Lopes notes this in his narrative with "começou dizer que lhe chamassem as trombas para tamger" (297–98) (he requested the trumpets to be called forth and played), and, within the lines of the first stanza of his song, Sousa invites his wife to dance "a ssoom destas trombas." Elsewhere in the *CDJI* (and other chronicles), the playing of horns is a sign of military triumph or peace, but here they are the accompaniment to the poetically-staged "dance" as a ludic, satiric celebration of defeat. Moreover, as Menéndez Pidal points out, horns and trumpet players in medieval Iberian poetic culture were characteristic of one of the lowest classes of *juglar*, so this corroborates the allusion to *vilão* (43). The ludic debasement is completed (again by drawing on the idiom of the satiric, medieval poetry) by Sousa's allusion to being sodomized and by denouncing his wife as a whore. While there are numerous references to sodomitic imagery in the medieval joke poetry, Sousa's *cantiga* is the only one in which the poetic first-person identifies *himself* as a passive sodomite.[14] The language of sodomitic penetration and meretriciousness, of sexual deviance and licentiousness, symbolically restates the historical scene of political defeat and disempowerment. Fernão Gonçalves de Sousa lays the blame for his ousting as mayor of Portel on his wife's insistence that he side with Castile, rendered in his poem as a whoring of Portuguese interests which leaves him passively *fodudo no cuu*.[15]

We have seen thus far that the *CDJI* is a multi-voiced historiographic space, and in the Portel episode Lopes provides an example of how historical circumstances are rendered into the formal genre of poetry, or how a shift is effected from an expository, chronistic narrative to a symbolic, poetic one. There is a playful antagonism, or at least tension, between event and *cantiga*: while the episode tells of political defeat and humiliation, it is one of textual triumph, and demonstrates how certain *notabilia facta* flourish in(to) different genres of discourse. Rhetorically, we might consider this to be an episode of *peristasis*, an amplification achieved through the description of circumstances. In the *CDJI*, Fernão Gonçalves de Sousa is the only figure that is at once historical subject and author of a text on an event in which he is directly involved. Poetically, he is the author of a *cantiga de mal dizer* while also one of the targets of the satire. Sousa's co-occupation of different spaces within the chronistic text—as author and subject in both historiographic and poetic narrative—is a brief but revealing exposition of the relationship between historical event and its discursive representations. I repeat my earlier observation that the Portel episode foregrounds the process by which an event is metamorphosed into narrative, because here we clearly see that Lopes's account of this historical scene and Sousa's poetic recapitulation of it in the creation and performance of a *cantiga* are independent, if complementary, textual practices. As we witness the mayor improvise his song, Lopes notionally relinquishes control of the narrative to the voice of one of his subjects and allows a past moment to take center stage in generating its own version of events. We do not know if Lopes found a record of the mayor's *cantiga* among his source materials (those "great number of books . . . and public documents" the chronicler says he consulted in the Prologue to the First Part) or if he composed the song himself, but the question is a moot one since the genre of discourse is ultimately at issue.[16] The device of the lyric insertion in the *CDJI* is limited to the two instances I have identified. Yet unlike other genres of texts in which lyric insertions occur, when they appear in historiographic writings there is an implicit claim to the ethos of *verdade* that governs the overall narrative, or to the "historicity" of poetry.[17] Lopes demonstrates how poetry can present an alternate version of events. This transformation hinges on the verb *cantar*, which first signals the rendering of history into a symbolic idiom, but even more importantly establishes the *cantiga* as another kind of historical discourse in that, leaving aside the question of its referentiality to "actual" events, is part of a culture of narrative and historiographic speaking. Thus the historicity of poetry means that *cantigas* pertain to the activity of memory-creation exemplified by the chronicler. Lyrics, as Lopes's careful detailing of the circumstances leading to their creation attests, are another kind of historical memory generated by those outside the confines of official, textual culture, couched as that memory might be in the idiom of poetry and of the *cantigas*.

The Portel episode in chapters 157 and 158 brings to a conclusion one fundamental component of the *CDJI*—the reconnaissance mission of Nuno Álvares Pereira through the Portuguese countryside to discover supporters of the Master of Avis. In chapters 159–162, Lopes pauses the narrative proper to list the citizens and members of the nobility (where it is possible to reconstruct such names) loyal to João's cause. At the head of this list is Nuno Álvares Pereira himself, whom Lopes compares to St. Peter—as Peter was the foundation of the Church, so was Pereira the "salvaçom da terra que seus avoos gaanharom" (299) (salvation of the land won by his ancestors). Pereira was the "gloria e louvor de todo seu linhagem" (299) (pride and glory of his entire lineage). Lopes's references to lineage (*linhagem*), both in the case of Pereira and the other Portuguese listed in this chapter, is a strategic narrative move that, in part, tacitly refers back to Sousa's *cantiga* and invests it with a level of meaning bearing on genealogical history. D. Pedro's *Livro de linhagens* (c. 1340–44) establishes genealogy as one of the structures of Portuguese history and historical narrative. Spiegel discusses some concepts underlying genealogical narrative as a genre: the elaboration of lineages are based on consanguinity, and therefore "genealogy functioned to secularize time by grounding it in biology" (*Past as Text* 104, 107). Moreover, "[r]aised to the royal level, genealogy took on the overtones of a dynastic myth" (104). We can apply these observations on twelfth-century French genealogy to the case at hand. In legitimating João's accession to power, Lopes was invested in establishing as much of a lineage or genealogy (indeed, a founding myth of Portuguese history) surrounding the House of Avis as possible. So it is that the chronicler's catalogue of loyal nobles and citizens in chapter 159 is tantamount to a vindication of certain Portuguese family lines and a dismissal, by exclusion, of others (i.e., those loyal to Castile). In this, the episode of Fernão Gonçalves de Sousa performs a metaphoric function in Lopes's adjustment of Portuguese family trees. For, if we accept Spiegel's claim that "a medieval genealogy displays a family's intention to affirm and extend its place in political life (104)" then Lopes's selection of certain families in his catalogue of Portuguese loyalists validates those families as present and future participants in Avis Portugal. The mayor and his wife Teresa stand as a case study of the loss of such a validation, which might explain the placement of the Portel episode before chapter 159 as a sort of prologue to the recitation of (genealogical) names. Lopes's *Crónica de D. Fernando* (on Fernando I) provides additional insight. We learn in chapter 45 of Queen Leonor's socially graceful demeanor, under which lurked ambition and a duplicitous personality. In order to strengthen her political support, Leonor arranged marriages and granted castles; among these arrangements, "casou Fernam Gonçallvez de Sousa com dona Tareija de Meira, e fez-lhe dar o castello de Portell" (229) (she approved the marriage of Fernão Gonçalves de Sousa with Teresa de Meira, and arranged for [Sousa] to be given the castle of Portel). This establishes Sousa's place in what will become the anti-Avis camp. The mayor's *cantiga*, then, expresses the violence done to ancestral lineage and continued political power through references to prostitution and sodomy. Teresa's success at persuading Sousa to take sides with Castile, as noted above, is a prostitution of Portuguese loyalty, for which Teresa is maligned as a "puta velha" (old whore). She no longer holds a place in ancestral generation because her meretriciousness has made it impossible for her to be part of legitimate familial/political structures; in the misogynistic vocabulary of much of the medieval joke poetry, her status as a *puta* means she can have no part in legitimate, ancestral bloodlines. Likewise, Sousa's status as a "villaão fodudo no cuu" (a common man buggered in the ass) contextualizes sodomy as that which disrupts (heterosexual) consanguineous lineages. In effect, as a result of his political loyalties, the mayor can no longer perpetuate his name within the Portuguese genealogical sphere, so he is as barren as a sodomite.

After the recognition of the individuals loyal to João (and therefore to Portugal), Lopes briefly comments on the course of world history, beginning with Adam, in writers such as Eusebius and Bede. These earlier authors proposed that world history was divided into six ages. Lopes announces that, with the reign of João I, a Seventh Age has begun. He explains that "per comparaçom, fazemos aqui a septima hidade; na quall se levamtou outro mumdo novo, e nova geeraçom de gentes; porque filhos dhomeẽs de tam baixa comdiçom . . . per seu boom serviço e trabalho, neste tempo forom feitos cavalleiros, chamamdosse logo de novas linhageẽs e apellidos" (308) (in comparison, we propose here a Seventh Age, in which a new world arose, and new family lines; because sons of men of lowly status, for their good service and work, in this age were made knights, proclaiming new ancestry and taking on new surnames). Rebelo notes that this Seventh Age represents not the end, but the beginning of history, signalled by a far-reaching solidarity with the new king among the Portuguese nobility and citizenry (67). Lopes's Seventh Age is thus political in nature, and the participation of the common people in the genealogical structure of Portuguese history allows for new branches of ancestry and, consequently, new configurations of political power to emerge. The *CDJI* is the first written testimony of this "new world." In outlining the political nature of the Seventh Age, the chronicler reaffirms an inseparable connection between the political and the historiographic. In this scenario, Fernão Gonçalves de Sousa's *cantiga* is political, not only because of its theme but because of its inclusion in chronistic discourse and in its capacity as an example of a truncated, ancestral line. Sousa's branch of the family has been disavowed within a revitalized, genealogical consciousness heralded by the Seventh Age. It is part of Lopes's "simprez verdade" (simple truth) because it is one possible and plausible way of speaking about historical events. It is part of the *res gestae* of the newly-validated Avis dynasty.

Notes

1. I have summarized in a few lines what was a complex political situation that involved Portugal, Spain, and England. For two recent analyses with further details, see Disney 117–26 and Newitt 39–47.
2. For the full document in which Duarte assigns Lopes this historiographic duty, see Lopes, *CDJI* xlv. All translations are mine.
3. The Third Part was written by Lopes's successor to the post of *cronista-mor*, Gomes Eanes de Zurara (c.1410–c.1474), more commonly known as the *Crónica da tomada de Ceuta*.
4. For studies of this Prologue, see Amado, *Fernão Lopes* 77–81, and Blackmore, "*Afeiçom* and History-Writing."
5. Lopes quite probably had in mind partisan readers of the *Crónica del Rey Don Juan, Primero de Castilla e de León* by the Castilian Pero López de Ayala (1332–1407?). This text, of course, relates the history of Juan I, João I's adversary.
6. Pereira would later take religious vows and become a mystic after entering the Carmelite monastery (Convento do Carmo) in Lisbon. He was canonized in 2009.
7. Editors of the *CDJI* present the lyric as beginning with "Pois Marina baillou" (So Marina danced), but in fact all of Sousa's speaking is lyrical, so that his initial words constitute the first stanza: "Amdaae per aqui, boa / dona, e hiremos balhamdo / vos e eu, a ssoom destas / trombas; vos por maa puta / velha, e eu por vilaão / fodudo no cuu, ca / assi quisestes vos. / Ou cantemos desta guisa, / que será melhor." This rearrangement of Sousa's words into a poetic stanza follows the metric scheme of "Pois Marina baillou," composed in *redondilha menor*.
8. A group of "moças sem nehuũ medo" (fearless girls) sing a song as they pick up rocks to help defend the city: "Esta he Lixboa prezada, / mirala e leixalla. / Se quiserdes carneiro, / quall derom ao Amdeiro; / se quiserdes cabrito, / quall deram ao Bispo" (198) (This is treasured Lisbon, / gaze upon it and leave. / If you'd like mutton, / as they gave to Amdeiro; / if you'd like kid, / as they gave to the Bishop). The references to Amdeiro and the Bishop are to figures killed in João's uprising against the incumbent monarchy.
9. Amado, for her part, proposes a Genettian understanding of "voice" in Lopes (*Fernão Lopes* 39).
10. Pedro of Barcelos was one of the leading intellectual and literary figures in Portugal in the fourteenth century. It is his death in 1354 that marks, according to many scholars, the definitive end of the Galician-Portuguese lyric school.
11. The Portel episode also occurs in the anonymous *Coronica do Condestabre*, on the life of Nuno Álvares Pereira, composed c. 1440 and printed for the first time in 1526. In this text, the chronicler downplays Sousa's language talents and emphasizes instead the negotiations between the mayor and Pereira. Even so, at episode's end, the chronicler elevates Sousa to "hũu do mais gracioso homeem do mundo" (92) (one of the wittiest men in the world), and provides the text of his *cantiga*, which is slightly

different from Lopes's version: "Poys Maryna balhou, tome o que ganou. Milhor era Portell e Villa Ruyva, puta velha, que com Çaffra e Segura. Tome o que ganou" (92) (So Marina danced, take what she earned. Better would be Portel and Vila Ruiva, than Zafra and Segura, take what she earned). The prologue to Sousa's *cantiga* is absent. The inclusion of the poem might be evidence of Lopes's participation in the chronicle, or of the *CDJI* as source material.

12. Rodrigues Lapa identifies the alcaides of Sancho II as one of the six main thematic foci of the *cantigas de escarnho e mal dizer* (8).
13. The term *sabor* is one of a group of words in Lopes's chronicles that can direct a reading toward the humorous (Amado, *O passado e o presente* 86n.1). Amado also notes the many factors that bear on laughter in Lopes, including gender, social position, psychological disposition, and narrative situation ("Fiction as Rhetoric" 40), some of which are present here.
14. For a study of these references, see Blackmore, "The Poets of Sodom."
15. Sousa gives his wife a satiric *senhal* (Marina) in his song. This name, and its variations, was common in the Galician-Portuguese joke poetry as a name of a *soldadeira* or camp prostitute. For some examples, see the *cantigas* by Pero da Ponte in Lapa (222, 224).
16. To date I have been unable to find independent corroboration in pre-Lopes sources of this *cantiga* or the one in chapter 115.
17. For example, see Boulton's study of lyric insertions in medieval French narrative. The lyrics Boulton studies are love lyrics interpolated into longer, narrative texts, but none of these texts are chronicles.

Works Cited

Alfonso el Sabio. *Primera crónica general de España*. Ed. Ramón Menéndez Pidal. 1955. Madrid: Gredos, 1977.

Amado, Teresa. "Belief in History." *A Revisionary History of Portuguese Literature*. Ed. Miguel Tamen and Helena C. Buescu. New York: Garland, 1999. 17–29.

———. "Crónica de D. João I." *Dicionário da literatura medieval galega e portuguesa*. Ed. Giulia Lanciani and Giuseppe Tavani. Lisbon: Caminho, 1993.

———. *Fernão Lopes, contador de história: sobre a* Crónica de D. João I. Lisbon: Estampa, 1991.

———. "Fiction as Rhetoric: A Study of Fernão Lopes' *Crónica de D. João I*." *The Medieval Chronicle* 5 (2008): 35–46.

———. *O passado e o presente: ler Fernão Lopes*. Lisbon: Presença, 2007.

Blackmore, Josiah. "*Afeiçom* and History-Writing: the Prologue of the *Crónica de D. João I*." *Luso-Brazilian Review* 34.2 (1997): 15–24.

———. "The Poets of Sodom." *Queer Iberia: Sexualities, Cultures, and Crossings from the Middle Ages to the Renaissance*. Duke University Press, 1999. 195–221.

Boulton, Maureen Barry McCann. *The Song in the Story: Lyric Insertions in French Narrative Fiction, 1200–1400*. Philadelphia: University of Pennsylvania Press, 1993.

Crónica geral de Espanha de 1344. 4 vols. Ed. Luís Filipe Lindley Cintra. Lisbon: Academia Portuguesa da História, 1951–1990.

Disney, A.R. *A History of Portugal and the Portuguese Empire*. Vol. 1. Cambridge: Cambridge University Press, 2009.

Estoria de Dom Nuno Alvrez Pereyra. Edição crítica da "Coronica do Condestabre." Ed. Adelino de Almeida Calado. Coimbra: [University of Coimbra], 1991.

Jensen, Frede. *The Earliest Portuguese Lyrics*. Odense: Odense University Press, 1978.

———. ed. and trans. *Medieval Galician-Portuguese Poetry: An Anthology*. New York: Garland, 1992.

Lapa, M. Rodrigues, ed. *Cantigas d'escarnho e de mal dizer dos cancioneiros medievais galego-portugueses*. Lisbon: João Sá da Costa, 1995.

Livro de linhagens do Conde D. Pedro. Vol. 2, pt. 1. Ed. José Mattoso. Lisbon: Publicações do II Centenário da Academia das Ciências, 1980. Portugaliae Monumenta Historica, New Ser.

Lopes, Fernão. *Crónica de D. Fernando*. Ed. Giuliano Macchi. Lisbon: Imprensa Nacional-Casa da Moeda, 1975.

———. *Cronica del Rei Dom Joham I de boa memoria e dos Reis de Portugal o decimo*. Parte primeira. Ed. Anselmo Braamcamp Freire. 1915. Pref. Luís F. Lindley Cintra. Lisbon: Imprensa Nacional-Casa da Moeda, 1977.

López de Ayala, Pero. *Crónicas*. Ed. José-Luis Martín. Barcelona: Planeta, 1991.

Márquez Villanueva, Francisco. *El concepto cultural alfonsí*. Rev. ed. Barcelona: Bellaterra, 2004.

Menéndez Pidal, Ramón. *Poesía juglaresca y orígenes de las literaturas románicas: problemas de historia literaria y cultural*. 6th ed. Madrid: Instituto de Estudios Políticos, 1957.

Newitt, Malyn. *Portugal in European and World History*. London: Reaktion, 2009.

Rebelo, Luís de Sousa. "Providencialismo e profecia nas crónicas portuguesas da expansão." *Bulletin of Hispanic Studies* 71 (1994): 67–86.

Russell, P.E. "Archivists as Historians: The Case of the Portuguese Fifteenth-Century Royal Chroniclers." *Historical Literature in Medieval Iberia*. Papers of the Medieval Hispanic Research Seminar 2. Ed. Alan Deyermond. London: Dept. of Hispanic Studies, Queen Mary and Westfield College, 1996. 67–83.

Spiegel, Gabrielle M. *The Past as Text: The Theory and Practice of Medieval Historiography*. Baltimore: Johns Hopkins University Press, 1997.

———. *Romancing the Past: The Rise of Vernacular Prose in Historiography in Thirteenth-Century France*. Berkeley: University of California Press, 1993.

9

The *Most marueilous historie of the Iewes*: Historiography and the "Marvelous" in the Sixteenth Century

Eleazar Gutwirth

A compendious and most marueilous history of the latter times of the Iewes commonweale beginning where the Bible, or Scriptures leaue, and continuing . . . is the title of a book printed in London in 1558 and some twelve times afterwards. Written by Peter Morwyn, it was published by Richard Jugge. It is sometimes described as a translation of the twelfth-century abstract of the Mediterranean Jewish chronicle *Yosippon* by the Toledan Abraham ben David.[1]

The study of Morwyn's *History*—which could confirm such views—would need to establish as a priority the question of original and translation. But the critical interest in Morwyn does not begin with the Wissenschaft or Moritz Steinschneider (*Die Geschichtsliteratur*). Nor did it begin with Anglo-Jewish studies in the mold of Lucien Wolf.[2] Peter Morwyn's book began to arouse wider interest as early as the eighteenth century, when attempts were made to find a background or precedents revealing an interest in historical texts in the century that led to *King John*'s "Do like the Mutines of Ierufalem . . ."[3] Morwyn, then, was seen as proof of the existence of a reading public for historical writings in the vernacular in sixteenth-century England. The questions that could be (and—albeit much later—were) asked of Morwyn's Jewish history book were manifold: what was his attitude to the Jews? How did his original work differ from the later and colonial versions? What was the *vorlage*?[4] Was the English text based on an unknown Hebrew version of *Yosippon*? Could he be counted among the relatively early generation of Christian Hebraists? (Gutwirth, "L' accueil"; Wolf).

Credible answers to some of these questions would require more knowledge about his life, a revision of the sources, and some basic historical research. This has not attracted many critics. The question of how exactly Morwyn was influenced on the continent and by whom would depend on this and much work still needs to be done.[5] Nevertheless, all this refers to his work as translator. Given the origins of the field this is not unexpected. The focus here is not on the translation but rather on the less polemical, briefer texts which are incontestably Morwyn's own work, his personal contribution. They are at least two: the *Epistle to the Reader* and the title of the English translation. The Epistle/ Prologue will be dealt with below, but the use of the adjective "marvelous" in the title of a Jewish history book seems significant. In Morwyn's time, there were indeed various available reactions—and, therefore, adjectives—to historiography on the Jews, but the category of "the marvelous" is not among them. This leads directly to the question: what does "marvelous" mean and imply in a sixteenth-century context and, since Morwyn's book is concerned with Jewish history, what could "marvelous" mean in the context of Jewish historiography in the sixteenth century? To answer such a question, three other works of sixteenth-century Mediterranean historiography on the Jews may also be considered: *Shevet Yehuda* (*The Staff of Judah*); the *Consolation for the Tribulations*; and the so-called *Crónica de los reyes otomanos*. These are works published or written around 1552–1566, roughly contemporary with Morwyn's *History*. Like Morwyn's, all of them are concerned with Mediterranean history. Given the realities of the early modern period in Jewish history—Iberian expulsions and intensified migrations, itineraries which include Italy and the flourishing of the Ottoman Jewish communities—readers are not surprised to find that they are all linked in one way or another to the Ottoman Empire and the Mediterranean, and that such links are reflected in the texts (Gutwirth, "Jewish Bodies"). The first, *Shevet Yehuda*, is a book of Jewish history that, despite the usual qualifications and doubts, seems to enter print culture in 1554 in Adrianople. That is to say that it is somehow connected to the city in Eastern Thrace, the westernmost part of Turkey, close to the borders with Greece and Bulgaria. Known as Edirne, it served as the capital city of the Ottoman Empire from 1365 to 1453. In addition, the text of this Hebrew chronicle shows traces of the hand or pen of Joseph ibn Verga, usually described as a Turkish rabbi and historian who lived at Adrianople in the sixteenth century, author of the *She'erit Yosef* published in Adrianople in 1554. The second work of Jewish history to be considered, Samuel Usque's *Consolation* of 1553, culminates, as will be seen, with a kind of panegyric to Turkey (and, by implication, the Porte) and it reflects the *ambiente* of the Mediterranean itineraries of exiles and ex-*conversos* on their way from the Iberian Peninsula to the Ottoman Empire. Finally, the Ottoman author, Moses Almosnino, devotes his Judeo-Spanish chronicle, the *Crónica de los reyes otomanos*, to the Ottoman Empire. A later version of it is the *Extremos y Grandezas de Constantinopla*—a frequently mentioned and noteworthy publication—printed in Madrid in 1638.

By now, attention to the category of the marvelous in the sixteenth century hardly needs an apology.[6] As Paul Julian Smith remarks, "the rise of meraviglia . . . points to the eventual eclipse of traditional Aristotelianism" (138). Lorraine Daston, for example, reminds us that

> Marsilio Ficino's revival of magic, both natural and demonic, imbued scholarly Neoplatonism with a strong affinity for the occult; the new printing centers north and south of the Alps spewed out edition after edition of books of secrets retailing household recipes, virtues of herbs and stones, tricks of the trades, and "natural magic"; the witchcraft trials concentrated theological and legal attention on the precise nature of demonic meddling in human affairs; the voyages of exploration brought back tales and trophies of creatures and landscapes more marvelous than anything in Pliny or Mandeville; the religious and political upheavals set in motion by the Reformation also triggered an avalanche of crude broadsides and learned Latin treatises that anxiously interpreted comets, monstrous births, rains of blood, and any number of other strange phenomena as portents. Although portents were the very prototype of signifying events, spectacular and unsettling messages sent by God to herald triumph or catastrophe . . . (100)

Numerous studies have succeeded in elevating the status of inquiries on the marvelous in the sixteenth century, frequently relating the marvelous to problems of philosophy, metaphysics, science, and creativity in the literary and visual arts (Park and Daston, Platt, Daston, Biow). That is to say, the works on the marvelous are presented by implication as transnational, multinational, and universal. And yet at times their reader would hardly suspect the richness of the materials and the scholarship on, for example, the marvelous in Hispanic texts (Arellano, Arellano and Reyre).[7] To be sure, much of the work on the latter is concerned with texts from a later age, the baroque of Giambattista Marino's "*E' del poeta il fin la meraviglia*" (Smith 44, 138, 141, 166). There are, however, exceptions that focus on medieval Iberian Christian travelers, for example (Beltrán). More immediately relevant to our subject are the late medieval observations written down by Hispano-Jewish authors who traveled to "the Orient." These have been neglected because they are embedded in texts that are not obviously travel narratives, but rather seem to belong to other genres. A case in point is that of the fourteenth-century Zaragozan, Joseph ben Eleazar (Gutwirth, "Ibn Ezra"). However, such works do not touch on Jewish historiography.

The above mentioned studies of the marvelous and monstrous do not consider the latter in the *The Staff of Judah/ Shevet Yehuda*, a book of Jewish history printed around 1554 (Gutwirth, "The Expulsion"). Nor do they explore the relationship between the marvelous/monstrous in *Shevet Yehuda* and the garden of monsters created by the Italian architect Pirro Ligorio for Prince Francesco Orsini (Vicino) in Viterbo, in the mid-sixteenth century and known as Bomarzo (fig. 1). Indeed, the act of positing such a connection in 1988 probably owed less to Augustin and Aquinas's views on the marvelous than to Alberto Ginastera's dodecaphonic opera *Bomarzo* (1967) and, of course, to his source, Manuel Mujica Lainez' somewhat experimental novel *Bomarzo* (1962) (Gutwirth, "The Expulsion"). Mujica Lainez himself was indebted to the fascination with Bomarzo and its garden of monsters expressed by Jean Cocteau, Salvador Dali, and Mario Praz. The extent to which academic scholarship has followed or led these mainstream figures is another question.

Like the overgrown, ruinous gardens of Bomarzo, the *Shevet Yehuda* did not lend itself to direct, spontaneous understanding. But the restoration of Ligorio's Bomarzo garden of monsters in the 1970s seems to have been followed by a number of studies on the monstrous/marvelous in the sixteenth century, and one of the directions these studies has taken is to explore the question of the marvelous before Bomarzo, that is to say, the medieval and Renaissance sources, antecedents, or precedents of the garden's monsters (Frommel; Von Henneberg, "Bomarzo," "Vicino"). This is fundamental if one is to begin to understand the garden. For the subject at hand this is particularly useful because the garden itself cannot possibly have "influenced" the *Shevet Yehuda*, a book of Jewish history that existed in print at least by 1554. Although Orsini and Ligorio might have conceived of the project of the garden of monsters in Bomarzo by 1552, it was completed only in 1580, decades after the printing of the *Shevet Yehuda*. Earlier (pre–1552) heraldry, pageantry, romance, epic, travel, and medical literature contributed to this "conceiving" of the garden and cannot be discarded as irrelevant to the texts studied here any more than to the program leading to the Sacro Bosco and its analogues.

To this end a consideration of the Italian romance, *Orlando Furioso*, is rel-

Figure 1. *Ogre* in Garden of Monsters/Il Sacro Bosco. Pirro Ligorio and Francesco Orsini. Bomarzo, Viterbo, Italy. Photo Alessio Damato.

evant to understanding the marvelous in the Bomarzo garden and in sixteenth-century European culture in general. In his poem, Ariosto compares a garden—in his case a garden of love—with the wonders of the ancient world. The influence of *Orlando Furioso* on Ligorio and Orsini is clear in the inscription on the pedestal of one of a pair of sphinxes in the physical garden of Bomarzo: "He who does not visit this place with raised eyebrows and tight lips will fail to admire the seven wonders of the world." *Orlando Furioso* was also read by Judeo-Spanish readers of the sixteenth century and exists in a Judeo-Spanish version in Hebrew *aljamiado*. The latter was misidentified in the Bodleian catalogue of MS Canonici, Oriental 6 (Neubauer, # 2001) as "Italian transcribed into Hebrew characters" or as "Judeo-Italian." Laura Minervini, though, has since studied it as "'An *aljamiado* version of *Orlando Furioso*: a Judeo-Spanish transcription of Jerónimo de Urrea's translation" ("Una versión aljamiada"; "*Aljamiado* Version"). Of course, the question of transcription systems—interesting in terms of diachronic phonology or linguistics—is not entirely relevant for us. The question from our perspective is not one of transliterations but, rather: what does the very existence of such a MS codex tell us about sixteenth-century Mediterranean Judeo-Spanish reading communities, their cultural/intellectual history and "taste"? And this taste included the marvelous. In other words, after 1549 there were Hispanophone Jewish readers of *Orlando Furioso*, a work which intends to lead to "lips compressed and arched eye-brows" or, as the original stone inscription at Bomarzo has it: "CIGLIA INARCATE /ET LABBRA STRETTE." To understand the implications we might attend to at least one critical reaction. Judith Lee, for example, explains that the use of the marvelous is a central critical question of the early modern period and asserts that "Ariosto used the . . . marvelous to dramatize the inadequacy of the idealized Romance vision. In particular, he used the marvelous to dramatize not the spiritual and moral potential of human power but its limits" (78). "Monsters" and the "marvelous" are united not only intrinsically (by the premises of sixteenth-century thought and philosophy) but, much more relevantly, by the specific history of reading among the exiled Hispano-Jewish, Hispanophone communities in Italy.

The *Shevet Yehuda* is not in Italian, English, or any of the other languages usually examined in studies on the marvelous in the last two or three decades. It is a work in Hebrew, the language of the Bible, the same Bible that has shaped the interest in monsters to such an extent that other languages have fully assimilated its *behemoth* and *leviathan* (Driver, Gutmann, Penchansky). It was argued some time ago that the *Shevet Yehuda* presents the readers with various cases of code switching which are worth noticing from a perspective anchored not in a purely linguistic approach, but in *histoire de la lecture* (Gutwirth, "Expulsion"). The first general point has to do with cultural complicity between public and author. The Hebrew-Romance code switching is an example of a presupposed reading public from specific linguistic communities. If we think about the numerous, by no means purely linguistic, discussions on communication, translations and understanding or misunderstanding the Other in the sixteenth century—from the 1490s (i.e., from the time of the encounters with the New World) and onwards—we can begin to understand the possible ramifications.[8]

One could further argue that code-switching in *Shevet Yehuda* reflects surrounding contemporary cultural directions and categories. There are various discrete semantic fields where code switching from Hebrew to Spanish occurs in the text. The marvelous is one of these defined semantic fields. The pertinent references occur in a specific chapter of the *Shevet Yehuda* which represents a conversation, a dialogue at court:

A story of don Pedro and Nicolau of Valencia
. . . Seventh question:
"Why did he not give humans the strength of the lion?"
. . . Nicolau replies . . . "We have found [cases] where a man has more strength than the lion, for David smote the lion [I Sam 17:35]."
The king said: "At that time David had not yet spoken by virtue of what we call *espiritu* so why should we believe him? . . ."[9]
Nicolau said: "And I have seen an even greater thing and that is a *mostruo* (sic) whose height was two *ammot* and his width was one *ammah* and his head had no skin only the bone of the vertex and he had no ears but he had one hole in the back of his head and they said that he heard from there and in each hand he had two fingers and his feet were like the feet of the horse . . ." [10]
. . . said the King: "You have abandoned the borders of wisdom and entered the borders of the fools. Are you trying to strengthen one lie with another lie?" (85)

The sixteenth-century interest in monsters which explains the interest in the marvelous in *Orlando Furioso*—and in other sources of monsters, such as, for example, the sirens in the sculptures of Bomarzo—was the interest that conforms to the wider context of the code switching from the Hebrew to the Spanish terms, *mostruos, salvaje, centauro*, and *sirena del mar* in the *Shevet Yehuda.* Of course, some antecedents go back to the Bible. This is not entirely surprising. Early on, it was realized that there were monsters in the Bible and that the biblical text could offer a repertory of monstrous figures to the interested reader as do the later Talmudic and Midrashic sources on monsters.[11] But the words used in the *Shevet Yehuda* are clearly in Spanish and they come neither from the Bible, the *kentaurus* (and not *centauro*) of the Midrash, nor the siren in medieval Hebrew texts (Rashi or Ravad, etc.). In the *Shevet Yehuda* the code switching from Hebrew into Romance drew the attention of an Hispanophone reading public to the Castilian *mostruos* (monsters) in the middle of a Hebrew book.[12] This did not happen in the other, older Hebrew texts. This also happens with the story about the *salvaje* (savage) in the *Shevet Yehuda* where the Spanish refers to a marvelous being characterized by excessive hair. We do find vaguely similar Hebrew references to hairy beings in works composed before the *Shevet Yehuda*. As Haviva Pedaya recently affirmed referring to Hebrew/Aramaic mystical texts, "Anyone familiar with the Idra Raba and with the Idra Zuta has encountered the . . . symbol of the beard and the hair" (325). Similarly, as is well known, the *Historia de Preliis* existed in Hebrew versions in the Middle Ages. In one of these, the Hebrew *Gests of Alexander,* we also find excessive hair mentioned (Bonfils, *Hebrew Alexander*). But in these works, hairiness is frequently attributed to women rather than men as in the *Shevet Yehuda*.[13] The Hebrew versions of the *Historia de Preliis,* however, are not related to the House of Mendoza (as is *Shevet Yehuda*), nor do they feature code switching to Spanish. Such texts can therefore, barely be taken into serious consideration. At best, they could be seen as drawing attention—by such sharp and numerous contrasts—to the different and specific cultural tradition that frequently developed literary figures such as the *salvaje* from at least the *Libro de Alexandre* onward. This is a tradition which has been studied intensively in Hispanic, non-Hebraic Christian texts (Deyermond, López-Ríos, among others).

Code switching into Spanish in the Hebrew text of *Shevet Yehuda*, then, was not entirely chaotic and was not a fortuitous result of spontaneous generation, but had a certain direction. It is related to the link between the fascination with monsters and the category of the marvelous in the sixteenth century. What has become increasingly clear, as I hope I have shown, is that the sixteenth century provides numerous examples of interest in the marvelous and the monstrous and that the two were related.

The passage on the *mostruo,* the *sirena del mar*, and the *centauro* contains other non-Hebraic Romance terms. For A. Schochat, the work's modern editor, this passage was a humorous parody either of the thirteenth-century *Gate of Heaven* by Rabbi Gershon Ben Shlomoh d'Arles (possibly written between 1242 and 1275) or of other, unnamed and unspecified, medieval allegorizing exegetes. There is no attempt in Schochat's notes, however, to develop or prove this point or compare the two texts in order to support this argument.[14] Given such acute problems with the *Quellenforschung,* I turn instead to an analysis of the function of the marvelous and the monstrous in the story and the resonances of the Romance terms in the Hebrew text.

The section of the *Shevet Yehuda* in which we find these monsters is entitled "*Sippur haya me-ha-melekh don Pedro ha-zaqen 'im he-hakham Nicolau de Valencia*" (79ff) (The Story of What Happened to the Old King Don Pedro with the Scholar Nicolau of Valencia). The section is of significance also because it contains possible early traces of skepticism and is a version of a story that has attracted authors from Boccaccio's *Decameron* (or earlier) to Lessing's *Nathan der Weise*, namely, the so-called "three rings" story.[15] The same section is also the site of Ytzhak Baer's spectacular discovery of Alfonso de la Torre and Antonio de Guevara as sources of the *Shevet Yehuda* ("Prologue").

The general frame of the section or chapter in the *Shevet Yehuda* is that provided by the story of the rings; namely, tales where the Jew manages to evade the trap set by the king's question: which is the true faith? Judaism or Christianity? Once this is understood, the questions on natural philosophy in that section may no longer constitute as incongruous a list as might seem on a spontaneous reading. Indeed, little effort has been invested in discovering the unity of this section that appears as disjointed fragments of incongruous themes. And yet, it could be argued that there is an overriding concern and that this is stated—albeit obliquely—at the beginning of the section. When Nicolau of Valencia tries to convince the King to kill the Jews, he supports his argument as follows:

> When a Gentile comes towards the Jew, the Jew says: "He came in a bad hour." When he comes nearer, the Jew says: "Peace be with you my lord! May God grant you life!" And when he has left [and is out of hearing] he says: "Go to hell like Qorah! And like Pharaoh to the sea! . . ."
> The King asks: "Have you heard it with your ears?" Nicolau replies: "I heard it from one of the converts." The King says: "They are not to be believed." (79)

So that the question of evidence ("have you heard it with your ears") sets the tone for the rest of the section and informs every component of the section. The human issues of epistemology, *ratio*, and skepticism constitute a common basis for dialogue between Jew and Gentile/Christian; between courtier and King. This might give us a clue as to the apparently frivolous quality of the dialogues in the book. It could be argued that the question of witnessing, trust, believing a statement—of the distance between the said and the unsaid or meant or said outside hearing range—is not exclusive to this story. The Tower of Babel, the Epimenides paradox, and, in the twentieth century still in the work of Freud (as in his analysis of the Minsk/Pinsk joke) or even in treatments of *The Body in Pain*, this is one of the dominant concerns (Scarry). So that this section of the *Shevet Yehuda* touches upon questions which are not quite frivolous. In a Romance context relevant to the *Shevet Yehuda*, with its Romance code switching, we may recall the problems of communication and meaning raised by the *Libro de buen amor* and "la disputación que los griegos et los romanos en uno ovieron" (*coplas* 44–69) (the Dispute between the Greeks and the Romans). Pointedly relevant is its moral: "La patraña de la vieja ardida: / No hay mala palabra si no es a mal tenida; / verás que bien es dicha si bien es entendida" (Ruiz 17) (The wise old woman's proverb goes: "No evil word is spoken, if it's not thought to be evil." You will see that something is well said if well understood; MacDonald 27).

Within this general frame—faintly reminiscent also of the *Kuzari* and other precedents—we have here in *Shevet Yehuda* a case of a courtier who is a Christian and one who is a Jew. The King is old and seems to despise both. He asks a question which is far from innocent: he chooses the irrational quality of stories which may be defined as seafarers'/wayfarers' tales. This may be analogous to what in other cultures and languages of antiquity is classified as *Reisefabulistik* (Ehlen). More precisely the question alludes to a *sugyya* or discussion unit from the Talmud (bBB 73b), notoriously and obviously monstrous/marvelous: A frog as large as sixty houses was swallowed by a *tanin* (sometimes translated "sea monster") which was swallowed, in its turn, by a raven, which then flew to a tree. So that in this 1550s Hebrew text, the character of the Christian King introduces the category of the marvelous into a section saturated with philosophy and theology. What the Jew answers has to do with this category of the marvelous and his introductory remarks do not come from the *Gate of Heaven*. The ancients, he argues, would explain their teachings with the help of music. The Jews, who did not know music, used an alternative to music, namely parables or rhetoric. That is to say, he attempts an explanation of the *aggada*, of the marvelous and monstrous, in terms of natural philosophy. His attempt is precipitated by the introduction of the marvelous and the monstrous into the discussion. The marvelous does not contradict philosophy or reasoning but leads to reason. It is for the *'am* (people): *le qarev et ha 'am:* to attract "the people" or bring them closer. In other words, there is something attractive—to the readers—about the marvelous. It could, conceivably be argued that there is a self-reflective aspect to this passage. Indeed the question of parable and message, of allegory and allegorized, of language and meaning—as has been seen—could be relevant to *Shevet Yehuda's* project.

The resonances for Hispanophone readers of the Hebrew book (with its code switching to Ibero-Romance) should be examined further. Here we note that the concern with *mostruos* in texts written in the Romance is more pronounced after roughly 1400. It comes to the fore in texts of travel and in texts of medicine. In our case, the Escorial manuscript of the anonymous Spanish translation of the travels of John of Mandeville is relevant. Without entering into the complex problems of textual transmission we can understand that the original, written in Anglo-Norman (and finished between 1357 and 1371) is not relevant, as The *Shevet Yehuda* shows no contact with that linguistic and literary tradition. The translation into the Romance is usually dated to c. 1400. It includes a paragraph on monsters in Egypt. It describes the encounter in the deserts of Egypt between a saintly hermit and a beast that was like a man with two great horns that came out of its forehead, but who had the body of a man. "[E]t la bestia o mostruo respondio que eill hera creatura mortal assi como dios & natura lo auian formado / Et fincaua enlos desiertos" (fol. 6v)

([A]nd the good man asked him what he was and the beast or monster gave him a reply. He was a mortal creature as God and Nature had made him / and he stayed in the deserts). The translation adds: "Et encora es la cabe[ç]a daqueill mostro con sus cuernos en Alexandria *por la maraueilla . . .*" (fol. 6v) (And the head of that monster with its horns is still in Alexandria *because it is marvelous*).

A second text which shows this concern with *mostruos* comes from medicine; more precisely from the translation known as *Compendio de la humana salud* of Johannes de Ketham. The Madrid MS of it is usually dated to the fifteenth century. Like the *Shevet Yehuda,* it is presented in the form of a dialogue, or rather, of questions and answers. One of these has to do with strength: "*Porque los beçones o que nascen de vna ventrada no son tan esforçados como los que nascen vno a vno*" (Why are twins or those that are born together at the same time not as strong as those that are born one by one), namely, why are twins weaker (24). The answer has to do with the semen, which leads to a consideration of how the place where the semen falls affects the nature of the embryo as in the case of the hermaphrodite, at which point the narrative asserts: "*Llamamos la fembra hombre . . . monstruo en natura . . .*" (24) (We call the hermaphrodite . . . monster of nature).

The most widely known example of a text on *marauillas* in the Romance of Castile is Christopher Colombus's first letter to Luis de Santángel (1493). The letter has been mentioned so frequently that I forgo its analysis, except to raise the point that letters are usually written with the recipient in mind and that rich documentation studied from Manuel Serrano y Sanz and onwards attests not only to Santángel's probable roots in the Jewish Aragonese communities of the fifteenth century, but to the contacts and relations between the Santángels and various Jewish men and women in the second half of the fifteenth century.[16]

The question of resonances reminds us that the marvelous is not purely a textual issue—in the sense of purely textual written sources—because in the fifteenth/sixteenth centuries, we find the marvelous/monstrous in non-textual environments as in the case of heraldry, architecture, ornamental features of buildings (e.g., door-knockers), gardens or landscape designs. This can be further understood by attending to the field of the visual. Centaurs appear in Jewish art from medieval Spain, for example, in the artwork of Hebrew manuscripts. At least six examples could be mentioned. As in the case of code switching or explaining the monsters of Bomarzo, attention to precedents, including late medieval works, is necessary. This is so, partly, of course, because early modernists have been frequently criticized for not attending to the roots of phenomena in previous centuries. But it is also the case in Hispano-Jewish history and culture despite the dramatic changes after the late fifteenth century.

The image of a centaur appears in the artwork of a Hebrew manuscript from c. 1299 Cervera or Soria. It is sometimes called the Cervera Bible, but the centaur appears in a non-biblical section: Radaq's *Mikhlol.* Despite numerous discussions on the relations between text and image in medieval manuscripts, it seems that there is as yet no explanation of its location in a distinct section of the *Mikhlol* (Lisbon, Bibliotheca Nacional. Ii Ms. 72, fol 442v). Particularly interesting is the centaur in another Hebrew manuscript, the Bible of Pamplona, and not only because it is nearer chronologically to the *Shevet Yehuda* than the thirteenth-century codex. It is a Hebrew Bible with Masorah. This Hebrew Bible manuscript, usually dated to 1400, was bought by the bishop of Pamplona in the fifteenth century and today is preserved in the Archivo Capitular of the Cathedral of Pamplona. The centaur in the Bible is composed of Masoretic micrography, i.e., the scribes have used the text to create images with the words of the text. Again, art historians seem to have been unable to explain the location of the image, in other words to link or relate the image of the centaur to the text of this particular section of the Masorah. It appears in the illuminations to Ex. 40, i.e., the description of the anointing of the Temple. One of the most salient features is that the centaur in the Pamplona Cathedral Hebrew manuscript codex echoes the centaur in that cathedral's artwork (Silva y Verástegui). More comprehensible is the location of the image of the centaur in another Hebrew manuscript that used to belong to the Sassoon collection, and was described not only in the *Ohel David,* but also in the *Catalogue* for the Sotheby's sale in Zurich (Sassoon).[17] The manuscript (MS Sassoon 823) was produced in Spain, probably around 1361–62 in Catalonia, perhaps by a scribe named Moshe. It consists of a number of Hebrew texts, but the relevant one here is the final and longest one, the *Sefer Ha'Mivharim* on fols. 93–228. The centaur with a bow and arrow appears on fol. 129 among the signs of the zodiac. The zodiac is the more common area of visual representations of the centaur. Also from Catalonia in the fourteenth century comes the next image of a centaur on fol 29b in the so-called John Rylands Haggadah. The illumination of a centaur with a bow and arrow has a comprehensible location—it is next to *harag et bekhoreihem (He killed their first born)* in the poem for that occasion during the Passover liturgy (Dayeinu). In addition, on fol. 33b we find a marginal drollery or grotesque: a centaur dressed as a jester.

The six centaurs mentioned may not all have a single explanation or symbolic value. More research is needed to establish basic questions of the relations

Figure 2. *Sirena del mar.* Mermaid. Catalan Atlas. Abraham Cresques. c. 1375. Bibliothèque nationale de France, Département des manuscrits, Espagnol 30.

between patron and artist and also between text and visual image. But the six cases of centaurs discussed above represent rich evidence for the presence and resonance of the centaur in Hispano-Jewish culture. One may mention also that in the *Catalan Atlas* dated to 1375 we find that to the south of China lie 7,548 islands on which Cresques locates some of the monstrous races of antiquity and the Middle Ages (Edson). He describes them as people of great size, like giants, without intelligence, who eat men and strangers if they can catch them. The same interdisciplinary method of researching texts, language, geography and image could be applied to the *Shevet Yehuda*'s *sirena del mar*, which, incidentally, is also to be found in the same Atlas (fig. 2). There is therefore no need to posit a unique, textual, "lost source" for the focus on (and code switching to) *mostruos* in the *Shevet Yehuda*.

The concern with the marvelous in sixteenth-century historiography on the

Jews, then, can be explained partly by the general concern with the marvelous in the sixteenth century; it may be related to the concern with the marvelous in more specific cultural phenomena such as the tastes of readers of Judeo-Spanish *aljamiado* literature after 1549. The attention to code switching may reveal an intellectual indebtedness to immediately preceding periods and explain the resonances of the categories employed. These would include texts on travel and medicine in the Romance language of the *le 'azim* in the *Shevet Yehuda*. It could be related to non-textual phenomena such as Hebrew manuscript illuminations from late medieval Spain. In the passage selected from the *Shevet Yehuda,* it is associated with natural philosophy; epistemology and skepticism, but also, possibly, with some echoes of Pythagorean theories about music and numbers.

The *Shevet Yehuda* is only one history book in a century famous for its rich creativity in the field of Jewish historiography. Therefore, attention to other sixteenth-century Mediterranean exponents of the genre is possible. Two more examples may not only attest to the marvelous in other texts, but also widen and qualify our perspectives on the marvelous in Jewish historiography. If the *editio princeps* of the *Shevet Yehuda* really is from 1554, as seems to be the consensus, we may recall a history work from 1553, a year earlier, but composed in Portuguese. This is the *Consolation for the Tribulations of Israel (Consolação às Tribulações de Israel)* (*Consolation*) authored by Samuel Usque and published in Ferrara. Like Morwyn and the *Shevet Yehuda*, it is linked to medieval Iberia, and it also raises questions of influence by earlier Mediterranean historians: Josephus and the author of the *Yosippon*. As in the case of Morwyn and the *Shevet Yehuda*, interest in the book does not originate in the Wissenschaft. Given the old and widespread notion that such readings begin only in nineteenth-century Germany, the point may need some brief explanation. The reference here is not to the *conversos* of England or Southern France in the sixteenth century, who seem to have read it and treated it as a sacral text. It is, rather, to the scholars of the eighteenth century, the *siglo de las luces*. Although, undoubtedly, many present day studies on the work follow on Heinrich Graetz's nineteenth-century questions, there was attention to the work evident even in the eighteenth-century sources Graetz uses. Indeed, José Rodríguez de Castro devotes several columns of his *Biblioteca* to him. Considering the tone of Usque's passages on the Inquisition and on the persecution of the Jews, José Rodríguez de Castro is surprisingly objective in his description of the book's contents. Equally interesting—for those who are aware of the role of Francisco Pérez Bayer in eighteenth-century Hebrew and Jewish studies in Spain in general and his contribution to Hebrew and Samaritan numismatics in particular—is the fact, revealed by Rodríguez de Castro, that the Valencian had a copy of Usque's *Consolation* in his library. This gives us a somewhat unusual perspective on the eighteenth-century peninsular history of reading and its contacts with Jewish texts.

If, as in the case of the *Shevet Yehuda*, we focus on the theme of the marvelous/monstrous in Usque's *Consolation*, we have to attend to passages such as the following on the Inquisition:

> The king and queen sent to Rome for a wild monster of such strange form and horrible mien that all Europe trembles at the mere mention of its name. Its body, an amalgam of hard iron and deadly poison, has an adamantine shell made of steel and covered with enormous scales. It rises in the air on a thousand wings with black and poisonous pinions and it moves on the ground with a thousand pernicious and destructive feet. Its form is both the awesome lion's and the frightful serpent's. (228)

The *Consolation* contains various passages (circa 23) that work with this concept of *maravilhas*. These are frequently rewritings or retellings of biblical stories that try to represent the Bible in new, fresh ways. The wider frame is the new genre of the pastoral in the post-Sannazaro age. In the passage on the Inquisition, the marvelous is removed from the biblical, it is present by way of the monster and it seems to have an intensely visual quality. Equally contemporary, rather than biblical, is his account of the Ottoman Empire:

> [T]he eighth and most signal way by which you will rise to a higher degree of consolation is in the great nation of Turkey. This country is like a broad and expansive sea which our Lord has opened with the rod of his mercy as Moses did for you in the exodus from Egypt so that the swells of your present misfortunes which relentlessly pursue you in all kingdoms of Europe like the infinite multitude of Egyptians might cease and be consumed in it . . . (231)

In the *Consolation,* when reading explicit references to *maravilhas*, we wonder whether they are different from the rest of the chronicle; whether the whole of the book is not suffused with this notion, whether the whole of Jewish history is not presented as a history of the marvelous. When we read about the hybrid monster that represents the Inquisition, we are reading about the monstrous/marvelous even when the word itself is not used. The representation of the hybrid monster in Usque's work cannot but recall contemporary visual materials—both woodcuts and copper engravings—in the field of Catholic/Protestant polemics (Scribner, Watt). It is perhaps significant that Scribner's study of forms of propaganda—such as illustrated broadsheets, picture books, title pages, and book illustrations—during the Reformation is entitled *For the Sake of Simple Folk*, especially if we bear in mind the *Shevet Yehuda*'s "*'am*" (people). In the field of Hispanic texts one recalls that such hybrid animal/monstrous images—within the specific parameters of religious polemics and the vernacular—appear in the fifteenth-century *Libro del Alborayque*. These are only some aspects of the discourse of the marvelous. In Usque's text the analogy of Turkey to a biblical miracle lends it an air of the supernatural.

A reappearance of the marvelous and Turkey occurs in yet another work of Jewish history that is not usually taken into account, namely the so-called *Crónica de los reyes otomanos* by Moses Almosnino (Gutwirth, "*Acutissima patria*"). It was written in the decade following the *Consolation*, in 1566. In it, we find descriptions of Constantinople, its buildings, its civil service, its qadis and muftis. The references to the marvelous are particularly repetitive in Almosnino's account of the royal *entrada* (entrance) into Constantinople on the 27th of November, 1566. Almosnino asserts that he is responding to a request to report in writing about the event. The avid curiosity of the public and the intense attention of Almosnino are reflected in the ample space devoted to the ceremonial *entrada* and in the detailed descriptions. The army, court and bureaucracy of the Ottoman Empire were, of course, topics commented on by other European travelers of the early modern period. But such royal or noble *entradas* are also part of a tradition in both medieval Hispano-Jewish history and literature (Gutwirth, "Jews"; "Song"). In the *entrada* section, Almosnino refers to various *maravillas*. Among others, there is a description of the Ottoman armies in a parade: "Una lanza cada cual de ellos pulida y labrada a maravilla . . ." (Almosnino 82). (Every one of them had a spear which was marvelously finished/polished and crafted). Or, again: "Toda esta flota de gente era mucho para ver a maravilla en la cantidad y calidad de ellos . . ." (Almosnino 83) (The number and quality of this sea of soldiers was a marvel to behold). The marvel here seems related to *labrar* (to craft) and *pulir* (to polish); to Renaissance views (ultimately traceable to Aristotle) of *arte* as a trained ability, skill or techne and that has a clearly human quality.[18] Here the marvelous is not superhuman. The twin preoccupations of medieval Jewish historiography—martyrology and scholarship—are less prominent than usual. Recent work has emphasized Almosnino's introduction of fields and themes such as engineering, fiscal policy, optics, wine, and others into the highly traditional parameters of this genre. Given the date of the work—and what that implies—this is worth noting (Gutwirth, "Acutissima patria").

Before concluding, we may come back briefly to Morwyn's *Marvelous His-*

tory. As mentioned, there is little solid evidence of Morwyn's activities during the Marian exile (1553–1558). If we knew where he stayed—in Basel or Geneva, in Germany or Italy—we might possibly try to reconstruct the specific Christian Hebraists' circles in which he traveled, or the circles surrounding the printing presses with their attested interest and investments in Jewish historiography around that period when, for example, the Toledan Ibn Dawd's twelfth-century chronicles were being printed by various sixteenth-century presses. We are now more aware of the quality and quantity of Christian Hebraists on the continent in these decades and also of the—sometimes hidden—converts and Jews who in one way or another, as correspondents, teachers, secretaries, consultants, correctors, and editors, took part in the projects of Christian Hebraism in the 1540s and 1550s (Gutwirth, "History"). As it is, there does not seem to be a great interest in the question, let alone an explanation for the hybrid sources of Morwyn's translation. Attention, therefore, may be directed to a rereading of his less problematic prologue entitled, *Epistle to the Reader*. In it he invokes for his translation the precedent or model of the Septuagint and links his book to the field of Bible translations into emerging languages:

> [A]s there is amongst us already in our native tongue the original beginning of that nation and the continuance also for a long space in the Bible and annexed to the same so there might be likewise an understanding and declaration to all men in the English tongue as well as in other of the destruction of so famous a commonweale . . . (1)

The question of original and translation, of origins (beginning) and "continuance," of texts which are "for all men in the English tongue" and others (those which are for the few, in other tongues) is relevant to the whole work. The question of such relations between different things—usually binaries—reappears in possibly curious guises. Thus, for example, Morwyn tackles the question of what is the relation between the two Mediterranean authors, that of the *Yosippon* and Josephus:

> [Y]ea written by the same Josephus as the tenor and contents of both the books do import although the name [is different—son of Mattathia and son of Gorion] is a thing common in the Jews' genealogies that men need not seek far for the like for one man to deduct his dissent from diverse names of father grandfather . . . now taking the name . . . of the most noble of his kindred . . . the histories do so agree that they may well be thought to be written by one man. (2)

The history of scholarship or fifteenth and sixteenth-century scholarly debate on the *Yosippon*/Josephus question is far from simple and, despite attempts and appearances, still needs to be reconstructed. Vague general references to the Renaissance interest in historiography or in the beginnings of critical readings of texts are far from satisfying. In many cases, reconstructions of such a history would depend upon a close examination of precise texts and formulations of that period. Attention would have to be paid not only to Sebastian Munster, but also to vernacular translations and to Abraham Zacut and Isaac Abravanel. Morwyn does not say that one Jew is pretty much like another, but he implies something of the sort when arguing that different names do not denote difference. In the Prologue or *Epistle to the Reader* this argument forms part of a set of questions about the quality of relations between different binaries and, therefore, it is not dissonant to find that the question of veracity versus history is also touched upon, as is the question of patron/client or request and performance, in other words, publisher and author.

That brings up the question of religious factors. Morwyn states explicitly that religion is one of the motivations of his work and critics mention the Reformation and its attitudes to the Bible and original languages as the background to his work. For us, this is an added element leading to the marvelous. But it does not detract from the significance of the printing project or "industrial" aspect. Indeed, the *Epistle to the Reader* itself is only one reminder of the constant presence of the reader in the mind of the collaborators in the project. Even such a visible and basic element as the typography—with its changes when citing biblical verses—reveals that they have the readers in mind. Defending his work, Morwyn asserts that, in comparison with Josephus Flavius, his own work is "far more brief much less costly" (Prologue). Therefore, although unconventional, it is only reasonable to pay attention to the other project in which Morwyn is involved, i.e., "The treasure of Evonymvs, conteyninge the vvonderfull hid secretes of nature . . . Translated (with great diligence & laboure) out of Latin, by Peter Morvvyng. Imprinted at London by Iohn Daie, dvvelling ouer Aldersgate, beneath Saint Martines. (1559)." It is a year later than the *Marvelous History*. The apparently incommensurate qualities of the two fields treated by Morwyn had repercussions on subsequent, modern studies of them. Work on Morwyn, such as it is, does not deal with his two works in a symmetrical, proportionate manner. The attention to the *Marvellous History* exceeds, by far, that bestowed upon the *Evonymus*, as can be discerned by a mere glance at the bibliography. And yet the two works are not completely unrelated. The printer of the *Marvelous History*, Richard Jugge (d. 1577), who kept a shop at the sign of the Bible at the North door of St Paul's Cathedral, has been replaced by John

Day as printer of the *Evonymvs*.[19] Better known as the printer of John Foxe's *Actes and Monuments*, he is described as stationer and he lived over Aldersgate, and is mentioned as churchwarden of St. Anne's under the date 1574.[20] Both printers, then, are Londoners and connected to the church and, crucially, both belong to the small elite of the licensed. The *Evonymvs*, like the *Marvelous History*, is also linked to the continent and to sixteenth-century concerns. In the *Evonymvs*, again, we find the invocation of the marvelous and the wonderful. In both, the readers' attention is drawn to the commercial quality of the enterprise by the explicit mention of the addresses and names of the printers and the connections between cause and text, between patron and translator, as well as to questions of "much less costly" with regard to the *Yosippon*, or to "travails and expenses" or the "covetousness of apothecaries" in the *Evonymvs*. In both there is an *Epistle to the Reader.* In both, the vernacular is mentioned in such a way that it amounts to an argument or apologetic explanation for not writing in Latin and for writing for a wider audience. In both, the labors of translation are emphasized as in the claim that the work has been "Translated (with great diligence & laboure . . .)." The diligence, labors, and value of the translation are articulated and arguments constructed: "notification *in our tongue* of the fulfilling of the same," or again and more explicitly:

> In the translation thereof what paynes is taken not only in rendering diverse words that were depraved and corrupted in the Latin text and some whole members of sentences left out which were expressely in the Hebrew but also that hebraical forms of speech so discrepant from our phrase and accustomed manner of speaking might be framed unto our vulgar and familiar communication that they might be better understanded I refer it unto the judgment of them that be experts in the tongues . . . to confer both the texts . . . that shall everywhere espy a great dissimilitude between the words of both and sometimes find whole members of sentences transposed . . . (Morwyn 3)

Finally, if in the *History* or *Yosippon* "marvelous quality" is introduced into the title, the *Evonymus* is presented as containing "wonderful hid secrets" and as dealing with chemistry, a skill that causes "marvelous change."

To conclude, the "marvelous" in the texts mentioned here includes the distillation of wine into *aqua vitae* (Morwyn's translation of Gessner). It also includes the ironwork for the Ottomans' swords and the organization of an Ottoman military parade, and it is also the adjective applied to Jewish history. No single slogan or formula will delimit the category. We could posit an "Other" or a stranger who is marvelous/monstrous, but such classifications themselves are in flux, ephemeral, or misleading. The Christians imagined in the *Shevet Yehuda* are not marvelous, but the marvelous constitutes a space which is established as a space for dialogue between Jews and Christians. This dialogue is possible because—despite numerous disagreements—there is a range of shared beliefs, traditions and resonances, sometimes in precise Castilian Romance or Portuguese, or in Judeo-Spanish manifestations. The monstrous in Usque is not identical or synonymous with Christian Europe. On the contrary, for Usque, Europe, like the *conversos* and the Jews, trembles at the mention of the Inquisition. If Ottoman Turkey is constructed as marvelous, it is so by analogy to the Bible rather than by opposition.

It has been suggested also that, among various particular uses of the marvelous, there is possibly a common ground which is perhaps clearer in Morwyn, with the explicit articulation of the names and addresses of publishers, with his references to the price and weight of the books: "Far more brief much less costly." Perhaps the age of the Marqués de Santillana's *Carta et proemio* to the Constable of Portugal or Moses Arragel's Prologue/ Epistle to the Master of Calatrava gives way to the age of the Epistle to the Reader; the age when the *Shevet Yehuda* explains the marvelous as a way of attracting the *`am*, the "people," and Usque addresses a community of readers by discussing what is the appropriate language for reading. The age of the marvelous seems roughly contemporary with the age of licensed printers and their desire to reach a wide audience.

Notes

1. See further references in E. Gutwirth, "L'accueil."
2. Lucien Wolf was skeptical as to Morwyn's contacts with the original and thought that the *Marvelous history* was a version of Munster's version.
3. Malone's essay appeared in the Variorum of 1778. The reference is to *King John* (ii, I, 328): "Your Royall prefences be rul'd by mee, Do like the Mutines of Ierufalem . . ." See also Mary Dormer Harris (93).
4. Here one must mention the thesis of Jacob Reiner, who seems to have attempted a confrontation of certain, selected passages in *Yosippon* and Morwyn. See Reiner, "The Original Hebrew *Yosippon*"; "The Jewish War"; "The English *Yosippon*"; and the bibliography in his notes.
5. The question had been already posed by Israel Baroway, "During the Marian reign, who instructed Home, Anthony Gilby, Humphrey, and Morwyn, at the University of Basle?" He assumes that Basle was indeed the only relevant location. If we were certain that Morwyn's destination during the Marian exile had been Basle, we could

sensibly reconstruct a probable context for his interest in and access to Hebrew, Jewish works, particularly historiography and particularly the Toledan Ibn Daud. This is the case, first and foremost, of course, because of the work of Prijs. See *Die Basler Hebräische Drucke*. After Prijs, we now have the work of Carlos Gilly which is highly innovative in many respects. It attempts to present a cross section of Spanish intellectual history seen from the vantage point of a European printing center. It therefore attends to the reception of works from medieval Iberia—Muslim, Jewish, and Christian. He reinforces the claims of Basle as a haven for dissidents, which, for him, relates to Spain but which, for us, is of interest as lending added probability to Morwyn's sojourn there. Basle emerges as a center for transmission and arbiter of European intellectual life. A focus on Basle serves to recreate the intellectual life of Spain. For him, there is a growing interest by humanists in Hebrew as a critical language for biblical scholarship. At the same time, there is the image of the Spanish humanists as heretics and victims of the Inquisition. The section on historiography includes the works of Ibn Daud but little on the *nachleben* of the Toledan's historical books and the scholarship on them.

6. Also relevant is John Onians, "A Short History of Amazement."
7. To recall this wealth of materials and the continuity of scholarship on coeval and (mostly) later manifestations in Spanish, it may suffice to mention among numerous others *Loca Ficta* and *El mundo maravilloso de los autos de Calderón*.
8. These concern a variety of disciplines and differing theoretical approaches which go far beyond the scope of this study; see, for example, Eric Mount, Sylvia Molloy, Tzvetan Todorov, and Stephen Greenblatt.
9. Despite the opinions that the work was written in Italy the *le 'azim* are not Italian but clearly Iberian. Note the *aleph yod*, i.e., initial vowel before the sibilant in *espiritu*.
10. *Mostruo* is written without the /n/.
11. See among others, for example, Natan Slifkin's *Sacred Monsters*.
12. On code switching in Hispano-Hebraic texts of the fifteenth century see E. Gutwirth, "La España," and "The Toldot Ishaq."
13. As is well known, the Hebrew work includes tales of Alexander's encounters in the forests of India with strange and grotesque human beings, beasts, monsters, and birds. Thus, for example, "Alexander departed thence and came to the bank of a river where they found men and women who were covered with hair like the beasts of the forest." Or again, elsewhere: "He departed thence with all his troops and they came into other forests. There they found women whose teeth were as sharp as those of the wolf and as large as those of the wild boars. Their hair reached down to their navels. They were as hairy as camels and had tails like oxen," or, again, "They departed thence and came into another of the forests of India. There they found women whose hair came down to their feet and whose feet were like those of the horse" (Bonfils, *Hebrew Alexander* 131). Note the (threefold?) incremental series: "covered with hair"; "hair to the navel"; "hair to their feet."
14. *Le 'azim* do appear in the *Gate*, as was already clear from Bodenheimer's appendixes.

Bodenheimer referred to work in progress or a forthcoming study on the *le`azim* by L. Kopf. I have not been able to locate that study. *Mostruos, salvajes, sirena del mar, centauro* seem to be absent from the *le`azim* in the *Gate*.

15. A sustained publication on this theme is Friedrich Niewöhner, *Veritas sive varietas*. For the *Shevet Yehuda*, the works of Baer are still indispensable. See, among others, his "Prologue" to the Schochat edition.
16. Both Serrano y Sanz and his followers were interested particularly in questions of genealogy. For us the question of cultural contacts with Jews by members of the family is foremost.
17. Although this catalogue is anonymous it represents the work of Ch. Abramsky. See *Catalogue of Thirty-eight Highly Important Hebrew and Samaritan Manuscripts: From the Collection Formed by the Late David Solomon Sassoon, the Property of the Family of David Solomon Sassoon, which Will be Sold at Auction by Sotheby & Co.* at Baur Au Lac Hotel, Zurich, on Wednesday, 5th Nov., 1975. (Lot 15).
18. Attention to Turkish steel swords crafting may have a precedent around 1431 in the famous travel account by Bertradon de la Bro(c)quière.
19. Jugge's biography and bibliography is relevant in that reaffirms our perspective on the need to take into account the industrial aspects: He was admitted a freeman of the Stationers Company in 1541 and was its warden and master in the 1560s and 1570s. He was evidently interested in the institutional aspects of the craft. He was heavily involved in the printing of the Bible in the vernacular in the 1550s, something which lends added resonance to Morwyn's attempts to link the Bible and *Yosippon* and his attention to the question of the vernacular and translation. See "Jugge, Richard." This would mean that the Reformation and Christian Hebraism and such trends were only part of the context of his and Morwyn's work. See also E. J. Devereux (42).
20. John Day, like Jugge, is relevant in so far as he also reflects the intersection between politics, religion and printing under Queen Elizabeth. But the aspect to be emphasized here is the "industrial," since after the Marian persecution he benefited from the patronage of officials and nobles, including William Cecil, Robert Dudley, and Matthew Parker (Evenden).

Works Cited

Almosnino, Moisés. *Crónica de los reyes otomanos*. Ed. Pilar Romeu Ferré. Barcelona: Tirocinio, 1998.

Arellano, Ignacio. *Loca Ficta: los espacios de la maravilla en la Edad Media y el Siglo de Oro*. Madrid: Iberoamericana, 2003.

Arellano, Ignacio and Dominique Reyre, eds. *El mundo maravilloso de los autos de Calderón*. Estudios de Literatura 107. Calderón: Autos sacramentales completos 62. Kassel: Reichenberger, 2007.

Baer, Ytzhak. "Prologue." *Shevet Yehuda*. Ed. A. Schochat and Y. Baer. Jerusalem: Mosad Bialik, 1946–1947.

Baroway, Israel. "Towards Understanding Tudor-Jacobean Hebrew Studies" *Jewish Social Studies* 18 (1956): 3–24.

Beltrán Llavador, Rafael, ed. *Maravillas, peregrinaciones y utopías: literatura de viajes en el mundo románico*. Valencia: Universitat de Valencia, 2002.

Bonfils, Immanel ben Jacob. *A Hebrew Alexander Romance According to MS London, Jews' College 145*. Ed. Wout Jac. van Bekkum, Louvain, 1992.

Biow, Douglas. *Mirabile Dictu: Representations of the Marvelous in Medieval and Renaissance Epic*. Ann Arbor: University of Michigan Press, 1996.

Cervera Bible. Lisbon, Bibliotheca Nacional. Ii Ms. 72.

Crescas, Abraham. *Catalan Atlas. Atlas des cartes marines*. 1375. Bibliothèque nationale de France. Département des manuscrits. MS Espagnol 30. Gallica online (bnf.fr). Web. 28 Nov. 2012.

Daston, Lorraine. "Marvelous Facts and Miraculous Evidence in Early Modern Europe." *Critical Inquiry*. 18.1 (Autumn 1991): 93–124.

Devereux, E. J. "Empty Tuns and Unfruitful Grafts: Richard Grafton's Historical Publications." *The Sixteenth Century Journal* 21.1 (1990): 33–56.

Deyermond, A. D. "El hombre salvaje en la novela sentimental." *Filología* 10 (1964 [1966]): 97–111.

Driver, G. R. "Mythical Monsters in the Old Testament." *Studi Orientalistici in onore di Giorgio Levi Della Vida*. Roma: Instituto per L'Oriente, 1956. 234–49.

Edson, Evelyn. *The World Map, 1300–1492: The Persistence of Tradition*. Baltimore: Johns Hopkins University Press, 2007.

Ehlen, Oliver. "Leitbilder und romanhafte Züge in apokryphen Evangelientexten. Untersuchungen zur Motivik and Erzählungsstruktur anhand des Protevangelium Jacobi und der Acta Pilati Graec. B." Ph.D. Diss., University of Jena, 2000.

Evenden, Elizabeth. "The Michael Wood Mystery: William Cecil and the Lincolnshire Printing of John Day." *Sixteenth Century Journal* 35.2 (2004): 383–94.

Frommel, Sabine, ed. con la collaborazione di Andrea Alessi. *Bomarzo: il Sacro Bosco*. Convegno Internazionale di Studi. Milan: Electa, 2009.

Gilly, Carlos. *Spanien und der Basler Buchdruck bis 1600*. Basler Beitrage zur Geschichtswissenschaft I 5 I. Basel: Verlag Helbing, 1985.

Ginastera, Alberto and Manuel Mujica Lainez. *Bomarzo: An Opera in Two Acts and Fifteen Scenes*. New York: Boosey and Hawkes, 1967.

Greenblatt, Stephen. *Marvelous Possessions: The Wonder of the New World*. Oxford: Clarendon, 1991.

Gutmann, J. "Leviathan, Behemoth and Ziz: Jewish Messianic Symbols in Art." *HUCA* 39 (1968): 219–30.

Gutwirth, E. "L'accueil fait a Abraham ibn Daud dans l'Europe de la Renaissance." *Tolede et Jerusalem*. Ed. Shoham and Rosensteil. Lausanne: L'age d'Homme, 1992. 97–110.

———. "La España de Isaac Caro." *Actas IV Congreso internacional: Encuentro de las tres culturas*. Ed. C. Carrete Parrondo. Toledo: Ayuntamiento, 1988. 51–56.

———. "The Expulsion of the Jews from Spain and Jewish Historiography." Ed. Ada Rapoport-Albert and Steven J. Zipperstein. *Jewish History: Essays in Honour of Chimen Abramsky*. London: Peter Halban, 1988. 141–61.

———. "History, Poetry and the Trilingual Question in Habsburg Spain." *CALÍOPE* 17.1 (2011): 69–96.

———. "Jewish Bodies and Renaissance Melancholy: Culture and the City in Italy and the Ottoman Empire." *The Jewish Body. Corporeality, Society, and Identity in the Renaissance and Early Modern Period*. Ed. G. Veltri. Leiden: Brill, 2009. 57–92.

———. "*Acutissima patria*: Locating Texts before and after the Expulsions." *Hispania Judaica Bulletin* 8 (2011): 19–38.

———. "The *Toldot Ishaq* in his Time." *Miscelánea de Estudios Arábes y Hebreos* 40.2 (1991): 119–30.

———. "Ibn Ezra Supercommentaries as Historical Sources." *Abraham ibn Ezra and his Age*. Ed. F. Díaz Esteban. Madrid: Asociación española de orientalistas, 1990. 147–54.

———. "The Jews in Fifteenth century Castilian Chronicles." *Jewish Quarterly Review* 84.4 (1984): 379–96.

———. "A Song and Dance: Transcultural Practices of Daily Life in Medieval Spain." *Jews Muslims and Christians In and Around the Crown of Aragon Essays in Honour of Professor Elena Lourie*. Ed. Harvey J. Hames. Leiden: Brill, 2003. 207–228.

Harris, Mary Dormer. "Note on the Mutines of Jerusalem in Shakespeare's *King John*." *Notes and Queries* (1931): 93.

Henneberg, Josephine von. "Bomarzo: Nuovi dati e Un'intepretazione." *Storia dell'Arte* 13 (1972): 43–55.

———. "Vicino Orsini's Sacro Bosco and the Literature of his Time." *Aquila* 4 (1979): 219–28.

"Jugge, Richard." *Dictionary of National Biography*. Sir Leslie Stephen and Sir Sidney Lee. London: Macmillan, 1899.

Ketham, Johannes. *Compendio de la humana salud*. Ed. María Teresa Herrera. Madrid: Arco Libros, 1990.

Lee, Judith. "The English Ariosto: The Elizabethan Poet and the Marvelous." *Studies in Philology* 80.3 (1983): 277–99.

López-Ríos, Santiago. "El concepto de 'salvaje' en la Edad Media española: algunas consideraciones." *Dicenda: Cuadernos de filología hispánica*. 12 (1994): 145–56.

Mandeville, Jean. *Libro de las maravillas del mundo y el viaje a Jerusalén, de Asia y África*. Real Biblioteca del Monasterio de San Lorenzo de El Escorial. MS. M.III.7. Ed Juan Luis Rodríguez Bravo and María del Mar Martínez Rodríguez. Hispanic Seminary of Medieval Studies (Madison), 1995.

Minervini, L. "Una versión aljamiada del *Orlando Furioso* de Ludovico Ariosto." *Los judaizantes en Europa y la literatura castellana del Siglo de Oro*. Ed. F. Díaz Esteban. Madrid: Letrúmero, 1994. 295–98.

———. "An *Aljamiado* Version of 'Orlando Furioso': A Judeo-Spanish Transcription of Jerónimo de Urrea's Translation." *Hispano-Jewish Civilization after 1492: The Fourth International Congress for Research and Study of Sephardi and Oriental Jewish Heritage*. Ed. M. Abitbol et al. Jerusalem: Misgav Yerushalayim, 1997. 191–201.

Molloy, Sylvia. "Can We Talk?" *Profession* (2002): 4–6.

Morwyn, Peter. *A compendious and most maruelous history of the latter times of the Iewes commonweale beginning where the Bible, or Scriptures leaue, and continuing*... London. 1558.

Mount, Eric. "Can We Talk? Contexts of Meaning for Interpreting Illness." *Journal of Medical Humanities* 14.2 (1993): 51–65.

Mujica Lainez, Manuel. *Bomarzo*. Bs.As.: Editorial Sudamericana, 1968.

Niewöhner, Friedrich. *Veritas sive varietas. Lessings Toleranzparabel und das Buch Von den drei Betrügern*. Bibliothek der Aufklärung 5. Heidelberg: L. Schneider. 1988.

Onians, John. "A Short History of Amazement." *Sight and Insight: Essays on Art and Culture in Honour of E.H. Gombrich at 85*. Ed. J. Onians. London: Phaidon Press, 1994. 11–33.

Park, Katharine and Lorraine Daston. "Unnatural Conceptions: The Study of Monsters in Sixteenth- and Seventeenth-Century France and England." *Past and Present* 92 (1981): 20–54.

Pedaya, Haviva. "The Great Mother." *Temps i espais de la Girona jueva*. Ed. Silvia Planas Mercè. Girona: Patronat Call de Girona, 2011. 311–28.

Penchansky, David. "God the Monster: Fantasy in the Garden of Eden." *The Monstrous and the Unspeakable: the Bible as Fantastic Literature*. Ed. George Aichele and Tina Pippin. Sheffield: Sheffield Academic Press, 1997.

Platt, Peter G. *Wonders, Marvels, and Monsters in Early Modern Culture*. Delaware: University of Delaware Press, 1999.

Prijs, Joseph. *Die Basler Hebräische Drucke (1492–1866)*. Ed. Bernhard Prijs. Olten and Freiburg Breisgau: Urs Graf-Verlag, 1964.

Reiner, Jacob. "The Original Hebrew *Yosippon* in the *Chronicle of lerahmeel*." *Jewish Quarterly Review* 60 (1969/70): 128–46.

———. "The Jewish War: Variations in the Historical Narratives in the Texts of Josephus and the *Yosippon*." Ph.D. Diss., Dropsie University, 1972.

———. "The English *Yosippon*." *The Jewish Quarterly Review* New Series 58.2 (1967): 126–42.

Rodríguez de Castro, José. *Biblioteca española: Tomo primero que contiene la noticia de los escritores rabinos españoles desde la época conocida de su literatura hasta el presente*. Madrid, 1781.

Rossebastiano, A. *La tradizione ibero-romanza del Libro de las maravillas del mundo di Juan de Mandavila*. Alessandria: Edizioni dell'Orso, 1997.

Ruiz, Juan. *Libro de buen amor*. Ed. Alberto Blecua Madrid. Cátedra, 1992. *The Book of Good Love*. Trans. Elizabeth MacDonald. London: Everyman, 1999.

Sassoon, D. S. *Ohel David. Descriptive catalogue of the Hebrew and Samaritan manuscripts in the Sassoon Library*. 2 vols. Oxford, 1932.
Scarry, Elaine. *The Body in Pain*. New York: Oxford University Press, 1985.
Scribner, R. W. *For the Sake of Simple Folk. Popular Propaganda for the German Reformation*. Oxford: Clarendon, 1994.
Serrano y Sanz, Manuel. *Orígenes de la dominación española en América*. Madrid: Bailly-Bailliere, 1913.
Ben Shlomoh, Gershom. *The Gate of Heaven. Shaar ha-Shamayim*. Ed. and trans. F.S. Bodenheimer. Jerusalem: Kiryath Sepher, 1953.
Shevet Yehuda. Ed. A. Schochat, A. and Y. Baer. Jerusalem: Mosad Bialik, 1946–1947.
Silva y Verástegui, Soledad. *La miniatura medieval en Navarra*. Pamplona, 1989.
Slifkin, Natan. *Sacred Monsters: Mysterious and Mythical Creatures of Scripture, Talmud and Midrash*. New York: Zoo Torah, 2007.
Smith, Paul Julian. *Quevedo on Parnassus*. London: Modern Humanities Research Association, 1987.
Steinschneider, Moritz. *Die Geschichtsliteratur der Juden in Druckwerken und Handschriften*. Frankfurt: Kaufman, 1905.
Todorov, Tzvetan. *The Conquest of America: The Question of the Other*. Trans. Richard Howard. New York: Harper and Row, 1984.
Usque, Samuel. *Consolação às Tribulações de Israel* (*Consolation for the Tribulations of Israel*). Trans. Martin A. Cohen. Philadelphia: Jewish Publication Society of America, 1965.
Watt, Tessa. *Cheap Print and Popular Piety, 1550–1640*. Cambridge, UK: Cambridge University Press, 1993.
Wolf, Lucien. "'Josippon' in England." *Transactions of the Jewish Historical Society of England* 6 (1908–10): 226–89.

10

Reading *Amadís* in Constantinople: Imperial Spanish Fiction in the Key of Diaspora

David A. Wacks

Introduction

Garci Rodríguez de Montalvo's *Amadís de Gaula* (Zaragoza, 1508) was the most important Spanish novel of chivalry to be published in the sixteenth century, and inspired dozens of sequels and imitations. It was responsible for an international boom in chivalric novels in the sixteenth century that was brought to an end only by the publication of Cervantes's *Don Quijote*.[1] The translation of *Amadís* into Hebrew is a significant cultural moment, a reappropriation of the values of the chivalric novel in a Sephardic setting. It is a simultaneous deployment of Spanish culture as an engine of Sephardic prestige and a rejection of imperial Spanish culture, substituting in its place a reading that reflects the values of a diasporic minority. In the face of the Sepharadim's rejection from and abjection by the Spanish imperium, Jacob Algaba's *Amadís* duplicates aspects of Spanish cultural imperialism within the Jewish communities of the Ottoman Empire. We can therefore read Algaba's *Amadís* as product of what I will call Sephardic humanism, a response to the Imperial culture of letters promulgated by the Catholic Monarchs.[2]

As in the case of writers associated with the court of Ferdinand and Isabella, Sephardic humanists worked across and between historiography and fiction. The translator Jacob Algaba was a proponent of a counter-humanism that flourished in Sephardic communities during the sixteenth century. Sephardic humanism is not often studied in relation to configurations of Spanish imperial power. More often scholars see it as a precursor to a modern Jewish national history rather than as an obscure counter-history of the emergent Spanish nation state.

Amadís de Gaula as Imperial Hero

Every culture has its knight in shining armor, its Superman and Captain America. In sixteenth-century Spain this was the tradition of literary knights errant inaugurated in print by *Amadís de Gaula*, protagonist of a wildly successful franchise of chivalric novels. Along with the Arthurian legends that arrived in the Iberian Peninsula from France during the late twelfth and early thirteenth centuries, tales of Amadís had been circulating in Iberia for hundreds of years when Garci Rodríguez de Montalvo published his authorized, updated recension of the deeds of Amadís de Gaula in Zaragoza in 1508.[3] The book was a huge success, and Montalvo and his successors capitalized on it by bringing out some ten sequels chronicling the adventures first of Esplandián, son of Amadís, and then of a series of related sequels in what was the *Star Wars* franchise of sixteenth-century Spain at the dawn of its so-called *Siglo de Oro* (Golden Age) (Lucía Megías 597–98). One need go no further than Cervantes's *Don Quijote* to find evidence of the tremendous hold *Amadís* had on the popular imagination. In a scene where the town barber and the priest are preparing to burn protagonist Alonso Quijano's library, they debate the fate of *Amadís*, eventually saving from the flames (ed. Rico 61; trans. Grossman 46).

This cult of the hero that sprung up around Amadís and his successors was a product of the times. In the sixteenth century the struggle with the Ottoman Empire was the stage on which Amadís made his entry. The Spanish knight errant became, in the popular imagination, a hero for the times, one who (like Captain America during and after World War II), would serve as a fictional avatar of popular fears of military defeat and invasion (Saemann 71–72; Dittmer).[4] In the second part of the *Quijote*, Cervantes lampoons this very notion of the Spanish knight errant as Christian Imperial soldier. When Don Quixote is discussing an impending Turkish attack on Spain with the barber and the priest, he suggests that King Philip assemble a crack unit of super soldiers to defend Spain against the Ottomans:

> ¿Hay más sino mandar Su Majestad por público pregón que se junten en la corte para un día señalado todos los caballeros andantes que vagan por España; que, aunque no viniesen sino media docena, tal podría venir entre ellos, que solo bastase a destruir toda la potestad del Turco? Estenme vuestras mercedes atentos y vayan conmigo. ¿Por ventura es cosa nueva deshacer un solo caballero andante un ejército de doscientos mil hombres, como si todos juntos tuvieran una sola garganta o fueran hechos de alfenique? Si no, díganme cuántas historias están llenas destas maravillas. ¡Había, en hora mala para mí, que no quiero decir para otro, de vivir hoy el famoso don Belianís o alguno de los del inumerable linaje de Amadís de Gaula! Que si alguno de éstos hoy viviera y con el Turco se afrontara, a fe que no le arrendara la ganancia. (Cervantes 552)

> What else can His Majesty do but command by public proclamation that on a specific day all the knights errant wandering through Spain are to gather at court, and even if no more than half a dozen were to come, there might be one among them who could, by himself, destroy all the power of the Turk. Your graces should listen carefully and follow what I say. Is it by any chance surprising for a single knight errant to vanquish an army of two hundred thousand men, as if all of them together had but one throat or were made of sugar candy? Tell me, then: how many histories are filled with such marvels? If only—to my misfortune, if not to anyone else's—the famous Don Belianís were alive today, or any one of the countless descendants of Amadís of Gaul! If any of them were here today and confronted the Turk, it would not be to his advantage! (trans. Grossman 461)

Heroes embody the values that are important to a given society, and Amadís and his successors were avatars of Spanish imperial desire.[5] Accordingly, Montalvo's introduction to *Amadís* paints the knight hero as a man who, had he been born a real knight and not a fictional character, might have fought alongside the Catholic Monarchs as they reclaimed the last redoubts of Islamic sovereignty on the Iberian Peninsula, before setting their sights across the Mediterranean on the Ottoman seat of power, Constantinople.

In this propagandistic turn, Montalvo was following the lead of humanists working at the court of the Catholic Monarchs who actively promoted a program of imperial imagery that very deliberately deployed tropes from Imperial Rome, mixing these with specifically Iberian and Catholic elements to create a narrative of temporal and spiritual imperial renovation.[6] According to this narrative, the Spanish crown is a renewal of the Holy Roman Empire, itself a renewal of Classical Rome. Just as the Holy Roman Empire was renewed through Christian salvation, the Spanish Empire is renewed through a spiritual discipline that transcends the Roman example in that not only is Christianity to be the guiding force of government, but of the souls of all imperial subjects as well (Rojinksy 119–20; Pagden 32).

Like the humanist historians of the court of the Catholic Monarchs, in his introduction Montalvo stresses that the value of history is to study the deeds of great men.[7] He legitimates his work by placing *Amadís* on the same stage as his king, Ferdinand of Aragón, suggesting that the orators of classical antiquity would be equally inspired by Ferdinand's deeds as by those of Caesar. He frames the deeds of Amadís within a discussion of those of the great (historical/mythical) heroes of antiquity, next to those of Ferdinand in the present day. What connects fictional Amadís, mythical Achilles, historical Caesar, and contemporary Ferdinand? The rhetorical excellence with which their deeds are celebrated, the "flowers" and "roses" planted in their honor by great orators in the tradition of courtly, martial rhetoric:

> Pues si en el tiempo destos oradores, que más en las cosas de la fama que de interesse ocupavan sus juizios y fatigavan sus spíritus, acaesciera aquella santa conquista que el nuestro muy esforçado Rey hizo del reino de Granada, ¡cuántas flores, cuántas rosas en ella por ellos fueran sembradas, assí en lo tocante al esfuerço de los cavalleros, en las rebueltas, escaramuças y peligrosos combates y en todas las otras cosas de afruentas y trabajos, que para la tal Guerra se aparejaron, como en los esforçados razonamientos del gran Rey a los sus altos hombres en las reales tiendas ayuntados, y las obedientes respuestas por ellos dadas, y sobre todo, las grandes alabanças, los crescidos loores que meresce por haver emprendido y acabado jornada tan cathólica! (219–20)

> So then, if in the time of these [classical] orators, who in matters of reputation than in personal gain applied their intelligence and wearied their spirits, should have taken place that holy conquest that our very brave King made of the kingdom of Granada, what flowers, what roses might they have planted on its occasion, as concerns the bravery of the knights in the battles, skirmishes, and dangerous duels and all the other cases of confrontations and travails that were performed in the course of that war, as well as of the compelling speeches made by the great King to his nobles gathered in the royal campaign tents, the obedient replies made by them, and above all, the great praises, the lofty admirations that he deserves for having taken on and accomplished such a divinely inspired task!

Montalvo projects upon the fictional Amadís the very real desire to continue the trajectory of imperial holy war begun by the elimination of Islamic political power on the Iberian Peninsula. If the Christian conquest of al-Andalus had long been framed as a domestic crusade, and the Pope himself gave them the title "Catholic Monarchs," it follows that what made them so 'Catholic' was their military commitment to expand Christendom and diminish *Dar al-Islam.*[8] Constantinople, only recently conquered by the Ottomans, would replace Granada as the object of imperial desire. In the *Amadís* the former Byzantine capital emerges in the novel as a site of Christian Imperial fantasy, an alternate past in which the Byzantine Christians successfully fight off the Ottomans.[9]

In Montalvo's sequel, Esplandián, son of Amadís, falls in love with the daughter of the Byzantine Emperor of Constantinople, then successfully leads the Byzantines in routing an attempted Muslim invasion. After the great victory, the Emperor abdicates in favor of Esplandián, who himself ascends to the throne.[10] Subsequent Amadís sequels feature protagonists, descendents of Amadís, who likewise rule over or defend a Christian Constantinople.[11]

In this way, Montalvo maps the values of a new kind of Catholicism, one yoked to imperial aspirations that are mapped onto the mostly secular figure of the Arthurian knight errant as a means of redemption. This happens precisely at the time when the mode of combat the knight errant represents—individual combat in the name of one's lady—is passing into a ceremonial, symbolic practice that no longer has pride of place in real warfare and that has been surpassed by mass warfare carried out by professional armies on a grand scale.[12]

As we have seen in Montalvo's introduction to Amadís, the author frames the exploits of his (fictional) chivalric hero in terms of the military victories of Ferdinand over the Muslim enemy Granada. Once the boundaries of the peninsula are secure against the infidel, and the North African coast pacified, the next logical grand imperial gesture would be to recuperate Constantinople for Christendom. The Ottoman Turks had, after all, conquered Constantinople in the not-so-distant past, and their looming presence on the Mediterranean was seen as a serious threat to Spanish political power in the region and even on the Iberian Peninsula itself.[13] Contemporary chroniclers confirm that the loss of Christian Constantinople was, during the reign of the Catholic Monarchs, still a fresh wound. Diego Enríquez del Castillo, writing before 1503, writes that "el dolor de la perdiçión de Constantinopla, que el turco avya tomado, estava muy rreçiente en los coraçones de todos" (156) (the pain of the loss of Constantinople, that the Turk had conquered, was very recent in the hearts of all). It is a natural move, especially after the Fourth Crusade (1204) for the chivalric hero to be cast in a crusading role.[14] Crusade chronicles, a well represented genre, were an important influence in determining the shapes of chivalric romance, and vice versa.[15]

This sort of conflation of history and courtly narrative was common in Peninsular literature of the late fifteenth and early sixteenth centuries. Chivalric novels such as *Amadís de Gaula* and its successors represented themselves as a kind of history, or at best as offering some of the same benefits to be had from reading 'real' histories of kings who actually lived and acted.[16]

Montalvo's mapping of the fictional knight errant onto political concerns of the day was very much in keeping with the history of chivalric romance. His innovation is his deliberate and explicit application of the fictional exploits of Amadís and Esplandián to the specific exploits of the rulers of an emergent nation state.[17] The fantasy of recuperating Constantinople is played out with abandon in the fictional literature of the reign of the Catholic Monarchs, even if it is minimized in the royal chronicles of the time. The literary sources of the times give voice to Iberian memories and anxieties of struggle with the Turk and desire to recuperate Constantinople, notably in the fifteenth-century Catalan romance *Curial e Güelfa*, and most pointedly in *Tirant lo Blanc* (Díaz Mas 343–44). If documents emanating from the royal chancery did not voice specific imperial designs on the Ottoman capital, there was a significant artistic trend fantasizing a Christian Constantinople. Despite the fact that the Catholic Monarchs were never in a position to consider a full-on invasion, the dream of the Reconquest of Constantinople was a powerful idea, one that was conveniently suited to the articulation of an Imperial identity. This is the *Amadís* that Jacob Algaba set his pen to translate while living in the very Constantinople that many readers of Amadís imagined the knight might one day conquer in the name of Spain.

The Sepharadim in the Imperial Spanish Context

The publication of Jacob Algaba's Hebrew translation of *Amadís* is a sort of ironic restoration of Amadís to Constantinople, albeit one that differs from Montalvo's vision of a Constantinople restored to Christendom. The publication of this Ottoman Hebrew *Amadís* will serve as a focal point for my discussion of the Sephardic role in the Hispanic cultural imaginary of the sixteenth century, precisely during Spain's emergence as a global imperial power. We have mentioned the chroniclers and authors working at the court of Ferdinand and Isabella and their task to construct an imperial identity. What is the role of Sephardic Jewry in this imperial idea? Why are they worth mentioning, seeing as how they had been cut off from Spain by the Edict of Expulsion?

In light of recent calls for more global approaches to early modern Hispanic studies, critics have been studying traditional topics in broader contexts, using approaches that de-center the idea of an author representing a single national culture or ethos. Carroll Johnson, the distinguished North American Cervantes scholar, held that the future of his field lay in the study of Cervantes's works in the context of Spanish Imperialism in the New World and in Islam. This sentiment has been echoed and carried out by younger scholars who argue for more transnational, transterritorial approaches to European national literature and history.[18] The Sephardic context widens the scope to include the Mediterranean context, and the disasporic context of the Sepharadim, who settled in communities from the Americas to India, affords the scholar of Spanish narrative a much more cosmopolitan scope than a focus merely on the Hispanic world.

Early modern Sephardic culture is very much a product of imperial Spain, and reproduces aspects of it in its own way. We can think of it as a kind of parallel shadow imperialism that the Sepharadim brought to bear on the Jewish communities of the Ottoman Empire where many of them settled.[19] The idea that the Sepharadim were deterritorialized 'Spaniards' was a common, if controversial, idea among Spanish liberals in the late nineteenth and twentieth centuries.[20] One might even venture that the Ottoman Sepharadim were performing their Spanishness in what could be argued was a form of colonization of the Ottoman Jewish world.

Significant numbers of Sepharadim had emigrated to the Ottoman Empire since the fourteenth century, with a spike after the anti-Jewish violence of 1391 and a larger one following the 1492 expulsion. Sepharadim and *conversos* continued to arrive over the course of the sixteenth century as well, some coming directly from Spain and Portugal, others from North Africa, Western Europe, and other points.[21] The Ottoman Empire was a popular destination for Spanish and Portuguese *conversos* who, although well situated materially in Spain and Portugal, sought to practice Judaism openly. By the mid-sixteenth century the Sepharadim had largely overwhelmed the native Greek-speaking Romaniote and other Jewish groups living in the Ottoman Empire. Judeo-Castilian came to dominate the Romance languages spoken by Ottoman Jews of Provencal, Portuguese, Catalan, and Italian origin, and Sephardic customs and liturgical rite dominated those of other groups as well (Levy 23–27, 60–63).

Contemporary (Sephardic) sources bear out this characterization of the Sepharadim as the socially and culturally dominant group within Ottoman Jewry, imposing their liturgy, rabbinic jurisprudence, cuisine, language, and social customs on the wider community. Writing in 1509, Rabbi Moses Aroquis of Salonika bears witness to this phenomenon:

> It is well known that the Sepharadim and their scholars in this empire, together with the other communities that have joined them, make up the majority, may the Lord be praised. To them alone the land was given, and they are its glory and its splendor and its magnificence, enlightening the land and its inhabitants. Who deserves to order them about? All these places too should be considered as ours, and it is fitting that the small number of early inhabitants of the empire observe all our religious customs . . . (Aroquis 44, cited in Hacker, "Sephardim" 111)

The Ottoman embrace of the Sepharadim only underscores this point. They effect a massive *translatio studii* from Spain to the Ottoman Empire that spans commercial, industrial, military, and intellectual spheres.[22] This fact was certainly not lost on Sultan Bayazid II, who is famously rumored to have marveled at the foolishness of the Catholic Monarchs for impoverishing their own kingdom while enriching his own.[23] Neither was it lost on outside observers such as Nicholas de Nicolay, a French traveler and diplomat who marveled at the extent of the Sephardic economic domination of the Ottoman scene:

> [The Jews] have amongst them workmen of all artes and handicraftes moste excellent, and specially of the Maranes [Marranos] of late banished and driven out of Spaine and Portugale, who to the great detriment and damage of the Christianitie, have taught the Turkes divers inventions, craftes and engines of warre, as to make artillerie, harquebuses, gunne powder, shot, and other munitions: they have also there set up printing, not before seen in those countries, by the which in faire characters they put in light divers bookes in divers languages, as Greek, Latin, Italian, Spanish, and the Hebrew tongue, beeing too them naturall, but are not permitted to print the Turkie or Arabic tongue. (Nicholay 93a, cited in Levy 26)

Such reports of the overwhelming successes of the Sepharadim were couched in messianic terms. The increased proximity of the exiled Sepharadim (who were said to descend from Jerusalemite Hebrews) to the Holy Land was seen as a harbinger of the Messiah (Levy 19–20). Both the imperial discourse of the Catholic Monarchs (Liss 65) and the destiny of the Sepharadim in the Ottoman Empire were couched in millenarian and prophetic terms. This went back at least to the Ottoman conquest of Constantinople, which Jewish writers understood in a messianic sense. This gathering messianism was accelerated by the Expulsion of the Jews from Spain and the subsequent annexation of the Holy Land, *Eretz Yisrael*, to the Ottoman Empire in 1516 (Goldish 41–42, 50–51; Silver 110–50).

Despite the many historical and cultural continuities between the Sepharadim and Imperial Spain, most scholarly formulations of Spain's Imperial culture center on *conversos* (who were permitted to remain Spanish subjects) and omit discussion of unconverted Sepharadim (Fuchs, "Imperium" 74). The Sepharadim are *involved* in Spanish Imperial culture, but not as Imperial subjects or objects. They enact Spanish culture on the Ottoman stage in a kind of Sephardic counter-nationalism that mimics and remixes Spanish imperial culture.[24]

How did Sephardic intellectuals react to this exclusion? By refashioning the tropes of the traditions of imperial humanism in their own image; by producing a Sephardic humanism that refracted their love for and alienation from Spain through a mixture of humanist and Jewish habits of expression. Just as Montalvo's *Amadís* flowed from the context of Spanish humanism, Algaba's *Amadís* is a product of Sephardic humanism, the scholarship of the Sephardic abjection from Imperial Spain.

The Hebrew *Amadís*: Knight Errant in Diaspora

The project of the Sephardic intellectual is twofold: on the one hand, he sought to legitimize their work by drawing on the prestige of Spanish humanism; on the other, he reshaped this humanism into one that reflected the values of the community in a diasporic, transimperial context. Algaba's Hebrew *Amadís* accomplishes by recasting the heroic values of Montalvo's book to bring them more fully in line with Sephardic sensibilities (Piccus 210 n42, 211 n43; Ashkenazi 367).

Both versions were of course shaped by market considerations. Montalvo tailored the story to fulfill popular expectations of Christian, chivalric behavior. This he accomplished without a doubt. But Algaba's challenge was different. He was assured of the popularity of the narrative franchise—this was never in question, and the popularity of the *Amadís* narrative among Sepharadim is well documented. The figure of Amadís was so compelling in the Sephardic imagination that he acquired a certain symbolic universality. There is a large corpus of popular ballads in the Sephardic tradition that, although they are largely unrelated to the story of Montalvo's *Amadís,* still call their heroic protagonist by his name. The name *Amadís* becomes emblematic of any "knight in shining armor" type.[25] To the Sepharadim, as to the Spanish, *Amadís* was the archetypical hero, and therefore every hero was *Amadís*.

Even well before Algaba's Hebrew translation appeared, Ottoman Sepharadim were avid readers of Spanish editions of *Amadís* and other chivalric novels. In the early sixteenth century, Jerusalem Rabbi Menahem di Lonzano chastised his community for reading *Amadís* and *Palmerín* on Shabbat (the Sabbath), when they should have been reading religious books.[26] Unlike the bootleg Spanish copies of *Amadís* and *Palmerín* mentioned by Lunzano, a Hebrew Amadís would need to bear the imprimatur of the Rabbis of Constantinople in order to see the light of day, and that would require some revisions.[27] Sephardic authors and translators therefore had to recast chivalric heroes in values that were consonant with those of the community, or at the very least they had to *say* that's what they were doing.

The culture of Montalvo's *Amadís,* with its exaggerated religious rhetoric and rarefied standards of courtliness, rejected Algaba's religious culture, and Algaba happily returned the favor, refashioning Amadís as a Sephardic hero: one who springs from Iberian tradition but who is free of the restraints of official Spanish culture as practiced by the courts and propagated by Christian authors of chivalric novels, court histories, and manuals of conduct. Here I would like to talk more directly about the text of the translation itself, in order to demonstrate what Algaba's translation *does* as a translation made by and for members of a culture in diaspora.

Diaspora and the Chivalric Imagination

First-wave modern theorists of diaspora writing in the 1970s and 1980s argued that the cultural imagination of diasporic populations vacillates between two geographical territories, constantly mediating between the symbolic value of their homeland and the lived reality of their current hostland. Later theorists of more recent diasporas have criticized this 'dual-territorial' model. Sudesh Mishra, one of the harshest critics of this approach, argues that it cannot address the complexities of the modern diasporas of Indian, African, Chinese, and other populations (30).

Montalvo's *Amadís* was a natural favorite for Sephardic Jews who, while living in Constantinople, Salonika, or elsewhere, spoke Spanish and still identified strongly with the vernacular culture of their land of origin. Its reception by Sephardic Jews and its translation into Hebrew offers us a glimpse into the literary practices of the Sephardic diaspora. The Hebrew *Amadís* can help us to better understand the diasporic cultural production of the Sepharadim, particularly in how it drew on print technology and translation from Spanish in order to promulgate their own version of Spanish culture throughout the Sephardic Diaspora.

The Hebrew print industry was active in Spain from the late fifteenth century, and presses in Spain produced a great number of religious works (Bibles, Talmuds, biblical commentaries, liturgical and moralistic texts, etc.) but also volumes of philosophy, science, and what we might call secular prose such as histories and fiction. In the early sixteenth century Hebrew printing continued to flourish first in Italy and then in Ottoman cities such as Salonika, Adrianopolis, and Constantinople.[28] For most of the sixteenth century nearly all titles with any discernible Jewish content were published in Hebrew (in Salonika printers brought out a few titles in Judeo-Spanish, and Italian printers published some in Italian or in both Italian and Hebrew) but for the most part Hebrew had pride of place as the prestige language of the Jewish press.[29]

In Ottoman Jewish society, Hebrew was the academic and religious *lingua franca* of a number of different ethnic groups who had settled in Ottoman cities. While Salonika in the sixteenth century was overwhelmingly Sephardic, the indigenous Greek-Speaking Romaniote Jews had significant communities in the cities and were joined by Ashkenazi Jews from Western and Eastern Europe as well as some Mizrahi (Eastern) Jews from the Arabic, Persian, and Turkic-speaking areas of the Ottoman Empire and beyond. But by their numbers, their superior cultural level, and their considerable network of commercial and diplomatic contacts, the Sepharadim quickly emerged as the prestige subculture of Ottoman Jewry. This, along with the fact that Sepharadim conversant in Spanish would have no need of a Hebrew translation in order to read *Amadís*, suggests that the translation was made either for Greek-speaking (but Hebrew-reading) Romaniote Jews in Ottoman lands or perhaps for non-Spanish-speaking Jewish readers in any country that Algaba's edition eventually might have reached. At this time Jewish merchants, diplomats, and scholars traveled widely throughout the Mediterranean and beyond. While we have no documentary evidence of the reception of Algaba's translation, it is not unreasonable to think that copies may have ended up in the hands of readers in Cairo, Tunis, Venice, Troyes, or Cochin for that matter. Sephardic intellectual culture (in the broad sense) had long history of prestige in the East, going back to Maimonides, who retained the sobriquet 'Ha-Sefardí' long after leaving his native Cordoba (Zohar 9). As we read Algaba's text we should keep two things in mind: he was in all likelihood writing for non-Sephardic Jews, and he was consciously representing Sephardic culture to them in choosing to translate a Spanish (European) novel, a genre that had yet to be introduced to Hebrew.[30]

As is often the case with translations into Hebrew, a certain amount of adaptation is necessary in order to predispose the text for Jewish religious and cultural sensibilities. The medieval translations made by the Ibn Tibbons, followed by those of Judah al-Ḥarizi and others developed differing approaches toward the translation of Arabic texts from a Muslim milieu (Robinson). While Jewish translators brought over numerous scientific and medical texts from Latin into Hebrew during the Middle Ages, translations into Hebrew of literary fiction were scarce. Apart from the thirteenth-century *Melekh Artus* (King Arthur), there were very few models to follow.[31]

Let us now turn to the text and see how Algaba worked with Montalvo's version to appeal to Jewish audiences and (it must be said) to *sell* copies of his translation. One common strategy of Algaba is to de-Christianize the text, removing references that might offend Jewish sensibilities. It is noteworthy that in most of these cases he avoids substituting specifically Jewish terms or concepts. Algaba's *Amadís* is the first major narrative work in a register of Hebrew that is largely free of the dense weave of *shibbutzim,* clever Biblical and rabbinical allusions that was characteristic of nearly every other work of Hebrew prose being published at the time, and only the histories of Joseph Hakohen and Solomon ibn Verga, roughly contemporary original works composed in Hebrew, shared Algaba's relatively plain prose style.[32]

In Algaba's translation, priests become laymen, oaths are secularized, and moralizing digressions (to which Montalvo was famously inclined) are simply omitted (Piccus 187). Most of these examples are superficial and predictable. When Amadís exclaims "¡Sancta María!" (235) Algaba substitutes 'Long live my Lord the King!' (7) Montalvo has the Queen lead Amadís into her "capilla" (chapel) (276), which Algaba renders as 'chamber' (28). Elsewhere, Amadís comes upon a wounded knight in the road who asks to be taken to an "hermitaño" (Anchorite) who might 'tend to his soul' ("que curará de mi alma") (280), which Algaba renders as 'someone who might heal me' (29).

Occasionally Algaba changes the moral valence of a term that is not specifically Christian but that might have been unseemly to Montalvo's target readership. When Amadís comes upon a damsel who has been sexually assaulted, in Montalvo's version she relates that she was "escarnecida" (dishonored) (293) by her attacker, while Algaba's damsel simply says "he lay with me" (38).

Most of the examples of Algaba's de-Christianization of the text are similarly routine; but some merit interpretation.[33] When King Languines orders a traitorous woman burnt to death, Algaba instead has her thrown to her death from a high tower. His reluctance to depict her being burned may be out of respect to victims of the Spanish Inquisition. Instead he supplies a ready-made phrase from the Hebrew Bible describing the fate Jezebel meets as punishment for her sins (2 Kings 9:30–37, especially 33) (301, trans. Algaba 42).

Despite his secularizing tendency, there are some moments in which he (for lack of a better, less-charged term) 'Judaizes' the text, inserting references to Jewish texts, cultural concepts, and observances. A few of these replace Christian references, but many appear to be spontaneous, whether out of a desire to appeal to his audience or, occasionally, for ironic effect.

In one particularly playful rabbinic allusion, Amadís deals his enemy a crippling blow to the thigh. In addition to the direct translation for thigh (*yareakh*) Algaba adds a technical term drawn from the rabbinic discourse on koshering animal carcasses: *maqom tsomet hagidin*, (the place where the tendons come together).[34] This is Algaba's ironic response to the episode in Genesis where the angel, tired of wrestling with Jacob all night long, finally "wrenched Jacob's hip at the socket" (32: 26). The biblical text then explains "that is why the children of Israel to this day do not eat the thigh muscle that is on the socket of the hip [i.e. sirloin, top loin, etc.], since Jacob's hip socket was wrenched at the thigh muscle" (32:33). Where the biblical texts derives its dietary ruling from the battle between Jacob and the angel, Algaba playfully writes the language of dietary restriction back into the battle between Amadís and his opponent. Here Algaba inserts a rabbinic sensibility into a chivalric text, in a move that parallels and challenges Montalvo's Christian moralizing tendency, but substituting a jurisprudential mode for a moralistic one.

An important part of the appeal of Montalvo's *Amadís* was its representation of Arthurian chivalric manners and speech. Part of the fantasy that Montalvo was selling to his readers was to clothe the fictional chivalric hero in the courtly mores of Montalvo's time, to blend in his protagonist the imagined courtly world of the knights errant of Arthurian imagination with the speech and courtly habits of the Spanish élite.[35]

This presented a particular problem for Algaba's readers, who were likely unfamiliar with the European traditions of chivalric behavior common to both chivalric fiction and to the social life of the Western European upper classes.[36] His challenge was to render Montalvo's frequent representations of the chivalric imaginary intelligible to non-Sephardic Ottoman Jews while still retaining the cultural cachet and novelty of the world it represented to his readers. It stands to reason that non-Sephardic Jews, who had never lived in Christian Europe would be unfamiliar with the institutions and practices of chivalry that form the fabric of the social world of *Amadís*. You cannot, of course, trade on foreign *caché* that is totally incomprehensible to your audience. To this end Algaba tailors Montalvo's references to the institutions of chivalry, social conventions, and courtly practices that may have fallen outside the experience of his non-Sephardic readers. As in the examples of de-Christianization, some such examples are superficial, but telling of differences of expectations of what 'courtly' or 'chivalric' might mean to non-Sephardic, Jewish audiences.

Some of these differences pertain to aspects of material culture portrayed in the chivalric novel that do not resonate with Ottoman Jewish expectations. In one such example, a character named 'la doncella de la guirnalda' (the damsel of the garland), so named because she always wore a garland of flowers to accentuate her beautiful hair, becomes in Algaba's version the 'damsel of the crown,' an accessory that ostensibly made more sense to the Ottoman readers to whom a garland of flowers might have seemed more rustic than idyllic. Algaba often renders declarations couched in elevated courtly language (which abound), in Biblical Hebrew, which better emphasizes their high register. When Amadís declares "¡muerto soy de corazón!" (290) (I shall die of heartbreak!), Algaba renders *mah anokhi, she-nitraf libi!* (35) (What will become of me, for my heart is torn asunder!), deploying the rarer first-person singular pronoun *anokhi* found in the Hebrew Bible. When a rival knight mocks Amadís as unworthy to love Oriana, he challenges Amadís: "Quiero que me digáis quién es y amarla he" (307) (tell me who she is, so that *I* may love her). Algaba puts into the knight's mouth the instantly recognizable words of the *Song of Songs* (6:10): *Haged na li mi ha-nishkafa-kemo shahar* (46) (Please tell me, who is she that shines through like the dawn). Again Algaba shows a bit of playfulness in his ironic deployment of biblical language, emphasizing the intensity of the discussion between Amadís and his rival in a way that makes sense to his audience. His deployment of the very well known phrase from the Song of Songs calls attention to the Hebrew poetic tradition in a Hispanic context in which descriptions of beloveds were more typically based on troubadouresque and Petrarchan ideals and language of female beauty.

Algaba also translates some of the specific conventions and practices of Spain's chivalric culture into more familiar, general terms. When Amadís swears an oath of service to Helisenda, he does so "en esta cruz y espada con que la orden de cavallería recebí" (234) (upon this cross and sword which I received with the Order of Chivalry), referencing a specifically Christian, chivalric practice of swearing upon a sword planted point down so that the handle and guard resemble a cross. The reference to the Order of Chivalry would most likely be opaque, and swearing on the cross unacceptable to a Jewish audience. Algaba has him swear simply upon his sword as a kind of shorthand (6). In replacing the strictly temporal symbol of the sword for the religious-temporal symbolism of the cross formed by the sword, he substitutes the values of the diasporic minority community for those of the sovereign majority.

When Helisena appeals to the honor of King Perión's squire, she asks him if he is an *hidalgo* (nobleman of low rank) (235); by this she means 'are you an honorable individual with whom I can trust my secret?' Algaba preserves the equation of high birth and good moral conduct implied by the word *hidalgo* but his Helisena asks the squire 'who are you and your family? Are they high born?' (*me`olah*, literally 'superior' or 'fine') (7).

Very occasionally, Algaba demonstrates his familiarity with courtly and chivalric discourse by introducing elements of them into the Hebrew when they are absent from the Spanish. In one such example, Amadís is complaining to Oriana about the difficulty of deferring his sexual desire for her. His complaint is couched in standard language of the courtly lover. He claims it is an impossible task, because his "juizio no puede resistir aquellos mortales deseos de quien cruelmente es atormentado" (385) (better judgment cannot resist those mortal desires by which it is cruelly tormented). What is interesting is that Algaba's Hebrew rendering introduces a different trope of the courtly lover, one that is also characteristic of Montalvo's day but that is absent from prior Hebrew tradition. He writes: "My heart is bound and tied in iron chains" (89), an image very much consistent with the late medieval Western European poetic convention of love as a form of slavery or imprisonment (Spanish books on amorous topics of the late fifteenth century included *Siervo libre de amor* 'Free Slave of Love' and *Cárcel de amor* 'Prison of Love'). Here Algaba proves himself a knowledgeable reader of Spanish tradition who actively seeks to reconcile, integrate, and mediate between Hebrew and Spanish literary traditions. His insertion of this courtly trope speaks to his biculturality and more importantly to his role of translator mediating between diasporic communities, the Sepharadim who represented the prestige of European courtly culture, and the Greek- and Arabic-speaking Jews who were his target audience.

Conclusion

Algaba's translation project was ultimately a commercial failure. His translation of the first book of Montalvo's *Amadís* was of very low quality and for whatever reason did not appear to have stimulated demand for subsequent installments (Dan 183). We have no concrete data to explain this fact, but we may speculate. Perhaps the time had not yet come for 'light literature' in Hebrew. Algaba's *Amadís* was nearly alone in that respect: apart from Jacob Tsarfati's 1509 translation of Fernando de Rojas' *Celestina*, it is the only Hebrew edition of its times of a popular novel.[37] The other secular works that were published in the sixteenth century were more 'serious' literature: difficult rhyming prose narratives that were showy displays of erudition and arcana, histories of Jewish persecutions or of the regimes that persecuted them, and a smattering of philosophical and scientific works. Algaba's test balloon novel was either an aberration or the lone survivor of a healthy tradition of such translations; we may never know which. In any event, the modern European novel would not make a significant début in Hebrew until the eighteenth century (Dan 181). Nonetheless, Algaba's *Amadís* does tell us a great deal about how he sought to represent Sephardic popular culture to the other communities of the Jewish diaspora in the Ottoman Empire of his day. His adaptation of Montalvo's iconic work for a non-Sephardic Jewish audience is an illuminating example of how Sepharadim chose to articulate their relationship with the land from which they found themselves in a second, Sephardic diaspora.

Notes

1. For an overview of *Amadís* studies, see Wendell Smith's introductory essay to the critical cluster of essays he edited in *La Corónica* 40.2 (2012).
2. My understanding of 'Sephardic humanism' differs somewhat from that of David Shasha, for whom it is the counterpoint to what he views as the anti-intellectualism of the Ashkenazi majority during medieval and early modern periods. It is more along the lines of what Ryan Szpiech ("Between Court and Call") proposes in his discussion of fifteenth-century Sephardic authors writing in the environment of Catalan humanism in the Crown of Aragon. See also the comments of Eleazar Gutwirth on the humanistic tendencies of Sephardic historiographer Solomon Ibn Verga ("Expulsion") and philospher Isaac Abravanel ("Abravanel" 642–44). Cedric Cohen Skalli, editor of Abravanel's correspondence, writes of "an authentic literary parallelism" (10) between Abravanel's Portuguese and Hebrew letters, both of which bear the imprint of the humanist *ars dictaminis* of his times.
3. Arthurian romances were known in the Peninsula since the mid-twelfth century, when Catalan troubadours began to make mention of Tristan and Lancelot. In the following century, Alfonso X mentions Tristan, Arthur, and Merlin in the *Cantigas de Santa Maria* (Entwistle 12, 119). See also Thomas (21–23) and Lida de Malkiel. Montalvo's *Amadís* (books 1–4, which would later become known as part 1 of the series) was extremely popular, and went through some twenty editions between 1508 and 1588 (Lucía Megías 127–28). This makes it the most published Spanish chivalric novel in the Sixteenth century, leaving aside for the moment the very many translations into languages other than Spanish.
4. For a study of Amadís as an early modern superhero, see Harney.
5. Eisenberg notes that Spanish chivalric novels in particular reflected and reinforced Spain's religious, crusading sensibilities (44).
6. See Tate (292). Martin Biersack (41–42) explains that the cultivation of a Roman

Imperial legacy by the Catholic Monarchs was meant to shore up their position before the nobles of Castile and Aragon.

7. Eisenberg notes that this strategy was common to nearly all Spanish chivalric romances, whose heroes "offered to the readers the supposedly beneficial picture of the ideal medieval ruler" (45). See also Cacho Blecua (198). The blurring of historical and fictional modes also common to the genre contributed to the exemplary value of the protagonists in that they were presented by their authors as historical characters. According to Fogelquist, part of the function of chivalric novels in general is to bridge the historical gap between antiquity and the late medieval period, which also contributes to the genre's ambiguous historicity (30).
8. The Catholic Monarchs were hardly the first Iberian Christian rulers to benefit from papal support of domestic 'crusades.' Even before the First Crusade, Pope Alexander II (1062–1073) established the Christian campaigns in al-Andalus as holy wars, in which participation might be repaid by remission of sins and relief from penance (O'Callaghan 24–26).
9. Literary sources of the times give voice to Iberian memories and anxieties of struggle with the Turk and desire to recuperate Constantinople, in the fifteenth century Catalan romance *Curial e Güelfa*, and most pointedly in *Tirant lo Blanc* (Díaz Mas 343–44; Piera). This desire to 'recuperate' Ottoman (formerly Byzantine) lands was not entirely fantastic. In the thirteenth century, the Crown of Aragon held significant territories in the so-called Latin kingdoms of the Eastern Mediterranean, and we should remember that the flag of the Crown of Aragon flew over the Duchy of Athens from 1311 to 1388. In fact, there had been a continuous presence of Western Christian forces, including Aragonese in parts of Byzantium going back to the crusades. On the Crown of Aragon in the Eastern Mediterranean, see Hillgarth.
10. Rodríguez de Montalvo (*Sergas* 696–98). The narrator of Sergas makes frequent exhortations in favor of Christian unity before the Turkish menace (Giráldez 24–25).
11. No fewer than six protagonists of medieval and Early Modern chivalric romances were crowned Emperor of Constantinople: Partinoples, Tirante, Esplandián, Palmerín de Olivia, Primaleón, and Claribalte (Rodilla León 307–08).
12. Fallows points out that the type of single combat portrayed in chivalric novels and ritualized in formal tournaments was fully obsolete by the mid-sixteenth century. He gives the sobering example of the Marquis of Saluzzo, "who, at the siege of Carmagnola in 1537, against the advice of his officers and man, cantered on his horse before the walls of the heavily defended city, lance in rest, openly defying the enemy harquebusiers. . . . Instead of being admired for his impetuosity or of being afforded the dubious privilege of exhibiting a battle scar at some future date . . . [he] was blasted out of the saddle at close range by a volley of harquebus fire and was killed instantly" (266).
13. Susan Giráldez (24) points out that ever since 1481, Aragonese writers were preoccupied by the possibility of a Turkish invasion of the Peninsula.

14. Authors of some thirteenth-century French romances included representations of crusading activities to cater to the tastes of patrons who had themselves participated in the Fourth Crusade as well as for propagandistic reasons (Trotter 169).
15. In his biography of French crusader Robert Curthose, William Aird points out that successive waves of crusade chronicles demonstrate increasing influence of chivalric romance (156). Sharon Kinoshita argues, with more intensity, that historicity and fictionality are difficult to separate in Robert de Clari's *Conquête de Constantinople* (139). Marina Brownlee writes that romance is a reaction to historical events and trends, "a continuous and sophisticated reinvention of itself as a response to an ever-changing historico-political configuration" (119). Barbara Fuchs likewise registers the complementarity of Romance and Chronicle, holding that "Romances simply have a different purchase on the truth" that has "little to do with empiricism; it connotes instead a moral stance towards political and historical events" (*Romance* 103).
16. Montalvo compares his work 'chronicling' the deeds of the fictional Amadís to that of the classical writers who chronicled the great deeds of Hector, Achilles, and Ajax. What we can glean from these (fictional) stories of chivalric adventures, he explains, are "los Buenos enxemplos y doctrinas que más a la salvación nuestra se allegaren . . . tomemos por alas con que nuestras animas suban a la alteza de la Gloria para donde fueron criadas" (22) (good examples and guidelines that bring us that much closer to our salvation . . . We use them as wings upon which our souls might fly up to the height of Glory whither they are destined). Medieval chroniclers had long included epic and chivalric material in supposedly 'historical' works. See, for example, David Arbesú's notes that the compilers of the *Primera crónica general* produced for Alfonso X (1252–1284) took greak pains to " intertwine reality with legend" (30) in including the story of Flores and Blancaflor in their account of Umayyad Cordoba.
17. Susan Giráldez writes that book 5 of *Amadís*, the *Sergas de Esplandián*, is "una obra propagandística, portavoz de la ideología de la monarquía católica de Fernando e Isabel" (4) (a work of propaganda, spokesperson for the ideology of the Catholic monarchy of Ferdinand and Isabella). Court chroniclers had long incorporated traditional and epic materials into their works of official history going back at last to the thirteenth century in Iberia, and historians of the sixteenth and seventeenth centuries affirm that such materials were valid sources for works of history (Sieber 293).
18. Fuchs, for example, proposes readings that emphasize "the transatlantic or international dimension of texts previously read within narrow national traditions" ("Imperium Studies" 71). Kinoshita questions the usefulness of modern categories of "nationalism, Orientalism, and postcolonialism," calling for "alternate genealogies of a medieval West that can no longer simplistically be adduced as the moment of origins of a 'clash of civilizations'" (12).
19. In 1964 the Spanish Hebraist Federico Pérez Castro argued that the greatest evidence of the Sepharadim's 'Spanishness' was their Spanish-style cultural imperialism: "No sólo siguieron viviendo según nuestros modos, sino que los impusieron allí donde

fueron a establecerse; fenómeno espiritual y social éste tan perfectamente español, que acaso sea el que más netamente defina su honda identificación con España" (Pérez Castro 84) (Not only continued to live according to our ways, but also imposed them wherever they settled; a spiritual and social phenomenon so perfectly Spanish, that might be what most clearly defines their profound identification with Spain).

20. Early-twentieth century Spanish Sephardist Ángel Pulido titled his book on Sepharadim *Españoles sin patria* (Spaniards Without a Fatherland). On this tendency, see also Bush (14) and Wacks (324–26). Beckwith notes that Pulido's pro-Sephardism was "superficial" (186) and was predicated on their linguistic assimilation to modern Castilian (187).
21. Levy points out that "the migration of the jews from the Iberian Peninsula, as well as from Italy and France, to the Ottoman Empire was, therefore, a gradual process that spanned many decades" (4). See also Ray (45–47) and Hacker, "Links."
22. The Sultans incentivized the Sepharadim to settle in secondary and tertiary commercial centers with generous concessions and tax relief. This policy was designed to stimulate economic development of provincial centers throughout the Ottoman Empire (Hacker, "Sürgün" 3). They were also key players in promoting international trade (Shmuelevitz 129). Just as Ottoman policy enabled Sephardic elites to reproduce the favorable economic conditions they had enjoyed in Spain, Sephardic intellectuals and printers saw it as their duty to reproduce the intellectual ferment of Spain in their new Ottoman context (Schmelzer 261–62 and 264).
23. Seventeenth-century Sephardic author Immanuel Aboab reports (*Nomologia* Amsterdam 1629) relates the famous yet likely apocryphal anecdote: "Can you call such a king wise and intelligent? He is impoverishing his country and enriching my kingdom" (Benbassa and Rodrigue 7).
24. Nadia Altschul has written on the concept of mimicry (*chez* Fanon and Bhabha) as a useful theoretical lens for studying cultural exchange in al-Andalus. According to her, "mimicry is not merely an appropriation but a form of mis-imitation; and in contrast to imitation it shows ambivalence between deference and defiance" (60).
25. Some of these ballads are sung well into the twentieth century. Samuel Armistead records a robust tradition of ballads featuring the exploits of *Don Amadí*, *Amalvi*, and other variants ("*Amadís*" 29–30).
26. Francisco Vásquez, *Palmerín de Olivia* (Salamanca 1511). See the modern edition of María Marín Piña. On Rabbi Lonzano's reaction, see Malachi (39). Lonzano's text, the moralistic poem *Tovah Tokhehat* (*The Best of Remonstrations*) is found in his *Shete Yadot* (*Two Hands*), a modern facsimile of the 1618 Venice edition (Lonzano f.135v.)
27. In her study of a fragmentary Judeo-Spanish chivalric novel, Alla Markova points out that social values of the Spanish Christian nobility associated with the heroes of chivalric novels were incompatible with Sephardic mores and tastes, and this discrepancy was responsible for the acculturation of the chivalric hero to the Sephardic context (160).

28. On the Hebrew book in Italy, see Hacker and Shear. On the Hebrew press in Constantinople, see Ya'iri. Wilkinson also lists a number of titles printed in Judeo-Spanish in Salonika, all of which are later than Algaba's translation. Wilkinson, *Iberian* 817.
29. Other than Moshe Almosnino's *Regimiento de la Vida* and *Tratado de los suenyos* (1564) and *Extremos y grandezas de Constantinopla* (actually an excerpt of Almosnino's inedited *Crónicas otomanas* published only in a transliteration by Jacob Cansino in Oran in 1638) very few (if any) secular volumes in Ladino were published during the sixteenth century.
30. Joseph Dan argues very forcefully that it was Algaba's translation of *Amadís de Gaula*, and not the novels of the eighteenth- and nineteenth-century *maskilim* (proponents of the *Haskalah* or 'Hebrew Enlightenment'), that was "the first European novel to see light in Hebrew clothes in print" (188). As such arguments often do, Dan's takes on a political cast in which he accuses the Ashkenazi (Eastern European Jewish) dominated Israeli literary establishment of revisionism: "There is no truth in the claim that it was the Jews of Ashkenaz that brought European culture to the tents of Israel" (181).
31. The anonymous translator of *Melekh Artus* felt it necessary to write a lengthy apology for his work of secular fiction, despite the fact that (as the editor of the text points out) Sephardic authors had cultivated secular fiction for over a century by the time the Hebrew Arthur appeared in Italy in 1279. Like Algaba, he was careful to de-Christianize the text and to insert numerous biblical and Talmudic allusions in order to make the romance more palatable to Jewish literary sensibilities (Leviant 61–72; Drukker 125).
32. On the poetic value of Biblical *shibbutzim*, see Kozodoy (117). Ross Brann similarly notes that "the emotional impact of the sacred history and other writings recorded in the Hebrew Bible thus inspired and fertilized the poets' literary imagination, religious and secular . . . " (25).
33. On de-Christianization in the Sephardic Romancero, see Armistead and Silverman ("Christian"). They note elsewhere that by contrast, 'judaization,' or the substitution of Jewish terminology and concepts for specifically Christian terms is relatively rare (*En torno* 138).
34. Karo, *Shulkhan Arukh, Yoreh De'ah*, 55:1.
35. Eisenberg notes that Charles V promoted the popularity of the chivalric novel through his personal interest in them as well as his enthusiastic support for tournaments and "chivalric spectacle" (95).
36. Here Algaba faces the challenge of communicating concepts for which his audience has no stable referent. Elsewhere Jewish translators, must coin a neologism for a concept with which his (European) audience is familiar, but that has no available form in Hebrew. To wit, in order to render 'to be knighted' into Hebrew the anonymous translator of the medieval Italian Arthur narrative inflected a Hebrew word for 'horseman' into a reflexive verb form (Leviant 53 n45).

37. All that remains of Tsarfati's translation of the *Celestina* is the introductory poem he himself composed. The poem was first edited by Cassuto. Carpenter translated it into English, and Hamilton studies it in the context of medieval Hispano-Hebrew prose.

Works Cited

Aird, William. *Robert "Curthose," Duke of Normandy*. Woodbridge: Boydell and Brewer, 2007.

Aboab, Imanuel. *Nomología, o, discursos legales*. Ed. Moisés Orfali Levi. Salamanca: Ediciones Universidad de Salamanca, 2007.

Almosnino, Moses. *Crónica de los reyes otomanos*. Ed. Pilar Romeu Ferré. Barcelona: Tirocinio, 1998.

———. *Regimiento de la vida; Tratado de los suenyos* (Salonika, 1564). Ed. John Zemke. Tempe: Arizona Center for Medieval and Renaissance Studies, 2004.

Altschul, Nadia. "The Future of Postcolonial Approaches to Medieval Iberian Studies." *Journal of Medieval Iberian Studies* 1.1 (2009): 5–17.

Arbesú, David. "Introduction." *Crónica De Flor y Blancaflores*. Tempe: ACMRS (Arizona Center for Medieval and Renaissance Studies), 2011. 1–47.

Armistead, Samuel G. "*Amadís de Gaula* en la literatura oral de los sefardíes." *La pluma es lengua del alma: Ensayos en honor de E. Michael Gerli*. Ed. José Manuel Hidalgo. Newark, Del.: Juan de la Cuesta Hispanic Monographs, 2011. 27–32.

Armistead, Samuel G., and Joseph Silverman. "Christian Elements and De-Christianization in the Sephardic Romancero." *Collected Studies in Honor of Américo Castro's Eightieth Year*. Ed. Marcel Hornik. Oxford: Lincombe Lodge Resarch Library, 1965. 21–38.

———. *En torno al romancero sefardí: Hispanismo y balcanismo de la tradición judeo-española*. Madrid: Seminario Menéndez Pidal, 1982.

Aroquis, Moses. *The Responsa of Zera Anashim*. [Hebrew] Ed. D. Frankel. Husyatin, 1902.

Ashkenazi, Assaf. "El *Amadís de Gaula* en su versión hebrea del siglo XVI." *Amadís de Gaula 1508: Quinientos años de libros de caballerías*. Ed. José Manuel Lucía Megías. Madrid: Biblioteca Nacional de España, 2008. 364–68.

Beckwith, Stacy N. "Facing Sepharad, Facing Israel and Spain: Yehuda Burla and Antonio Gala's Janus Profiles of National Reconstitution." *Sephardism: Spanish Jewish History and the Modern Literary Imagination*. Ed. Yael Halevi-Wise. Palo Alto: Stanford University Press, 2012. 169–88.

Benbassa, Esther, and Aron Rodrigue. *Sephardi Jewry: A History of the Judeo-Spanish Community, 14th–20th Centuries*. Berkeley: University of California Press, 2000.

Biersack, Martin. "Los Reyes Católicos y La Tradición Imperial Romana." *eHumanista* 12 (2009): 33–47. Web. 3 Aug. 2012.

Brann, Ross. *The Compunctious Poet: Cultural Ambiguity and Hebrew Poetry in Medieval Spain*. Baltimore: Johns Hopkins University, 1991.

Brownlee, Marina. "Iconicity, Romance and History in the *Crónica Sarracina*." *Diacritics* 36.3–4 (2006): 119–30. Web. 3 Aug. 2012.

Bush, Andrew. "Amador de los Ríos and the Beginnings of Modern Jewish Studies in Spain." *Journal of Spanish Cultural Studies* 12.1 (2011): 13–34.

Cacho Blecua, Juan Manuel. "Introducción." Rodríguez de Montalvo, *Amadís* 17–208.

Carpenter, Dwayne E. "A Converso Best-Seller: Celestina and Her Foreign Offspring." *Crisis and Creativity in the Sephardic World*. Ed. Benjamin Gampel. New York: Columbia University Press, 1997. 267–81.

Cassuto, Moses D. "From the Poetry of Joseph Ben Samuel Tsarfati: The First Comedy in Hebrew" [Hebrew]. *Jewish Studies in Memory of George A. Kohut. 1874–1933*. Ed. Salo Wittmayer Baron and Alexander Marx. New York: Alexander Kohut Memorial Foundation, 1935. 121–28.

Cervantes Saavedra, Miguel. *Don Quijote*. Ed. Francisco Rico. Madrid: Alfaguara, 2005.

———. *Don Quixote*. Trans. Edith Grossman. New York: Ecco, 2003.

Cohen Skalli, Cedric. "Introduction." *Isaac Abravanel: Letters*. Ed. Cedric Cohen Skalli. Berlin: Walter De Gruyter, 2007. 1–78.

Dan, Joseph. "The First Hebrew Novel: Jacob Algaba's *Amadís de Gaul*." [Hebrew] *Moznayim* 45 (1977): 181–88.

Díaz Mas, Paloma. "El eco de la caída de Constantinopla en las literaturas hispánicas." *Constaninopla 1453: Mitos y Realidades*. Ed. Pedro Bádenas de la Peña and Inmaculada Pérez Martín. Madrid: Consejo Superior de Investigaciones Cientificas, 2003. 318–49.

Dittmer, Jason. "Retconning America: Captain America in the Wake of World War II and the McCarthy Hearings." *The Amazing Transforming Superhero! Essays on the Revision of Characters in Comic Books, Film and Television*. Jefferson, NC: McFarland, 2007. 33–51.

Drukker, Tamar. "A Thirteenth-Century Arthurian Tale in Hebrew: A Unique Literary Exchange." *Medieval Encounters* 15.1 (2009): 114–29. Web. 3 Aug. 2012.

Eisenberg, Daniel. *Romances of Chivalry in the Spanish Golden Age*. Newark, Del.: Juan de la Cuesta, 1982.

Enríquez del Castillo, Diego. *Crónica de Enrique IV de Diego Enríquez Del Castillo*. Ed. Aureliano Sánchez Martín. Valladolid: Secretariado de Publicaciones Universidad de Valladolid, 1994.

Entwistle, William. *The Arthurian Legend in the Literatures of the Spanish Peninsula*. New York: Phaeton Press, 1975.

Fallows, Noel. *Jousting in Medieval and Renaissance Iberia*. Woodbridge, Suffolk: Boydell Press, 2010.

Fogelquist, James Donald. *El Amadís y el género de la historia fingida*. Madrid: José Purrúa Turanzas, 1982.

Fuchs, Barbara. "Imperium Studies: Theorizing Early Modern Expansion." *Postcolonial Moves: Medieval Through Modern*. Ed. Patricia Clare Ingham and Michelle R. Warren. New York: Palgrave Macmillian, 2003. 71–90.

———. *Romance*. New York: Routledge, 2004.
Giráldez, Susan. Las sergas de Esplandián *y la España de Los Reyes Católicos*. New York: P. Lang, 2003.
Goldish, Matt. "Patterns in Converso Messianism." *Jewish Messianism in the Early Modern World*. Dordrecht: Kluwer, 2001. 41–63.
Gutwirth, Eleazar. "Don Ishaq Abravanel and Vernacular Humanism in Fifteenth Century Iberia." *Bibliothèque d'Humanisme et Renaissance* 60.3 (1998): 641–71.
———. "The Expulsion from Spain and Jewish Historiography." *Jewish History: Essays in Honour of Chimen Abramsky*. London: Peter Halban, 1988. 141–61.
Hacker, Joseph. "The Sephardim in the Ottoman Empire in the Sixteenth Century." *The Sephardi Legacy*. Vol. 2. 2 vols. Jerusalem: Magnes Press, 1992. 108–33.
———. "The Links Between Spanish Jewry and Palestine." *Vision and Conflict in the Holy Land*. New York: St. Martin's Press, 1985. 111–39.
———. "The Sürgün System and Jewish Society in the Ottoman Empire." *Ottoman and Jewish Turkey: Community and Leadership*. Ed. Aron Rodrigue. Bloomington: Indiana University Press, 1992. 1–65.
Hacker, Joseph and Adam Shear. *The Hebrew Book in Early Modern Italy*. Philadelphia: University of Pennsylvania Press, 2011.
Hamilton, Michelle M. "Joseph ben Samuel Sarfati's *Tratado de Melibea y Calisto*: A Sephardic Jew's Reading of the *Celestina* in Light of the Medieval Judeo-Spanish Go-between Tradition." *Sefarad* 62.2 (2002): 329–47.
Harney, Michael. "Amadís, Superhero." *La Corónica* 40.2 (2012): 291–318.
Hillgarth, Jocelyn. *The Problem of a Catalan Mediterranean Empire, 1229–1327*. London: Longman, 1975.
Johnson, Carroll B. *Transliterating a Culture: Cervantes and the Moriscos*. Ed. Mark Groundland. Newark, Del.: Juan de la Cuesta Hispanic Monographs, 2010.
Karo, Joseph ben Ephraim. *Shulhan `arukh Yoreh De`ah*. Ed. Ya`akov Hayim Sofer. Yerushalayim: M. Sofer, 1966.
Kinoshita, Sharon. *Medieval Boundaries: Rethinking Difference in Old French Literature*. Philadelphia: University of Pennsylvania Press, 2006.
Kozodoy, Neal. "Reading Medieval Hebrew Love Poetry." *Association for Jewish Studies Review* 2 (1977): 111–29. Web. 3 Aug. 2012.
Leviant, Curt. *King Artus: A Hebrew Arthurian Romance of 1279*. Assen: Van Gorcum and Co., 1969.
Levy, Avigdor. *The Sephardim in the Ottoman Empire*. Princeton: Darwin, 1992.
Lida de Malkiel, María Rosa. "La literatura artúrica en España y Portugal." *Estudios De Literatura Española y Comparada*. Buenos Aires: EUDEBA, 1966. 134–48.
Liss, Peggy. "Isabel, Myth, and History." *Isabel la Católica, Queen of Castile*. Ed. David A. Boruchoff. New York: Palgrave, 2003. 57–78.
Lucía Megías, José Manuel. *Imprenta y libros de caballerías*. Madrid: Ollero y Ramos, 2000.
Lonzano, Menahem. *Shete Yadot*. Jerusalem: [s.n], 1969.
Malachi, Zvi. *The Loving Knight: The Romance:* Amadís de Gaula *and Its Hebrew*

Adaptation (Turkey, c. 1541). Trans. Phyllis Hackett. Lod: Haberman Institute for Literary Research, 1982.

Markova, Alla. "Un fragmento manuscrito de una novela de caballerias en Judeo-espanol." *Sefarad*. 69.1 (2009): 159–72.

McPheeters, Dean. "Una traducción hebrea de la *Celestina* en el siglo XVI." *Homenaje a Rodríguez-Moñino*. Ed. Antonio R. Rodríguez Moñino. Madrid, 1966. 299–311.

Mishra, Sudesh. *Diaspora Criticism*. Edinburgh: Edinburgh University Press, 2006.

Nicolay, Nicholas. *The Navigations, Peregrinatians and Voyages, Made into Turkie by Nicholas Nicolay*. Trans. T. Washington. London, 1585.

O'Callaghan, Joseph F. *Reconquest and Crusade in Medieval Spain*. The Middle Ages Series. Philadelphia: University of Pennsylvania Press, 2003.

Pagden, Anthony. *Lords of All the World: Ideologies of Empire in Spain, Britain and France C. 1500–c. 1800*. New Haven, Conn.: Yale University Press, 1995.

Pérez Castro, Federico. *Aspectos de La cultura hebraicoespañola*. Santander, 1964.

Piccus, Jules. "Corrections, Suppressions, and Changes in Montalvo's *Amadís*, Book I." *Textures and Meaning: Thirty Years of Judaic Studies at the University of Massachusetts Amherst*. Ed. Leonard H. Ehrlich et al. Amherst: Department of Judaic and Near Eastern Studies, University of Massachusetts, 2004. 179–211. Web. 3 August 2012.

Piera, Montserrat. "Tirant Lo Blanc: Rehistoricizing the 'Other' Reconquista." *Tirant Lo Blanc: New Approaches*. Ed. Arthur Terry. London, England: Tamesis, 1999. 45–58.

Pulido Fernández, Ángel. *Españoles sin patria y la raza sefardí*. Ed. facs. Granada: Universidad de Granada, 1993.

Ray, Jonathan. "Iberian Jewry Between West and East: Jewish Settlement in the Sixteenth-Century Mediterranean." *Mediterranean Studies* 18.1 (2009): 44–65.

Robinson, James. "The Ibn Tibbon Family: a Dynasty of Translators in Medieval Provence." *Be'erot Yitzhak: Studies in Memory of Isadore Twersky*. Ed. Jay Michael Harris. Cambridge: Harvard University Center for Jewish Studies, 2005. 193–224.

Rodilla León, María José. "Troya, Roma, y Constantinopla en *El Claribalte*." *Amadís y Sus Libros: 500 Años*. Ed. Aurelio González and Axayácatl Campos García Rojas. Mexico City: El Colegio de México, 2009. 303–11.

Rodríguez de Montalvo, Garci. *Amadís De Gaula*. Ed. Juan Manuel Cacho Blecua. Madrid: Cátedra, 1987.

———. *'Alilot Ha-abir*. Ed. Tzvi Malachi. Trans. Jacob Algaba. Tel Aviv: Tel Aviv University Press, 1981.

———. *Sergas de Esplandián*. Ed. Carlos Sainz de la Maza. Madrid: Castalia, 2003.

Rojinsky, David. *Companion to Empire: a Genealogy of the Written Word in Spain and New Spain, c.550–1550*. Amsterdam: Rodopi, 2010.

Saemann, Björn. *How Comics Reflect Society: The Development of American Superheroes*. Munich: GRIN Verlag, 2011.

Schmelzer, Menahem. "Hebrew Manuscripts and Printed Books Among the Sephardim Before and After the Expulsion." *Crisis and Creativity in the Sephardic World*. Ed. Benjamin R. Gampel. New York: Columbia University Press, 1997. 257–66.

Shasha, David. "Sephardic Literature: The Real Hidden Legacy." *Zeek*. Sept. 2005. Web. 13 June 2012.

Shmuelevitz, Aryeh. *The Jews of the Ottoman Empire in the Late Fifteenth and the Sixteenth Centuries: Administrative, Economic, Legal, and Social Relations as Reflected in the Responsa*. Leiden: E.J. Brill, 1984.

Sieber, Diane. "The Frontier Ballad and Spanish Golden Age Historiography: Recontextualizing the *Guerras civiles de Granada*." *Hispanic Review* 65.3 (1997): 291–306. Web. 3 Aug. 2012.

Silver, Abba. *A History of Messianic Speculation in Israel from the First Through the Seventeenth Centuries*. New York: Macmillan Co., 1927.

Smith, Wendell. "Amadís De Gaula, the Undiscovered Country: An Introduction." *La Corónica* 40.2 (2012): 177–86.

Szpiech, Ryan. "Between Court and Call: Catalan Humanism and Hebrew Letters." *eHumanista/IVITRA* 1 (2012): 168–84. Web. 3 Aug. 2012.

Tate, Robert Brian. *Ensayos sobre la historiografía peninsular del siglo XV*. Madrid: Gredos, 1970.

Thomas, Henry. *Spanish and Portuguese Romances of Chivalry: The Revival of the Romance of Chivalry in the Spanish Peninsula, and Its Extension and Influence Abroad*. Cambridge: University Press, 1920.

Trotter, D. *Medieval French Literature and the Crusades (1100–1300)*. Genève: Librairie Droz, 1988.

Vásquez, Francisco. *Palmerín de Olivia: (Salamanca, Juan de Porras, 1511)*. Ed. María Carmen Marín Piña, Giuseppe Di Stefano, and Daniela Pierucci. Alcalá de Henares, Madrid: Centro de Estudios Cervantinos, 2004.

Wacks, David A. "Is Spain's Hebrew Literature 'Spanish'?" *Spain's Multicultural Legacies: Studies in Honor of Samuel G. Armistead*. Ed. Adrienne Martin and Cristina Martínez-Carazo. Newark, Del.: Juan de la Cuesta Hispanic Monographs, 2008. 315–31.

Wilkinson, Alexander S. *Iberian books: Books published in Spanish or Portuguese or on the Iberian Peninsula before 1601*. Leiden: Brill, 2010.

Ya'iri, Abraham. *The Hebrew Press in Constantinople* [Hebrew]. Jerusalem: Y.L. Magnes, 1967.

Zohar, Zion. "A Global Perspective on Sephardic and Mizrahi Jewry: An Introductory Essay." *Sephardic and Mizrahi Jewry: From the Golden Age of Spain to Modern Times*. Ed. Zion Zohar. New York: New York University Press, 2005. 3–22.

◆ 11

Apocalyptic Sealing in the *Lozana Andaluza*

Ryan D. Giles

Antonio de Nebrija, in his *Introductorium Cosmographiae* (c.1500), followed the ancient Romans in designating the body of water that separates the peninsulas of Iberia and Italy as *mare nostrum* (our sea) and the *mare interius* (interior sea) (Flórez Miguel 198). He also includes the later name, *Mediterraneo*, to signify its orientation in the middle or in-between lands. This emphasizes the way in which the sea offers a medium for international trade, and a meeting point and crossroads for linguistic and religious groups living in the region. Nebrija spent ten years studying at the University of Bologna, and then brought the new humanistic and classical learning back with him to Spain. Decades later, one of his most well-known students would make the journey to Italy for different reasons and write a literary classic that embodies other kinds of cultural exchange between people and places connected by the Mediterranean.

Francisco Delicado, author of the 1528 *Retrato de la Lozana andaluza* (*Portrait of the Lusty Andalusian Woman*), seems to have journeyed to Rome in order to escape persecution resulting from his status as a *converso*, or Christian descendant of Jews. He may have also hoped to further his career as a priest and medical practitioner.[1] The Spanish exile not only wrote the *Lozana andaluza*, but also a manual for treating syphilis, *El modo de adoperare el legno de India* (On the Use of the West Indies Wood, 1529). It is clear from his two extant works that Delicado suffered for decades from this disease, known among Spanish speakers as the *mal francorum* (French malady).[2] This illness had spread through the region via sea routes, and, not suprisingly, other Romance speakers sometimes attributed its scourge to the Spanish and Italians. He also exhibits an intimate familiarity with a criminal underworld of pimps and whores working in early sixteenth-century Rome.[3] In fact, Delicado apparently wrote most of the *Lozana andaluza* while recovering in a Roman hospital, and finished it in Venice after escaping from Charles V's invading, mutinous army in 1527.[4] Combining Spanish and Italian dialects, the narrative tells the story of an Andalusian *conversa* who sails through the Mediterranean with her lover, making stops at various ports, before being abandoned by him. Lozana later makes her way to the Eternal City, where she gains notoriety as a sex worker, procuress, and healer. Lozana performs the various duties of a midwife, but is also known for her ability to alleviate the symptoms of syphilis, a disease from which she herself suffers. Characters in the dialogue call attention to the syphilitic scar that marks her forehead, referred to as her "estrella" (star) or "estrellica" (little star) (186, 193). This sign of the French disease or "greñimón," together with Lozana's deformed nose, is used to identify her on the streets of Rome (192). In the pages that follow, we will see how it also relates to the outcome of the narrative, reflecting apocalyptic expectations shared by Romans and newly arrived exiles from the other side of the western Mediterranean.

A number of critics have linked this scar to Lozana's Sephardic background. For example, both Manuel de Costa Fontes and Carolyn Wolfenzon have suggested that the "estrella" or "estrellica" could allude to the star of David, and in this way signal her Jewish ancestry and/or possible adherence to crypto-Judaism (*Art* 186; "*La Lozana*" 112).[5] Meghan McInnis-Domínguez has more recently related the mark on Lozana's face to emerging notions of impure Jewish blood and the "alterity" of *conversos* introducing a "social disease" within the imperial state (311–13). One potential problem with such theories is that a woodcut in the book depicts the "star" or "little star" as an asterisk detached from Lozana's body, and not a Davidic hexagram (fig. 1).

In fact, it resembles the kind of *astriscus* used by printers to indicate omissions, but also to mark places in the text containing essential truths or *sententia* (Parkes 57). Similarly, Lozana's facial scar might be expected to reveal something about her that is not explicitly stated, but of the utmost importance—whether or not the mark was in some way meant to draw attention to her Jewish background.

Further light can be shed on this question by turning to another woodcut in which the scar appears on Lozana's forehead as an inverted *T* or tau. The im-

Figure 1. "Una estrellica" woodcut. *Retrato de la Lozana andaluza, editio princeps* (Venice, 1528), fol. 6r.

age is particularly significant, as it is the only visual portrait of the title character in the *Retrato* (fig. 2).

There are a number of reasons to believe that its rendering of Lozana's scar is intentional. Since the book ends with the sacking of the Eternal City and surrender of the pope, it could be argued that this upside-down tau refers to the inverted cross of St. Peter as a symbol of the Roman Church in crisis. Lozana has come to embody a worldly, sexualized decadence that was seen as leading to the destruction of the city. Her literary depiction epitomizes the sinful decadence of *Roma*, personified as a whore whose name written backward spells *amor* (505). The Church taught that a treasure of divine grace, won by Christ's loving sacrifice on the Cross, had been entrusted to the Roman Curia until the end of time. Delicado, however, portrays a worldly love of the flesh being bought and sold in the same Holy City where the freely given *caritas* or charity of the Holy Spirit was supposed to reign supreme. Thus, the cruciform, venereal scar on Lozana's forehead, feeds into a sense of Rome's doomed, meretricious faithlessness. Early sixteenth-century Spanish and Italian audiences would have been familiar with the idea that bodily signs could be interpreted as a means of predicting disaster. During this period, there was a growing interest across Europe in reading these *signa* as political and religious portents. A number of surviving woodcuts and texts claim that, prior to catastrophic events, mystical letters and cross shapes appeared on the bodies of monstrous men and women living in Renaissance Italy.[6] In late medieval Spain, Jews were sometimes said to have converted to Christianity after seeing cruciform signs, as in the case of Abner de Burgos (Williams 259).

In consideration of her identity as a New Christian, the mark might have taken on further connotations, beyond its connection with St. Peter's cross. Shortly after baptism, the confirmation ceremony for new Christians and their children involved anointing the forehead with the sign of the cross.[7] Through what was called *signaculum, sigillum*, or the "Sacrament of the Seal," the body and soul of the believer were sealed by God to receive the divine love of the Spirit, "unto the day of redemption" (Scannell; Eph. 4:30). As explained in the medieval Spanish legal code called the *Siete Partidas* (*Seven Divisions*), this practice signified an open and unhindered disclosure of belief, in accordance with the Gospel promise: "Everyone therefore that shall confess me before

Figure 2. Lozana's House in Rome (detail), fols. 1v and 32v.

men, I will also confess him before my Father who is in heaven" (1.23; Matt. 10:42).[8] Apparently, Inquisitorial officials suspected false converts would not heed the warning given in the subsequent biblical verse: "But he that shall deny me before men, I will also deny him before my Father who is in heaven."[9] David Gitlitz has demonstrated that sixteenth-century *conversos* were sometimes accused of trying to remove chrism oil following the conferral of this sealing sacrament (147–48).[10] Such accusations bring to mind Lozana's attempt to conceal her scar by wearing a hood, as well as an earlier scene in which she claims to have struck herself on the forehead, ironically causing the mark to become more pronounced (186, 192–93).

The ritual of anointing that *conversos* allegedly sought to undo reflects an interpretation of the Book of Ezekiel that was central to the Christian understanding of sacred history. When the prophet foresees the siege of Jerusalem and pillaging of the Temple by the Babylonians, God tells him to mark the sorrowful witnesses so they might be spared. St. Jerome translated the Hebrew letter ("ת") made on their foreheads as a Greek tau (9:4). The mark in Ezekiel ("signa thau super frontes") (9:4) (set a mark upon the foreheads) (724) was interpreted as a prefigurement of the same sign—now identified with the *sigillum* of the Cross—sealing the foreheads of children of Jerusalem and faithful servants of God in Revelation. In John the Divine's vision, the tau on their foreheads protects against punishments that include plagues and an outbreak of grievous wounds and sores ("factum est vulnus saevum ac pessimum") (7.1–8, 16.2) (there fell a noisome and grievous sore) (1321). This might explain why the *signum thau* was often utilized as an apotropaic on medieval textual amulets, and specifically believed to confer protection against pestilence on fifteenth- and early sixteenth-century parchment and broadside charms. Its power "contra pestilentiam" or "contra peste" is explicitly invoked on Italian examples from the period (Skemer 180). For example, an apotropaic cross appears on a *nómina* or paper amulet that was discovered in the Spanish town of Barcarrota (Extremadura), together with books in Spanish, Portuguese, Italian,

French, Latin, and Hebrew that have been connected to a *converso* physician like Delicado. Like the *Lozana andaluza*, this find is emblematic of the Mediterraneanized cultural context of the sixteenth century. An Italian inscription on the back of the paper indicates that it was written in Rome during the year 1551, and carried on a return sea voyage to Iberia (Torrico 225). The amulet features written elements thought to protect against leprosy and the plague, including the Trisagion or thrice-holy prayer from Revelation. In the text of the Apocalypse, sores are said to afflict those who instead bear the mark of the Beast, a sign ("character") that also appears on the forehead ("in frontibus suis") (13:16–17) (in their foreheads) (1268). Lozana's inverted tau scar is thus suggestive both of the pestilent mark of the condemned and, ironically, the divine sealing of those who will be spared. In other words, the mark on her forehead could be viewed as a damning curse or a kind of amuletic inscription, consistent with the character's role as a carrier and healer of syphilis.[11] It is both synecdochic and proleptic in relation to the book's ongoing characterization of Lozana.

Consonant with the apocalyptic expectations of Christians, Jews living in Italy during the Middle Ages were sometimes obliged to wear tau-shaped badges (Damiani 59).[12] The cruciform letter was made to function as a mark of shame recalling the crucifixion of Christ and alleged perfidy of the Jews, as well as a sign of their protected status in expectation of a final conversion at the end of time.[13] This context sheds light on the way in which Lozana's bodily inscription anticipates the Last Judgment, as depicted for example in Alfonso X's apocalyptic song to Mary, "terrán escrito nas frentes quanto fezeron" (422, v. 37) (all have written on their foreheads what they have done). Over the course of the narrative, Lozana is marked as an outrageously sinful New Christian. Her "estrella" at the same time recalls the fallen star prophesized to open the smoldering, bottomless pit in Revelation, leading to the destruction of those deemed unworthy to receive the divine seal first envisioned in Ezekiel ("non habent signum Dei in frontibus") (9:4) (only those men which have not the seal of God in their foreheads) (1266). Parallels between the devastation of wicked cities in the Hebrew Bible, New Testament doomsday prophesies, and the 1527 sacking of Rome did not go unnoticed by witnesses like Delicado. In keeping with the significance of Lozana's upside-down tau, characters in the dialogue make comparisons between the coming invasion of City of St. Peter and the End of Days. Notably, Lozana and another syphilitic *conversa* named Divicia invoke the sixth angel of Revelation who was prophesized to unleash a demonic army, after a plague of festering sores has afflicted those who bear the mark of the Beast (Mamotreto 54; 16:2–14).[14]

Delicado's treatise on the *mal francorum* further clarifies his eschatological understanding of the disease that marks Lozana's forehead, and the devastation of Rome at the end of her portrait. The author paraphrases and cites from the Old and New Testaments, translating the Latin *vulnus* (wound), *plaga* (blow, wound, or resulting scar) and *ulcus* (sore) with the Spanish word "plaga."[15]

> En Roma hizieron el año de mill y quinientos y veynte y siete los armigeros los quales no solamente pusieron sus sacrilegas manos en los pobres y en nos, los sacerdotes, y en las yglesias, hasta en la *Santa santorum*, temerariamente, por cierto, no guardando que Dios dize en el Salmo 7: "Como tomará el tiempo, las justicias juzgará." El Apocalipsis asimismo dize en el capítulo sesto décimo: "Porque blasphemaron el nombre del Altíssimo . . . y derramaron la sangre de los prophetas . . . es hecha la plaga [*vulnus*], seva e péssima." Esaías dize, primo capítulo: "Guay a la gente peccatrice . . . blasphemauerunt sanctum . . . enferma . . . [con] plaga [*vulnus . . . et plaga*] hinchada . . . no es ligada ni medicada con medicina ni ungida con olio" . . . En el Deuteronomij, capítulo vigésimo octavo, dize . . . "*[Percutiat te Dominus]ulcere pessimo . . . sanarique non possis a planta pedis usque ad verticen tuum*" . . . que quiere dezir claro de una plaga incurabile como ésta de que aquí tratamos. (Damiani, "*El modo*" 265)[16]

> (Armies entered Rome in the year one thousand five hundred and twenty seven, that not only placed their sacrilegious hands on the poor, on we the priests, on the churches, and even the *Sancta sanctorum*; fearfully, to be sure, not obeying what God says in Psalm 7: 'As He will overtake time, judging right and wrong.' The Apocalypse likewise says in chapter sixteen: 'Because they have blasphemed the name of the Highest . . . and spilled the blood of the prophets . . . there fell upon them a wounding plague, fierce and grievous.' Isaiah says, chapter one: 'Woe to the sinful people . . . they blasphemed the Holy One . . . sickened . . . [with] swelling plague wound that can neither be bound with ligatures, treated with medicine, nor anointed with balm' . . . In Deuteronomy, chapter twenty eight, it says: '[May the Lord strike thee with] a very sore ulcer . . . and be thou incurable from the sole of the foot to the top of the head' . . . which is to clearly to say with an incurable plague wound like this one we are treating here.)

Delicado's epilogues to the *Lozana andaluza*, the "Epístola" and "Digresión" create similar links between wounding venereal disease, the destruction of Rome, and the fulfillment of punishments and judgments described in Scripture:

> Oh Roma, oh Babilón . . . ¿pensólo nadie jamás tan alto secreto y juicio? . . . después del saco y de la ruina, pestilencia . . . el fin de los munchos juicios que había visto y escrito . . . mira este retrato de Roma . . . '¡*Ve tibi civitas meretrix*!' . . . ¡Oh gran juicio de Dios!, venir un tanto ejército '*sub nube*' . . . para castigar los habitatores romanes . . . corrigiendo nuestro malo y vicioso vivir. (489–91, 507)

> (Oh, Rome, oh Babylon . . . did anyone ever consider so lofty a secret and judgment? . . . after the pillage and destruction, pestilence . . . the end of the numerous judgments that I had foreseen and written about . . . Look at this portrait of Rome . . . 'Woe to you, city of strumpets' . . . Oh, great judgment of God! To permit such an army to come 'beneath a cloud' . . . to punish the Roman inhabitants . . . for our evil and corrupt lives.)

By identifying "Roma putana" (Rome, the whore) with Babylon, the author not only evokes the city destroyed by God in Genesis, but more importantly its refiguration in Revelation as "the great whore . . . on her forehead a name was written, a mystery: Babylon the great, Mother of the fornications and abominations" (43; 17:1–5).[17] This would suggest that the meaning of the symbol on Lozana's forehead extends beyond her status as a *conversa*, and the tradition of seals protecting or condemning the saved and the iniquitous in Ezekiel and Revelation. The sign is crucial to the ongoing personification of the Eternal City's corruption in the *Lozana andaluza*, through the apocalyptic mode of thinking and fictionalizing that Frank Kermode called a "sense of an ending." Thus, a "shadow of the end" is cast by the inverted cross of St. Peter when it appears portentously on the forehead of an unrepentant whore and hypersexual convert who is neither faithful to the new nor the old religion (Kermode 5).

Drawing parallels between the doomed whoredom of Rome and the divinely ordained ending of biblical cities, Delicado's epilogues to the *Lozana andaluza* also correspond with other testimonies of the 1527 sacking. For example, his image of troops advancing as if "sub nube" or under a cloud appropriates language from Isaiah's apocalypse to describe the thick fog that purportedly enveloped the city on the morning of the assault (25:5).[18] The Old Testament prophet foresees the annihilation of a corrupt city, and the coming of a Messiah who will restore justice and resurrect the dead—inaugurating a millennial age that the Church had long interpreted as the Second Coming: "thou hast reduced the city to a heap, the strong city to ruin, the house of strangers . . . Thou shalt bring down the tumult of strangers . . . as with heat under a burning cloud ['calore sub nube'] . . . He shall cast death down headlong forever: and the Lord God shall wipe away tears . . . and the reproach of his people he shall take away . . . And they shall say in that day: Lo, this is our God, we have waited for him, and he will save us" (25:1–9).[19] Comparable imagery can be found in an anonymous Spanish letter that likens Rome to Sodom awaiting God's wrath, or a prediction made by the papal adviser Pietro Corsi that Christ would soon return to drive out the invaders, together with other sinners, and purify the desecrated city or *Civitas diaboli*. Scholars like Pamela Brakhage and John Edwards have found that, following the exile of 1492, Messianic expectations of this kind proliferated and circulated among Jewish as well as Christian communities in Rome, and elsewhere on the Italian and Iberian Peninsulas.[20]

The author makes another telling reference to the *topos* of the fallen *Civitas diaboli,* deserving of God's punishment, when he cites the first part of St. Jerome's condemnation of Alexandria in the ever-popular *Vitae Patrum* or *Lives of the Church Fathers*: "Vae tibi, ciuitas meretrix, in qua totius orbis daemonia confluxere" (213) (Woe to you, harlot city, into which have flowed together the demons of the whole world!).[21] This allusion to converging demonic forces comes as no surprise, considering that witnesses like Corsi and historian Marino Sanuto described how the 1527 sacking transformed the Eternal City into Hell on Earth and the entrance to Hades.[22] In addition to the assault itself, the mouth of Hell is pictured in a woodcut near the end of the text, receiving sinners who are characteristically dressed as fools (figs. 3 and 4).[23]

This infernal entryway is presided over by the demonic figure of Pluto who will also be evoked in Lozana's dream about the coming destruction. In her prophetic nightmare, the ruler of the underworld is accompanied by Mars and Mercury—gods who were associated with war and the treatment of syphilis, respectively: "Veía a Plutón caballero . . . veía venir a Marte debajo una niebla, y era tanto el estrépito que sus ministros hacían . . . sin otro ningún

Figure 3. Invasion of Rome, fol. 53r.

Figure 4. Dream of "Plutón," fol. 51r.

dentenimiento cabalgaba en Mercurio . . . Finalmente desperté . . . consideraba cómo las cosas que han de estar en el profundo, cómo Plutón que está sobre la Sierra" (478–79) (I saw Pluto as a rider . . . I saw Mars coming beneath the mist, and his ministers making such deafening noises . . . without delay, I rode Mercury . . . Finally, I awoke . . . considering how things must be in the infernal depths, and how Pluto is atop the Mountains).[24]

Like other eyewitnesses, Delicado emphasizes that this armed advance of Mars and hellish defilement of the city extended to "even the *Sancta sanctorum*" of the Lateran chapel—this in contrast to Pompey's famous refusal to violate the Holy of Holies in the tabernacle of the Jerusalem temple.[25] In fact, the same precedent can be found in contemporary disputes over whether the sacking should be blamed primarily on worldly excesses of the Church, or the insatiable evil of her enemies. For instance, the papal defender Baldassare Castiglione observed that, while Pagans left the inner sanctum of Solomon's temple intact, Christian mercenaries violated the sanctuaries of their own Church.[26] According to Delicado, this sacrilege was worse than might be expected of the "great Turk" (504). In his 1527 *Diálogo de las cosas ocurridas en Roma* (*Dialogue on Things that Have Happened in Rome*), on the other hand, the imperial apologist Alfonso de Valdés provides an explanation for why God would allow Roman altars to be profaned: "Son templos muertos . . . si quisiese, ¿no podría hacer cient mil templos más suntuosos y más ricos quel templo de Salomón?" (29) (these are dead temples . . . if He so wished, could He not build a hundred thousand temples more sumptuous and richer than the temple of Solomon?). Valdés instead urged believers to create a new Rome, filled with "living temples" of Christ, in keeping with the timeless city of peace envisioned by John of Patmos: "I, John, saw . . . the new Jerusalem . . . prepared as a bride . . . I saw no temple therein. For the Lord God Almighty is the temple thereof . . . the Alpha and the Omega" (21:2–22, 22:13).[27]

Just as the tau seal from the beginning of Revelation is implicated in an earlier woodcut depicting Lozana, this eschatological combination of the first and last Greek letters is reproduced at the close of Delicado's book (51v). Following her prophetic dream, the title character decides to retire on the island to Lipari with her "peers," then promises to send her lover, Rampín, a mysterious gift: "Yo quiero ir a paraíso, y entraré por la puerta que abierta hallare . . . si veo la Paz, que allá está continua, la enviaré atada con este ñudo de Salomón, desátela quien la quisiere. Y esta es mi última voluntad" (480) (I want to go to paradise, and will enter through the door that I find open to me . . . if I see that peace is continuous there, I will send it tied with this knot of Solomon, let whoever wants to untie it. And this is my last wish).[28] The woodcut showing this

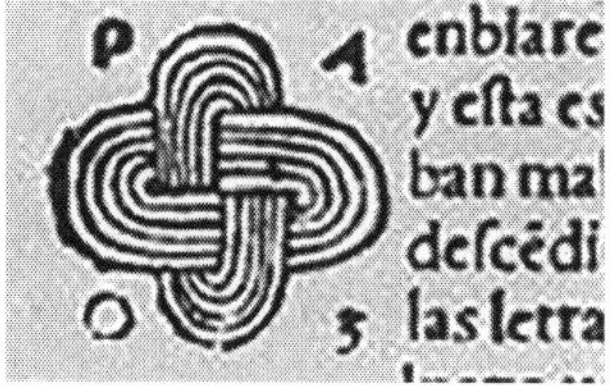

Figure 5. "Este ñudo de Salamón," fol. 51v.

cross-shaped knot (fig. 5) includes the mystical Alpha Omega in Latin script, symbolizing eternity as the beginning and the end, together with the letters "P" and "Z" to spell out the Spanish word "PAZ."

Several critics have offered explanations for the inclusion of this esoteric image. For Costa Fontes, the cross-shaped, Solomonic knot subverts the supersessionist relationship between Christianity and Judaism in a way that supports his theory that Delicado was a crypto-Jew. Comparing uses of Solomon's seal as a hexagram or six-pointed star in Jewish Cabbala, Carla Perugini reaches a similar conclusion. On the other hand, Claude Allaigre and Ian Macpherson have related Lozana's "ñudo" to variations of the seal in which a pentagram or five-pointed star—consisting of lines interwoven without beginning or end—represents the eternal wisdom and power entrusted to the first temple builder.[29] As Macpherson points out, medieval and early modern Christians also understood this star as a representation of the five wounds of Christ that could be employed as a healing charm.[30] He goes on to demonstrate how the *Lozana andaluza* knot relates to Christograms that combine the alpha omega with the first two letters of the Savior's name in Greek, X and P—letters that Delicado seemingly changed to Z and P, so as to read to "PAZ." Macpherson notes that the quadripartite form of the woodcut, with divine letters configured around its four corners, mirrors "four points . . . as the compass . . . the fourfold design of Solomon's temple . . . constructed on the model of the Tabernacle" (214). He finds that configurations of Solomon's seal were sometimes associated by poets with the "indissoluble ties" of love knots during the late Middle Ages, visualized as endless loops like those of Lozana's "ñudo" (219).[31] Finally, Macpherson agrees with other critics that the word "PAZ" on the woodcut anticipates Lozana's journey to a supposedly paradisiacal Lipari.

What has yet to be considered is the significance of powers attributed to Solomonic seals and knots in the late medieval imaginary, and how these might relate to the "sense of ending" that is conveyed by the earlier inverted tau woodcut. Solomon's attributes can be traced from the *Historia* of Josephus and biblical passages, to the pseudepigraphic *Testament of Solomon*, Latin dialogues, and hagiographic legends.[32] The king was famous for his attainment of divine knowledge and ability to command demonic spirits during the construction of the first temple. As a consequence of what was described as his insatiable lust for foreign women, however, Solomon fell under malevolent influences and allowed himself to be seduced into idolatry, risking the future of his kingdom and his own salvation. We have seen how a similarly perilous seduction is represented by Delicado's Spanish prostitute. Solomon's legend was further developed in popular books of magic attributed to this wise, yet dangerously flawed king, such as the *Liber iuratus or Sacer* (*The Sworn Book of Honorius*), the *Ars Notoria* (*Notary Art*), and especially the *Clavicula Salomonis* (*Key of Solomon*).[33] These texts emerged from ancient Jewish and Christian traditions, and were also influenced by the related Islamic story of "Sulaiman" commanding an army of devilish "jinn" (spirits). Variations claimed to offer esoteric knowledge, recorded by Solomon, kept hidden under his throne, and later buried with him. The most widely disseminated among these was the late medieval *Clavicula*, which provided instructions for drawing on the power of invocations, pentacles, and other sealing formulas to call forth and bind demons.[34]

Julio Caro Baroja has documented early references to this work circulating on the Iberian Peninsula. Already in the fourteenth century, the General Inquisitor of Aragon ordered the destruction of a text called the *Liber Salomonis* (*Book of Solomon*).[35] Subsequent burnings took place in Cuenca in 1434, again in Barcelona in 1440, and decades later in Salamanca. Not long after Delicado finished the *Lozana andaluza*, the reformer Pedro Ciruelo condemned Solomonic books for invoking demonic forces, and they were placed on the Index of Forbidden Books during the 1550s.[36] During the second half of the sixteenth century, the theologian Martín del Río explains how the *Clavicula* was first copied by Iberian Jews and Muslims, and later widely disseminated by Christians, in spite of failed attempts by the Church to confiscate and destroy all existing copies.[37] Warnings issued by Renaissance censors attest to the continued popularity of the *Clavicula* among Spanish speakers, strongly suggesting that a learned bibliophile like Delicado would have been aware of this text when he created Lozana's Solomonic "ñudo."

It is also clear that elements from the *Clavicula* were reproduced on textual amulets intended to be carried as a means of conjuring and protecting believers from demonic influences. This tradition would suggest that, like the tau's purported efficacy against the plague, Lozana's knot could be interpreted as an amuletic shield.[38] Specifically, the image might be understood as offering protection against the violent incursion into Rome that the bawd foresees in her dream—and that Delicado and his contemporaries compared to an opening of the mouth of Hell and a demonic convergence on the city. Such an interpretation is supported by the prevalence of Solomonic features on amulets that were either produced in or brought to Spain from the High Middle Ages to the mid sixteenth century.[39]

The efficacy commonly attributed to these kinds of seals is specified on a medieval amuletic parchment that has been preserved in the Canterbury Cathedral: "Hoc este signum regis Salomonis quo demones . . . signalauit, qui super se portauerit . . . saluus erit, et si demon ei apparuerit iubeat ei quicumque uoluerit et obediet ei . . . Salomon ut demones compelleret" (Skemer 302) (This is the sign of the king Solomon that . . . summons demons; he who wears it . . . is safeguarded, and if any demon whatsoever appears to him, he commands it and it obeys him . . . as Solomon summoned demons).[40] Similarly, the Solomonic knot in Delicado's book might be construed as summoning or safeguarding against the demonic. Versions of the king's *signum* were often copied together with the tau and alpha omega, to indicate divine and eternal protection. For example, Don Skemer has brought to light a textual amulet that was produced in Italy during the early sixteenth century, and features a knotted cross with the divine acronym, "AGLA," flanked by the five-pointed star along with other Solomonic keys and *caracteres* (214–17).[41] Another characteristic element found on such objects is the Latin "pax," recalling the Vulgate pronouncements of Christ: "Peace I leave with you, my peace I give unto you," and "peace be in this house," a blessing that is parodically repeated by Lozana (John 4:27, Luke 10:5).[42] This might suggest that the efficacy of the word "PAZ" on the knot should also be taken ironically, calling into question the assumption that Lozana will peacefully escape to the island of Lipari.

The most relevant analogue for Lozana's "ñudo," however, can be found in a 1527 Spanish translation of the *Clavicula*. This manuscript was surrendered to authorities on the Canary Islands weeks before the sack of Rome, and preserved in the archives of the Spanish Inquisition. It begins with a series of promises and conjurations: "Con esta atan todos los demonios que son en el mundo y son los que contratan los abysmos . . . 'conjuro vos prynçepes de los demonios que morays en quatro partes del mundo'" (fol. 34r) (With this all demons are bound that occupy the world and those that are sworn to the abyss . . . 'I conjure you rulers of the demons that occupy the four parts of the world'). In accordance with the "ñudo," the vernacular text invokes "alpha" and "O," and shows how to unbind "en paz con la vendyçión" (in peace with your blessing) (135–36). The text demonstrates how the obedience of demons can be ensured with threats: "De las maldyçiones que dyó sobre Sodoma y Gomorra . . . y sobre la gran çibdad de Babylonia . . . venga sobre vos las doze maldyçiones que son y an de ser en el dya del juiçio" (136) (Of curses that befell Sodom and Gomorrah . . . and the great city of Babylon . . . may the twelve curses fall on you that are and will be on the Day of Judgment).[43] Because the Spanish grimoire and Delicado's work both correlate Solomon's binding with the topic of punishing the *Civitate diaboli*, we might expect the tying and untying of Lozana's "ñudo" to implicate an apocalyptic threat, together with the power to summon and control demonic spirits. Like the mark that anoints and curses the lover's forehead, the woodcut could potentially shield against war and plague, or invite punishment and destruction.

The sign of Solomon in the *Clavicula* manuscript, comparable to Lozana's endless knot, is created by tracing the lines of a pentagram, without start or finish, and inserting a cross in the center, surrounded by mystical letters that are difficult to decipher: "Este syno de Salamón y en medyo vna cruz . . . y estas letras que tiene escrypto derredor" (Lamb 136–37, fig. 6) (This sign of Solomon with a cross in the middle . . . and these letters that have writing around them)

What follows are directions for casting spells and producing amulets, overwhelmingly intended to bind or unbind lovers, but also effective in conjuring armed avengers and healing various ailments.[44] The inclusion of this material once more attests to Solomon's reputation for compelling demons to submit to his will, yet proving himself powerless to resist the temptation of illicit lovers—and, in particular, exotic women from other nations like Lozana. Not surprisingly, at one point in Delicado's work, his title character calls a doctor "Salomón" in a speech on the pleasures of sexual activity (461). Near the end of the *Clavicula* manuscript, instructions are provided for binding lovers, just as the magician king controlled evil spirits who, according to end-time prophecy, will torment humankind before being vanquished by the Lord. This section explains the potency of Solomon's "nudos" in way that further clarifies the significance of the "ñudo de Salomon" in the *Lozana*:

> Para ligar cualquyer persona, toma filo de alanbre . . . y faz . . . nudos y quando los dyeres dyrás ansy . . . 'enlego a fulana o fulano . . . en nel nombre de . . . quantos

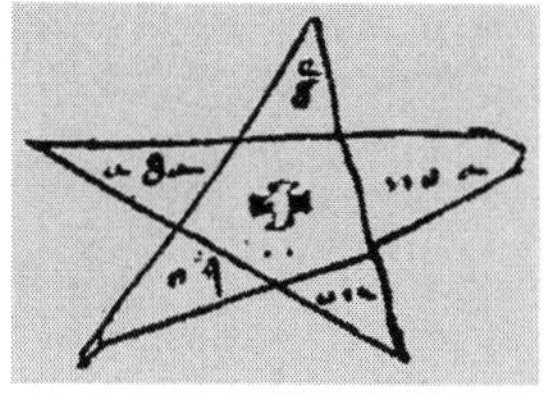

Figure 6. "Este syno de Salamón." *Un çerco general desde Salamón.* Bute, *Inquisición testificaciones*, Ms. 4.1, fol. 38 (rep. Lamb p. 117).

> demonios nel mundo son . . . ansy como lygó Salamón a los demonios . . . ansy sea ligado fulano o fulana que no pueda ser deslygado de onbre ny de muger del mundo fasta que yo mismo los deslygue . . . a cada nudo . . . Conjuro vos dyablos todos los nombrados y por quantos soys por todas las quatro partes del mundo y por el juyçio que ha de ser sobre vosotros el dya temeroso del juyçio . . . ansy como están ligados los nudos deste fylo' . . . Para desfazer este ligamiento . . . desfáz los nudos. Dyrás estas palabras . . . 'Christus vicat, Chrustus rreyna, Christus enpera'" (Lamb 142–43)[45]

> (To bind anyone, take a wire thread . . . and make . . . knots and when they are made you will say this . . . 'I bind such a person . . . in the name of . . . all of the demons of the world . . . just as Solomon bound the demons . . . thus will the person be bound so that they cannot be unbound by any man or woman in the world until I myself undo . . . each knot . . . I conjure you, all of the devils so named, as many of you as exist in the four parts of the world, and by the justice that will be dealt to you on the Fearful day of Judgment . . . just as the knots of this wire are tied' . . . To undo this binding . . . undo the knots. You will say these words . . . 'Christ conquers, Christ reigns, Christ rules.')

In light of this contemporaneous explanation, the woodcut in the *Lozana andaluza* on the one hand seems to represent an efficacious object that can be tied like a wire, while on the other inserting a textual amulet into the literary narrative itself. This material presence is created by printing the sigil of a Solomonic *ligatura*, complete with divine names, onto the paper of the first and only 1527 edition.[46] Within the logic of the text, the "ñudo" is instilled with a fictional power to bind and unbind, conjure and release lovers from the seductive deceit and apocalyptic violence of demons that will precede the Second Advent of Christ. Revelation can be unveiled from the four corners of the "ñudo," in accordance with the fourfold layout of Solomon's temple and quadripartite directionality of John the Divine's vision. In this way, Lozana's knot works in conjunction with the inverted tau woodcut, to mark performatively the prophesized division between the damned and the saved, and signal pestilence and healing. The dual seals placed at the beginning and the end of the book are efficacious in stigmatizing conversion as well as the unconverted, exposing the corruption of the Church, and heralding the sacrilegious approach of its enemies.

In the end, the irony of Lozana's escape from the hellish fate that awaits Rome cannot be fully appreciated without considering Lipari's fame as infernal entryway, as opposed to the open "puerta" to "paraiso" that she imagines.

This idea stems from a pseudo-patristic work that was widely read throughout the Middle Ages and Renaissance, the *Pseudo-Gregorian Dialogues*. It is highly likely that Delicado would have been exposed to its well-known accounts of the punishment that awaited departed souls. The *Dialogi* was "the medieval equivalent of a bestseller," to the extent that no other eschatological work attributed to the Fathers of the Church "was more eagerly transcribed and read" (Clark 2.3).[47] According to this text, an opening to Hell was located among the volcanic peaks of the Mediterranean island of Lipari: "To those craters were ferried the doomed souls of the young and dissolute . . . because the Arian king Theodoric the Ostrogoth had persecuted unto death Pope John I . . . he was justly condemned to torments there . . . We read how a hermit of great holiness saw the impious king being thrust down into hell in one of the craters of Lipari, watched by two of his illustrious victims" (Clark 2.645–46). This sixth-century pope was held prisoner by heretical, Barbarian invaders of Italy, as was Clement VII in 1527 after fleeing to the Castel Sant'Angelo. For early audiences who were familiar with this "bestseller," Delicado's reference to Lipari could be understood as implicitly cursing the persecutors of the pope and plunderers of Rome—called by Lozana "teutónicos bárbaros" (Teutonic barbarians)—while at the same time consigning the city's "doomed" and "dissolute" inhabitants to the flames (503). Lozana's final destination links her knot with an open entrance to Hell, contributing to its literary power to summon a demonic army and conjure the sacking of Rome. Delicado's own escape to Venice, on the other hand, seems to correlate with the supposed effectiveness of the tau "contra peste" and the apotropaic protection of Solomon's seal against "demon ei apparuerit." One of the woodcuts in the dialogue even depicts a Venetian gondola, conducting the characters of the novel as the creation of their author. These two seals and synecdochic disclosures at the start and finish of the narrative can be viewed as safeguarding the author from his own creation, since he claims to have found solace from the cursed, diseased city of the *Lozana andaluza*. For the syphilitic profligates that inhabit Delicado's book, however, any doorway or sea route that might bring peace has been closed off. It was the openness of *mare nostrum* and *mare interius* that first facilitated the circulation of the disease, along the textual and cultural fluidity and exchange that mark Delicado's novel and this historical moment as a whole. Fittingly, at the close of the narrative, the waters of the Mediterranean on the one hand flow toward the Aeolian mouth of Hell, and on the other represent the relative freedom and safe passage afforded to exiles who made their way to port of Venice.

Notes

1. The papal court of Alexander VI accepted thousands of Jewish refugees that arrived from Spain and Portugal. In the prologue to the *Lozana andaluza* (169–70), Delicado cites Hernando de Pulgar, who lamented the treatment of *conversos* in Andalucía (see MacKay).
2. He also also wrote a third, related work, now missing, that was entitled *De consolatione infirmorum* (*On Consoling the Infirm*).
3. This hospital was known as Santiago de Carreteras. On Delicado's later editorial work in Venice, see especially Lucia Binotti.
4. The Imperial forces had defeated the French army, and then mutinied after never receiving their pay. They were able to compel their commander, the Duke of Bourbon, to continue the march to Rome.
5. In the introduction to his edition (118), Allaigre relates Lozana's scar to marks made on the foreheads of Roman slaves as recorded by Martial and in the lexicography of Covarrubias (537, 178).
6. A notable example would include the monsters of Ravenna and Bologna (see Niccoli 30–59). The former is described at the beginning of *Guzmán de Alfarache* (1599) with portentous features, letters, and a cruciform marking. This disfigured creature was said to foreshadow the defeat of the papal army by the French in 1512. Another was supposed to have washed up in the river Tiber in 1496, with features of an ass, scales, a pig hoof, a bird claw, female breasts, and an old man's face. It purportedly reflected the state and fate of the papacy (Edwards 294–95).
7. In the Roman Rite, the words of the Sacrament for anointing the forehead were "Signo te signo crucis, et confirmo te chrismate salutis" (Jackson 104) (I sign you with the sign of the cross, and confirm you with the chrism of salvation).
8. Receiving Confirmation was also an imitation of the Savior, as *Christos* means "the anointed one."
9. The words in the Vulgate, Matthew 10:32–33, were: "Omnis ergo qui confitebitur me coram hominibus confitebor et ego eum coram Patre meo qui est in caelis. Qui autem negaverit me coram hominibus negabo et ego eum coram Patre meo qui est in caelis."
10. The custom was not to remove the oil for seven days. During the medieval and early modern period in Spain, confirmation generally occurred as soon as a bishop could be present to conduct the ceremony—in any case, within a year of the baptism.
11. Syphilis was commonly associated with *amor eros* or lovesickness, as can be seen when Delicado implies that his dialogue can either relieve or exacerbate the erotic passions (167, 170, 173). In contrast to Lozana's Galenic, coital therapy, moralizing preachers and medical authorities, insisted that syphilitics be made to suffer "the just rewards of unbridled lust" (Allen 41–60). Accordingly, Delicado's *De modo adoperare* calls for a forty-day fast and sudorific infusions made from the sawdust of guaiacum wood that were meant to cure "ogni piaga" (485) (all sores).

12. The wearing of badges by Roman Jews is pointed out to Lozana shortly after she arrives, although not described in detail (240).
13. Later, circular badges were introduced that presumably symbolized coins. See Damiani and Patai (59; 156). Jeremy Cohen has studied the eschatological belief in the final conversion of the Jews, which was supported by the writings of Augustine and hearkens back to St. Paul's Epistle to the Romans (11:25–26).
14. Witnesses also report how the Tiber flooded the same year, leading to a famine and further epidemics (see Partner 80–81). Delicado recalls these further disasters in his "Epístola" (490).
15. The Spanish word for wound, "llaga," was itself derived from the Latin *plaga*.
16. This treatise combines Castilian, Latin, and Italian. A modern Spanish translation has been recently completed by Ignacio Ahumada.
17. Rome is first portrayed as full of brothels, and personified as a "putana" (whore) when Rampín gives the recently arrived Lozana a tour of the city (216).
18. The same anonymous letter in the anthology of Rodríguez Villa describes this situation: "Hizo una neblina al entrar, que apenas se conocían los unos a los otros" (141) (A fog developed as we entered [the city], so that we could barely tell one from another).
19. Delicado makes another millennial allusion earlier in the narrative, when he evokes the legend of the Wandering Jew. This figure was known in Spanish as "Juan espera en Dios" (John who awaits God) and legendarily cursed to walk the earth until the return of Christ. On the figure of the "judío errante" in early modern Spain, as attested in the Cristóbal de Vallalón's *Crotalón* and other sources, see Caro Baroja (355–65).
20. In a satirical poem at the end of Delicado's book, Cupid condemns an unnamed lady to suffer "tan gran maldición / de Sodoma y Gomorra" (such a great curse as Sodom and Gomorra), and then consigns each her bodily charms to ruin, including "la resplandeciente frente" (her resplendent forehead) (493, 499–500). See the studies by Brakhage and Edward on the Jewish messianism of contemporary figures like Solomón Molcho, David Reubeni, and Asher Lemmlein. They also consider how the eschatology of Spiritual Franciscans influenced works like the *Libro de profecías* of Columbus and the *Apocalypsis Nova* attributed to João Mendes de Silva (known as "Amadeo").
21. The *Vita Pauli primi eremitae* (*Life of Paul the First Hermit*) and Jerome's other *Vitae* of the Church Fathers were frequently reprinted during the sixteenth-century by Latin hagiologists like Laurentius Surius (Lorenz Sauer).
22. Corsi's apocalyptic, mythographic allusions have been unpacked by Kenneth Gouwens (86–87). In the words of Sanuto, "Tutta questa città è in tanta tribulatione" (This whole city is in so much tribulation) that the urban landscape resembles "l'inferno" (qtd. in Gouwens xviii) (hell).
23. As Perugini has pointed out, this woodcut, together with another one showing

characters from Delicado's dialogue on a Venetian gondola share visual parallels with the pictorial scheme of the late fifteenth-century *Stultifera Navis* (Ship of Fools).

24. Lozana describes these mountains in the dream as the Andalusian *Sierra Morena.* As in other instances, such as the digression concerning the appearance of the Magdalene in province of Córdoba (396–98), events in Rome are conflated with the author's homeland.
25. This well-known account of Pompey's conquest first appears in Josephus.
26. Castiglione was a papal ambassador in Madrid, engaged in an open dispute with Alfonso de Valdés, who was a member of the Imperial court and twin brother of the more famous Spanish humanist, Juan de Valdés.
27. Compare to Paul's first letter to the Corinthians: "Or know you not, that your members are the temple of the Holy Ghost, who is in you, whom you have from God" (6:19).
28. Characteristically, Delicado engages in a pun that associates the name of the island with the Spanish word for pairs and peers, "pares" (487).
29. Allaigre and Macpherson also discuss related adaptations of the myth of the Gordian knot, including its use in the royal heraldry of the Catholic Monarchs were responsible for the 1492 expulsion of the Jews from Spain. The fourfold layout of the temple was thought to reflect the creation of the universe, and also interpreted on the basis of Pythagorean ideas. It is possible that Delicado saw the common endless knot motif on an ancient Roman mosaic during his time in Italy.
30. Both he and Allaigre cite the note made in Luis de Usoz y Rio's nineteenth-century edition of earlier mentioned "pregunta" from the *Cancionero de obras de burla*: "Áludese aquí al llamado sello, sigilo o signo de Salomón cuya figura es . . . el famoso pentalfa que significa salud, y que antiguamente tenía en España el vulgo por amuleto, y preservativo contra las brujas" (115–17) (Referring here to the said seal, sigil or sign of Salomon whose figure is . . . the famous pentalpha that signifies health, and that formerly was in Spain commonly held to be an amulet and apotropaic against witches).
31. Such a connection can be seen, for example, in Fray Íñigo de Mendoza's "invención" (invention) addressed to "un signo de Salomón" (Rodríguez-Puértolas 347) (a sign of Solomon). The sign is used in different ways in another *Cancionero* work by the same author, punning the word "signo," as well as by the poet known as Serrano and in an anonymous "Pregunta" (associated it with a dishonorable facial scar) (see Macpherson 205–9; Allaigre 142).
32. According to Josephus: "He obtained also by inspiration the art of magic . . . and left the method of conjuration in writing whereby the devils are enchanted and expelled" (qtd. in Hattaway 204). The most detailed scriptural portrayal of Solomon's submission to women can be found in 1 Kings: "Solomon loved many strange women . . . And to these was Solomon joined with a most ardent love . . . and the women turned away his heart . . . to follow strange gods . . . the Lord was angry

with Solomon" (11:1–9). This story is also mentioned elsewhere in the Hebrew Bible: "Did not Solomon king of Israel sin in this kind of thing . . . women of other countries brought even him to sin" (Neh. 13:26). Written during the first centuries of the Christian era, the *Testament* gives an account of Solomon's sealing of demons and portrays the Queen of Sheba as a witch. In medieval Latin dialogues, Solomon engages in a dispute with a carnivalesque fool named Marcolf who subverts his famed wisdom (see the edition of Ziolkowsi). In Renaissance Spain, these traditions were recorded as vernacular legends, such as the "Vida de Salomón y duda si se salvó" (Life of Solomon and doubt whether he was saved) by Alonso de Villegas.

33. On the knowledge of Solomonic magic in medieval Spain, see also the *Liber Razielis* (*Book of Raziel*) that was translated by Alfonso X during the 1250s.
34. Christopher Marlowe's *Doctor Faustus*, written and first performed at the end of the sixteenth century, famously stages a use of this kind of magic: "Within this circle is Jehovah's name / Forward and backward anagrammatized; / The abbreviated names of holy saints" (3.8–10).
35. This version of the text was apparently attributed to Ramon Llull. The Aragonese Inquisitor, Nicolau Eymerich was best known for writing the *Directorium Inquisitorum*, which provides instruction in uncovering witchcraft and sorcery.
36. Ciruelo singles out the *Ars notoria*: "Fingen los que la usan, que por ella el Rey Salomón supo todas las sciencias humanas y divinas en una noche; y después, él dexó escriptura de un librito para enseñar cómo se hacía de exercitar esta arte" (61) (Those that use this [art] pretend that through it the King Solomon learned all human and divine sciences in one night; and after, he left written down a little book to teach how this art was practiced).
37. "A quien atribuyen . . . otro gran volumen . . . lleno de sacrificios y encantamientos de demonios. Los judíos y alárabes de España dejaban por derecho hereditario a sus sucesores este libro, y por él obraban algunas maravillas y cosas increíbles. La Inquisición entregó a las llamas cuantos ejemplares pudo haber de estas obras" (qtd. in Fernández Guerra y Orbe 320) (To whom is attributed . . . another great text . . . full of sacrifices and demonic enchantments. The Jews and Arabs of Spain passed this book on to their heirs by right of inheritance, and with it worked great marvels and incredible things. The Inquisition consigned to the flames as many copies of these works as could be had).
38. Famously, the shield of Gawain in the fourteenth-century Arthurian romance features a version of the seal of Solomon (Green 186).
39. See, for example, the exorcistic prayer that is included in the thirteenth-century *Razón de amor* manuscript studied by Enzo Franchini. A pentagram and seal can be found on the earlier-mentioned paper *nomina* from Barcarrota.
40. It is clear that the Canterbury parchment was meant to be folded in a particular way and carried. As in the case of other amulets, the folds correspond to sacred numbers that were believed to contribute to the object's power.

41. AGLA was an acronym common used on textual amulets that was derived from the Hebrew blessing, התא רובג םולעל ינודא or “Atta gibbor leolam adonai” (Thou, Lord, are forever might) (Skemer 112).
42. Celestina also utters this benediction when visiting Melibea’s house (Rojas 151). The words from the Gospel of John are found in the Roman rite, and pronounced during for preparation of Communion. During the Middle Ages, celebrants could participate by kissing a *pax*-board that featured an image of the Savior or Mary.
43. Details in these instructions correspond with aspects of Celestina’s famous hex, such as the use of bat’s blood. They also coincide with Ciruelo’s description of *nóminas*, as when the *Clavicula* claims that virgin parchment must be used (137, 139, 140).
44. These include avoiding sudden death and becoming invisible. In several instances, specifics are given on how the inscribed material object is to be worn or carried: “Sy quisyeres dormir con la muger quantas vezes quisyeres, escryve en plegamyno vírgen estas letras y mételas devajo de las espaldas” (Lamb 137, 139, 140) (To sleep with a woman as many times as you like, write on virgin parchment these letters and place them under the back).
45. These words were also invoked by crusaders during the Middle Ages. Later in the sixteenth century, Pope Sixtus V had this acclamation of *Laudes regiae* inscribed on an Egyptian obelisk that was placed at the center of St. Peter’s Square in Rome.
46. During the late Middle Ages, different kinds of wire were used for making for wool cards, pins, and for a number of other purposes (including jewelry). Metal thread and fine, pliant wires like the one described in the *Clavicula* were produced either by cutting strips of foil or drawing “short rods of cast metal . . . through successively diminishing holes in a draw plate” (Campbell 134).
47. This *Dialogi*, as Clark points out in his study, had marked influence on everything from medieval folklore, to sermons, religious literature, and art for centuries to come. Disputes of the authenticity of its authorship began with the work of sixteenth-century humanists and continued for centuries.

Works Cited

Alfonso X. *Cantigas de Santa María*. Ed. Walter Mettmann. Madrid: Castalia, 1986.

———. *Siete Partidas*. 5 vols. Trans. Samuel Parsons Scott. Ed. Robert I. Burns. Philadelphia, University of Pennsylvania Press, 2001.

Allen, Peter Lewis. *The Wages of Sin: Sex and Disease, Past and Present*. Chicago: University of Chicago Press, 2000.

Bible. Douay-Rheims Version. New York: Benziger Brothers, 1941.

Biblia Sacra. Iuxta Vulgatam Versionem. Ed. Robert Weber. 4th ed. Stuttgart: Bibelgesellschaft, 1994.

Binotti, Lucia. *Cultural Capital, Language and National Identity in Imperial Spain*. Woodbridge, UK: Tamesis, 2012.

Brakhage, Pamela S. *The Theology of "La lozana andaluza."* Potomac, MD: Scripta Humanistica, 1986.

Campbell, Marion. "Gold, Silver and Precious Stones." *English Medieval Industries*. Ed. John Blaire and Nigel Ramsey. London: Hambledon, 1991. 107–66.

Caro Baroja, Julio. "El libro mágico: La *Clavícula* de Solomón." *Vidas mágicas e inquisición*. 2 vols. Madrid: Taurus, 1967. 1.159–76.

Clark, Francis, ed. *Pseudo-Gregorian Dialogues*. 2 vols. Leiden: Brill, 1987.

Cohen, Jeremy. *Living Letters of the Law: Ideas of the Jew in Medieval Christianity*. Berkeley: University of California Press, 1999.

Costa Fontes, Manuel de. *The Art of Subversion in Inquisitorial Spain: Rojas and Delicado*. Purdue Studies in Romance Literatures 30. West Lafayette, IN: Purdue University Press, 2005.

Covarrubias Orozco, Sebastián de. *Tesoro de la lengua castellana o española*. Madrid: L. Sanchez, 1611. Web. 9 Sep. 2012.

Damiani, Bruno M. *Francisco Delicado*. Twayne World Author Series 335. New York: Twayne, 1974.

_____, ed. "*El modo de adoperare el legno de India Occidantale*: A Critical Transcription." *Revista Hispánica Moderna* 36.4 (1970): 251–71.

Delicado, Francisco. *El modo de usar el palo de la India Occidental, saludable remedio contra toda llaga y mal incurable*. Ed. and trans. Ignacio Ahumada. Jaén: Universidad de Jaén, 2011.

———. *Retrato de la Lozana andaluza*. Venecia, 1528. Web. 7 Sep. 2012.

———. *Retrato de la Lozana andaluza*. Ed. Claude Allaigre. Madrid: Cátedra, 1985.

Edwards, John. "The Friars and the Jews: Messianism in Spain and Italy, circa 1500." *Friars and Jews in the Middle Ages and Renaissance*. Ed. Steven J. McMichael and Susan E. Myers. Leiden: Brill, 2004. 273–98.

Flórez Miguel, Cirilo. "Las ciencias y la Universidad de Salamanca en el siglo XV." *Salamanca y su universidad en el primer renacimiento: Siglo XV*. Ed. Luis Enrique Rodríguez-San Pedro Beza and Juan Luis Polo Rodríguez. Salamanca: Universidad de Salamanca, 2011. 179–202.

Fernández Guerra y Orbe, Aureliano. *Obras de Don Francisco de Quevedo Villegas*. Vol. 1. 3 vols. Madrid: Rivadaneyra, 1852. Web. 9 Sep. 2012.

Franchini, Enzo. *El manuscrito, la lengua y el ser literario de la "Razón de amor."* Madrid: Consejo Superior de Investigaciones Cientificas, 1993.

Gitlitz, David. *Secrecy and Deceit: The Religion of the Crypto-Jews*. Albuquerque: University of New Mexico Press, 2002.

Green, Richard Hamilton. "Gawain's Shield and the Quest for Perfection." *Sir Gawain and Pearl: Critical Essays*. Ed. Robert J. Blanch. London: Indiana University Press, 1966. 176–94.

Gouwens, Kenneth. *Remembering the Renaissance: Humanist Narratives of the Sack of Rome*. Leiden: Brill, 1998.

Harrison, Keith, trans. *Sir Gawain and the Green Knight*. Ed. Helen Cooper. Oxford: Oxford University Press, 2008.

Hattaway, Michael. "Paradoxes of Solomon: Learning in the English Renaissance." *Journal of the History of Ideas* 29.4 (1968): 499–530.

Jackson, William. *History of Confirmation*. London; Oxford: James Parker, 1877. Web. 9 Sep. 2012.

Jerome. *De probatis sanctorum historiis. Vita Pauli primi eremitae [Vitae Patrum]*. Ed. Laurentius Surius. Cologne: Agrippinae, 1570. Web. 9 Sep. 2012.

———. *Vita Pauli primi eremitae [Vitae Patrum]*. Vol. 6. Trans. W.H. Fremantle, G. Lewis, and W.G. Martley. *Nicene and Post-Nicene Fathers, Second Series*. Ed. Philip Schaff and Henry Wace. 14 vols. Buffalo: Christian Literature Publishing, 1893. Web. 9 Sep. 2012.

Kermode, Frank. *A Sense of Ending: Studies in the Theory of Fiction*. Rpt. Oxford: Oxford University Press, 2000.

Lamb, Úrsula, ed. "La Inquisición en Canarias y un libro de magia del siglo XVI." *El museo canario* 24 (1963): 113–44. Web. 9 Sep. 2012.

Mackay, Angus. "The Whores of Babylon." *Love, Religion, and Politics in Fifteenth-Century Spain*. Ed. Ian Macpherson and Angus MacKay. Leiden: Brill, 1998. 179–87.

Macpherson, Ian. "Solomon's Knot." *Love, Religion, and Politics in Fifteenth-Century Spain*. Ed. Ian Macpherson and Angus MacKay. Leiden: Brill, 1998. 205–22.

Marlowe, Christopher. *Doctor Faustus and Other Plays*. Ed. David Bevington and Eric Rasmussen. Oxford: Oxford University Press, 1995.

McInnis-Domínguez, Meghan. "The Diseasing Healer: Francisco Delicado's Infectious *La Lozana andaluza*." *eHumanista* 17 (2011): 311–33. Web. 9 Sep. 2012.

Niccoli, Ottavia. *Prophecy and People in Renaissance Italy*. Princeton: Princeton University Press, 1990.

Parkes, M.B. *Pause and Effect: Punctuation in the West*. Aldershot, UK: Scolar, 1992.

Partner, Peter. *Renaissance Rome 1500–1559: A Portrait of a Society*. Berkeley: University of California Press, 1980.

Patai, Raphael. *The Jewish Mind*. Detroit: Wayne State University Press, 1977.

Perugini, Carla. "Contaminaciones ideológicas en *La Lozana andaluza*." *Ínsula: revista de letras y ciencias humanas* 635 (1999): 10–11.

———. "Las fuentes iconográficas de la *Editio Princeps* de la *Lozana andaluza*." *Salina: Revista de la Facultat de Lletres de Tarragona* 14 (2000): 65–72.

Río, Martín del. *La magia demoníaca: libro II de las Disquisiciones mágicas*. Ed. Jesús Moya. Madrid: Hiperión, 1991.

Rodríguez-Puértolas, Julio, ed. *Cancionero*. Madrid: Espasa-Calpe, 1968.

Rodriguez Villa, Antonio. *Memorias para la historia del asalto y saqueo de Roma en 1527*. Madrid: La biblioteca de instrucción y recreo, 1875. Web. 9 Sep. 2012.

Rojas, Fernando de. *La Celestina*. Ed. Dorothy Severin. Madrid: Cátedra, 1990.

San Pedro, Diego de. *Cárcel de amor*. Ed. Enrique Moreno Báez. Madrid: Cátedra, 1982.

Scannell, Thomas. "Confirmation." *The Catholic Encyclopedia*. Vol. 4. New York: Robert Appleton Company, 1908. Web. 1 Aug. 2012

Shalev-Eyni, Sarit. "Solomon, his Demons and Jongleurs: The Meeting of Islamic, Judaic and Christian Culture." *Al-Masāq* 18.2 (2006): 145–60. Web. 9 Sep. 2012.

Skemer, Don C. *Binding Words: Textual Amulets in the Middle Ages*. University Park: Pennsylvania State University Press, 2006.

Torrico, Benjamín. "Hiding in the Wall: Lazarillo's Bedfellows: The Secret Library of Barcarrota." *The Lazarillo Phenomenon: Essays on the Adventures of a Classic Text*. Ed. Reyes Coll-Tellechea and Sean McDaniel. Lewisburg, PA: Bucknell University Press, 2010. 210–38.

Usoz y Rio, Luis, ed. *Cancionero de obras de burlas provocantes a risa*. London: Luis Sánchez, 1841.

Villegas de, Alonso. *Flos sanctorum, y historia general, en que se escrive la vida de la Virgen Sacratíssima . . . y de los Santos Antiguos*. Rpt. Barcelona: Rafael Figuero y Juan Iglis, 1691. 455–88. Web. 9 Sep. 2012.

Voragine, Jacobus de. "The History of Solomon." *Golden Legend [Legenda aurea]*. Trans. William Caxton. 7 vols. Philadelphia: Temple University Press, 1900. 2.2–23.

Williams, Arthur Lukyn, ed. *"Adversus Judaeos": A Bird's-Eye View of Christian Apologiae until the Renaissance*. Rpt. Cambridge; Cambridge University Press, 2012.

Wolfenzon, Carolyn. "La *Lozana andaluza*: Judaísmo, sífilis, exilio y creación." *Hispanic Research Journal* 8.2 (2007): 107–22.

Ziolkowsi, Jan M., ed. *Solomon and Marcolf*. Cambridge, MA: Harvard University Press, 2008.

◆ 12

Expanding the Self in a Mediterranean Context: Liberality and Deception in Cervantes's *El amante liberal*

Luis F. Avilés

The main focus of this essay is to explore how a Mediterranean experience is the main vehicle for personal transformation in *El amante liberal*, a novel written by Miguel de Cervantes. More specifically, I am interested in the ways in which a character with limited resources and a narrow sense of the world and of himself is able to change through an experience of captivity and hybridity overseas. What is significant about this novel is that it proposes an evolution of what I call a limited sense of self through a series of events that demand two distinct and divergent activities: liberality and deception. The main character, named Ricardo, needs to evolve ethically, but does so not only by becoming liberal, but also by learning to lie and deceive. In order to comprehend the seemingly contradictory nature of these practices, I will propose the need for a reinterpretation of the meaning and significance of liberality, a theme of considerable importance across the Cervantine corpus. Its appearance in the novel, I will argue, while not inconsistent with historical and philosophical approaches to the virtue of liberality, nevertheless requires a more complex and nuanced understanding of the term than that traditionally granted to it in critical studies of the novel. Crucially, it is Cervantes's expanded conception of liberality that restitutes an ethical component to the novel's ending, precisely where many recent studies have found only irony.

As such, the purpose of this essay is to explore how the protagonist's ethical evolution, accomplished in a Mediterranean context of captivity and contact with otherness (mainly Turks), can produce a development that can be assessed as an ethical way of being. How is it possible for deception to work alongside liberality in order to accomplish a moral evolution in Ricardo? How can they be integrated and still retain a moral value in the novel? What is the significance of the Mediterranean context and, more specifically, the demands of captivity, for the articulation of such an evolution of character? Why liberality? Why deception and lies? These are some of the questions that guide my analysis of the novel. I will begin by identifying the limitations of Ricardo at the beginning of the narration, proceeding to analyze in detail how liberality and deception expand the protagonist's sense of self. After demonstrating how a libidinal economy comes to define human relations and communities in the early modern Mediterranean—as well as threaten their destruction—I will propose a reading of the novel as a representation of an ethical management of the self as an alternative to the aggression and captivity experienced overseas. From my perspective, *El amante liberal* proposes a different possibility to the forceful possession and the assignment of a price to human life that eschews normative standards of masculinity while ultimately preserving human will and agency through a recognition of the other's right to freedom.

One-Dimensional Sense of Self

In *El amante liberal,* Cervantes introduces the reader into a Mediterranean experience that will allow the protagonist Ricardo to survive captivity and to overcome the restrictions of his own personality. A Sicilian nobleman and soldier who has been held captive in Cyprus, Ricardo tells Mahamut (a renegade and friend) his story of love for Leonisa, the most beautiful woman in Sicily. Unfortunately for Ricardo, Leonisa seems to prefer the company of Cornelio, an effeminate, delicate young man of "blandas manos y rizos cabellos, de voz meliflua y de amorosas palabras, y, finalmente, todo hecho de ámbar y de alfeñique, guarnecido de telas y adornado de brocados" (114–15) (soft hands and curled hair, a honeyed voice and loving words, and, in short, made all of ambergris and soft almond paste, attired in fine clothes and adorned with brocades).[1] One day, Ricardo finds out that Leonisa will accompany Cornelio and his family to Ascanio's garden near the coast, where they will enjoy each other's company in public view. Intensely affected by jealousy, Ricardo finds the pair and proceeds to insult the younger suitor. A duel ensues in which Cornelio is assisted by members of his family. It is at this moment that a pirate ship appears and abducts Leonisa and Ricardo, among other captives.

In the story he narrates to Mahamut, Ricardo (already in a melancholic state) represents himself as a choleric individual who finds difficulty controlling his emotions. His anger has its source in strong feelings of self-worth and entitlement based on an idealized conception of the self that closely follows paradigms of masculine honor and reputation. For example, his reaction to Cornelio is caused by insurmountable differences he perceives between himself and the rival, differences that stem from opposing conceptions of masculinity. These oppositional differences have to do with dress ("galán"), cleanliness ("atildado"), strength ("blandas manos," "alfeñique"), voice ("voz meliflua"), age (young man as opposed to a mature one), and sexuality (the comparison with Ganymede; 115–16). Ricardo's fury is the result of the distance between these two seemingly irreconcilable versions of masculinity. At the beginning of the narrated events (ordered chronologically), he emphatically rejects what Cornelio stands for vis-à-vis what he perceives to be his sole "possession" and his sense of entitlement. Along these lines, I fully agree with Clamurro when he states that "Ricardo's impulsive, egocentric nature and his obsession with his own quite limited view of things, his self-absorbed love for Leonisa, and his inability to understand her true feelings, create the principal obstacle that must be overcome in the *novela*" (43).

Another instance of this one-dimensional way of dealing with his personal life shows clearly when he tells Leonisa that Cornelio will not be able to appreciate her properly, nor estimate her true worth (in Spanish "estimar" has both meanings). According to Ricardo, this is due to the fact that Cornelio is too young, rich, and beautiful, characteristics that can only produce "necedad" or folly (117). A woman's *value* is measured in both personal and economic semantic fields, and apparently a man must be able to judge it correctly in order to deserve her love. From Ricardo's point of view, Cornelio is too young and too rich, two obstacles for the proper valuation of a lady. In conclusion, Ricardo scolds Leonisa and warns her not to expect "estimación" from Cornelio, "porque no tiene otra cosa buena el mundo, sino hacer sus acciones siempre de una misma manera, por que no se engañe nadie sino por su propia ignorancia" (116–17) (for humankind has only one virtue and that is that it always works in the same way so that no one is deceived except as a result of his own ignorance). Here Ricardo is justifying a reduction of the world's complexity in order to better avoid the possibility of mistakes. To him, actions always appear in the same manner, with clear and established meanings, and those who are unable to see or understand those meanings are defined as ignorant. According to Ricardo there is one good thing about the world: actions are easy to interpret because the world provides ample evidence of reality upon which to base one's actions. A young man from a rich family will not be able to appreciate the true value of his loved one because this conforms to the expectations set by the masculine ideals for his class (not to mention all other factors pertaining to sexuality and beauty mentioned above).[2] It is Ricardo's conception of how to manage the world and conform to Spanish masculine ideals of behavior that will be eventually overcome by a Mediterranean experience defined by its diversity, complexity, and difference. In sum, Ricardo's choleric personality and one-dimensional view of action in the world compromise his ability to be a lover. His emotional attachment to Leonisa and his discontent with Cornelio undermines any cultured attribute that he may have, defining her, in an unreasonable gesture, as ignorant due to her inability to interpret action in an effective way. Even more significant, Ricardo is the first character who argues for a correct estimation of women, something Cornelio is incapable of doing in the novel.

This one-dimensional view of action also affects Ricardo's melancholic phase in the novel. Cervantes allows the character to search for aesthetic and literary *topoi* in order to cope with the separation and presumed death of Leonisa. But the way in which he articulates these *topoi* underscores his limitations when it comes time to deal with sadness and loss. For example, at the beginning of the novel Ricardo directs an apostrophe to the ruins of Cyprus that is criticized by the narrator himself (a common practice of Cervantes's narrators): "Propia condición de afligidos que, llevados de sus imaginaciones, hacen y dicen cosas ajenas de toda razón y buen discurso" (110) (This condition is natural in those afflicted who, carried away by their imaginings, do and say things alien to all reason and sound sense). Similar instances of this type of questionable management of emotion indicate a melancholic vulnerability in Ricardo, the constant reference to his own personal loss through imagination.[3] This vulnerability will initially be solved thanks to his relationship with Mahamut, a good friend despite being a renegade. One of the roles assigned to Mahamut in the novel is precisely to "rescue" Ricardo from his flights of fancy and his self-absorption. In the case of the apostrophe, the renegade puts the emphasis on the historical context of the ruins by alluding to the absent soldiers and captives that unsuccessfully defended the fortifications from the Turks in the year 1570 (110–11).[4] He effectively separates the emotional unity forged by Ricardo's rhetoric of suffering and tears from the historicity embedded in the ruins. By working against the unifying (metonymic) force of the apostrophe, Mahamut urges his friend to plant himself on more solid ground: "Pero dejemos estas cosas, pues no llevan remedio, y vengamos a las tuyas, que quiero ver si le tienen" (111) (But let us leave these affairs for they have no remedy and let us come to yours, for I want to see whether they have one). He separates the ruins (a representation of a sad historical event that has already been decided) from the condition of Ricardo (an unresolved personal suffering that may have a practical solution). At another moment of imaginative flight and self-absorption, Ricardo narrates to Mahamut an anecdote that his father told him during Charles V's campaign at Tunis in 1535. Again, Mahamut needs to scold Ricardo for his extreme praise of Leonisa, waiting for a future moment in which they can talk about "otras cosas que sean de más gusto, y aún quizá de más provecho" (137) (other things more to our liking and even, perhaps, more to our profit). We can thus conclude that one of the central functions of Mahamut in the story is to continue managing Ricardo's emotional situation in a more practical, efficient, and beneficial manner, controlling his tendency to concentrate excessively on his own self and not allowing him to succumb to his melancholic fits.[5]

Expanding the Self: Liberality and Deception

I have delved in some detail into the constraints that limit a diverse sense of self in the protagonist so that I can illustrate the changes he will undergo during his captivity overseas. From my perspective, there are two distinct areas in which Ricardo is able to expand his sense of self and his worldview. First, he will become generous ("liberal"), and second, he will learn to deceive. What is interesting and highly complex about this proposition is that the narrative deploys two personal characteristics that, from a moral or ethical perspective, would seem to work in opposition. How can liberality and deception be helpful and desirable traits in order to solve the problems confronted by the protagonist and his limited sense of his own self and the world?

In the early modern period, liberality was considered a moral virtue that had the function of moderating the need to give riches and resources to others. Giving too much and in an indiscriminate way was considered a vice defined at the time by the word *prodigality*. The other extreme (having resources but being unwilling to distribute them to others) was known as avarice.[6] *Autoridades* defines the liberal person as "generoso, bizarro, y que sin fin particular, ni tocar en el extremo de prodigalidad, graciosamente da y socorre, no solo a los menesterosos, sino a los que no lo son tanto, haciéndoles todo bien" (396) (generous, gallant, and to no particular end nor reaching the extreme of prodigality, graciously aids and gives not only to those in need, but to those who are not so needy, doing for them all manner of good deeds). It is important to keep in mind two basic meanings intended in this definition. First, that the act of generosity must not include a "particular end" or a selfish gain. It must be an act that is independent of an individual profit on the giver's part, a way of giving "graciosamente" (with happiness, willingly) in order to do good unselfishly.[7] Second, this act of giving must be done carefully so as not to become an act of prodigality, or a wasteful spending of the household. Covarrubias defines the prodigal man as a "desperdiciador de la hacienda, que la gasta sin orden, cuando, como y con quien no debe" (1,378) (squanderer of the estate who spends it without order when, how, and on whom he should not). Prodigality then means a giving away of resources without the proper consideration of the reasons for giving, to whom one gives, and for what purpose.

Liberality is thus a complex approach to a specific situation, and Ricardo must follow several parameters in order to be considered a fully generous person. First of all, he must choose well to whom he gives, since the recipient must be a worthy person (see Leocata 25). Second, he should also give according to a correct and measured value assigned to the need of the other. In other words, he must demonstrate that he has the virtue of correctly assessing the need of those to whom he wishes to provide assistance. Third, he must do all of this with a moral purpose and without expecting a reward, more or less following the idealizing tendencies of gift-giving.[8] Fourth, he must be careful that his giving does not become a wasteful spending of resources that will end up in an excessive loss. I would propose that of these four requirements, the more complex in *El amante liberal* are the assignment of value to the needs of the other and the elimination of self-interest from the act of generosity. With regard to the other two requirements, it is understandable that Ricardo would feel the need to help Leonisa and her family, since he believes that he is somewhat responsible for the unfortunate events in Sicily and for the abduction by Turkish pirates. He is also in love with her. However, the problem of the loss of his *hacienda* is avoided thanks to their escape to Christian lands, and consequently no ransom is ever paid.

I believe that a complex approach based on the concept of liberality is necessary to fully understand *El amante liberal*. There has been a tendency in recent criticism of the text to question Ricardo's true intentions at the end of the novel, consequently obviating the theme of liberality and its importance. This has resulted in a consistent questioning or downright deconstruction of the references to liberality, affecting not only the main theme of the text, but also the two main characteristics that Cervantes assigns to the protagonist and that are included in the title of the novel (a "liberal lover").[9] The problem I see with an interpretation of the ending as a hidden rhetorical strategy on the part of Ricardo is that once scholars arrive at this conclusion, they must postulate that what Ricardo learned in his Mediterranean ordeal is the mastering of a deceitful rhetoric for the purposes of conquering the heart of the woman he loves. It would be a more sophisticated use of power than the mostly open management of money and desire he experienced in Cyprus. The end result would be the complete elimination of the exemplary, ethical component of liberality announced both in the title of the novel and in the main themes that guide the narrative. However, the Mediterranean experience is cumulative in the novel, and the transformations undergone by Ricardo support a reading that focuses on how it is the ethics of liberality rather than the cunning use of rhetoric that allows him to acquire what he desires. Deception is part of a paradoxical effect on the main character that, in tandem with liberality, explains the complexity of Cervantes's proposed rendition of a Mediterranean experience of captivity.[10]

The question, then, is how does Ricardo become a liberal person? How is he able to judge the correct value of the needs of Leonisa and avoid self-interest in the process? In other words, how does he begin to expand his restricted and limited sense of self? What we may call the irruption of a Mediterranean experience involves the capture and captivity of both lovers by Turkish pirates. Both characters are immediately introduced into a series of economic transactions that will include the complete spectrum of possible exchanges and negotiations in the market for human life. As soon as they are captured, Ricardo's first decision is to assume sole responsibility for Leonisa's ransom. In contrast, Cornelio remains silent even though his family is richer and with more economic resources.[11] This is the first instance in which the accusation leveled by Ricardo against his competitor can be evaluated in the novel. Obviously, the young Cornelio does not know the true value of Leonisa in the same way Ricardo does, or at least he lacks any initiative to share in her rescue. As stated clearly by Hutchinson, facts corroborate Cornelio's negative image (90). There is no apparent explanation for Cornelio's silence and no clear reason why he should not offer assistance. This is highly important because Leonisa's subsequent change of opinion regarding Ricardo's personality is based on the inaction of Cornelio in Sicily, his unwillingness to openly enter the Mediterranean economy of captivity at a moment of crisis. This is the first instance in which there is some truth to what Ricardo stated during his emotional speech that the rich, young and beautiful rival is unable to esteem Leonisa's value correctly. At this moment, one version of masculinity that has evolved thanks to the appearance of liberality begins to gain ground over another in the narrative, since despite being of a lower social origin Ricardo is more than willing to enter this imposed economy without hesitation, assuming responsibility for the welfare of another human being.

The Turks, who proceed to assign a high value for Leonisa due to her extreme beauty and the sexual desire she constantly awakens, further complicate the context of liberality. By having Ricardo be aware of the very high price assigned to Leonisa, Cervantes communicates to the reader both that this price far exceeds the price set in similar transactions involving women captives, and that Ricardo is someone capable of recognizing and who knows the value assigned to human beings in the context of an economy of captivity.[12] I need to make clear that the value given to Leonisa (or any other captive, independent of feelings or emotional considerations) is an estimation given to the impossibility to assign worth to human life. What I mean to say is that in the particular economy of captivity and ransom an estimation of value is attached to what should not be given value, especially if it is a person one loves.[13] Captivity affects the proper estimation of human value, or may even be considered a dehumanizing procedure of assigning value to human life. This is important because we must distinguish between different aspects of the diverse economic map presented in the novel. In this map we must include the inestimable worth of another human being (especially the person one loves). This valuation is present in the novel, but not fully developed. When Ricardo accuses Cornelio of not knowing the true value of Leonisa, he states that he will not know how to "estimar lo inestimable" (116) (esteem the inestimable). This exceptional worth of a person, or the impossibility of giving a measurable value to a human being, should be considered the true estimation of life and should also remain outside any economy. I consider this to be the other (ethical) extreme in relation to the assignment of value when a person enters the particular economy of captivity. Suddenly the captured person is given a value for the purposes of a ransom or as an object to be exchanged for other human beings. He or she may become a slave or may be transferred from one owner to another at any time. The economy of captivity may also expand and be affected by an excessive assignment of value because the captive has now become an object of desire.[14] This libidinal economy has a tendency to complicate the economy of captivity because it now assigns an exceedingly high value to captives, becoming an obstacle to "measured" and "reasonable" exchanges of human life. This latter economy within the economic particularity of captivity affects the majority of characters from other cultural and religious backgrounds (from the Jewish merchant to the Turks).[15]

What follows is an illustration of how the libidinal economy works in the novel. Leonisa suffers a continuous shift in the assignment of worth given to her, a fact that complicates her trajectory (from owner to owner). At first, the Greek renegade Yzuf requests 6,000 "escudos" for Leonisa, later reduced to 5,000 thanks to the effective bargaining of Ricardo's steward (120). Later on, during the partition of the Turkish booty on the island of Pantanalea, Yzuf will give his counterpart Fetala an enormous amount of human life for the possession of Leonisa. He gives away Ricardo, two Christians who will serve as rowers, and two very beautiful Corsicans ("dos muchachos hermosísimos, de nación corsos"), implying sexual favors and for that reason of higher value (121). Later on, the Jewish merchant requests a price of 4,000 "doblas" (2,000 ducats) for Leonisa, plus the price of her beautiful dress, which amounts to another 1,000 ducats, paid in this case by the qadi (130–32). Originally, he had paid 2,000 "doblas" for her, effectively making a 100 percent profit on the transaction (144). The Turks that sold Leonisa to the Jew are the only characters that exchange her without being affected by the libidinal economy. This is due to the fact that the Turks that inherit Leonisa after the death of Yzuf treat her as if she were their sister (143). They assign a value to her that could be considered the standard value for a captive woman, without the interference of sexual desire.[16]

As the narrative proceeds, the desire for Leonisa intensifies and her value enters the most dangerous and inherently destructive realm of the libidinal economy. Suddenly, value is increased in an utterly inordinate manner. For example, the sexual possession of Leonisa becomes of such importance to the qadi that his own life is at stake: "Antes pensaba morir mil veces que entregalla una al Gran Turco" (139) (He was resolved to die a thousand deaths rather than deliver her up once to the Great Turk). At this moment, a series of propositions involving the killing of other human beings in order to possess Leonisa become operative in the novel. The qadi (aided by the false council of Ricardo and Mahamut) proposes that during the voyage to Constantinople they should feign the mortal sickness of Leonisa, but using instead the body of a previously bought Christian woman that will be dumped in the ocean. But this slave is later substituted by the qadi's own wife Halima, because she is the primary obstacle to the final possession of Leonisa (148). The qadi can now weigh the sexual possession of Leonisa with Halima's life. This is another version of masculinity that plunges into the Mediterranean economy of human life and is willing to assign values that imply life and death.

The end result of this continuous and chaotic fluctuation of human value in a libidinal economy is the civil strife among the Turks, as well as the destruction of the social fabric of those possessing (and sharing) a political and religious function in the Turkish society of the eastern Mediterranean. The libidinal economy of desire evolves into an extreme manipulation of the value of human life, making possible a radical lowering of human worth to the category of being expendable. Once the combination of sexual desire and a particular economy of captivity irrupts within the fabric of Turkish political structures in the occupied territories, relationships of respect, friendship, and shared religious values are incapable of containing the destructive forces of desire. The political and social fabric in the colonial possessions of the Turkish empire is effectively demolished. When Hazán's men approach the ship of the qadi too aggressively and attack it, the narrator states: "Sin respetos de las banderas de paz, ni de lo que a su religión debían, embistieron con el del cadí con tanta furia, que estuvo poco en echarle al fondo" (150) (Without respecting the flags of truce nor what they owed to their religion, they rammed the Cadi's boat with such fury that it was almost sunk). When the voice of the qadi assumes his authority and scolds both attackers, the men recognize for a moment who they really are: "A estas palabras suspendieron todos las armas, y unos y otros se miraron y se conocieron" (151) (At these words they all put down their arms and, looking at each other, they recognised each other). Unfortunately, this truce is very short, since Alí, with eyes and ears closed ("cerró los ojos y los oídos a todo"), attacks and almost kills the qadi. This reduction of human life to an economy of desire and possession affects the Turkish elites in the novel, those who have almost unlimited resources in terms of both power and money.[17] The figure of the qadi is also crucial in this respect, since he is the appointed voice of religious and social judgment that succumbs to desire and is willing to traffic in expendable human life. Although his words carry authority, that authority has lost the respect of the men he is supposed to spiritually guide.

The desire to be liberal must then be understood as a moral economy that values freedom more than monetary possession, and consequently is willing to spend large sums of money because it recognizes the value of human life (a value that is always superior to any imposed worth from the perspective of the economy of captivity or the libidinal economy). This is the nature of Ricardo's intentions when he volunteered to be responsible for the freedom of Leonisa. But despite his efforts, liberality does not provide the moral solution to the problem of the abduction by the Turkish pirates. The narration does not allow Ricardo to accomplish this within the imposed economy of captivity in Sicily. We must wait till the end of the novel for liberality to accomplish its full ethical potential. Since Ricardo's intentions are not fulfilled at the beginning of the novel, all captives must counteract their lack of freedom through other means, including deception. To respond to the unbridled desire of the majority of Turkish characters (especially those that are part of the political elite), the captives deploy deception as the only mechanism they have to escape the cycles of life and death instituted by the libidinal economy. The imperative to lie and deceive intensifies once Leonisa is found alive in the hands of the Jewish merchant and becomes the possession of the qadi. The moment when Ricardo tells his friend Mahamut that the Christian captive is Leonisa, the renegade begins to show his superiority over Ricardo, who is still affected by his limited perspective. Mahamut immediately tries to control the latter's excess of emotion: "Pues calla y no la descubras . . . , que la ventura va ordenando que la tengas buena y próspera, porque ella va a poder de mi amo" (132) (Then be silent and do not give her away . . . Fortune is beginning to smile on you, for she is now in my master's possession). At that moment, Ricardo asks a question that continues to illustrate his lack of a careful, strategic approach to the new context: "Parécete . . . que será bien ponerme en parte donde pueda ser visto?" (132) (Do you think that I should place myself where she can see me?). To this imprudent question Mahamut reacts immediately: "No . . . , porque no la sobresaltes o te sobresaltes, y no vengas a dar indicio de que la conoces ni que la has visto" (133) (No . . . in case you distress her or indeed yourself and reveal that you know her). Once again, Mahamut compensates for Ricardo's continued lack of contextual skills. Mahamut is able to understand that secrecy empowers their status as captives, even if they lack freedom from their owners. He also understands the dangers of Ricardo's lack of self-control when it comes to his emotional state.

On the way to the city, Mahamut is able to judge Leonisa's affections toward Ricardo by telling her a false story that includes Cornelio's captivity and Ricardo's death. Leonisa immediately reacts by displaying her disdain for Cornelio, even when Mahamut tells her that he has become a captive and is now owned by a Turkish merchant who "fiaba de Cornelio toda su hacienda" (134) (entrusted him with the care of all his possessions). Her response is quite eloquent: "Bien se la sabrá guardar—dijo Leonisa—, porque sabe guardar muy bien la suya" (134) (He will certainly safeguard them, said Leonisa, for he is well used to safeguarding his own). Leonisa shows her displeasure for Cornelio's incapacity to be liberal during the first moments of her captivity on the Sicilian shore. She has begun to reject that model of masculinity predicated on being overtly passive and too protective of possessions. Mahamut carefully observes her disdain, and decides not only to test her further on the issue, but also takes the opportunity to expand on his lies in order to actively help Ricardo gain her favor. Leonisa asks Mahamut if Cornelio mentioned her to him, and he replies:

> me preguntó [Cornelio] si había aportado por esta isla una cristiana dese nombre, de tales y tales señas, a la cual holgaría de hallar para rescatarla, si es que su amo se había ya desengañado de que no era tan rica como él pensaba, aunque podía ser que por haberla gozado la tuviese en menos; que como no pasen de trecientos o cuatrocientos escudos, él los daría de muy buena gana por ella, porque un tiempo la había tenido alguna afición. (135)

> (He asked me whether a Christian woman of that name and of such a description had come ashore anywhere on the island, for he was eager to find her and ransom her provided her owner had finally realized that she was not as rich as he had thought, although it might in any case turn out that, having enjoyed her favors, he valued her less highly. And so long as the sum demanded for her did not exceed three or four hundred crowns, he would willingly pay it, for he had once been quite fond of her.)

The rhetorical strategy implemented by Mahamut devastates the figure of Cornelio as a lover in the eyes of Leonisa. In the false account of a conversation that never took place, Cornelio is said to have wished for the revelation of the lower economic status of Leonisa's family; insinuated the possibility that her owner had fulfilled his sexual desire with her and for that reason lowered her exchange value; proposed to pay the insignificant amount of 300 to 400 "escudos" for her; and stated that he had once felt some kind of affection for her. In Mahamut's narrative, Cornelio appears to almost desire the loss of Leonisa's virginity in order to lower the price of her rescue. We are clearly very distant from the 5,000 "escudos" that Ricardo was willing to pay for her ransom in Sicily.

In Mahamut's narrative, deception works both as a tool to examine other people's thoughts and as a clear manipulation of desire in favor of a friend. This is done at a personal level that will definitely affect the future relationships between characters in the narrative. There is no question that Mahamut affected Leonisa's opinion of Cornelio, one that will manifest itself in all its importance at the end of the novel. Later on the use of deception will also play a key role as part of a strategy for survival and gaining freedom from captivity. Along these lines, one of the main strategies proposed by Mahamut is the need to be trusted by their owners. The sexual desire that both the qadi and Halima develop for Leonisa and Ricardo (now named Mario) will lead to promises of freedom and generous contractual agreements. But despite the clear need to play a role in a performance of deception against their owners, it is surprising to encounter Ricardo's resistance to it. Up to this moment in the novel, he has remained a character in need of direction and help. Moments after the difficult encounter between a living Ricardo and Leonisa (a beautifully constructed scene worthy of a master narrator), he will still display his clumsiness and be advised quickly on the strategic way to behave. In his excitement to see Leonisa, he begins to talk, and Leonisa responds accordingly: "Púsose Leonisa en esto el dedo en la boca, por lo cual entendió Ricardo que era señal de que callase o hablase más quedo" (141) (At this Leonisa raised her finger to her lips, which Ricardo took to mean that he should be silent or lower his voice). She even commands him to do as she says: "Habla paso, Mario, que así me parece que te llamas ahora, y no trates de otra cosa de la que yo te tratare" (142) (Speak quietly, Mario, for this I believe is now your name, and only of those things of which I speak). After Leonisa communicates to Ricardo the love that Halima feels for him, she indicates that even if he does not want to accept her sexual favors, "es forzoso que lo finjas, siquiera porque yo te lo ruego" (142) (It is imperative that you pretend you do if only because I ask you to). Ricardo's response illustrates his difficulty in accepting this proposition, even if what he is asked to do is to act for his own benefit:

> Jamás pensé ni pude imaginar, hermosa Leonisa, que cosa que me pidieras trujera consigo imposible de cumplirla, pero la que me pides me ha desengañado. ¿Es por ventura la voluntad tan ligera que se pueda mover y llevar donde quisieren llevarla, o estarle ha bien al varón honrado y verdadero fingir en cosas de tanto peso? Si a ti te parece que alguna destas cosas se debe o puede hacer, haz lo que más gustares, pues eres señora de mi voluntad; mas ya sé que también me engañas en esto, pues jamás la has conocido, y así no sabes lo que has de hacer della. Pero, a trueco que no digas que en la primera cosa que me mandaste dejaste de ser obedecida, yo perderé del derecho que debo a ser quien soy, y satisfaré tu deseo y el de Halima fingidamente, como dices, si es que se ha de granjear con esto el bien de verte; y así, finge tú las respuestas a tu gusto, que desde aquí las firma y confirma mi fingida voluntad. (142)

> (Never did I think or could imagine, lovely Leonisa, that anything you asked of me would prove impossible to comply with. But what you ask of me now has taught me otherwise. Is desire per chance so fickle that it can be moved or redirected at will or does it become an honest and honorable man to feign in such weighty matters? If you believe that either of those things can or ought to be done, do as you prefer, for you are mistress of my will. But I know that in this you also deceive me, for you have never known my will and so you cannot know what you must do with it. Nevertheless, so that you may not say that you were disobeyed in the first thing which you commanded me, I shall surrender the right which binds me to be

who I am and I shall satisfy your desire and that of Halima falsely, as you say, if by so doing I shall earn the blessing of seeing you. So falsify my replies as you wish, for henceforth they will be ratified and verified by my false desire.)[18]

This is a very complex passage, one that has not been sufficiently examined by critics. Ricardo reacts negatively to the manipulation of two aspects of the self that, in his mind, should be fixed and unmovable. The first concerns the will ("voluntad"), which he claims Leonisa does not know. The second obstacle that he encounters has to do with his conception of himself as a "varón honrado y verdadero" (an honest and honourable man) that needs to remain consistent even if circumstances require the performance (or improvisation) of an alternate self. In other words, Ricardo not only displays a restricted sense of self from the beginning of the novel, but also a reluctance to explore other possible self-presentations in order to deal effectively with particular circumstances, especially those related to imprisonment and captivity. In fact, Ricardo seems to communicate to Leonisa that if she knew that he was an honorable and truthful man, then she would not ask such a behavior from him. He reacts as if the imitation of feigning love for somebody else would transform him into that other person (a man that is not truthful and has no honor). This is an ancient fear that we may trace back to Plato's discomfort with performance, representations and images. In fact, we may understand Ricardo's attitude as a manifestation of what Rancière has called the ethical regime of images. In this regime one needs to know "in what way images' mode of being affects the *ethos*, the mode of being of individuals and communities" (21). It represents a fear of a peculiar visibility and the forces that insist on maintaining the invisibility of certain possibilities. It is as if imitating a negative model of behavior will jeopardize his own self and leave him prey to the malleable opinions of the community. The right to be himself is then forfeited ("yo perderé del derecho que debo a ser quien soy") (I shall surrender the right which binds me to be who I am). For him, a strategy or performance always has the problem of appearing to be reality, not necessarily in the Platonic fear of transforming oneself into another, but in the public and visible existence of opinion. We need to recall that Ricardo wants to live in a world of transparent realities, a world in which will and self are open to all so that no one can be deceived, recalling Ricardo's statement about the world: "porque no tiene otra cosa buena el mundo, sino hacer sus acciones siempre de una misma manera, por que no se engañe nadie sino por su propia ignorancia" (144) (for humankind has only one virtue and that is that it always works in the same way so that no one is deceived except as a result of his own ignorance). Since action is related to will, both the long passage I am discussing here and the quote related to human action are intimately related. He remains frustrated by what he claims is Leonisa's lack of knowledge of his will in a similar way that he was frustrated by her lack of knowledge of Cornelio's. A deceptive performance would imply that he will act in a way that is different from the way he believes a man should act. In the end, however, he accepts her request with reluctance.[19]

Later on in their conversation, Leonisa convinces him of the need to deceive: "Es menester usar en esto lo que de nuestra condición no se puede esperar, que es el fingimiento y el engaño" (145) (It is necessary for us to resort to what is not to be expected of people of our station, namely trickery and deception). She understands what Ricardo is saying (they share the same moral imperatives of honor and truthfulness), but she also recognizes that their situation requires a way of acting that deviates from their natural disposition. Leonisa's function here is very similar to Mahamut's, in the sense that they help expand Ricardo's limitations during their captivity. The context imposes on a particular "condición" (a particular way of being) the need to act differently, to act in a way so that others remain ignorant of the true intentions against them. Once they agree on a strategy, Leonisa imposes the conditions for their continued interaction, which on the brighter side includes a new recognition of Ricardo's personality: "No me dará, como solía, fastidio tu vista, porque te hago saber, Ricardo, que siempre te tuve por desabrido y arrogante, y que presumías de ti algo más de lo que debías. Confieso también que me engañaba . . . " (145) (The sight of you does not repel me as it used to, for I can tell you that I always considered that you were unpleasant and arrogant and that you valued yourself more than you ought). During the whole experience of captivity, Leonisa has begun to see what she was unable to see before in her suitor, and Ricardo has begun to enjoy the fruits of his new behavior toward her: "Quedó Leonisa contenta y satisfecha del llano proceder de Ricardo, y él contentísimo de haber oído una palabra de la boca de Leonisa sin aspereza" (146) (Leonisa remaining pleased and satisfied with Ricardo's straightforward manner and he delighted at having heard a word from Leonisa's mouth that was not unkind).

The Lessons of the Mediterranean

After the disasters brought about by excessive desire, which culminated in the deaths of the majority of the Turkish sailors, Ricardo and his company (now including Halima) are finally able to begin their return home. At the sight of the coast of Sicily, "renovóse la alegría en sus corazones; alborotáronse sus espíritus con el nuevo contento, que es uno de los mayores que en esta vida se puede tener" (154) (joy renewed itself in their hearts and their spirits soared with this new delight, which is one of the greatest one can experience in this life). In his understandably euphoric state, Ricardo decides to play a joke on Leonisa's parents (a "graciosa burla"). He proceeds to decorate the ship with Turkish banners, and also encourages everybody to dress in Turkish robe. He pleads with Leonisa to wear the same dress that she wore in Cyprus, and she accepts. The protagonist's decision to play a joke has been approached in interesting ways by many critics. For example, Cardaillac, Carrière, and Subirats believe that the change of dress is a sort of liberation from the Turkish experience (22). Díaz Migoyo cleverly reads the scene not as a genuine return home but as a theatrical representation of a return home (131). With a different perspective, Clamurro interprets the scene as a "symbolic reiteration of the marvel and wonder that is the mixture of the fearful and the beautiful: the European vision of the Ottoman Empire" (66). Barbara Fuchs considers it a case of perversion, born of the "powerful attraction of the East for European readers," finding no apparent reason for what she considers a "superfluous disguise" in her reading of scenes of passing (73).

From my perspective, the performance organized by Ricardo responds not only to the general happiness experienced by the returning party, which has a physiological effect in the movement of their spirits, but also must be understood as a playful willingness to openly display the changes they endured after surviving captivity in the Mediterranean.[20] I believe that the performance is not intended as a statement on Turkish (or Christian) culture on the part of either Ricardo or Cervantes. It is rather the public, visual display of Ricardo's change and, consequently, it is a scene that must be contrasted to the way he acted in the same place and on the same Mediterranean shore at the beginning of the novel.[21] What does Ricardo display with his game? A willingness to adopt an alternate appearance not guided by the strict social concerns that constrained his behavior in the past, and the eagerness to accept deception as part of human action (but in a harmless display). The performance effectively illustrates his expanded self by overcoming the Platonic fears of experimenting with false images. It vividly illustrates how Ricardo embraces the complexity and diversity of human life, a life that now includes a Turkish component (the visible mark of an experience with the other). He has gone from a choleric and highly possessive man, to a more cheerful and complex personality. His ludic representation is not a deception that should be categorized as malicious or perverse. This type of deception, which functions quite well in this performative illustration of individual change, can be better understood within the category of jocose lies (*jocosus*) originally proposed by Thomas Aquinas in his *Summa Theologica*. Aquinas reduced the kinds of lies categorized by Augustine to three: "officious, or helpful, lies; the jocose lies, told in jest; and the mischievous, or malicious, lies, told to harm someone" (Bok 34). It is true that Ricardo experiences these three types of lies in the novel (the helpful lie that will free him from captivity, the lies intended to harm another person such as the qadi, and the jocose lie that he articulates in his performance). However, his dramatic enactment of his change does not constitute a dangerous lie, nor is it represented as such by the narrator.[22] Ricardo's decision to arrive this way in Sicily can be understood as the end result of his Mediterranean experience of captivity, but formulated in a way that is not harmful to others. It brings otherness into a culture, but in a manageable way because it is an imitation, a representation. Therefore, his performance, as an act, remains from an ethical standpoint on the opposite side of the libidinal economy of captivity, the other face of Mediterranean reality. I would argue that it represents the playful joy of freedom, feelings of desire, and change outside the chaos suffered under an economy of possession.

This jocose use of deception at the end of the novel functions as the prologue for the re-appearance of liberality as the correct response to both captivity and the libidinal economy of desire. We must recall that Ricardo does not pay the ransom at the beginning, so he is unable to fully accomplish on his own his intention of paying Leonisa's assigned value. However, we must also remember that his intentions left a mark on Leonisa. It is only at the end that Ricardo can demonstrate how much he has been transformed by his experience. The first thing he does is truly remarkable. In front of the whole city ("no quedó gente en toda la ciudad que dejase de salir a la marina" [155] [there was nobody in the entire city who did not come down to the harbour]), he grabs the hands of both Cornelio and Leonisa and begins to address the crowd that has gathered. After acknowledging the happiness felt upon the return to his homeland, Ricardo begins to speak about Leonisa in a way that suggests that despite all she has suffered, she never changed. She has endured all with "valor y entereza" (valour and integrity), and has not changed her "costumbres" (habits), and for that reason Ricardo thinks that her desire for Cornelio has remained the same.[23] That is why he offers Cornelio to Leonisa: "te doy al que tú siempre has tenido en la memoria" (157) (I give you to the one you have always carried in your memory). What Ricardo wants desperately to do is to define his act as the true definition of liberality: "Esta sí quiero se tenga por liberalidad, en cuya comparación dar la hacienda, la vida y la honra no es nada" (157) (This indeed I wish to be deemed an act of generosity, compared with giving one's wealth, one's life and one's honor is as nothing). He even offers to give Cornelio his share of the booty taken from the Turkish ship, around 30,000 "escudos," six times the highest value assigned to Leonisa in the libidinal economy of captivity. Now it is true that Ricardo is making a mistake, and he will immediately recognize it. But critics should not dismiss this initial gesture for the following reason. When Ricardo grabs the hand of Cornelio and offers to give Leonisa to him, assigning to himself the functions of parental authority, what in reality he is doing is restituting the right of Cornelio's masculinity not only to exist as such, but also to be acknowledged in public view by all. The rejection of his model of masculinity at the beginning of the novel is reversed and given full recognition in front of the whole city. Instead of injuring Cornelio verbally, he now understands that this young man cannot be excluded from the possibility of having the right to marriage.[24] More importantly, I believe that the character of Ricardo has to acknowledge Cornelio's subjectivity (and masculinity) precisely because he wants to act with "liberalidad." He correctly identifies the imperative of liberality as a need to recognize what he insistently (and aggressively) rejected at the beginning of the story. Now, in full view of the city, Ricardo appears truly as a changed person.

Despite his intentions, however, Ricardo has made the mistake of assuming, as I already stated, the paternal functions within the institution of marriage. But the significance of what he has done cannot be forgotten. He rightfully corrects himself, saying that he cannot give what is not his:

> No es posible que nadie pueda mostrarse liberal de lo ajeno. ¿Qué jurisdición tengo yo en Leonisa para darla a otro? O ¿cómo puedo ofrecer lo que está tan lejos de ser mío? Leonisa es suya, y tan suya, que, a faltarle sus padres . . . ningún opósito tuviera a su voluntad. (158)
>
> (It is impossible for anyone to be generous with what does not belong to him. What authority do I have over Leonisa to give her to another? How can I offer what is so far from being mine? Leonisa is his, and so much so that if she did not have her parents . . . she would have no resistance to Cornelio's will.)

At the moment when Ricardo wants to grant Cornelio the possibility of marrying Leonisa, he simultaneously fails to recognize Leonisa's freedom, which he reveals in the second part of his speech. This is precisely what I consider the ethical gesture of liberality, which can be defined now as the recognition of the liberty of the other. This act of liberality represents the opposite of the libidinal economy that affected Ricardo as well as all Turkish characters dominated by excessive passion (including the Jewish merchant). The value of freedom now corresponds to the high value of a human life, and it does not matter if that human being is different from a normative conception of masculinity (Cornelio). In fact, Ricardo's gesture toward Cornelio deconstructs that normality demanded by a code or culture. True, it is provisional and tentative in the story, but it is still present. In the end, Leonisa requests from her parents what Ricardo has tried to give her: "Me den licencia y libertad para disponer de la que tu mucha valentía y liberalidad me ha dado" (158) (To grant me freedom and license to exercise that freedom which, thanks to your great courage and generosity, I now enjoy). The parents, of course, grant her the freedom to choose, and she selects Ricardo over Cornelio. Her selection is not an absolute corroboration of a normative subjectivity, but rather a recognition of the liberality demonstrated by Ricardo and that was lacking in Cornelio. Furthermore, Leonisa mentions the valor ("valentía") just demonstrated by Ricardo, and that word must be defined in this instance as the courage of appearing as a changed person, in front of the entire city, recognizing his mistakes in public, and even more remarkable, recognizing Cornelio as well.

I agree with Hutchinson when he concludes that Leonisa retains her agency at the end, and is not the victim of a rhetorical ploy (92). If her decision was clouded, it was due to Mahamut's deception, not necessarily by Ricardo's "strategic" or "rhetorical" generosity at the end. I prefer to read the novel from a non-ironic perspective because of the ethical content I have just described in this essay. I believe that this content enriches the novel and reflects a consistent exploration of liberality on the part of Cervantes.[25] Doing otherwise would lead to conclude that in this novel it is not possible to grow ethically in contact with the other, and that, on the contrary, the Mediterranean provides for the Western subject only the tools to gain even more power over others. That would mean that what Ricardo learns may have changed him, but instead of an ethical transformation, he learns instead to possess what he wants by using strategy, secrecy, rhetorical entrapment, and deception. In reality, if we follow this reading, he would become a true example of a Machiavellian personality. I cannot agree with this conclusion.

What I have called a Mediterranean experience in *El amante liberal* is a complex fictional representation of Ricardo's ethical evolution. It is an experience characterized by the interaction with other cultures overseas, within the context of captivity, and framed as well as the story of lovers separated and eventually united. These events imprint themselves in a limited personality, opening up opportunities for an expanded sense of the world and of the self. I believe I have demonstrated that Ricardo's growth stems from the acquisition of two seemingly divergent human activities that expand the limitations of the main character of the story. What they share in common is that both are actions directed at others, but for different reasons. Learning to deceive is a tool of survival that covers a diverse spectrum of approaches to the other: from the intention to defend oneself against the harm inflicted by an enemy, sometimes reaching the need to aggressively act against the other's will, to finally deceive in a way that is not harmful to others. The lessons provided by learning to deceive help overcome an overly simplistic understanding of human action, experiencing how humans hide their true intentions and how this complexity needs to be acknowledged. It also suggests that despite the best intentions misunderstandings and misjudgments of other people's character may occur, and that experience of others is limited and even problematic. This is precisely what Ricardo and Leonisa experienced with each other (he thought that Leonisa loved Cornelio, and she believed that Ricardo was arrogant and choleric). Deception may lead to freedom, or it may lead to total war (*bellum omnium contra omnes*). But deception is needed in the novel in order to change an erroneous and overly simplistic view of the world. Deception must be tempered by the joy of freedom, but also by liberality. In the novel, liberality is a kind of economic activity that is able to restitute the true value of a person. The liberal man (or woman) is the one that always gives not expecting a reward because of a recognition of the other's endemic freedom. Liberality is a way to liberate the recipient from obligations and reciprocity. That is why it is such an important tool in a Mediterranean dominated by an economy of captivity, or for any context in which a libidinal economy of forced possession dominates human relationships. Deception teaches that in an urban environment of mutual affections severe judgments should not be made of human actions that are more complex than they appear (Ricardo's way of thinking about Leonisa and Cornelio). Furthermore, by accepting the complexity of humanity, Ricardo would be more willing to suspend judgment until more evidence is available. Once Ricardo knows that, liberality can only thrive because it can assign the proper value to the other, which is that such a valuation is impossible in material terms.[26] In both instances, deception's power to destroy may be managed and give way to forms of liberality that expand reality and, consequently, open up the possibility for a true recognition of the other in the human field of action.

Notes

1. I quote from the edition of Jorge García López, indicating the page number in parenthesis. I quote all English translations from Volume I of Ife's edition of the *Exemplary Novels.*
2. My argument here is that besides sexuality, a major difference between both men is determined by social status, bodily appearance and money. There are different versions of masculinity in the novel that manifest themselves by the way they estimate the value of Leonisa. Ricardo's argument is based on his understanding that Cornelio's social status, beauty, and privilege will not allow him to "estimar" (estimate) correctly the value of Leonisa, and his major complaint is that she shows ignorance of this "fact." For a reading of Cornelio based on sexual difference, see Paul Julian Smith and Adrienne Martin.
3. For a study of the emotional registers of captivity, see Paul Michael Johnson, who argues that in Cervantes's *The Captive's Tale* the captive must similarly confront "an excess of affect and affliction," or what he terms the "specter of captivity" (154).
4. For the historical background on Cyprus, see Hegyi and Carroll Johnson.
5. One must keep in mind that Ricardo has the ability to rescue himself from captivity at any time if he so desires. Even his current owner, Hazam Bajá, "me ha dicho muchas veces que me rescate, pues soy hombre principal" (153) (has told me more than once that as a man of distinction . . . I might do so), but he has not done so because he wants to live a short life of misery, uniting captivity and the sad memory of Leonisa: "Juntándose a la vida del cautiverio los pensamientos y memorias que jamás me dejan de la muerte de Leonisa" (153) (Life in captivity together with the memory and recollection of Leonisa's death, which haunt me constantly). His melancholic state will soon end once Leonisa reappears in the novel.
6. All this follows closely Aristotle's definition of generosity in *Nicomachean Ethics* IV, 1. Cervantes has worked extensively with these distinctions in other novels. For example, the father of Ruy Pérez de Viedma in *The Captive's Tale* suffers from prodigality, as does Carrizales in *The Jealous Extremaduran*. Other characters, such as Persiles, consistently act with liberality.
7. Thomas Aquinas states that a liberal act must always be done with happiness. See Leocata and Lázaro Pulido, who both mention the need to give in this manner in their articles on liberality.
8. The moral aspect of liberality, mentioned by Aristotle, is discussed in Leocata. Liberality is an activity that can be included in what Steven Hutchinson has called "economía ética" (ethical economy) in Cervantes.
9. I am of course referring to a number of critics that approach the novel from an ironic perspective. They include Gonzalo Díaz Migoyo, Georges Güntert, Theresa Ann Sears, Carroll Johnson, Adrienne Martin, and Barbara Fuchs.
10. This would also imply that I cannot agree with Márquez Villanueva when he states that in *El amante liberal* captivity is a mere "fondo convencional" (60–61)

(a conventional background) for the sentimental story of two lovers. From my perspective, the resolution of the sentimental aspects of the narrative are intrinsically related to captivity and the Mediterranean experience. One cannot be understood without the other.

11. Leonisa's parents were not against her relationship with Cornelio, because there was the hope that he "la escogería por su esposa, y en ello granjearían yerno más rico" (115) (would choose her as his wife and they, in this way, would gain a wealthier son-in-law than in me).
12. Hutchinson has noted correctly that there was a tendency to assign a higher value to women captives due to sexual considerations. See 88 and note 60 for bibliographical indications.
13. For example, there are innumerable instances of incalculability in the literature devoted to love and affection. Lovers are incapable of assigning a monetary value to each other. However, economic factors do appear when captivity and ransom affect one of the lovers, especially because monetary values are imposed by captors on the ones with the responsibility to pay the ransom. An interesting case of an inestimable value appears in *La española inglesa*, in which the Queen of England assigns to Isabela the same value as a daughter.
14. For an excellent discussion of the economic aspects of captivity in the novel, see Carroll Johnson and Hutchinson.
15. As I will discuss in a moment, not all the Turks assign value through a libidinal prism. Hutchinson distinguishes correctly between use value and exchange value, concluding that Leonisa is assigned a "máximo 'valor de uso' imaginable" (88) (highest use value imaginable), rendering insignificant the exchange value.
16. In reality, we must understand Leonisa's favorable judgment of the pirates solely with reference to the respect they showed for her virginity. Undoubtedly, they did not treat her as a sister when they decided to profit by selling her to the merchant Jew. This fact illustrates the gradations of ethical behavior that appear in the novel.
17. It did not affect, however, the Turkish pirates in Yzuf's ship. In the case of the Jewish merchant, he has the monetary resources but lacks the political or religious power (he does not have an army). Similar to the Jewish merchant, Cornelio has the resources but appears unwilling to use them at an opportune moment and for the purposes of helping a person that is close to him.
18. The translator at times translates "voluntad" with the word "desire." However the correct translation is "will."
19. This reluctance has a hint of parody when Ricardo implements the word "fingir" several times toward the end of the quote, including paronomasia with the sound /f/: "*satisfaré* tu deseo y el de Halima *fingidamente*, como dices, si es que se ha de granjear con esto el bien de verte; y así, *finge* tú las respuestas a tu gusto, que desde aquí las *firma* y *confirma* mi *fingida* voluntad" (142; my emphasis) (I *shall satisfy* your desire and that of Halima *falsely*, as you say, if by so doing I shall earn the blessing of

seeing you. So *falsify* my replies as you wish, for henceforth they will be *ratified* and *verified* by my *false* desire).

20. We must also keep in mind other similar instances in which characters who have solved a problem seem to enjoy expressing themselves through harmless jokes. We find an example in *La señora Cornelia*.
21. I do agree with Díaz Migoyo when he states that Ricardo wants all present to evaluate what he will do now and contrast it with the way he was before. However, I cannot agree with him when he states that both scenes are structurally the same (133).
22. On Aquinas's categories, see also the excellent books by Bettetini (26) and Zagorin (29). For a semiotic approach to lying in the *Exemplary Novels*, see Bianchi.
23. This is another misreading by Ricardo, since in effect we know that Leonisa has changed and will go from "desamorada" (loveless) to gaining the capacity to at least respond positively to Ricardo.
24. Here I am distancing myself from Adrienne Martin's view of Cornelio as an "impossible suitor," although I do agree with her that in many levels there is an "authorial repudiation" of his possibilities to be a viable suitor (154).
25. Examples abound, especially in novels like *La española inglesa*, *Don Quixote*, *El cerco de Numancia*, and especially in *Los trabajos de Persiles y Sigismunda*, among others.
26. We must not forget that Ricardo and Mahamut do not enter the economy of captivity by taking the qadi with them. He is given a choice, and the choice includes his freedom. They cure his wounds, prepare a boat and supply it for the necessities of his trip, returning to him some of his own money (153). As stated by El Saffar, he is even granted his wish to embrace Leonisa before he leaves (148). It is true that Christians take all his money, but not at the expense of human life. All Turks who died did so because of greed and lack of restraint in front of their own (including the lack of respect for a figure that commands it such as the qadi). However, not all Turks behave in this manner.

Works Cited

Aristotle. *Nicomachean Ethics*. Trans. Terence Irwin. Indianapolis and Cambridge: Hackett Publishing Company, 1985.

Bettetini, María. *Breve historia de la mentira. De Ulises a Pinocho*. Trans. Pepa Linares. Madrid: Cátedra, 2002.

Bianchi, Letizia. "Secreto y mentira en las *Novelas ejemplares*." *Actas de la Asociación Internacional de Hispanistas* 8 (1983): 235–42.

Bok, Sissela. *Lying: Moral Choice in Public and Private Life*. 2nd ed. New York: Vintage Books, 1999.

Cardaillac, Denise and Louis, Marie-Thérèse Carrièrre, and Rosita Subirats. "Para una nueva lectura de *El amante liberal*." *Criticón* 10 (1980): 13–29.

Cervantes, Miguel de. *Novelas ejemplares*. Ed. Jorge García López. Barcelona: Editorial Crítica, 2001.

———. "The Generous Lover" (*El amante liberal*). *Exemplary Novels I*. Ed. B.W. Ife. 4 vols. Warminster: Aris and Phillips, 1992.

Clamurro, William. *Beneath the Fiction: The Contrary Worlds of Cervantes's* Novelas ejemplares. New York: Peter Lang, 1997.

Covarrubias, Sebastián. *Tesoro de la lengua castellana o española*. Ed. Ignacio Arellano and Rafael Zafra. Madrid: Iberoamericana Vervuert, 2006.

Díaz Migoyo, Gonzalo. "La ficción cordial de *El amante liberal*." *Nueva Revista de Filología Hispánica* 35 (1987): 129–50.

Diccionario de Autoridades. Madrid: Gredos, 1990.

El Saffar, Ruth. *Novel to Romance: A Study of Cervantes's* Novelas Ejemplares. Baltimore and London: The Johns Hopkins University Press, 1974.

Fuchs, Barbara. *Passing for Spain: Cervantes and the Fictions of Identity*. Urbana and Chicago: University of Illinois Press, 2003.

Güntert, Georges. *Cervantes: Novelar el mundo desintegrado*. Barcelona: Puvill Libros, 1993.

Hegyi, Ottmar. *Cervantes and the Turks: Historical Reality versus Literary Fiction* in La gran Sultana *and* El amante liberal. Newark: Juan de la Cuesta, 1992.

Hutchinson, Steven. *Economía ética en Cervantes*. Alcalá de Henares: Centro de Estudios Cervantinos, 2001.

Johnson, Carroll B. *Cervantes and the Material World*. Urbana and Chicago: University of Illinois Press, 2000.

Johnson, Paul Michael. "A Soldier's Shame: The Specter of Captivity in *La historia del cautivo*." *Cervantes* 31.2 (2011): 153–84.

Lázaro Pulido, Manuel. "Justicia y liberalidad en los albores de la Segunda Escolástica Peninsular: Entre la Edad Media y el Siglo de Oro." *Justicia y liberalidad: Antecedentes medievales y proyecciones en el Siglo de Oro*. Ed. Corso de Estrada, Laura E. and María Idoya Zorroza. Pamplona: Ediciones Universidad de Navarra, 2012. 143–66.

Leocata, Francisco. "Justicia y liberalidad: la interpretación tomista de un pasaje aristotélico." *Justicia y liberalidad: Antecedentes medievales y proyecciones en el Siglo de Oro*. Ed. Corso de Estrada, Laura E. and María Idoya Zorroza. Pamplona: Ediciones Universidad de Navarra, 2012. 19–32.

Márquez Villanueva, Francisco. *Moros, moriscos y turcos de Cervantes: Ensayos críticos*. Barcelona: Ediciones Bellaterra, 2010.

Martin, Adrienne L. "Rereading *El amante liberal* in the Age of Contrapuntal Sexualities." *Cervantes and its Postmodern Constituencies*. New York: Garland, 1998.

Rancière, Jacques. *The Politics of Aesthetics: The Distribution of the Sensible*. Trans. Gabriel Rockhill. London: Continuum, 2004.

Sears, Theresa Ann. *A Marriage of Convenience: Ideal and Ideology in the* Novelas Ejemplares. New York: Peter Lang, 1993.

Smith, Paul Julian. "Cervantes, Goytisolo, and the Sodomitical Scene." *Cervantes and the Modernists: The Question of Influence*. Ed. Edwin Williamson. London: Tamesis, 1994. 43–54.

Zagorin, Perez. *Ways of Lying: Dissimulation, Persecution, and Conformity in Early Modern Europe*. Cambridge: Harvard University Press, 1990.

◆ 13

Intimate Strangers: Humor and the Representation of Difference in Cervantes's Drama of Captivity

Barbara Fuchs

Cervantes's captivity plays have often been read in an almost documentary vein, for the evidence they might provide of Cervantes's own experience in the bagnios or, more broadly, of that of European captives in North Africa and across the Mediterranean. Yet the plays are also sophisticated fictions that negotiate the Iberian imaginary of North Africa and Spain's own cultural complexities. As Javier Irigoyen-García has recently noted, even the most resolutely Christian representations within a play like *Los baños de Argel* are threaded through with hybrid cultural forms, as when the Christian captives in the bagnio perform a pastoral play enlivened by Moorish musicians (45–51). The ludic figures or *graciosos* who provide comic relief in these plays, I propose, also reveal the close engagements across confessional lines that marked the early modern Mediterranean. Even the most dismissive and satiric representations in these texts evoke the points of contact among the cultures of the Mediterranean, revealing via humor what may otherwise be unspeakable about early modern Spanish Christians: their profound hybridization in an enduringly mixed Spain. Even as the ludic figures vociferously mock Jews and Muslims, they betray an intimate knowledge of their confessional Others, whether in terms of customs or as erotic objects. The intimacy I explore here is above and beyond the religious contiguity between Islam, Judaism, and Christianity, or the "religious syncretism" between the latter two noted by Carlos Alvar (31), although Christianity's Jewish past is certainly one point of connection. As Moisés Castillo has observed, "En zonas de contacto cultural como Argel o Constantinopla no podemos preservar la fantasía social de que entre en Uno y el Otro haya una diferencia intrínsecamente radical" (220) (In cultural contact zones such as Algiers or Constantinople we cannot maintain the social fantasy that there is an intrinsically radical difference between Self and Other). I want to argue that such difference often proves illusory for the Spanish characters, wherever they may find themselves.

Both of the plays that concern me in the present study, *Los baños de Argel* and *La gran sultana*, feature a figure of misrule who voices the most explicit anti-Semitic and anti-Islamic prejudice in the text. Critics have struggled to characterize these figures: in ethical terms, their humor emphatically fails to translate for modern sensibilities and thus produces a profound discomfort. In formal terms, they do not match the characteristics of the Lopean *gracioso* or *figura de donaire*, who serves as the hero or heroine's aide and counsel and is generally a sympathetic figure. Instead, as Jean Canavaggio has argued, these Cervantine characters are more akin to a court buffoon or *hombre de placer*, charged with entertaining those in power (1985–86). Yet, as Aurelio González points out, Cervantes's ludic figures are not servants but instead function independently (32, 34). Hence they paradoxically enjoy far greater latitude in their actions, despite their status as captives.

Although I agree with Canavaggio and González that the Cervantine figures cannot be mapped precisely onto the Lopean model of the *gracioso*, it seems important to consider them within that framework, as audience expectations of the *gracioso*, first introduced by Lope in the 1595 *La francesilla* (González 31), would have colored the reception of Cervantes's analogous characters. Even though Cervantes's plays were read rather than performed, retaining the *gracioso* as a frame of reference sharpens the contrast between Cervantes's treatment of these figures and their more standard role in the *comedia nueva*, underscoring their unorthodox proceedings. For the Cervantine figures depart noticeably from the familiar transgressions of the *graciosos*, which involve primarily the breaching of class decorum in their relations with their masters. Cervantes's ludic figures instead invoke religious and civic hierarchies that they systematically transgress.

Most striking is the *graciosos*' negotiation of otherness while they are captives. In both *Los baños* and *La gran sultana*, Cervantes's *graciosos* betray an intimate understanding of such matters as Jewish dietary law, or the restrictions placed on Jews on the Sabbath, which they use to torture the Jews on stage. In both plays, too, they voice a low version of the erotic fascination with Muslim women that appears so often in Spanish texts. In their engagement with the abject and the forbidden, these Cervantine *graciosos* serve as a symptom of Spain's repressed cultural hybridity, which the texts must often discount in their efforts to construct a solid Christian identity in opposition to Islam or Judaism. Morevoer, their erotic attachments destabilize any effective othering of the Semitic. Although these figures are clearly humorous and meant to scandalize viewers as they entertain them, they voice a cultural and erotic proximity that is often unspeakable in more serious registers.

It is instructive to juxtapose these *gracioso* episodes to the slightly earlier discourse of maurophilia, which turned the Moor into an idealized figure of chivalric romance, and, frequently, an object of desire. As I charted in *Exotic Nation*, the maurophile print ballads of the later sixteenth century, in particular, were contested by a whole series of counter-ballads that adamantly denounced the idealization of Moors, pointing instead to the debased reality of the contemporary Moriscos (Fuchs 72–87). The satirical rebuttals are dismissive and cruel, yet they, too, speak of a familiarity with the Moriscos so viciously anatomized, detailing their abjection in contradistinction to the idealizations of literary maurophilia. In "Quien compra diez y seis moros," one of the more savage poems of Gabriel Lasso de la Vega, for example, a master scoffs at the association of Moorishness with fine *marlotas* and such, noting that slaves, who cart wood from the forest and sleep in the hayloft, have no need for such things (102–3). This kind of domestic, quotidian intimacy reflects the Moriscos' captivity and slavery after the repression of the Alpujarras uprising. It is important to remember that the captivity of Christians in North Africa is only half the story, as slavery became the fate of a large number of Moriscos remaining in Iberia after 1571. In Cervantes's version the intimacy is taken further: strong prejudice coexists with an enduring fascination not only with Muslims but with Jews, whom the *graciosos* cannot seem to leave alone, and not just within Spain, where Moriscos might function as a domesticated other, but in North Africa and Constantinople.

In the main plot of *Los baños de Argel*, the fascination with a veiled and forbidden Muslim femininity is explored through the figure of Zara, with whom Don Lope falls in love after she gives him money to rescue himself, and who, the logic of the plot demands, must prove to be a secret Christian.[1] As the play concludes, Zara leaves Algiers with the Christians, protesting, "Ya no Zara / sino María me llamo" (3080–81) (Zara no more; I am María now).[2] Her conversion neutralizes the exogamous fascination, reinscribing Christian dominance: whatever erotic entanglement develops between Zara and Lope is ultimately (and teleologically) in the service of Christian religion. At the level of the humorous subplots, however, there is no saving grace—no secret identity redeems the fascination. Thus the erotic thrall to the other remains far more disruptive. Although one might argue that humor itself defangs these moments, a psychoanalytic reading seems more appropriate, as a cultural repressed emerges via the joke.

In *Los baños*, the *gracioso* is an irreverent sexton named Tristán, allowing Cervantes to add a note of anti-clerical satire as he ironizes the character's role as a man of the Church. Pervasively identified with his role, he is always referred to as "Sacristán," from the *dramatis personae* on, even though he obviously performs no such function in Algiers, where no church requires his services. Instead, he is characterized by his appetites and his irreverence, even as he insistently—and quite possibly lewdly—underscores his role in ringing the bells to broadcast his religion and congregate the faithful. When the corsairs first attack his town to take captives, he laments: "Como persona aplicada a la Iglesia, y no al trabajo,/ mejor meneo el badajo/ que desenvaino la espada" (51–53) (As a person dedicated to the Church rather than to work, I can ring a clapper better than I unsheathe a sword). When interrogated by his captors on his profession, he explains: "Como yo soy sacristán/ toco el din, el don y el dan/ a cualquiera hora del día" (739–41) (I'm a sexton, so I play *ding, dong* at any time of day). And when he contemplates his return to Spain, it is once again with reference to his bells:

> ¡Oh campanas de España!
> ¿Cuándo entre aquestas manos
> tendré vuestros badajos?
> ¿Cuándo haré el tic y toc o el grave empino?
> ¿Cuándo de los bodigos
> que por los pobres muertos
> ofrecen ricas viudas
> veré mi arcaz colmado? (2860–67)
>
> (O bells of Spain! / When shall I hold / your clappers in these hands? / When shall I make the ding and dong or the solemn ascent? / When will I see my coffer filled / with the rolls that rich widows give / in remembrance of the poor departed ones?)

Beyond the ribaldry of Tristán's obsession with bells and clappers, these passages suggest a strong synecdochal association between the sexton and the Catholic Church, much like the synecdoche of *campana* for *iglesia* that Sebastián de Covarrubias notes.[3] Thus his symbolic association with the church is both emphasized and satirized, even as he transgresses in Algiers.

As Irigoyen-García has noted, the Sacristán is also the only character to emphasize his Old Christian origins: "Es mi tierra Mollorido,/ un lugar muy escondido,/ allá en Castilla la Vieja" (83) (My homeland is Mollorido, a very remote village in Old Castile) (Irigoyen-García 52). Yet in his encounters with the more earnest Christians in the *bagnio* the sexton insists that he will eat meat whenever his master gives him any, and not only on the permitted days, proclaiming, "Que no hay aquí teologías" (1160–66) (There are no theologies here). His concerned interlocutor, the *Viejo* whose young son will become a martyr by the end of the play, warns Tristán about the slippery slope of apostasy. His counter-example to the Sacristán's moral relativism is none other than the story of the martyred Maccabees:

VIEJO: ¿No te recuerdas, por ventura,
de aquellos niños hebreos
que nos cuenta la Escritura?
SACRISTAN: ¿Dirás por los Macabeos,
que, por no comer grosura,
se dejaron hacer piezas? (1167–72)

(OLD MAN: Don't you remember, by chance, those Hebrew children in Scripture? SEXTON: You must mean the Maccabees, who let themselves be sliced to pieces rather than eat pork.)

The story, which Tristán knows full well, is told in Maccabees 7:1–42, and features *Jewish* martyrs gladly embracing death rather than breaking dietary law—a highly ironic tale for two Chistian captives to recall, insofar as it invokes the contemporary Spanish persecution of *conversos* and underscores the continuities between Judaism and Christianity. Although, as Ruth Fine has perceptively noted, Spanish orthodoxy often distinguishes biblical Hebrews—God's chosen people, a foreshadowing of the Christian people—from the pertinacious and disgraced Jews who refused to recognize Christ as the Messiah (437–39), it is also the case that the two categories frequently collapse into each other. Thus within *Los baños*, this reference to the "Hebrew" Maccabees anticipates the portrayal of the Jew as the one who sticks to his law, and the Sacristán's testing of that resolve in the alimentary realm as he encounters the Jews of Algiers.

From dietary temptations, the Viejo turns to the erotic threat of Islamic women to Tristán's Christian identity: "Yo recelo / que si una mora os da el pie

/ deis vos de mano a ese celo" (1179–81) (I fear that if something's afoot with a Moorish woman, you'll hand over such zeal). The Sacristán claims he has already received such offers: "Luego no me han dado ya / más de dos lo que quizá / otro no lo desechara?" (1182–84) (Now, haven't two already given me what another might not reject?). Yet the Sacristán's most extensive reflection on the lure of the *mora* is spoken in jest, to discomfit the corsair captain Caurali, who is actually in love with a Christian.

When the Christians are allowed to present a play in the *bagnio*, Tristán derails it by launching into an extended praise of his (imaginary) Moorish beloved. This is an odd scene, in which he taunts Caurali either for *his* love for the Christian Costanza, or by conjuring an imaginary *mora* who is purportedly the object of his desire, or by pretending that he addresses his plaint to Caurali himself, thereby feminizing him. It is difficult to reconstruct exactly how the taunt is supposed to work, when all that the text gives us is the slim stage direction: "*Todo cuanto dice agora el Sacristán, lo diga mirando al soslayo a Caurali.*" (*Everything that the Sexton says now, he says looking sideways at* CAURALÍ). The sexton launches into an extended praise of the Muslim beloved:

De Mahoma es esta flecha
de cuya fuerza reniego.
Como cuando el sol asoma
por una montaña baja
y de súbito nos toma
y con su vista nos doma
nuestra vista y la relaja;
como la piedra balaja,
que no consiente carcoma,
tal es el tu rostro, Aja,
dura lanza de Mahoma,
que las mis entrañas raja. (2142–53)

(This arrow is from Mohammad, / whose force I renege. / Like the sun, which, when it peers / over a low mountain, / takes us unawares / and with its sight tames / and disarms our sight; / like the carbuncle, / which resists all decay, / so is your countenance, Aja, / a hard lance of Mohammed / that tears my entrails apart.)

The Sacristán here both ventriloquizes and satirizes exogamous desire, rehearsing a poem that Cervantes himself uses also in the novella *El amante liberal*, where two Spanish poets fall for a beautiful blonde Moor in a more earnest moment. Yet the iteration goes beyond the redoubled Cervantine moments: Pedro Córdoba has discovered that these lines are not original to Cervantes, but appear in a manuscript miscellany of the humanist Alvar Gómez de Castro. Córdoba argues that the verses are unlikely to be Gómez de Castro's own, but are more probably part of the miscellany of verses, songs, and sayings that he collected (50). They thus suggest the much broader currency of such exogamous fantasies, which Cervantes merely replays. Although Cervantes frames the verses for great effect, then, their prehistory suggests that a Christian directing love poems to a Muslim was hardly an extraordinary occurrence. The Sacristán's humorous evocation of this desire for a *mora* undercuts the ideological certainties of the main plot, in which Moors automatically fall for Christians, but Christians only love Moors if they turn out to be Christians in the end. Although it is spoken in jest, the evocation of exogamous love bespeaks a kind of erotic intimacy that the play, with its strong warnings against apostasy, would otherwise belie.

The intimation of Christian desire for a Moor that is deflected through humor in *Los baños* returns more forcefully in *La gran sultana*. The main plot of this play, as is well known, concerns the love of an Ottoman emperor for the Christian Spanish captive Catalina, who so enchants him that he agrees to let her remain a Christian. Yet whereas the main plot emphasizes the strength of Christian faith even at the heart of the Muslim world, the humorous subplot presents exogamous desire in a more complicated light. The *gracioso* figure in this play is the captive Madrigal, who, like the Sacristán, constantly pokes fun at Muslims and Jews. Also, like the Sacristán, Madrigal is granted a kind of official status as the Spanish voice of the text. Whereas the Sacristán refers constantly to his ringing of the bells, Madrigal tells his captors that he is a *pregonero*, or town crier (2162).[4] The play insistently links him both to ventriloquism and to privileged speech, as he invents a series of linguistic hoaxes to prolong his life, from promising the qadi that he will teach an elephant how to speak, to claiming that he can interpret the prophecies offered by the birds. Despite these perversions of his role as mouthpiece, moreover, Madrigal becomes by the end a veritable author figure, who will carry the story that the audience has just witnessed safely back to Madrid.[5]

This conclusion is by no means evident as the play begins. Madrigal, it appears, has been seduced by an "alárabe," a dalliance that makes him reluctant to escape captivity. In his first encounter with the spy Andrea, who offers to help him escape, the captive demurs, explaining, "Son las leyes / del gusto poderosas sobretodo" (502–3) (The laws of taste are powerful over all). This is not Andrea's first attempt to get him out, as he reminds Madrigal:

ANDREA: La memoria
tenéis dada a adobar, a lo que entiendo,
o reducida a voluntad no buena.
¿No os acordáis que os vi y hablé la noche
que recogí a los cinco y vos quisistes
quedaros por no más de vuestro gusto,
poniendo por excusa que os tenía
amor rendida el alma, y que una alárabe,
con nuevo cautiverio y nuevas leyes,
os la tenía encadenada y presa?
MADRIGAL: Verdad; y aun todavía tengo el yugo
al cuello, todavía estoy cautivo,
todavía la fuerza poderosa
de amor tiene sujeto a mi albedrío.

(ANDREA: Your memory's gone to rot, as far as I can tell, or been reduced to no good purposes. Don't you remember that I saw you and spoke to you the night I picked up those five, and you wanted to stay solely for your pleasure, with the excuse that your soul had surrendered to love, and that an Arab woman had imprisoned and chained it in a new captivity and new laws?
MADRIGAL: True; and I still have the yoke around my neck, I'm still captive, the great power of love still rules over me.)

Madrigal's *cautiverio*, it turns out, is much more of a Petrarchan metaphor than an actual hardship, and his willing servitude ironizes the earnest suffering on which a captivity plot would seem to depend. Madrigal languishes in Constantinople because that is what he desires.

Given Madrigal's erotic thralldom, and his reluctance to fight his *gusto*, Andrea taunts him: "¿No sois vos español?" (506) (Are you not a Spaniard?). Madrigal's lengthy and blustery bravado in response is clearly compensatory, an attempt by a subject fully hybridized to claim purity and separateness:

MADRIGAL: ¿Por qué? ¿Por esto?
Pues por las once mil de malla juro
y por el alto, dulce, omnipotente
deseo que se encierra bajo el hopo
de cuatro acomodados porcionistas,
que he de romper por montes de diamantes,
y por dificultades indecibles
y he de llevar mi libertad en peso

sobre los propios hombros de mi gusto,
y entrar triunfando en Nápoles la bella
con dos o tres galeras levantadas
por mi industria o valor, y Dios delante,
y dando a la Anunciada los dos bucos,
quedaré con el uno rico y próspero,
y no ponerme ahora a andar por trena,
cargado de temor y de miseria.

ANDREA: ¡Español sois, sin duda! (507–22)

(MADRIGAL: Why? Because of this? Well, by the eleven thousand coats of mail, and by the high, sweet, potent desire under the collar of four rich boarders, I swear that I will break through mountains of diamonds and unspeakable obstacles, and I shall hoist my liberty on the very shoulders of my pleasure, and enter triumphant into the beautiful Naples with two or three galleys that will have rebelled because of my cleverness and valor, and God willing, after giving two ships to the Annunziata, I'll live rich and prosperous with the other one, instead of wandering through the bagnios weighted down with misery and dread.
ANDREA: You're a Spaniard, there's no question!)

Madrigal protests too much. Despite Andrea's claim that the oath identifies Madrigal as a Spaniard, the latter's fantasy never sees him back to Spain, and instead leaves him in an in-between existence, plying the Mediterranean on a galley.[6]

Moreover, although the *gracioso* finally manages to tear himself away, presumably taking the story to Madrid, his tangential love-plot is never really resolved. Madrigal's *gusto* is interesting precisely because it does not align itself neatly with the large-scale ideological maneuvers of the text or its categorizations; instead, it remains personal, unpredictable and irrepressible. The class dynamic is arresting here, too. Madrigal recalls the figure of Launcelot in Shakespeare's *The Merchant of Venice*, who taunts Jessica about her imperfect conversion to Christianity—she will always be her father's daughter—while sleeping with a "blackamoor," whom he has impregnated. Through these figures of low humor, the texts invite us to reflect on the relation between class and other forms of social distinction. The permeability of race and religion varies according to the class or status of those who would breach their boundaries.

If eros establishes a paradoxical intimacy between Spaniards and their ostracized others in *Los baños de Argel* and *La gran sultana*, food quickly becomes similarly charged, as anticipated by the reference to the Maccabees noted above. In subplots that may have worked for early modern audiences but have not aged well, Tristán and Madrigal continuously taunt and torture the Jews of Algiers and Constantinople, respectively, who often appear even more abject than the captives. What interests me is the store of cultural knowledge that underlies their attacks, effective precisely because they understand the intricacies of Jewish dietary law. Though some elements on which these taunts depend are broadly popularized, as when Madrigal drops a chunk of boar-bacon (pork not being available) into the Jew's stew, for example—others reflect a more intimate understanding. As Fine puts it, the plays exhibit "un notorio conocimiento de . . . las leyes de *kashrut*" (442) (a striking knowledge of the laws of *kashrut*).

The episode in *La Gran Sultana* is fleeting, and occurs largely off stage. Given that it is no easy feat to procure pork in a Muslim city, its complicated provenance must be addressed explicitly:

MADRIGAL: Ciertos jenízaros
mataron en el monte el otro día
un puerco jabalí, que le vendieron
a los cristianos de Mamud Arráez,
de los cuales compré de la papada
lo que está en la cazuela sepultado
para dar sepultura a estos malditos,
con quien tengo rencor y mal talante:
a quien el diablo pape, engulla y sorba. (434–42)

(MADRIGAL: Some janissaries killed a wild boar in the forest the other day, which they sold to Mamud Arráez's Christians, from whom I bought part of the jowl that's now sunk in the pot to sink these wretches whom I resent. May the devil eat, devour, and sip them up!)

Despite the difficulty of procuring pork, Madrigal would rather use it to torture the Jews than consume it himself. Thus, his very deliberate prank is an attempt to mark his difference from both Jews and Muslims who surround him, in what Madera Allan terms a "self-conscious performance of national religious identity" (188). Such a performance might be particularly important not only vis-à-vis the Jews, but in relation to the janissaries—a military corps made up entirely of converts to Islam—invoked here. The excess of the scene, and Madrigal's protestations, cannot disguise the fact that this Spaniard refuses to leave from Constantinople, as we learn soon after.[7]

In *Los baños*, the negotiation of dietary law is more detailed and extensive. The sexton enters carrying a *cazuela mojí*, a vegetable dish with eggs and cheese, which he has stolen from the Jew and which he now offers for ransom ("Rescátame esta cazuela" [1682] [Ransom this stew from me]). Tristan's power depends on the religious prohibitions that circumscribe the Jew's actions and render him even more powerless than the Spanish captive:

JUDÍO:	Hoy es sábado, y no tengo qué comer, y me mantengo de aqueso que guisé ayer.
SACRISTÁN:	Vuelve a guisar de comer.
JUDÍO:	No, que a mi ley contravengo. (1677–81)

(JEW: Today is Saturday [Sabbath], and I have nothing to eat, so I feed myself with what I cooked yesterday.[8]
SEXTON: Cook something else.
JEW: No, for I'd go against my Law.)

The Jew cannot cook on the Sabbath, and thus depends on the now infinitely valuable *cazuela*, previously prepared, for his sustenance. As he is also forbidden from conducting business on the Sabbath, he depends on the Sacristán to assign a price to the *cazuela* and to take his payment, adding insult to injury.

The Sacristán knowledgeably mocks the prohibitions that delimit the Jew's behavior, interrogating the inanimate *cazuela* on its own worth, as though he, too, were forbidden from setting a price for what he has stolen: "Di, cazuela: ¿cuánto vales? / 'Paréceme a mí que valgo / cinco reales, y no más.' / ¡Mentís, a fe de hidalgo!" (1701–4) (Tell me, pot: what are you worth? "I think I'm worth five *reales*, and no more." You lie, by my faith as a gentleman!). Tristán's ventriloquizing outburst reminds the audience that part of what is at stake in this scene is the incommensurability between "*fe de hidalgo*" and the Jew's "*mi ley*." Yet there is a certain discomfort in that *fe* being summoned in such a ribald context: Tristán is emphatically not an *hidalgo*, and he has previously made it clear just how flexible he is where *teologías* are concerned. His ability to speak in different voices here, as in the episode where he ventriloquizes the love for a Moorish woman, also ironizes the notion of any self-identical *hidalgo* core. Moreover, Tristán's power in this scene is entirely dependent on the Jew's adherence to his own law, which clearly holds more sway over its adherents than does Christian *teología*, at least in the comic subplot.[9]

The injuries mount when the Jew must ask the Sacristán to take the money from inside his shirt to pay the "ransom" for the *cazuela*. He takes three times as much as he had claimed, vowing that this is giving the Jew "credit" for the *cazuelas* that he plans to steal from him in the future. Before turning over the dish, he further taunts the Jew, tasting it and detailing all the *tref*, that is, non-kosher elements that it does *not* contain: "¿Que hay tan gustoso guisado? / No es carne de landrecillas / ni de la que a las costillas / se pega el bayo que es trefe" (1716–19) (Is there any such delicious dish? It's not nerve meat, nor meat that sticks to the ribs of the bay horse, which is *tref*). This passage seems to me rather remarkable, as Fine also notes: it is one thing for the Sacristán to know that Jews cannot cook on their Sabbath, but the detail here, and the use of the Hebrew *trefe*, or *tref*, for forbidden meat bespeaks an intimate familiarity with Jewish dietary law, as does the detailed account of what meat can and cannot be eaten. Although Jewish law was paradoxically circulated by the Inquisition, in an attempt to help Spaniards denounce their crypto-Jewish neighbors, Tristán here adopts the subject position of one bound by that law.[10] In his mockery, the Sacristán speaks as a Jew. Recall that Tristán also uses ventriloquism to rehearse his proximity to the other in his faux plaint for a Moorish beloved, a few scenes after his exchange with the Jew (and of course ventriloquism features prominently in the Madrigal plot, as I note above).

Although Fine notes that commentators and lexicographers have missed the Hebrew origins of *trefe*, she fails to recognize the deliberate erasure of what was surely a widely recognized etymology, at least in some quarters (443). Francisco del Rosal, in his unpublished *Diccionario etimológico* (licensed in 1601), gives not one but two Greek etymologies: "Trefe: cosa sin jugo. Del griego *terphos* que es la corteza y cáscara de cualquiera cosa, porque ésta no participa del jugo y virtud de la planta. Y asimesmo *trefe de livianos*, enfermedad que dicen *tísica*. Pero de aquí infiero que debe decirse de *Atrophe*, que del griego será lo que no sustenta, nutre o mantiene" (293r) (*Trefe*: a thing without juice/essence. From the Greek *terphos* which is the crust or shell of something, because this does not form part of the essence or virtue of the plant. Similarly *trefe de livianos*, a sickness called consumption. But from this I infer that it should be *atrophe*, which in the Greek is that which does not provide sustenance, nurture or maintain).[11] Covarrubias gives as the definition "cosa ligera que facilmente se dobla, se ensancha, y encoge, por ser de cuerpo delgado y floxo: y assí el que está flaco y enfermo, dizé estar deble y trefe. Antonio Nebrisense dize assí: trefe de *livianos pulmunarius, a, um, phthisicus, a, um*. Trefedad, dolencia, phtisis is" (976) (a slight thing that is easily doubles its size, stretches and shrinks, since it is of a thin and light nature: and thus one who is thin and sick is said to be weak and *trefe*. Antonio de Nebrija claims that: he who is *trefe de livianos pulminarius* has consumption sickness). These Greek and Latin references classicize a term that has a very different origin, recognized, though only partially, by the *Diccionario de Autoridades*: "TREFE. Lo que es ligero, delgado, y floxo, por lo qual facilmente se ensancha, dobla, y encoge. Usase algunas veces por falso, o falto de ley. Es voz Hebrea, que significa enfermo, o dañado. Lat. *Levis. Spongiosus*" (6.347) (TREFE. That which is slight, thin, and weak, and thus is easy to stretch, increase, and shrink. It is sometimes used for a deceptive person who has no religion. It is from the Hebrew meaning sick or injured. Lat. *Levis. Spongiosus*).[12] Del Rosal and Covarrubias thus perform the etymological cleansing of what was surely a widely recognized term in early modern Iberia, given its frequency in accusations to the Inquisition and depositions before it, as historians and linguists have documented (Perry and Cruz 183–84; Dworkin 115; Eberenz and De la Torre 246–47).[13]

There are other ironies in the *cazuela* episode, of course: the dish must be ransomed from a captive, who himself requires freeing but whose captivity has taught him no sympathy for other marginalized figures, so that he ends by threatening that he will next take the Jew's child, presumably for ransom, or, as he insinuates, to consume him: "¡Vive Dios, / que os tengo de hurtar un niño / antes de los meses dos: / y aun si las uñas aliño . . . !/¡Dios me entiende! (1722–26) (By God, I shall rob a child from you before two months are up; and if I season its feet . . . God knows what I mean!). Between these two invocations of his God, the Sacristán terrifyingly threatens to steal a Jewish child and eat him, once he has improved the flavor.

His blustering threat is partially carried out in Act III, where he appears before the qadi carrying the Jew's baby son (2514 and following). As Or Hasson notes, the episode inverts the anti-Semitic chestnut that Jews steal Christian children (495). The stage direction that precedes this moment betrays the violence of the scene: "*(Entra el SACRISTAN con un niño en las mantillas, fingido, y tras él el JUDIO de la cazuela.)*" (*Enter the SEXTON with a baby in blankets, make-believe, and behind him the JEW of the casserole*). The direction specifies that no real child need be subjected to this experience, but what does that suggest about the joke to which the audience is treated here?

The Sacristán claims that although he wants the child for ransom, he will bring it up as a Christian if the Jew does not pay up:

CADI: ¿Para qué quiere el niño?
SACRISTAN: ¿No está bueno?
Para que le rescaten, si no quieren

que le críe y le enseñe el Padrenuestro.
Qué decís vos, Raquel o Sedequías,
Farés, Sadoc, o Zabulón, o diablo? (2517–21)

(CADÍ: What does he want the child for?
SEXTON: Isn't he a good one? So that they ransom him, if they don't want me to raise him and teach him the Our Father. What do you say, Rachel or Zedekiah, Pharez, Sadoc, Zebulon or devil?)

The more savage appetites insinuated earlier to scare the Jew have here been reduced to the question of the baby's delectability. And once again, as in the reference to the Maccabees, the Sexton reminds us of his broad knowledge of the Old Testament, even if he uses it to mock the Jew. Pharez and Sadoc, both ancestors of Jesus mentioned in Matthew (1:3 and 1:14, respectively), are particularly striking figures to invoke, as they recall the genealogical continuity between Judaism and Christianity. As Fine cogently puts it, "Lo judío, lo repudiado, contamina lo valorado, lo hebreo; ¿o acaso ocurre a la inversa y es lo hebreo lo que eleva a la 'canalla miserable' y la reinserta en su anulado estatus de pueblo elegido?" (Fine 444) (Does what is repudiated as Jewish contaminate what is valued as Hebrew, or is it perhaps the inverse, so that what is Hebrew raises the 'miserable rabble,' restoring them to their annulled status as a chosen people?). This instability haunts the text, as opposites collapse into each other and the intimate proximity of the Other is revealed.

The qadi quickly resolves the issue of the kidnapped Jewish child, demanding his return, although he agrees to make the Jew pay Tristán for the time he has spent "para robarle este hideputa" (2544) (to rob this whoreson from him), as his tormentor endearingly puts it. And yet despite the redoubled joke, on the Jewish scapegoat and the oblivious Muslim judge, the cruelty of the moment has not been fully resolved. Instead, it hangs in the air as the scene quickly changes to that of a most serious threat against a Christian child.

The uncomfortable humor of the kidnapping is further qualified by its juxtaposition with the most tragic and melodramatic of *Los baños*'s many plots: the martyrdom of young Francisquito, who refuses to convert to Islam. Immediately following the courtroom burlesque above, an aged father witnesses on stage his son's martyrdom and death, which the former anguishedly welcomes as an *imitatio Christi*. This extraordinarily heightened moment cannot but color what comes immediately before it. Even if in this case farce precedes tragedy, the analogies between the two episodes are unavoidable, adumbrating any Christian exceptionalism.[14] While one Christian jokingly threatens to raise his Jewish captive into forced Christianity, the young Christian's resistance to forced conversion leads to his bloody death. Here, the mirroring between Christians and their Muslim captors is no longer a matter of shared material culture or reciprocal attraction, but rather of their refusal to respect the faith of another. Yet the Christian's intimate knowledge of the Jew, whom both Christian and Muslims persecute in Algiers, complicates any simple binary. Christians and their Muslim captors share more that they realize, but the Christians, like the Muslims, also share a history with Jews.

Yet what significance can we ultimately ascribe to characters whom even the most sophisticated critics would marginalize as "limited to the sphere of the ridiculous and grotesque" (Mariscal 204)? I would argue that they need not be serious for us to take them seriously. Cervantes underscores their emblematic potential, if not their representativity: the Sacristán as synecdoche of the church; Madrigal as the mouthpiece of Spanishness, and offers in them a resolutely anti-idealizing vision of Mediterranean connectedness. At issue is not whether Cervantes is promoting or reflecting the anti-Semitism of his time, as critics from Ámerico Castro on have debated, but what the representation of the cultural and erotic intimacy between the Christian *graciosos* and their victims in Algiers reveals.

Elsewhere, I have explored at length the pleasurable taking from Al-Andalus that characterizes so much of early modern Iberia's aristocratic cultures, from the luxurious textiles and garments in Isabella of Castile's wardrobe to the dashing *juego de cañas* so favored by Philip II (Fuchs, *Exotic*). Cervantes's *graciosos* in *Los baños* and *La gran sultana* suggest how, beyond the realm of the aristocratic and the geographic confines of Spain, pleasure and appetite complicate any sense of distinction as Christian captives engage the Other in visceral detail and with great technical mastery. There is a broader, messier taking beyond the confines of aristocratic pleasure, as shared knowledge and shared preferences lead to actual entanglements. The *graciosos* are not merely continuing a multi-confessional *habitus*, or persevering in customs of Andalusi origin; instead, with their outsize appetites they actively consume Jews and their food, and sleep with Muslim women. Their embodied engagement, however qualified by humor, ironizes the most trenchant ideological stances that one might find in these plays of captivity, emphasizing instead how messily identity is constituted in an Iberia that is marked, as ever, both by its multi-confessional roots and by a Muslim Mediterranean.

Notes

I am grateful to Isabel Gómez for her research assistance on this essay.

1. Although this is the plot that Cervantes reprises in the Captive's Tale of *Don Quijote* I, between the Captive and a *mora* now named Zoraida, there is no *gracioso* figure in that version of the story. One might argue that the prose version allows Cervantes to develop other ways to qualify and complicate the story of conversion, such as the opacity of Zoraida's motives and the hugely sympathetic representation of her betrayed father, Agi Morato.
2. All translations of *Los baños* and *La gran sultana* are from Barbara Fuchs and Aaron Ilika's 2009 edition. I have made some small emendations for clarity or emphasis. All other translations are mine unless otherwise noted.
3. See Covarrubias's fascinating and extensive entry for *campana*, in which he both notes, "Campana se toma algunas vezes por la iglesia o parrochia" (279) (Bell is sometimes used for the church and the parish) and recounts the power of bells to promote insurgency, explaining, "el Gran Turco no las consiente ni usa, de temor que con su sonido no alteren ni convoquen la comunidad" (279) (the Great Turk does not approve of nor use them, out of fear that their sound might upset or disturb the community).
4. On the related figure of the herald or Pursevant as "the crown's roving tongue" (278), see Lezra *Unspeakable* 275 and Fuchs *Mimesis* 128–29.
5. As Jacques Lezra notes, Madrigal must leave Constantinople in order to profit from telling his story, yet he can only tell his story "by remaining, as his admirers will say, a 'captive' of the city." ("Translated" 177).
6. Despite noting the competing claims on Madrigal's allegiance, Lezra oversimplifies his relationship to Spain when he claims, "Madrigal then seems to embody the most assertive form of syncretism, its most licentious, instrumental, and thorough manifestation: he has abandoned his national character (he abjures being Spanish), he takes on a Muslim lover, he commands animal as well as human languages" ("Translated" 175).
7. The metatheatrical dimension also complicates the joke here. As Maryrica Ortiz Lottman notes in an essay on *La gran sultana*, repeated references to a *cazuela* would necessarily invoke the section of the theater of that same name, reserved for common women (77). What would it mean to throw pork into the theatrical *cazuela*? The reference to the audience itself as tainted or mixed is very suggestive.
8. Compare this use of *sábado* with Covarrubias's definition, which begins: "Cerca de los judíos era el día de fiesta, en el que cessavan de toda obra servil, aunque fuesse necessaria para su sustento" (918) (As concerns the Jews, it was the day of rest in which they ceased all type of labor, even if it was necessary for sustinence) and goes on to cite the Hebrew etymology. Unlike the definition for *trefe*, this one cannot avoid the trace of both Hebrew and of Judaism in Spanish quotidian experience.

9. Kanellos notes: "Whereas the Sacristán is inconstant in his faith, the Jew, like the rest of the Christian captives, will not give an inch on any matter of faith" (50).
10. See for example the Edict of Faith for the city of Cuenca, 1624, in David Gitlitz, *Secrecy and Deceit* (626).
11. I am grateful to Javier Irigoyen-García for this reference.
12. The reference to a Hebrew origin for *trefe* disappears after the 1739 entry in the *Diccionario de Autoridades*, never to return. The 1884 edition of the *Autoridades* adds a Greek etymology, from the word for "versátil, variable," which is not dropped until 1914, when it is noted that *trefe* might share an origin with *trifa*. The 1899 edition recognizes a Hebrew origin for the latter.
13. For an analogous case of etymological erasure, including Covarrubias, see my discussion of how the Moorish *juego de cañas* was classicized in *Exotic Nation* (99–100).
14. Kanellos notes the connection here, although he reads to very different ends: "But the most obvious, analogous incident in the play is the Sacristán's kidnapping of the Jew's son for ransom. This is exactly what the Arabs have done to the Spaniards. These episodes must be construed as veiled criticism of Spanish anti-Semitism" (50).

Works Cited

Allan, Madera. *Food Fight: Taste in the Inquisitorial Trials of Ciudad Real*. Diss, University of Pennsylvania. Philadelphia: Proquest, 2009.

Alvar, Carlos. "Cervantes y los judíos." *Cervantes y las religiones*. Ed. Ruth Fine and Santiago López Navia. Madrid: Iberoamericana/Frankfurt: Vervuert, 2008. 29–54.

Canavaggio, Jean. "Sobre lo cómico en el teatro cervantino: Tristán y Madrigal, bufones in partibus." *Nueva Revista de Filología Hispánica* 34.2 (1985/1986): 538–547.

Castillo, Moisés R. "¿Ortodoxia Cervantina? Un análisis de *La gran sultana*, *El trato de Argel* y *Los baños de Argel*." *Bulletin of the Comediantes* 56.2 (2004): 219–40.

Cervantes, Miguel de. *The Bagnios of Algiers and The Great Sultana: Two Plays of Captivity*. Ed. and trans. Barbara Fuchs and Aaron Ilika. Philadelphia: University of Pennsylvania Press, 2009.

———. *Teatro completo*. Ed. Florencio Sevilla Arroyo and Antonio Rey Hazas. Barcelona: Planeta, 1987.

Córdoba, Pedro. "Cita y autocita en Cervantes." *La réception du texte littéraire; 7*. Ed. Jean-Pierre Étienvre and Leonardo Castro Tovar. Zaragoza: Casa de Velázquez, 1988. 39–50.

Covarrubias Horozco, Sebastián. *Tesoro de la lengua castellana o española (1611)*. Ed. Martin de Riquer. Barcelona: Alta Fulla, 1993.

Dworkin, Steven N. *A History of the Spanish Lexicon: A Linguistic Perspective*. Oxford: Oxford University Press, 2012.

Eberenz, Rolf, and Mariela de La Torre. *Conversaciones estrechamente vigiladas:*

Interacción coloquial y español oral en las actas inquisitoriales de los siglos XV a XVII. Zaragoza: Libros Pórticos, 2003.

Fine, Ruth. "El entrecruzamiento de lo hebreo y lo converso en la obra de Cervantes: un encuentro singular." *Cervantes y las religiones*. Ed. Ruth Fine and Santiago López Navia. Madrid: Iberoamericana/Frankfurt: Vervuert, 2008. 435–51.

Fuchs, Barbara. *Exotic Nation: Maurophilia and the Construction of Early Modern Spain.* Philadelphia: U Pennsylvania P, 2009.

———. *Mimesis and Empire: The New World, Islam, and European Identities.* Cambridge, U.K.: Cambridge University Press, 2001.

Gitlitz, David. *Secrecy and Deceit: The Religion of the Crypto-Jews*. Albuquerque: University of New Mexico Press, 2002.

González, Aurelio. "El gracioso de Cervantes, un modelo alternativo." *Teatro de Palabras: Revista sobre teatro áureo* 2 (2008): 29–44. Web. 6 Sept. 2012.

Hasson, Or. "Los baños de Argel: un análisis del tratamiento cervantino de lo hebreo y lo judío desde un punto de vista kleiniano." *Cervantes y las religiones*. Ed. Ruth Fine and Santiago López Navia. Madrid: Iberoamericana/Frankfurt: Vervuert, 2008. 473–502.

Irigoyen-García, Javier. "'La música ha sido hereje:' Pastoral Performance, Moorishness, and Cultural Hybridity in *Los baños de Argel*." *Bulletin of the Comediantes* 62.2 (2010): 45–62.

Kanellos, Nicolas. "The Anti-Semitism of Cervantes' *Los baños de Argel* and *La gran sultana*: A Reappraisal." *Bulletin of the Comediantes* 27 (1975): 48–52.

Lasso de la Vega, Gabriel. *Manojuelo de romances*. Madrid: Saeta, 1942.

Lezra, Jacques. "Translated Turks on the Early Modern Stage." *Transnational Exchange in Early Modern Theater.* Ed. Robert Henke and Eric Nicholson. Ashgate, 2008. 159–178.

———. *Unspeakable Subjects: The Genealogy of the Event in Early Modern Europe.* Stanford: Stanford University Press, 1997.

Mariscal, George. "*La gran sultana* and the Issue of Cervantes's Modernity." *Revista de Estudios Hispánicos* 28.2 (May 1994): 185–211.

Ortiz Lottman, Maryrica. "*La gran sultana*: Transformations in Secret Speech." *Cervantes: Bulletin of the Cervantes Society of America* 16.1 (1996): 74–90.

Perry, Mary Elizabeth and Anne J. Cruz. *Cultural Encounters: The Impact of the Inquisition in Spain and the New World.* Berkeley and Los Angeles: University of California Press, 1991.

Rosal, Francisco del. *Diccionario etimológico. Alfabeto primero de Origen y Etimología de todos los vocablos originales de la Lengua Castellana*. Ed. facsimile Enrique Gómez Aguado. Madrid: CSIC, 1992.

Afterword

Ebbs and Flows: Looking at Spain from a Mediterranean Perspective

Luis Martín-Estudillo and Nicholas Spadaccini

In recent years students of the "Spanish" Middle Ages and early modern period have been reassessing their areas or fields of study at a vertiginous pace. Yet it is also the case that traditional approaches to the cultures and texts of those periods remain part of a larger discussion that has called into question the very concepts of Spanish literature and, indeed, what came to be known as Hispanism (Epps and Fernández Cifuentes; Moraña; Resina; Ugarte). As argued by the editors and some of the contributors to this latest *Hispanic Issues* volume, approaching the Middle Ages and the early modern period from a Mediterranean perspective implies a heightened awareness of the nuances of cross-cultural contacts, tensions, and exchanges, while at the same time highlighting the critic's interdisciplinary disposition and the fact that s/he too—like those who practiced the old philology—could be understood by her/his locus and time of enunciation. In the end, what we see in these current critical trends is a progressive attempt at a redefinition or reconfiguration of traditional fields, placing them under the larger hermeneutic umbrellas of Iberian and Mediterranean studies. These conceptual arrangements shift the focus away from Castilian literature and culture and its purported role in the construction of Spanish national identity in favor of a greater awareness of the diversity of cultures and complex relations both within Iberia and, above all, within the greater, imagined Mediterranean. The purported aim of the present volume is to demonstrate through a series of studies undertaken by literary cultural critics, historians, and scholars of religion working in an interdisciplinary mode from the perspective of their respective disciplines, that medieval and early modern Iberia are best assessed if seen as part of the Mediterranean, a frame of reference that is said to include Africa and the Middle East and which, according to the editors, would also serve the cause of combating the Eurocentric tendencies (Introduction 4–5) of more traditional approaches to the "Spanish" Middle Ages and the *Siglos de Oro* (or the Renaissance and Baroque periods). It is fair to say that, following trends that have led to a strong renovation of the humanities, our fields have moved beyond the limited horizon of "old-school" Hispanism, which has become an object of historical study (Faber) and whose relevance and legitimacy as a set of intellectual practices have been submitted to intense scrutiny (Epps and Fernández Cifuentes; Moraña; Resina; Ugarte).

With forty published volumes since its inception more than a quarter century ago, *Hispanic Issues* has also been a forum for this discussion, one that has been carried respectfully toward scholars of the past whose work was defined by their own present, traditions, and agendas. One thinks, for example, of Ramón Menéndez Pidal's monumental work on the *Cantar de Mío Cid* and his nationalistic drive to reinforce the notion of the autochthonous emergence of the Castilian epic, an editorial practice that spanned some six decades and began to be challenged in a meaningful way with the appearance of new editions during the waning years of the Franco dictatorship (Smith 1–21; see also Lacarra). Moreover, one need not limit oneself to the work of Menéndez Pidal or that of Marcelino Menéndez y Pelayo to underscore a nationalistic bent in the forging of a canon. For example, it is well known that already in the early modern period, the editorial fortunes of Garcilaso de la Vega—the great Castilian poet from Toledo—were tied to the projection of Spanish as a "'national' hegemonic language" (Zavala 52–73). We mention these examples because revisiting the issue of canon formation could prove to be a productive endeavor beyond the historical interest that they might hold for those who aim to illuminate the inner history of our disciplines. It is also the case that we can neither dismiss the philological work of the past nor fail to acknowledge the fact that issues related to cultural and religious diversity and transnationalism have long been of interest to practitioners within our disciplines, as can be seen in the illuminating work of scholars such as Américo Castro, Claudio Guillén, Luce López Baralt, and others (including scholars from other disciplines), who contributed so much to the emergence of a post-philological Hispanism. To be sure, university departments continue to offer courses on the literatures and cultures of specific countries and, in the case of Spain, some of them still privilege traditional readings of the Castilian classics. Yet it is also the case that in recent years courses have been reframed to highlight issues of cultural and "national" diversity, with a heightened awareness of the tensions that have always existed between centers and peripheries and between local and global concerns. Such changes have even affected the Spanish university, whose departments of *filología* (with some exceptions) were seen as bastions of traditionalist approaches well after American academia had turned to cultural studies. Many of those departments are now sites of initiatives that embrace the study of diversity.[1] One thinks of the work undertaken by José-Carlos Mainer and Fernando Cabo Aseguinolaza, who have argued that an understanding of Spanish culture necessarily requires familiarity with the cultural and literary production in Basque, Catalan, and Galician, and that centers of cultural activity are also to be sought beyond Madrid and Barcelona. Of course, the complexities of such diversity is even more manifest when examined from a Mediterranean perspective, especially at a time of increased circulation and migrations of people and capital, with Africa (especially, though not exclusively, North Africa) and the Middle East playing an important role in the way in which a new Spain is imagined through practices of quotidien life, popular culture, the electronic media, and new literatures generated by immigrant groups (Martín-Estudillo and Spadaccini).

The value of the present volume is to have shown through powerful arguments and case studies that the multiplicity of voices, languages, cultures, and traditions (including the reimagining of classical literary tropes) can be assessed productively from a Mediterranean perspective, one which, to our mind, also brings those texts in consonance with present-day concerns and interdisciplinary interests that go beyond parochial, national identification. This afterword is written with those concerns in mind and with the purpose of reading the past to illuminate the present.

In academia, Mediterranean studies, as well as other emerging lines of work, arose from an awareness of the limitations of approaches that are (self-) constricted by the political realities of the nation-state or by the predominance given to a handful of languages, topics, or forms of expression. While those constraints often originated in the need for specialized scholarship, they also became a hindrance for inquiries into the sophisticated and multifarious cultural landscapes of places such as Iberia. As many of the essays in this volume have shown, within the context of the broader Mediterranean, analyses that seek to address its complexities would do well to take into account the impact of the exchanges, points of contact, and tensions that have existed between its different populations and their many Others throughout history. These phenomena often transcend political borders, something which is as true in today's globalized world as in pre-1914 Europe. Thus, if at the end of the sixteenth century, after Lepanto and the encounters over Cyprus and Tunis, the Mediterranean "exits world history" (Braudel 469–514; qtd. in Ragionieri 84), such an exit was surely temporary, for it was to reenter it following the decline of the Ottoman Empire and, most especially, from the days of the Cold War until the present, with an ever-changing Middle East marked by identitarian conflicts along social, cultural, religious, and political lines (Ragionieri 84–85).

The present volume provides a stimulating discussion on the need to examine Spanish history, literature, and culture from a broader, interdisciplinary, and encompassing perspective, one that allows us to examine both the relative strength and limitations of traditional assumptions and approaches, as argued incisively by Brian A. Catlos in his critique of the well-known essentialist debate between Américo Castro and Claudio Sánchez Albornoz regarding the nature of Spain and/in its history and the fact that, in the end, "each of them reifies and essentializes Islam, Christianity, and Judaism" (in this volume). Mediterranean studies is a particularly appropriate framework for addressing the sort of cultural exchanges that preceded the emergence of nation-states, political entities that generated a variety of obstacles (military, administrative, judicial, etc.) to the kinds of interactions that often took place within cultural spaces that eschewed clear identitarian demarcations. This can be seen not only in some of the texts that are studied or referenced in this volume but also in well-known others. One thinks of Cervantes, whose "The Captive's Tale" in *Don Quijote* "highlights the important function of the renegade in the new societies created on the Mediterranean frontiers" (Garcés 546). It is within those cultural spaces (Homi K. Bhabha's "in-between") that Cervantes elaborates "new signs of identity" that question the basis of an imagined unitary Spain underpinned by blood statutes and xenophobia and that recall failed imperial ambitions in the Mediterranean forged in the name of a universal Christian empire. To some extent this same vision is at play in *Los baños de Argel* (probably reworked prior to its publication in 1615), which also deals with the theme of captivity and whose "action . . . echoes the fading or crumbling military dreams of the previous period, following the new course of Spain's Mediterranean politics" (Canavaggio 38; our translation), as attention shifted to northern Europe, thus deemphasizing the struggle against Islam (Domínguez Ortiz 78–79). In the texts mentioned above and in Cervantes's exemplary novella, *El amante liberal,* the space of captivity also propitiates a rethinking of the self through the redeployment of the concept of liberality, which "provides an ethical component to the novel's ending" (Avilés in this volume). At times the precariousness of one's identity is also represented through humor, as seen in *Los baños de Argel* and *La gran sultana,* through the deployment of the figure of the lowly *gracioso,* a stock type in the Lopean *comedia,* which Cervantes rejects for its propagandistic propensities and the likelihood of a non-discriminating reception (Spadaccini). Whether or not one accepts the interpretation that in the above-mentioned captivity plays Tristán and Madrigal are "granted a kind of official status as the Spanish voice of the text," it is clear that their attacks on Jews and Muslims depend upon an accumulated "store of cultural knowledge" about the other (Fuchs in this volume), something that could also be said regarding other types of engagements that transpire within the "in-between" space of captivity, one that is marked by constantly shifting identities and the need for personal survival.

The importance of refocusing our work today to encompass broader perspectives is made evident by recent trends in academia, especially in the humanities, with its turn to theory, cultural studies, and more regional and global concerns, and the fact that with shrinking faculties and job prospects (especially in areas other than Spanish) some of the old, narrow specializations are no longer as viable as they used to be. Interdisciplinary work goes a long way toward a revitalization of our disciplines, work which, to be fair, has been going on for some time and is now gaining added impetus. It is also the case that many of us working in Golden Age and Colonial have long crossed the Atlantic, and it is likely that today most people working in our disciplines ask themselves how we can make texts of the past meaningful to current audiences. In some ways we are helped by a series of factors, including the phenomena of broad migration, the globalization of trade and capital, the weight of identitarian politics, the right of minority voices to be heard, and so on. Relatively new political structures such as the European Union (EU) acknowledge the need to look beyond the borders of member countries to revive historical connections, even if they do not always live up to stated promises. Such is the case of the proposal for the Barcelona Process, or "Union for the Mediterranean" (1995), which intended to deepen "relations between Europe and other Mediterranean countries as part of a strengthened Euro-Mediterranean partnership which produces tangible results for citizens in the region." One of the three key aspects of the agreement was the establishment of a "Partnership in social, cultural and human affairs: developing human resources, promoting understanding between cultures & exchanges between civil societies." In somewhat typical EU rhetoric, the Declaration "recognized that the traditions of culture and civilization throughout the Mediterranean region, dialogue between these cultures and exchanges at human, scientific, and technological levels are an essential factor in bringing their peoples closer, promoting understanding between them, and improving their perception of each other." Yet it is also the case that the benevolent rhetoric of the declaration regarding North-South relations was accompanied by references to problems of migration, terrorism, and drug trafficking. Thus, what was proposed as an opening to the larger Mediterranean came to be seen as concerted containment policies regarding immigration from so-called third countries: those not belonging to the Union. Because of its proximity to Africa, Spain is a key element in the containment and control efforts of Fortress Europe.

Official attempts at regulating human traffic through the Mediterranean have often proved futile and even counterproductive. Italians and Spaniards are especially aware of the plight of thousands of migrants who try to reach the coasts of Europe by avoiding governmental controls. The Italian island of Lampedusa was the site of dramatic episodes during the Arab Spring revolts of 2011, when thousands of Tunisians arrived there during the events that are now part of the global memory of migrations. To this day thousands make the trip from Africa and many die before they reach shore. The same tragedy is replicated in Spain and it is estimated that since 1988, when the first corpse appeared in one of its southern beaches, between six thousand and eighteen thousand immigrants lost their lives—something that is met with anguish, solidarity, and indifference by the Spanish citizenry.

As a response to the growing flow of African immigrants, the EU and the Spanish government began to take measures to seal the southern border. Their initiatives included the construction of a wall around Ceuta (a city "belonging" to Spain that is located in Northern Africa) in 1993, and the "total exterior surveillance system" designed in 1999 (one of the gems of Spain's own military-industrial complex.) This system comprises the use of long-range radars, thermal imaging cameras, night vision devices, helicopters, and patrol boats.

Literary and artistic works offer views on these human relations and movements as well as on the role and impact of governments that seek to regulate them. In the case of Spanish culture, the oeuvre of Juan Goytisolo is probably the best-known example of the rich possibilities and important insights derived from an informed and powerful literary approach to these issues. His writing has illuminated many aspects of the social and cultural reality of different areas of the Mediterranean region since the 1950s. Goytisolo's reflections are deeply rooted in historical knowledge along the lines of Américo Castro's reading of Spanish history, and that reading serves as a basis of his work about contemporary migrant movements between Africa and Europe, one of his most salient preoccupations. According to Goytisolo, Andalucía, Spain's Iberian southernmost region, has become a new "Hispanic March," a land with a newfound border-like and defensive vocation ("La Marca Hispánica que es ya Andalucía se aferrará entonces a su nueva vocación fronteriza y defensiva. Los *moros* de la otra orilla seguirán encarnando la amenaza virtual de la temida invasión de los bárbaros" (Goytisolo VIII: 868) (The Spanish March that Andalucía has already become will then stick to its new border and defensive calling. The Moors from the other side of the sea will continue to embody the virtual threat of the feared barbarian invasion). This barrier function that the EU seems to have destined for southern Spain is particularly striking considering not only the region's history as the focal point of Muslim culture in Europe up to the early modern period, but also its economic and demographic developments during the not so distant past, and how that history is publicly used nowadays.

Goytisolo's crucial contribution has been widely discussed and has exerted a deep influence on academics and artists alike. However, the policies of Fortress Europe have been made visible and contested by a number of other intellectuals and artists whose work is equally deserving of critical attention, especially within the framework of Mediterranean Studies. Valeriano López (Huéscar, 1963) has been a pioneer among those who have done openly political work on these issues, as seen in his foundational video piece on the topic of current cross-Mediterranean migrations called *Estrecho Adventure* as well as other works on the same subject. One could say, following Italo Calvino, that López's work engages a subject that is grave and largely invisible through lightness and visibility. Behind a screen of seeming frivolity or superficiality, through his particular approach (which embraces the language of so-called lesser forms such as video games and folktales), López reveals the historical depth and political reach of the migration phenomenon.

His first piece, *Estrecho Adventure* (1996), deals with the network of fantasies that feed this phenomenon. This work has received many awards internationally, and has been shown in numerous festivals, among them those in Tetouan (Morocco) and Kelibia (Tunis). The video has the format of a video game in which Abdul, a young Moroccan, crosses the Mediterranean avoiding official controls and establishes himself in Spain as a migrant worker. One of López's preferred practices is the resemantization of official symbols. In the video, he does so with the seal and flag of Andalucía and the flag the European Union. The stars of the EU flag rise on the horizon of the British and Spanish landscape in front of him as Abdul (or the player) skillfully pilots his raft across the Strait of Gibraltar. The stars may be guiding him on his trip to that promised land, but they also stand for the institution that tries to prevent him from succeeding in his adventure. We also hear a few bars from the Eurovision anthem, the Prelude to the *Te Deum* by Marc-Antoine Charpentier.

The Andalusian seal is animated as it comes out from an official form. Hercules becomes an unimpressive vigilante in charge of controlling the access to the gate located in the wall of barbed wire and brick that impedes Abdul's advance. His two mythic lions are here turned into mastiffs, or some other guard dogs wearing thorny collars. "Non plus ultra" is the motto that Hercules inscribed over the two pillars resulting when he separated Africa and Europe. Note that it is not the motto that appears in the actual Andalusian seal (which reads *Dominator Hercules Fundator*), nor the one in the Spanish seal (*Plus ultra*). By recovering the adverb of negation, the slogan recovers its original dissuasive meaning. But, while in classical antiquity it marked the limit of the sea that was known to navigators, here it is a warning to those who try to access that Europe that claims to be the heir of that prestigious classical past.

The second piece by López that we will briefly discuss here is titled *Confabulación*. The piece was produced in 2007 as an ironic celebration of the tenth anniversary of *Estrecho Adventure* and as a complementary look at the ongoing European contradictions vis-à-vis its growing population of African origin. One of the video's clearest intertexts is the most famous version of the Pied Piper of Hamelin, the one rendered by the Grimm brothers, in which a musician is commissioned by the Hamelin authorities to get rid of a plague of rats. He does the job, haunting the rodents with a magic melody, but he is not paid his due. The piper retaliates by taking away the town's children using the same harmonious method. One may initially think that López is recreating this latter part of the story, but the matter is a bit more complex than that.

In a rhetorical move whose etymological density is usual in López's titles, the Grimms' *fable* becomes a *confabulation*. Both words come from the Latin *fabula* (discourse, story, narration). López's piece shares some of the canonical traits of the fable, such as brevity, didactic intention, and a moral. Interestingly, in the English language a "confabulation" is a rather innocuous chat. But in Spanish, "confabular" is "to get to an agreement to carry out a plan, generally of an illicit nature": that is, to conspire. In it, López responds to some worrying developments related to the migration dynamics and policies that have been previously discussed in these pages. Paradoxically, parallel to the development of Fortress Europe to prevent those youngsters from accessing the continent, European governments were taking measures to promote the growth of their native populations due to the precipitous decline in birth rates throughout most of Europe. In the summer of 2007, at the height of Spain's economic boom, Socialist Prime Minister Rodríguez Zapatero announced that the State would give 2,500 euros for every child born in Spain. The combination of increasingly strict immigration control and these fertility stimuli policies could be seen as a form of xenophobia in agreement with the "immunitary paradigm" (Esposito) that the EU implicitly endorses.

The sounds in the film point to the economy of social prestige and belonging-ness at play in the context of Southern Europe. The melody that the piper plays is the main theme of the last movement of Beethoven's Ninth Symphony. It was chosen by the EU as its anthem so as to symbolize the union, diversity, and solidarity of its members. *An die Freude*, the Ode to Joy, the poem by Schiller that Ludwig van Beethoven set to music is a song that celebrates fraternity. The counterpoint to the high status that the German lyrics would have in Spain, a nation that is still dreaming about its Europeanness, is what the kids speak, a linguistic reminder of its Orientalized or, for some, less-than-European past. They use the dialect of Arabic spoken in Morocco; the only meaningful thing they say is another song of solidarity that they sing as they go down the streets following the flutist. The formulaic words *bir-ruh, bid-dam* (with soul, with blood) are cried out loud in protests throughout the Arab-speaking world, and are usually followed by the protest's slogan. In any case, the visual language of López's videos makes virtually unnecessary any knowledge of the languages spoken in them. We shall complete this analysis by looking at just one of the visible elements in this video.

The story filmed by López is set in his city, Granada, which has a particularly dense history, as it was the see of the last surviving Muslim kingdom in Spain until it was conquered by Isabella and Ferdinand in 1492. The artist sets the film in an old part of the city where urban decay is especially visible. Some walls have fallen, while others are full of graffiti—just the place where one could expect to see a rat or two. But instead of rats, we see children. The image of a pest that needs to be contained or managed was implicit in the opening scene of *Estrecho Adventure*, with the blurred depictions of a large number of Africans congregating in the North of the continent as they prepare their attempt to reach Europe. The children in *Confabulación* appear unexpectedly, and move in an anarchic way, even emerging from the cracks of walls. Those same walls that hid them become a trap; a funnel that channels them to their perdition.

However, the most prominent walls shown are probably those of the Alhambra, which look especially powerful from the perspective used. Thus López contradicts the usual imaginary of the monument, which is that of a luxurious palace surrounded by sensual gardens, emphasizing instead its fortress character. Disputing the paradisiacal image of the Spanish Middle Ages as a time of tolerance, but most especially the public use of that history as an historical antecedent for current multiculturalism, López undermines this current fable by denouncing a confabulation (in the Spanish sense, this is, a conspiracy) that reminds us of less edifying chapters of Spain's history, such as the expulsion of the Moriscos (1609–1614), the story of ethnic cleansing that Cervantes dramatizes so movingly in *Don Quijote* (54–63).

Four centuries later, the Muslim "other" still has a particularly relevant space in narratives about the Spanish role in the construction of European identity. Its presence in the debate is twofold. On the one hand, the centuries of Islamic rule in the Iberian Peninsula are privileged. On the other, great relevance is given to the migration to Spain of large numbers of Moroccans, especially evident since the second half of the 1990s. The former episode is seen from an ambivalent perspective, for it is often regarded as a period of great cultural refinement which left an unmistakable artistic legacy (with monuments such as the Great Mosque of Córdoba or the Alhambra in Granada, which are the source of generalized pride shared even by staunch Islamophobes), but also as an invasion which posed a threat to Spain's historical continuity, essentially determined by Christian faith. These conflicted views are conspicuous not only at a popular level, but also among leading intellectuals and academics. One does not have to refer to the books of prolific far-right revisionists such as Pío Moa or César Vidal to find a noticeable anxiety over the issue. Someone as well respected as José Luis Abellán, formerly professor and Chair of History of Spanish Philosophy at the nation's largest research institution, Madrid's Universidad Complutense, referred not too long ago to the eight-century-long Islamic presence in Iberia along the terms of Christian "resistance" against Muslim "intrusion" and "harassment." In Abellán's view, the historical function of an entity called "Spain"—portrayed as a functioning political unity—was to guard the borders of a nascent Europe from the barbarians coming from the other side of the Mediterranean, so as to allow the continental center to develop. The latter's culture, moreover, could not have been established without the decisive contributions of Spain, the abnegated peripheral nation, which was not only the military guardian of civilization, but also its intellectual ferment. For Abellán, Europe's debt toward Spain is double: he highlights the fact that, although "Spain" set the conditions for Europe's philosophical revitalization, "la necesidad de resistir a la absorción islamizante potenció . . . líneas anti-intelectualistas o, al menos, filosóficamente pauperizantes" (32) (the need to resist Islamizing absorption empowered attitudes that were . . . anti-intellectualist or, at the very least, philosophically poor). The notable level of exchanges between Christian and non-Christian cultures benefited only the rest of Europe, as "Spaniards" (identified exclusively with those who challenged Islam's expansion in the peninsula) were too busy "resisting" the "other" in order to safeguard the continent's essences. Abellán's schema of Spain as a periphery which repeatedly sacrificed itself for the stability of the center goes beyond the Middle Ages. Thus, the Renaissance and the (Counter-) Reformation are interpreted as two moments when Spain had to put aside its own advancement in order to fight for the preservation of Europe's unity. The triumphant European model of a nation-state based on Machiavellian political principles went against Spain's "fundamentos universalistas" (universalist principles), and the country isolated itself from the rest of the continent (35).

Recent Muslim immigrants have thus found a social landscape conditioned by an ambivalent perception of Spain's relationship to Africa and its own Islamic past. The latest colonial enterprises in Morocco and Equatorial Guinea, which lasted until the 1970s, allegedly served to remind Spaniards of their position in world affairs: they were conquerors, imposers of European ideals over so-called primitive peoples. The cases of Ceuta and Melilla—the two remaining major Spanish colonial outposts in Northern Africa—and the 2002 armed confrontation with Morocco over the tiny island of Tura, Laila, or Perejil (its toponym in Berber, Arabic, and Spanish, respectively), an uninhabited rock situated a slingshot away from the African coast, are good examples of the colonialistic values that are still present in Spain's official self-image.

The end of López's video piece reveals that the piper is acting in agreement with the authorities; he is one of the "confabulados," an agent of the European conspiracy to get rid of the presence of large numbers of boys and girls of African ascent, which the video presents as public health issue. The immunitary paradigm that directs EU immigration politics is nothing new, as Roberto Esposito has argued, although the pious rhetoric that tries to conceal it is. As the walls of Fortress Europe are full of cracks, permeable, and many of the Abduls trying to make it into the continent will succeed, officials contend that new measures need to be taken. Their policies are implemented as we speak, although fortunately not without forms of resistance which are often informed by the work of artists who make them visible and memorable.

The motivations to impose barriers in the Mediterranean vary, but not so much the rhetoric, which generally opposes what is presented as European wealth and intellectualism to African poverty and passion; or, in cruder terms, civilization and reason versus barbarism. However, we may do well remembering that very similar arguments have been at play within Europe as well. Roberto M. Dainotto has argued that the configuration of modern Eurocentrism since the mid-eighteenth century required a new arrangement of Europe's own border logic. The old East-West model prevalent until then would be substituted by an internal North-South divide that was necessary for the continent's self-sufficient dialectics of progress. Dainotto points to Montesquieu's *The Spirit of Laws* (1748) as the work in which that "theoretical event" was accomplished. Since then, "Asia is no longer an other of Europe—in fact, there is no other. In the totality that is Europe, even Asia, or its simile or equivalent value, can be found in Europe: in the South, that is, which is an Asia of sorts, a south that is itself Europe—but only a bad, defective, and pathological one" (Dainotto 47).

The notion of difference plays therefore a major role in the relationships between Europe and Iberia, most particularly Spain. European intellectuals used it to explain or excuse either their ignorance of Spain in their argumentations (be they historical or philosophical) or their passionate and often reductive engagements with matters Spanish. Their counterparts in Spain were complicit with a type of particularization that placed Spanish history and cultural productions in a separate category from those of the rest of modern Europe ("Spain is different"). While some were offended by it and its mention was usually followed by the enumeration of the qualities that made Spaniards superior to those Northern neighbors who pointed to Spain's "monstrosity," others assumed its historical reality as a challenge to be overcome and thus nullified—"difference" with Europe needed to turn into assimilation. One of the ways to achieve this goal would be to emphasize the points of contact with the center, but a more subtle and probably effective one in terms of local consumption was the exaltation of the "difference" between Spain and Africa, which was codified, not surprisingly, in terms of Spain's superiority over the peoples on the other side of the Mediterranean. The sea would no longer be exalted as an immemorial cradle of culture but regarded as a wall that was there to guard a higher form of culture.

The present volume shows how twists of cartography depend greatly on human imagination, prejudice, and political objectives. Academic alertness to the history of ebbs and flows in these complex relationships undoubtedly gains from constant self-examination and renovation of viewpoints that ultimately determine what we do from our disciplines. A "Mediterranean turn," with all of the implications discussed in this volume, allows for an engagement of those aspects of Iberian culture that can be more fully comprehended when they are not seen in relative isolation. Our approaches to the histories and cultures of (and in) the Mediterranean profit from an engagement of the work of scholars from various disciplines who are looking at similar issues and who are generating knowledge about them from places that often appear in the texts we study. Such an engagement also argues for a renewed emphasis on the notion that one is dealing with multiple loci of enunciation, and thus with the weaving of "Other" stories, often told from spaces in-between. Today, the persistent movement of people across the Mediterranean, especially from Africa to Southern Europe (with Spain being one of the major destinations) reminds us that the texts that interest us as scholars who work in the medieval and early modern periods speak of people, issues, and characters whose vast range of experiences have shaped, and continue to shape, the sea that is placed—as its toponym signals—"between lands."

Note

1. For a brief but incisive view of the ways Spanish philology is perceived from the North American academy, and alternatives to them, see Altschul and Nelson.

Works Cited

Abellán, José Luis. "El significado de la idea de Europa en la política y en la historia de España." *Sistema* 86–88 (1988): 31–44.

Altschul, Nadia R., and Bradley Nelson. "Transatlantic Discordances: The Problem of Philology." *Estudios Hispánicos: Perspectivas Internacionales*. Ed. Luis Martín-Estudillo, Nicholas Spadaccini, and Francisco Ocampo. *Hispanic Issues Online* 2 (2007): 55–63. Web.

Bhabha, Homi K. *The Location of Culture*. New York: Routledge, 1994.

Braudel, Fernand. *La Mediterranée et le monde méditerranéen à l'époque de Philippe II*. Vol. 2. Paris: Colin, 1966.

Cabo Aseguinolaza, Fernando. *El lugar de la literatura española*. Barcelona: Crítica, 2012.

Calvino, Italo. *Lezioni americane. Sei proposte per il prossimo millennio*. Milano: Garzanti, 1988.

Canavaggio, Jean. "Estudio Preliminar." *Los baños de Argel*. By Miguel de Cervantes. Ed. Jean Canavaggio. Madrid: Taurus, 1983.

Dainotto, Roberto M. "Does Europe Have a South? An Essay on Borders." *The Global South* 5.1 (Spring 2011): 37–50. Web.

Domínguez Ortíz, Antonio. *Desde Carlos V a la Paz de los Pirineos, 1517–1660. Historia de España*. Vol. 4. Barcelona: Ediciones Grijalbo, 1974.

Epps, Brad, and Luis Fernández Cifuentes, eds. *Spain Beyond Spain: Modernity, Literary History, and National Identity*. Lewisburg, PA: Bucknell University Press, 2005.

Esposito, Roberto. *Bios: Biopolitics and Philosophy*. Trans. Timothy Campbell. Minneapolis: University of Minnesota Press, 2008.

Faber, Sebastiaan. *Anglo-American Hispanists and the Spanish Civil War: Hispanophilia, Commitment, and Discipline*. New York: Palgrave, 2008.

Garcés, María Antonia. "'Grande amigo Mío': Cervantes y los renegados." *USA Cervantes. 39 cervantistas en Estados Unidos*. Ed. Georgina Dopico Black and Francisco Layna Ranz. Madrid: Consejo Superior de Investigaciones Científicas, 2009. 545–82.

Goytisolo, Juan. "De la migración a la inmigración". *Fronteras sur. Obras completas VIII. Guerra, periodismo y literatura*. Barcelona: Galaxia Gutenberg / Círculo de Lectores, 2007. 866–75.

Lacarra, María Eugenia. "La utilización del Cid de Menéndez Pidal en la ideología militar franquista." *Ideologies and Literature* 3.12 (1980): 95–127. Web.

López, Valeriano. *Estrecho Adventure*. 1996. Web.

_____. *Confabulación*. 2007. Web.

Martín-Estudillo, Luis, and Nicholas Spadaccini, eds. *New Spain, New Literatures*. Hispanic Issues 35. Nashville: Vanderbilt University Press, 2010.

Moraña, Mabel, ed. *Ideologies of Hispanism*. Hispanic Issues 30. Nashville: Vanderbilt University Press, 2005.

Ragionieri, Rodolfo. "Fragmentation and Order in the Mediterranean Area." *Identities and Conflicts*. Ed. Furio Cerutti and Rodolfo Ragioneri. New York: Palgrave, 2001. 81–120.

Resina, Joan Ramon. *Del hispanismo a los estudios ibéricos. Una propuesta federativa para el ámbito cultural*. Madrid: Biblioteca Nueva, 2009.

Smith, Colin. "Poema de Mio Cid." *The Politics of Editing*. Hispanic Issues 8. Ed. Nicholas Spadaccini and Jenaro Talens. Minneapolis: University of Minnesota Press, 1992. 1–21.

Spadaccini, Nicholas. "Metaficción, inscripción autorial, y crítica sociocultural en Cervantes." *USA Cervantes*. Ed. Georgina Dopico Black and Francisco Layna Ranz. Madrid: Consejo Superior de Investigaciones Científicas, 2009. 1053–56.

Ugarte, Michael. "Hispanism's Crisis and the Compitello Generation." *Capital Inscriptions: Essays on Hispanic Literature, Film, and Urban Space*. Ed. Benjamin Fraser. Newark: Juan de la Cuesta, 2012. 65–78.

Zavala, Iris. "The Art of Edition and the Techné of Mediation: Garcilaso's Poetry as Masterplot." *The Politics of Editing*. Hispanic Issues 8. Ed. Nicholas Spadaccini and Jenaro Talens. Minneapolis: University of Minnesota Press, 1992. 52–73.

Contributors

Luis F. Avilés is Associate Professor in the Department of Spanish and Portuguese at the University of California, Irvine. He has published a book entitled *Lenguaje y crisis: las alegorías del* Criticón (1998), and has also written a number of articles on Gracián, Garcilaso de la Vega, Cervantes, and Sor Juana Inés de la Cruz. He is presently finishing a book project entitled *Juegos visuales: espacio y mirada en la cultura literaria de los Siglos de Oro*. He is also working on another project that studies the relationships between ethics, war, and politics in Early Modern Spain.

Josiah Blackmore is Nancy Clark Smith Professor of the Language and Literature of Portugal at Harvard University. He specializes in the literature and culture of medieval and early modern Portugal. He has written *Manifest Perdition: Shipwreck Narrative and the Disruption of Empire* (2002), *Moorings: Portuguese Expansion and the Writing of Africa* (2009), and has edited *The Songs of António Botto* (2010). His current work focuses on the seafaring textual cultures of early modern Iberia.

Brian A. Catlos is Associate Professor of Religious Studies at the University of Colorado at Boulder, and Research Associate of Humanities at the University of California, Santa Cruz. He co-directs the Mediterranean Seminar/University of California Multi-Campus Research Project. His is the author of *The Victors and the Vanquished: Christians and Muslims of Catalonia and Aragon, 1050–1300* (2004); *The Muslims of Latin Christendom, 1050–1615* (2014), and *Faith, Power, and Violence in the Age of Crusade and Jihad* (2014).

Andrew W. Devereux is Assistant Professor of History at Loyola Marymount University. He is a historian of the medieval and early modern Mediterranean. He is currently working on a book project that takes an expansive view of Spanish rationales for empire by analyzing processes of Mediterranean expansion against similar episodes in the early sixteenth-century Americas. Devereux has published on the position of North Africa in early modern Spanish political thought (*Journal of Spanish Cultural Studies*, 2011) and is currently serving as co-Guest Editor of a special issue of *Medieval Encounters*.

Barbara Fuchs is Professor of Spanish and English at UCLA, where she also directs the Center for 17th- and 18th- Century Studies and the William A. Clark Memorial Library. She works on literature and empire in the early modern period, in both transatlantic and Mediterranean contexts. Her books include *Mimesis and Empire: The New World, Islam, and the Construction of European Identities* (2001), *Passing for Spain: Cervantes and the Fictions of Identity* (2003), *Exotic Nation: Maurophilia and the Construction of Early Modern Spain* (2009), and *The Poetics of Piracy: Emulating Spain in English Literature* (2013).

Ryan D. Giles is Associate Professor at Indiana University, Bloomington. He specializes in medieval and Renaissance Spanish literature, and is the author of *The Laughter of the Saints: Parodies of Holiness in Late Medieval and Renaissance Spain* (2009). Recent articles and book chapters have dealt with a variety of works, from *Milagros de Nuestra Señora* and *Libro de buen amor*, to the *Corbacho*, cancionero poetry, *Celestina*, and *Lazarillo de Tormes*. He is currently working on a book that explores the way in which prayers and incantations were simultaneously employed in literature and used as textual amulets in medieval and early modern Iberia.

Eleazar Gutwirth is Professor of Hispano-Jewish History and Culture at Tel-Aviv University. He is interested in the relations between Hispano-Jewish and other cultures in the age of transition from the medieval to the modern. He is editor of a special volume of *Jewish History* on Jews and Courts (2007). Other recent publications include: "Tendencias en la cultura judeocatalana medieval" in *Temps i espais de la Girona jueva* (2011); "History, language and the sciences in medieval Spain" in *Science in Medieval Jewish Cultures* (2012); "Lista notarial de libros judios (1415)" in *Biblias de Sefarad* (2012). He continues to work on Judeo-Spanish manuscripts and early printed books.

Michelle M. Hamilton is Associate Professor of Spanish and Portuguese at the University of Minnesota, Twin Cities, where she offers courses on religious studies, Jewish studies, and Spanish literature and culture. Her research focuses on the Romance, Hebrew, and Arabic literatures and cultures of medieval Iberia. Her publications include "The Sephardic Past in the Digital Future" (*Digital Philology*, forthcoming); *Representing Others in Medieval Iberian Literature* (2007), and *Wine, Women, and Song* (2004). Her current project deals with Jewish and *converso* cultural production in fifteenth-century Iberia.

Vicente Lledó-Guillem is Associate Professor of Spanish at Hofstra University in New York. His research focuses mainly on the history of the Spanish and Catalan languages, historical sociolinguistics, language ideology, and romance philology. He has published on medieval and Golden Age Spanish and Catalan Literature. His book, *Literatura o imperio: la construcción de las lenguas castellana y catalana en la España renacentista,* was published by Juan de la Cuesta in 2008. Some of his most recent publications are "Bernat Desclot's Response to Bernat d'Auriac's *sirventés*" in *La Corónica* (2011) and "¿Compañera o rebelde? La lengua y el imperio según Bernardo de Aldrete," *Bulletin of Hispanic Studies* (2010).

Manuela Marín is a former Research Professor at the Consejo Superior de Investigaciones Científicas in Madrid (Spain). She has worked mainly on the social and cultural history of al-Andalus and on gender in the Medieval Western Islamic lands. Her publications include *Mujeres en al-Andalus* (2000); "'Amar a cristianos moras': ecos de un tema cervantino en textos españoles sobre Marruecos (s. XIX–XX)," *Bulletin Hispanique*; "Una galería de retratos reales. Los soberanos omeyas de al-Ándalus (siglos II/VIII–IV/X) en la cronística árabe," *Anuario de Estudios Medievales*. She is currently working on hagiographical sources from the Maghrib and on Spaniards in Morocco from 1850 to 1956.

Luis Martín-Estudillo is Associate Professor of Spanish Literature at the University of Iowa. His publications include *La mirada elíptica: El trasfondo barroco de la poesía española contemporánea* (2007) and several co-edited and edited volumes, including *Hispanic Baroques: Reading Cultures in Context* (2005), *Post-Authoritarian Cultures: Spain and Latin America's Southern Cone* (2008), *Filosofía y tiempo final* (2010), *New Spain, New Literatures* (2010), and *Hispanic Literatures and the Question of a Liberal Education* (2011). He is the Managing Editor of the *Hispanic Issues* series and *Hispanic Issues Online*.

Nicholas M. Parmley is Assistant Professor of Spanish Literature at Whitman College. He completed his dissertation, *Imagining the Mediterranean: Disruption and Connectivity in Medieval Iberian Tales of the Sea* (University of Minnesota, Twin Cities) in June, 2013. Parmley has published on tales of the sea and seafaring in medieval Iberian Jewish literature and has forthcoming publications on the *ribera confusa* in Góngora's *Soledades* and on theories of translation in Cervantes's *Don Quijote*.

Simone Pinet is Associate Professor of Spanish and Medieval Studies at Cornell University, where she teaches medieval and early modern Spanish literature and culture. She is the author of *Archipelagoes: Insular Fictions from Chivalric Romance to the Novel* (2011), and articles on books of chivalry, visual culture, cartography, and medieval epic. She is currently completing *The Task of the Cleric*, a book manuscript on *mester de clerecía*.

Núria Silleras-Fernández is Assistant Professor at the Department of Spanish and Portuguese of the University of Colorado at Boulder. Her research focuses on Late Medieval and Early Modern Iberian literatures and cultures, and European history, particularly gender, politics, and religion. She is the author of *Power, Piety, and Patronage in Late Medieval Queenship. Maria de Luna* (2008), and several articles on topics such as queenship, courtly culture, patronage, and Humanism. Her current book project is entitled *Imagined Virtues: Francesc Eiximenis, Court Culture, and the Construction of the Feminine in Late Medieval and Early Modern Iberia*.

Nicholas Spadaccini is Professor of Hispanic Studies and Comparative Literature at the University of Minnesota. He has published books, critical editions, articles, and collective volumes on literary and cultural criticism, with an emphasis on early modern and contemporary Spain and colonial Latin America. His most recent published volumes (co-edited) are *New Spain, New Literatures* (2010), *Hispanic Literatures and the Question of a Liberal Education* (2011), and *Writing Monsters: Essays on Iberian and Latin American Cultures* (2014). He is Editor-in-Chief of the *Hispanic Issues* series and *Hispanic Issues Online (HIOL)*.

David A. Wacks is Associate Professor of Spanish at the University of Oregon. His research interests include Medieval Iberian literature and Sephardic Jewish culture. He is author of *Framing Iberia: Frametales and Maqamat in Medieval Spain* (2007), co-editor of *Wine, Women and Song: Hebrew and Arabic*

Literature in Medieval Iberia (2004) and of a special cluster of articles for the journal *eHumanista* on "Multilingual Medieval Iberia between the tongue and the pen." His current book project is titled *Double Diaspora: Sephardic Literature 1200–1550*. He blogs on his current research and teaching at davidwacks.uoregon.edu.

Gerard Wiegers is Professor of Religious Studies at the Faculty of Humanities of the University of Amsterdam. His research focuses on religious minorities in the Iberian Peninsula and North Africa. In cooperation with P.S. van Koningsveld he is preparing a historical study and critical edition of original Arabic texts of the Granadan Lead Books. Some of his publications include: "Moriscos and Arabic Studies in Europe," *Al-Qantara* (2010); "El contenido de los textos árabes de los Plomos" *Nuevas aportaciones al conocimiento y estudio del Sacro Monte* (2011); and *Los Moriscos. La expulsión y después* (co-edited with M. García-Arenal; 2012).

◆ Index

Compiled by Michelle M. Hamilton and Núria Silleras-Fernández

VOLUMES IN THE HISPANIC ISSUES SERIES

41 *In and Of the Mediterranean: Medieval and Early Modern Iberian Studies,* edited by Michelle M. Hamilton and Núria Silleras-Fernández

40 *Coloniality, Religion, and the Law in the Early Iberian World,* edited by Santa Arias and Raúl Marrero-Fente

39 *Poiesis and Modernity in the Old and New Worlds,* edited by Anthony J. Cascardi and Leah Middlebrook

38 *Spectacle and Topophilia: Reading Early (and Post-) Modern Hispanic Cultures,* edited by David R. Castillo and Bradley J. Nelson

37 *New Spain, New Literatures,* edited by Luis Martín-Estudillo and Nicholas Spadaccini

36 *Latin American Jewish Cultural Production,* edited by David William Foster

35 *Post-Authoritarian Cultures: Spain and Latin America's Southern Cone,* edited by Luis Martín-Estudillo and Roberto Ampuero

34 *Spanish and Empire,* edited by Nelsy Echávez-Solano and Kenya C. Dworkin y Méndez

33 *Generation X Rocks: Contemporary Peninsular Fiction, Film, and Rock Culture,* edited by Christine Henseler and Randolph D. Pope

32 *Reason and Its Others: Italy, Spain, and the New World,* edited by David Castillo and Massimo Lollini

31 *Hispanic Baroques: Reading Cultures in Context,* edited by Nicholas Spadaccini and Luis Martín-Estudillo

30 *Ideologies of Hispanism,* edited by Mabel Moraña

29 *The State of Latino Theater in the United States: Hybridity, Transculturation, and Identity,* edited by Luis A. Ramos-García

28 *Latin America Writes Back: Postmodernity in the Periphery (An Interdisciplinary Perspective),* edited by Emil Volek

27 *Women's Narrative and Film in Twentieth-Century Spain: A World of Difference(s),* edited by Ofelia Ferrán and Kathleen M. Glenn

26 *Marriage and Sexuality in Medieval and Early Modern Iberia,* edited by Eukene Lacarra Lanz

25 *Pablo Neruda and the U.S. Culture Industry,* edited by Teresa Longo

24 *Iberian Cities,* edited by Joan Ramon Resina

23 *National Identities and Sociopolitical Changes in Latin America,* edited by Mercedes F. Durán-Cogan and Antonio Gómez-Moriana

22 *Latin American Literature and Mass Media,* edited by Edmundo Paz-Soldán and Debra A. Castillo

21 *Charting Memory: Recalling Medieval Spain,* edited by Stacy N. Beckwith

20 *Culture and the State in Spain: 1550–1850*, edited by Tom Lewis and Francisco J. Sánchez

19 *Modernism and its Margins: Reinscribing Cultural Modernity from Spain and Latin America*, edited by Anthony L. Geist and José B. Monleón

18 *A Revisionary History of Portuguese Literature*, edited by Miguel Tamen and Helena C. Buescu

17 *Cervantes and his Postmodern Constituencies*, edited by Anne Cruz and Carroll B. Johnson

16 *Modes of Representation in Spanish Cinema*, edited by Jenaro Talens and Santos Zunzunegui

15 *Framing Latin American Cinema: Contemporary Critical Perspectives*, edited by Ann Marie Stock

14 *Rhetoric and Politics: Baltasar Gracián and the New World Order*, edited by Nicholas Spadaccini and Jenaro Talens

13 *Bodies and Biases: Sexualities in Hispanic Cultures and Literatures*, edited by David W. Foster and Roberto Reis

12 *The Picaresque: Tradition and Displacement*, edited by Giancarlo Maiorino

11 *Critical Practices in Post-Franco Spain*, edited by Silvia L. López, Jenaro Talens, and Dario Villanueva

10 *Latin American Identity and Constructions of Difference*, edited by Amaryll Chanady

9 *Amerindian Images and the Legacy of Columbus*, edited by René Jara and Nicholas Spadaccini

8 *The Politics of Editing*, edited by Nicholas Spadaccini and Jenaro Talens

7 *Culture and Control in Counter-Reformation Spain*, edited by Anne J. Cruz and Mary Elizabeth Perry

6 *Cervantes's Exemplary Novels and the Adventure of Writing*, edited by Michael Nerlich and Nicholas Spadaccini

5 *Ortega y Gasset and the Question of Modernity*, edited by Patrick H. Dust

4 *1492–1992: Re/Discovering Colonial Writing*, edited by René Jara and Nicholas Spadaccini

3 *The Crisis of Institutionalized Literature in Spain*, edited by Wlad Godzich and Nicholas Spadaccini

2 *Autobiography in Early Modern Spain*, edited by Nicholas Spadaccini and Jenaro Talens

1 *The Institutionalization of Literature in Spain*, edited by Wlad Godzich and Nicholas Spadaccini